SOUL SURVIVOR

SOUL SURVIVOR
A BIOGRAPHY OF AL GREEN

by *JIMMY McDONOUGH*

DA CAPO PRESS

Da Capo Press
Hachette Book Group
1290 Avenue of the Americas, New York, NY 10104
www.dacapopress.com

Printed in the United States of America
First Edition: August 2017
Published by Da Capo Press, an imprint of Perseus Books, LLC, a subsidiary of Hachette Book Group, Inc.

The Hachette Speakers Bureau provides a wide range of authors for speaking events. To find out more, go to www.hachettespeakersbureau.com or call (866) 376-6591.
The publisher is not responsible for websites (or their content) that are not owned by the publisher.

Print book interior design by Jeff Williams

Library of Congress Cataloging-in-Publication Data
Names: McDonough, Jimmy, author.
Title: Soul survivor : a biography of Al Green / by Jimmy McDonough.
Description: Boston, MA : Da Capo Press, 2017. | Includes bibliographical references and index.
Identifiers: LCCN 2017010283 | ISBN 9780306822674 (hardcover) | ISBN 9780306822681 (ebook)
Subjects: LCSH: Green, Al, 1946- | Soul musicians—United States—Biography.
Classification: LCC ML420.G843 M33 2017 | DDC 782.421644092 [B]—dc23
LC record available at https://lccn.loc.gov/2017010283

ISBNs: 978-0-306-82267-4 (hardcover), 978-0-306-82268-1 (ebook)

LSC-C

10 9 8 7 6 5 4 3 2 1

FOR BILL BENTLEY

blame him for my career

CONTENTS

Beware of men who speak well of you, my brother.
—AL GREEN

TALKING IN TONGUES

I'm a mystery. The people in my own church don't even know who I am. I'm not really sure if I know who I am half the time.
—AL GREEN

In 2000 Al Green wrote an autobiography. Excuse me—Davin Seay wrote the book and they slapped Al's name on the cover. Business as usual—celebrity tells writer his story, writer turns it into a book. In this case, though, everything about it was a little off. This was Al Green. *Reverend* Al Green, because by this point he'd been pastoring over his own Memphis-based house of worship, Full Gospel Tabernacle Church, for a decade and a half.

Green and Seay, a respected author with eight books to his name, among them other celebrity memoirs with Snoop Dogg and Dion, had been put together by the agency they had in common, William Morris. Davin shared more than an agent with the Reverend: "He liked to talk about God and salvation, and I'm a Christian myself." A deal was hatched, with Seay and Green receiving "a very decent advance" for Al's story. Signed, sealed, and delivered? Not quite. "I found out soon after what I was facing," said Seay.

Entering the kingdom of Green turned out to be "a really surreal experience. He would walk in and out of the real world. . . . As far as I could tell, he had three different personalities. One was Al, which was

1

his stage persona; one was Al Green, which was more normal; and then there was the Reverend Al Green." Seay quickly found out none of the three was interested in the book.

Green met with Seay only a handful of times that amounted to six hours of interviews, a paltry amount of time to cover such a rich and complex life. Davin admitted Al's involvement in the book was "minimal." Sometimes Green just didn't show up; he was at least an hour late when he did. During an interview at the Peabody Hotel, Green "broke into full-on Pentecostal tongues."

One meeting took place at Green's remote estate on the edge of the Shelby Forest fifty miles from Memphis. Seay drove up to encounter "locked gates—with musical notes, like Graceland." He buzzed and got Green, and then proceeded to wait outside two hours when Al couldn't find a key to the gates to his own home. An assistant had to be summoned from Memphis to let Davin in.

❖

It was during the one visit to Green's home that Al discussed in detail the most shocking and bizarre event of his life: Mary Woodson, an unstable woman he'd been romantically involved with, had come to visit Green in October 1974 and scalded him with boiling breakfast matter (mostly likely Cream of Wheat, often stated as grits) after he'd rebuffed her marriage proposal. Shortly thereafter she was found shot dead, lying next to one of Al's guns. After an investigation that involved the FBI, Mary's death was ruled a suicide. It appeared to Seay that this grim subject was one that Green, sitting in the very home Woodson had died in, actually wanted to talk about. "That was the most cogent he was in terms of a linear narrative," said Davin. "Maybe he was interested in setting the record straight. He never reflected on the personal consequences of it."

Getting much else out of Green proved next to impossible. "He definitely didn't want to do the work," said Seay. "There were some very tense encounters. Al had a nasty streak. He could turn on you on a dime in terms of just putting you in your place. It happened a lot. I was trying to push him, get information—at one point he told me, 'Just look at my clippings.' I said, 'Al, this is *your* story.' He wasn't interested."

Nor was anyone else around Green willing to help. When Seay tried to talk to Green's mother, Cora, she clammed up. Davin felt she "was terrified of Al. Instead of getting anecdotal stuff about his childhood, she just kept saying he was a great kid—'he loved me, I loved him.' It was really hard to get anything of substance from anybody."

Even though Green was in full-on Reverend mode, Seay still managed to get a fleeting glimpse of the "incredible sexuality" that has served Al so well. For some unknown reason, Green wanted to conduct one of their interviews at "a funky motel on the outskirts of Memphis . . . I don't know what he was doing there. We went back to my room to talk, there was a knock at the door, and it was the housemaid. She said, 'You got *Al Green* in there?' It was like she sniffed him out!" In response, Green "poured on the charm. In terms of his approach to women, he was like silk."

To Seay, the one place Al seemed at ease was at his church. When it came to Full Gospel Tabernacle Church, Green was "very dedicated. Not just to the preaching, but the pastoral role. He would deal with problems of the parishioners and listen to them. He could be very sweet."

Somehow Seay managed to squeeze a book out of his limited contact. *Take Me to the River* went on to become the go-to source on the subject of Green—you'll find it quoted in many an article, book, and album liner note. At best, *Take Me to the River* is a sketchy, dubious portrayal of Green's life. He mentions none of his wives, nor most of the studio musicians he's worked with (or his bands), and has little to say about his life post-1976. The book contains many factual errors. I don't hold Seay accountable for this; he did his best under trying circumstances. When Al was asked about his autobiography by one reporter, he burst out laughing, confessing he hadn't "read my own book." Clearly it was of little concern to him—"I'm the real person who lived the real life." The subject of *Take Me to the River,* the man who supposedly coauthored it, never bothered to look between the covers.

❖

This is probably not the Al Green you're expecting. You want the Love and Happiness man, that happy guy tossing roses to the ladies. Has any pop star ever seemed more charming? Look at any online interview. Witness that blinding smile, the seductive laugh. Al always seems to be laughing—the image presented is one of an easygoing, lovable guy.

"Let's Stay Together." "I'm Still in Love with You." "Tired of Being Alone." "Let's Get Married." "L-O-V-E (Love)." "Call Me." "Love and Happiness." We all know the songs. Forty years plus after they were recorded, it's still hard to walk through a supermarket, airport, or mall without hearing an Al Green song. They turn up in movies, TV shows, ads, and are sampled in hip-hop hits, burrowing into our collective consciousness. Green's run of classic seventies albums are, says musician, songwriter, and Vulgar Boatmen member Dale Lawrence, "the greatest make-out albums of all time." As Al likes to point out, countless people come up to him bearing wallet photos of their children, excited to confess that their child was conceived while his music was playing.

Green's potent combination of sex appeal and romance drove women berserk. Unlike Sly Stone, James Brown, or Marvin Gaye, Al shied away from the political. The message, he's said over and over, is love. And it was delivered with a tantalizing intimacy. "I want to get to *know* you," Green would proclaim to the rapt females lining the stage beneath him. Somehow Al made it sound like he really cared. That he'd be kind. Green projected the alluring confidence of a velvety-smooth gentleman suitor who'd attend to every need and desire. Given his blinding charisma, the fact that it would all end in the bedroom was a given. "Here I Am (Come and Take Me)" was the mere title of his song, but Al delivered the lyric as though it were a personal invitation hand delivered to the bedroom of your mind. Some of Green's vintage TV appearances can feel a bit wicked due to their lusty sexuality: here was a young, good-looking black man letting it all hang out, leaving all of America hungry for more.

How did Al pull that off? As Green's most impassioned, provocative (if incurably academic) critic Michael Awkward instructs, the persona Al often adopts in his songs "is that of an anxious, vulnerable, boyish supplicant begging not to be hurt." There it is—vulnerability. We feel like Al Green understands. That he is talking directly to us. There is a realness we believe.

Musically, Green "was the only one carrying that Southern deep-soul tradition into the 1970s. And he did it on his own terms, without ever imitating or sounding much like Otis or Wilson Pickett or anyone else you can name," said Dale Lawrence. "Soul was all over the charts in the early '70s, but except for Al, it was either funk, late Motown, Philly soul, or some other style where the drumming sits on top of the beat, anticipating disco. Al Green alone kept that deep groove, with the snare way behind the beat."

The man responsible for that deep groove was Willie Mitchell. Mitchell, aka Pops, was a laid-back, no-nonsense visionary who spent years perfecting the very distinct sound in his head, which he created with the Hi

Rhythm band, a bunch of youngsters that Willie taught to play (or maybe more importantly, what not to). Hi Records in Memphis was where it all happened, a scrappy independent label started by a bunch of white guys recording novelty R&B hits (and many more misses), only to be transformed by Mitchell into a hit-making machine that dominated soul and pop charts in the seventies, and that served as an oasis for African American singers, songwriters, and musicians.

Willie Mitchell, Hi Rhythm, and Hi Records: expect to find their stories within this book as well. They were essential to Al Green's greatness, and a happier part of this often dark tale.

❖

So who is Al Green? Different writers have experienced different Als. When Don McLeese interviewed him for the *Chicago Sun-Times* in 1985, he met an unassuming, low-key individual. Green, appearing at a gospel show in town, was staying at a Holiday Inn and driving a budget car. "This is the greatest R&B singer of his generation, and he's coming to this businessman's hotel. There was no one with him."

McLeese was used to quickie celebrity interviews where "you'd have an hour. I spent the afternoon with Green. There was no sense that he was in any hurry to get rid of me; the clock didn't seem to make much difference. He was just really, really charming and *on*. He talked a lot. You didn't have to pull anything out of him." Al didn't mind questions about the Mary Woodson incident. In fact, "the one thing he wanted to clarify was that it was Cream of Wheat."

David Nathan, interviewing Green in 1976 for the UK publication *Blues & Soul*, encountered a more outrageous Al. Delayed at the hotel for their scheduled interview, Green was about to hop in the shower and suggested that Nathan and the magazine's photographer come by, as they "might like a photo of him whilst he's taking the shower." Green would inform Nathan he was thinking of doing a tour of schools and universities, but only to "talk. As an orator."

In 1989 Kristine McKenna met a red-sunglassed Reverend clutching a family-sized pack of Juicy Fruit who broke into "Blue Suede Shoes" before kissing all the female members of his record label's publicity staff, then hollered at passersby on the street. "The man has a roving eye," she wrote. "Every woman who walks by the window distracts him." This Al was terminally upbeat. "I've never been unhappy," he insisted.

"I'm not happy," a melancholy Green had confessed to Lynn Norment thirteen years earlier. This was her first story for *Ebony* magazine, and there was a lot of pressure to deliver. "I put out my notebook, ready to interview him—this was before we were using tape recorders on a regular basis. And he said, 'Do you have to do that?'" "Do what?" asked Lynn. "Do you have to *write down* what I say?"

A nonplussed Norment informed him that was her job. "He would clam up if I started writing. If I put the notebook down, I could ask him anything and he would answer." She struggled to remember everything Green said, running off to the bathroom or waiting until he stepped out of the room to scribble everything down. "This went on and on throughout the afternoon. It was very, very odd." Norment got her story and has gone on to interview Green many times since. "There's a mystery and mystique about him. He was intriguing, all through the years. He leaves you feeling there's so much more he's not sharing."

Just about every interviewer has encountered Third-Person Al, famous for such pronouncements as: "Some of the things Al Green does, me doesn't agree with. 'Me' is always pressuring Al Green to follow the true line of light and perfection." Got that? Al not only does this in interviews but in day-to-day life. "He talks in the third person *a lot*," said Paul Zaleski, producer of some of Green's best eighties gospel. Renowned biographer Peter Guralnick declared interviewing Al "an exercise in forbearance, as he addresses himself with the eloquence of a Professor Irwin Corey to subjects never raised, jumps from topic to topic with the skittishness of a startled deer, and generally does not seem to be of this world."

Oddball behavior, or shrewd strategy? For all his erratic behavior, Green proved early in the game that he was extremely savvy about the press. "People don't need to know all about a performer," he said in 1972. "The less people know, the better. There's a whole psychological difference once you know about a thing or person . . . you say, 'Okay, I know that, so what else is there to know about now?'"

Al Green has made sure that plenty remains unknown. Details of court cases, run-ins with the law, his marriages and relationships (and their difficulties) have been kept out of the press for the most part. If questions turn personal, he deflects them with a smile. "I live in town, sometimes I live out of town, sometimes I live uptown, crosstown . . . I'm a loner, you know? I really don't hang out with a bunch of folks."

A complex, obtuse individual, yet the image Al promotes is a laughably simple one. "I'm just a guy that lives out in the country on a hill in Shelby Forest, [who] loves to read a book* and sing a song. That's all." Green likes to insist he is not a tragic figure. "We don't deal in that arena whatsoever, with the arena of tormented lives. So many pop stars have had unfortunate lives, but that's not our thrust."

As far as he's concerned, there's no need to question the Reverend—about anything. "I put the truth down in such a profound way it can't be denied. I'm a mystery and a miracle, and that's enough to write about."

❖

In 1976 Green bought a Memphis church and became its minister, forsaking his million-dollar career to return to the gospel music he'd been raised on. This transition is one that white music journalists love to overstate a la Robert Johnson selling his soul to the devil at the crossroads. The fact that Green sought refuge in the church not long after Mary Woodson's death neatly wraps up the tale.

Michael Awkward sheds light on the often predictable and reductive manner in which this part of the Green saga is told. "Knowledge of his eventual (albeit temporary) repudiation of secular music in favor of gospel music . . . motivates critics looking for an overarching interpretation of the meanings of the music to view it as reflecting a typical twentieth-century dilemma for vocalists trained in black churches who feel called upon to explore the pleasures and vicissitudes of romantic love rather than human struggles to achieve spiritual salvation."

As Awkward notes, the line writers love to quote is from "Belle," title song of the wonderfully idiosyncratic 1977 album that Green cowrote, coproduced, and performed directly after leaving Willie Mitchell for the gospel world. Addressing a young lady he covets (Mary Woodson, in fact, if Al is to be believed), he sings: "It's you that I want, but Him that I need." "Belle," writes Awkward, "is cited as evidence of Green's efforts to resolve his dialectical concerns after he has been born-again . . . these concerns are then grafted upon and seen as an animating force in his entire popular oeuvre."

---

* I've scoured every Green interview I could get my hands on, and the only book he ever mentions reading is the Bible. That one Al's studied so much he's told his congregation that every single word in his personal copy is underlined, prompting one of his sons to ask, "Daddy, if you underline everything, how you gonna know what's important?"

I believe Al's life is far more ambiguous, chaotic, and unsettled than the clichéd happy ending usually reported—and that he suggests in statements like: "The greatest thing that ever happened to me, to Al Green, the little boy from Arkansas, was that amidst all the doubts and speculation, I found peace."

❖

As much as Green has aided and abetted this simplistic telling of his life, he's also resented it. Al's quick to point out that he turned to the Lord due to an earlier conversion (at Disneyland, of all places), not because of Mary Woodson. Most interestingly, he rejects the idea that he has even been conflicted in any way. Al dismissed the idea of a divided soul in a remarkable interview he gave in 2000 while promoting his autobiography—a work that spent pages furthering that very notion. "It can only be one man in here," Green insisted. "This two people tuggin' at each other . . . they don't *exist* in *me* . . . it's good for sellin' books . . . the book creates this illusion. . . . Everything everybody want to know about Al Green, they already know."

At the same time, Green takes pride in the fact that no one knows who he really is. He's boasted of it his entire career—in songs, in interviews, even in sermons at his church. To a reporter in 1978: "I could be considered eccentric. I'm hard to figure out." To one in 1975: "I'm a weirdo. I don't hang around people. No one really knows me." To another in 1972: "I guess I really don't want anyone to know me as well as I know myself."

❖

I was warned this would not be an easy book to write. "Unless there's money involved, most people who've worked for him would rather not relive the experience," said one who'd been close to Green. Very few members of the Enterprise Orchestra, his classic, unsung seventies band, are even alive. "Playin' for Al Green is not that good for your health," joked one of the few surviving members, Reuben Fairfax Jr. More than a few people I spoke with seemed vexed by Al and grew agitated reliving their memories. Others felt there was no way to get to the bottom of the well. "There are so many different sides, I don't know how you're gonna do it," said Paul Zaleski. "There's ten personalities in him." The number of Als seemed to increase the more I dug.

Green makes it difficult to contact him, especially nowadays, when church seems to be his only concern. He has no manager, no label, no website, and is said to communicate via cheap phones that he tosses once the number becomes too popular. Those who know the intricacies of Al instructed me to send a letter to the post office box he'd kept for decades. No response. When I tried again, it was returned. The box had abruptly been closed, no forwarding address given. Subsequent letters to his church have gone unanswered. As *Take Me to the River* proved, he wasn't interested in telling his own story, let alone relinquishing any control over it to some stranger.

❖

I've had this book in mind for over twenty years, and as much as I relished the idea of interviewing Al, the fact that he wasn't interested was expected. There will be those who find the portrait that emerges in these pages somewhat bewildering, even disturbing. None of it diminishes his art for me, which I have tried to address in detail with admiration and honesty. Al is one of the greatest singers to ever grace this planet, and even though he's in his seventies, I believe this unruly genius is still capable of producing another masterpiece.

And make no mistake, Al Green *is* hard to figure out. Forget the usual calculated rock-star machinations, which inevitably boil down to some sort of cape, new hairdo, and a set of shades. Gaze upon a handful of Green's TV performances over the years—he really does seem to inhabit different *people,* not personas. At the risk of overusing Green's own favorite adjective for himself, he is one of the last great mysteries left in pop music.

What follows is what I managed to find out about him—about all the different Al Greens. I'm certain there is much more to be unearthed. For all his "I'm just a regular guy" jive, I do believe Al Green is a tormented soul.

As loath as I am to quote that old schoolmarm of rock criticism Robert Christgau, he's made a salient point about Green every now and then, most notably: "He demands to have his feet in the ground and walk in the water." That rang true when it was written in 1976, and I suspect it may still be on the money today.

Has Al Green found any love and happiness in this life, with or without the Lord? I wonder. As will you.

LITTLE AL, COUNTRY BOY

I was the black sheep of the family, the weirdo.
—AL GREEN

It feels right that Al Green comes from a place that can barely be located at all. Dansby, Arkansas, lies out in the farmland of Lee County, some fifty miles west of Memphis. It was just a tiny dot on the map of rural Arkansas. Al recalled visiting nearby Greasy Corner as a child and being wowed that it had a stop sign. Albert Leorns Greene was born in Dansby April 13, 1946,* although the family soon moved down the road to Jacknash, a hamlet that has disappeared completely. According to Cora, Al's mother, the historical museum in nearby Forrest City once exhibited a doctor's table Albert was supposed to have been born on, but she knew better. "I had that boy on the floor," she informed *Rolling Stone*.

Country life made a lasting impression on Green—or little Al, as he tellingly refers to himself in this period, even when he mentions his pre-stardom upbringing during sermons. In the opening chapter of his autobiography, Green points out that before he heard any R&B or gospel, it was the music of the land itself that called to him. He rhapsodizes

---

* Al would change his last name to Green once he moved to Memphis in 1968, even though he'd already had one hit record credited to Al Greene. "I dropped the 'e' because Greene with an 'e' stands for somebody's name. Green without an 'e' on the end, just g-r-e-e-n, is a color . . . I like the color. I'd rather be a color." For the sake of simplicity I'll refer to him as Green throughout unless noting the billing of his early groups/releases.

over rain on the windowpane and wind whistling through the cornfields.* Little Al loved the creatures that populated the farm and still finds himself entranced by nature programs on TV. "Animals make more sense than humans most of the time," he said in 2008. He'd claim that working with livestock would prepare him for his religious calling later in life. "I was taught to raise cattle and sheep . . . keeping a flock." For him, presiding over a ministry is "the same thing."

The simplicity of country life left its mark. One of the first things Al did upon achieving stardom was to buy a country estate and another nearby farm. He bought livestock and raised horses, just like his father had. "Really, I'm just a down-home country boy," Green insisted in 1996. "I like to get my pickup truck and load a few bales of hay."

❖

Albert was the sixth of ten children—five girls, five boys (Mary, Odessa, Margaret, Maxine, Cluster, Walter, William, Robert, Al, Lonel**). The family lived in a tiny two-bedroom house. The Greenes were dirt poor. "I learned what it means to hear your father say, 'Well, hey, you all can't have shoes at the same time, somebody will have to wait.' When I was a kid I always wanted a bike. And I never did get a bike." Hard times. "When I was young I decided I was not going to be poor," he said.

Robert Greene was an uneducated sharecropper employed by Paul Benton on the Red Gum Plantation. According to Al, four generations of Greenes had worked there before him. The Greene family was allowed to live on the property, partial payment for Robert's work. Like every other sharecropper, he worked hard and never got ahead. White plantation owners called the shots.

"My father was a jack of all trades and a master of none," said Al. As he saw it, Robert Greene "was just like me . . . a loner." In order to explore the complexities lurking in the son, one need look no further than the father. "My daddy was a man full of contradictions, secrets and sorrows," writes Al. Robert Greene also had a temper: "It was like he had a switch inside him and you could never quite be sure what was going to flick it." Those who know Al described him much the same way.

---

* In all my interviews for the book, I could find no one present for his very early years, so this is the one area of his autobiography relied on here, however uneasily.

** I've also seen his name spelled Lonell. In Green's book it is Larnell. In 1984 court records it is Lonel.

❖

"My mother and my father, they were Baptists," Green told Geoffrey Himes. "We were raised in church." Church was the one avenue of escape for African Americans in the area. As Green notes in his book, this was the one place they could relax, be themselves, and avoid "the eyes of the overseer." In a 1993 interview, gospel (and sometimes R&B) singer Marie Knight agreed with Green. "In those days the churches were loaded with young people . . . it wasn't as open as it is now, such as nightclubs and all that stuff. They weren't around. That was our only outlet—the church."

There were two churches in Dansby, Taylor's Chapel and Church of the Living God. The Greenes attended them both. The latter was a bit more formal and restrained; Taylor's Chapel was thumping with Pentecostal Holy Ghost ecstasy. "We used to have church down in the country," Green told his own congregation, relishing the memories. "We used to shout every time they stopped the music, you could hear the high heels that the mothers had on—*dit dit dit*—against the floor . . . a wooden floor."

Al felt church was more of an obligation to his father: "He wasn't all religious himself, but he tried to bring up a religious family." It was up to Mama Greene which church they attended each Sunday. Cora Lee Greene was a church bird, and later on she'd be very active in her son's church. When asked to describe his mother, Al chose these five words: "Diligence, forgiveness, humbleness, meekness, steadfastness." He was very close to her as a child and, while talking about her in 2008, preferred the word "mama" over "mother": "I measure other women by the stature of my mama."

Green's relatives were "old country folk," said bass player Reuben Fairfax Jr. "They had a slight belief in voodoo . . . they had funny ways." Mama Greene "couldn't sit in a chair without putting a handkerchief down, in case someone had thrown some voodoo dust on it." Everybody I talked to was plain crazy about Cora. They all called her Mama, and meant it. Mama Greene was "just great—a real person," said Fairfax. "So sweet, a beautiful lady," agreed Jackie Lee, widow of Al's longtime bandleader Larry Lee. And Cora was not without a sense of humor, apparently. In later years, Mama Greene would routinely ask Jackie why she hadn't married her son. "I'm with the guitar player," Jackie would inform her. "Every time I got pregnant she would think it was Al's baby, and I'd say, 'No it's not, it's Larry Lee's!' She was just playin'."

According to Al, Robert and Cora were distant cousins. There is scant information on the Greene clan in his book, other than the fact that they were descended from slaves and that Al had a great-great-grandfather who had escaped plantation life by being a professional gambler—one who, when bored, liked to fire off his pearl-handled revolvers to incite people to dance. Band member Johnny Brown recalled playing a funeral for Green's one-hundred-year-old grandmother "way out in the country in Forrest City." Al sang "Amazing Grace" at her service, and afterward they buried her not far from the church. "Al and his brothers, they all grabbed shovels and filled the hole up. They didn't use no tractor."

❖

Gospel music was a central part of church, and a big part of family life. "I was raised on it," said Green. "It was put in my cornbread." Singing was a family endeavor. "We'd just get together sometimes on Sunday evenings and sing. I mean *everybody* sang—my mom and dad sang *for real*." Al was particularly struck by Cora's talent. "My momma could sing like a jaybird!" The Greenes sang gospel music—and nothing but, unless they wanted to face the wrath of Robert. "My father played bass in different R&B groups, but he only played Christian music at home," recalled Al, who maintains that his dad had dreams of making it big in gospel. "Strangely enough about my dad, he always wanted to play gospel music but he'd still go out and get drunk on a Saturday night. I couldn't figure that." (Green, who can be a severe judge of character, goes as far as to call his father a hypocrite in his book.)

Robert formed a gospel group with his sons—except Al. Scraping funds together for a mail-order Rickenbacker guitar that Al's older brother Walter taught himself to play, the Greene Brothers developed a repertoire of such gospel standards as "Working on a Building," "Packing Up," and "Every Time I Feel the Spirit." They started making a name for themselves playing nearby churches. Seven-year-old Al watched with envy as the Greene Brothers rehearsed. When he asked to join the group, one of his brothers laughed in his face. "He looked at me and said, 'You must be kidding! Not only are you too young but you can't sing.' Needless to say my feathers were ruffled and I decided that I was going to show them."

Al's favorite gospel song as a child was "God Is Standing By," recorded by the Soul Stirrers and written by a contemporary of Greene's, Johnny Taylor. "I said, 'When I get big, I'm going to cut that song,'" Al recalled, and he'd do just that early in his career. Al Green might have been an erratic, ethereal being at times, but beneath the clouds lurked a will of iron. If he said he was going to do something, he usually did it—even if it took years. Al would later stress that whatever he learned to do, he had to do it himself. "Nobody ever did lend no helping hand . . . I always had to make it on my own, even as a little kid."

Green taught himself some rudimentary guitar on Walter's Rickenbacker despite the fact his brother "beat me over the head with it about nine times" for sneaking onto the guitar (and knocking it out of tune in the process) when Walter was out. "He'd say, 'You think you're T-Bone Walker?' I couldn't help it, man. I had the desire." The fact that his family excluded him from the group only spurred him on. "All I knew was that I wanted to sing so bad that I was going to sing on my own without anyone."

❖

Having a family gospel group didn't solve Robert Greene's problems. He was still stuck on the Red Gum Plantation, trapped in Jacknash, barely scratching out a living for his wife and ten kids. An understandably frustrated man, Robert dealt with the pressure by hitting the bottle. He'd throw Al and a few of his brothers into his old blue GMC pickup and tell Cora he was going to town. He'd tear off to the honky-tonks, leaving little Al behind in the GMC. "After a while he'd come out staggering and slurring, 'Now don't you tell your mama what I did, boy,'" Green told Larry Getlen. "He was so drunk, I wouldn't have to say anything."

At first these excursions were occasional detours Cora would overlook, but as Robert's frustrations mounted, they became more and more frequent, provoking intense rows with his wife. Al saw alcoholism, and he saw violence. Although Green could recall his father hitting him only once when he lunged for food at the dinner table, his mother wasn't so lucky. He'd witness his father "spitting curses and throwing punches, aiming to break Mama's jaw." The Greene children lived in fear "that one of them would grab for a knife or pull out a gun . . . one or the other was forever talking about leaving, and if it wasn't leaving, it was calling the police."

These were not easy times for little Al. By his own admission, he was a sensitive child, "the kid under a tree by himself." He wasn't good at sports and had just two friends—one of whom was crippled, picked on, and liked to sing Ben E. King's "Stand by Me" over and over, despite the fact he couldn't carry a tune. Al was a misfit, "always the weird one. Really . . . a very weird character. Always in trouble." Making matters worse was the fact he was surrounded by a set of mostly macho males, particularly Walter. "His brothers were real manly," said Johnny Brown. They were the "kind of guys who you don't want to be on the bad side of. Real tough guys with processed hair. And Al was the kind of guy they made fun of because he liked to hear birds sing. So he was close to his sisters."

Dealing with his dad presented its own problems for Al, who'd later reveal Robert could be capable of great cruelty. Al had a pet goat, Billy, and it kept getting loose. Despite his father's warnings, Billy kept escaping. Robert felt it was time to teach him a lesson. "We were having dinner one night and I'm thinking, 'Hmm, this stew tastes good, not like anything I've ever tasted before.'" Al asked his mom what kind of meat was in the stew. His mother remained silent, as did his father—until he started "cracking up with laughter . . . at that moment I knew it was Billy I was eating." It was a brutal thing to do to a little boy. "I've never eaten goat since," Al admitted to Jon Wilde.

Despite the conflicts, after Al became a star he employed most of his family members at one point or another. The only quote I've ever seen from his father was when he told the *Los Angeles Times* in 1974 that he "worried in the beginning if this life would be good for him or not—if it would be a bad influence." Al's kinfolk would later serve as his bodyguards. "They didn't let anybody get to the dressing room door," he boasted. "When somebody wanted to see me, they had to talk to 'Pop' Green. One time I took off in a rent-a-car and my brothers sent the highway patrol after me." And yet he'd keep all his family members at arm's length.

There was suspicion. Mistrust. "My brothers, they look at me as if I'm strange . . . I'm just different," said Al in 1975. And according to him, it's never gone away. "My brothers and sisters . . . they love me . . . but they don't really know how to show it," he'd say in 2008.

Different. That was Albert Leorns Green, and that's just what he'd been told when he was a child. "My momma said, 'You gonna be a little different than the rest of the children.'" And he wasn't going to change for nobody.

❖

There came a point when Robert Greene just couldn't take plantation life anymore: 1955. Al says it was when the money came in for that year's harvest. The payment for all the work he and his family had done amounted to only $800. Shortly thereafter Robert Greene rousted his family out of bed and instructed them to pack their things. They were leaving. Now. They filled up the GMC with their belongings, strapping a bed on top of it all. It was like "something out of the *Beverly Hillbillies*," writes Green.

Robert left the South in the dust, following the flight of so many African Americans by taking his family north to the factories of Grand Rapids, Michigan, "Furniture City." Walter had escaped Jacknash by marrying and moving there a year before—his father had grumbled about it when short a hand at harvest time—but it had planted a seed as well. Walter found work in a refrigerator plant, and soon the rest of the family was on his doorstep.

"When we got there, didn't have no job, no food, nowhere to go, no phone," Green told his church. "Dad said, 'Well, in the morning I'm gonna go out with my son and see if they need anybody." Al says he accompanied his father to the foundry, where his dad told someone in charge he had mouths to feed at home and needed work. "God made a way so the man gave my Daddy a job," said Al, although in his book he maintains relief didn't come so instantly. Robert was hired at Kaminder's Car Wash in downtown Grand Rapids, where most of his sons would work alongside him, eventually even his "black sheep" son.

To this day, Green rarely visits the city, although he's played there a few times. "He don't like to come here, 'cause Grand Rapids never really supported him back in those days," said Lee Virgins, who sang in Al's first two groups, the Creations and the Soul Mates. "We always had to get out of town to get our props."

Little Al did not take to Michigan. As he writes, the very name of the state can "still make me shudder." It was cold, gray, full of soot-covered buildings and desperate people. But Green learned to adapt. The day after he got beat up at Franklin Elementary School he conked the bully on the head with a Coke bottle until he bled. Al was learning the ways of the world. In high school he'd spend a month on the football team before getting kicked off for "repeated warnings of unnecessary roughness."

It was in Grand Rapids that Green's interest in music intensified. According to local choir member Larry Redd, Al made his debut with the Greene Brothers at a small Grand Rapids church shortly after moving there. The Greene Brothers did their set, and "at the end of the program, they indicated that their little brother had been wanting to sing with them and this was his debut, so they introduced Albert to the small crowd. We thought that this kid was all off-key—but he put so much heart and soul into it. It was an amazing performance."

However rough that first landing, Green quickly became star of the family group. "He was the talk of the town, don't think he wasn't," instructs Lee Virgins, who insisted that everybody was captivated by the little kid who could belt out Soul Stirrers tunes. "Al was electrifying, even when he was singing gospel as a kid in church." Outside of Al, the family group was "mediocre," he said. Brother Walter, reputed to be a good guitarist, "wanted to be an entertainer," according to George Lowe, one of the group of kids who sang around town. He was a "showman, a flashy guy, but he didn't have the talent. He tried to be a version of Al." When it came to the Greene Brothers, "Al was gifted," said Virgins. "It's like this: you got a yard full of chickens, and you walk out there and say, 'Well, which one's the best?' That was Al."

❖

Lee Virgins was the first person to believe in Al Green's talent. He encouraged him to sing, gave him food and shelter when he had nowhere to go, even sent funds his way after Al left Grand Rapids for Memphis. Four years older than Al, Lee had sung gospel with the Pilgrim Wonders as well as with various vocal groups around town. His father also worked at Kaminder's Car Wash, and he drove Robert Greene there when the family had no car. Lee met Al when he was around eleven or twelve, and they became fast friends. Al was "very, very shy" and knew little of the world outside of church. "I'd watch over him," said Virgins. "Al, he wasn't used to the streets like I was. I was sneakin' in the bars when I was fifteen years old. I loved Al like the younger brother I never had. If he had a problem, he'd come to me."

Though the Greene Brothers never recorded, live performances took them as far as New York and Canada. They'd cover gospel hits by the Swanee Quintet and the Sensational Nightingales, and would perform Alex Bradford's "Too Close," which Al would record a chilling version of early in his later gospel career. But the gospel artist that grabbed Green the most was Claude Jeter, the dazzling lead singer of the Swan Silvertones. His stirring falsetto on numbers such as "Savior, Pass Me Not" was an elemental influence on Green's style. "He's fantastic—his *highs,*" enthused Green on a 1972 TV appearance and then let rip a falsetto line from Jeter's "Mary, Don't You Weep."

The Greenes' apartment on Sycamore Street was next door to Mother Bates's House of Prayer, a lively storefront church that welcomed all and sundry through its doors. Mother Bates's selfless devotion to the Lord made an indelible impression on Al; she in turn was so impressed by his singing she took him on the revival circuit throughout the Midwest to belt out gospel numbers as the people flocked in. His father resented it, as he did anything that took his son away from the family band. It's clear that a calling to gospel music and church life pulled at Al from the very beginning. As a teenager he'd tell the Reverend Charlie Jones, the director of his youth choir at Macedonia Missionary Baptist Church, "'Deacon Jones, I'm going out and make a million, and then I'm coming back to Christianity.' I said I'd be praying for him 'till he gets back."

❖

Much to the consternation of his father, Green had also become immersed in R&B. "I first got really interested in pop music when my Dad said I couldn't bring it into the house." Al would "sneak away to the record shop until it was time to go home." First and foremost was Sam Cooke, who remains Al Green's favorite singer to this day. "He had such poise, control and smoothness. His voice could move mountains." Green was such a fanatic that when he was out on the road with his gospel band in the eighties, he'd repeatedly steal off with Reuben Fairfax Jr.'s cassette copy of *The Best of Sam Cooke.* Al would "knock on the door, come in to talk and go right over to the tape machine, get the tape, start to laughin', then go to his room. I probably bought it about ten times."

There was plenty for Al to relate to in Cooke. As a singer he possessed warmth and intensity, not to mention an ability to carry a tune into outer space. With matinee-idol looks and an easy charisma, Sam brought sexuality to gospel. Young female admirers would rush the stage to hear him intone such Soul Stirrers classics as "Jesus Gave Me Water." When Sam left the group in 1957 to record pop hits like "Cupid" and "You Send Me," many gospel fans never forgave him.

"I've long thought that Al makes more of that high, soaring Soul Stirrers style than Cooke himself does in his pop hits," maintained musician Dale Lawrence, who nonetheless points to Cooke's 1964 secular masterpiece "That's Where It's At" if you want to hear the roots of Al Green. "There's that double-tracked vocal that's all over Green's records. Yes, it's make-out music—but it's also a song *about* making out, about the end of an especially wonderful date, which I think you could also say about some of Al Green's records. Cooke even laughs during 'That's Where It's At,' another touch Al Green would be known for."

Another big influence on Green's singing was Jackie Wilson, the frenzied R&B star famous for belting out "Reet Petite" and "Lonely Teardrops." A former boxer from Detroit, "Mr. Excitement" was known for his four-octave vocal range and electrifying live performances. Wilson "hit the high notes and let them tingle," said Green. The "snappy sound" of James Brown was another that Al studied closely: "I dug James Brown for a good, strong stand." When Green went with Lee Virgins to see Brown perform in Grand Rapids, local deejay Roy Brown got them backstage. "We went to James Brown's dressing room, just me and Al," said Virgins, who felt witnessing Brown's organization in action made a lasting impression on Green.

Sam Cooke, Jackie Wilson, James Brown: those three names in particular would be mentioned by Al over and over in interviews. "I thought that if I could combine these three, I'd be great."

One rock and roll singer had a huge impact on Al—Elvis Presley. "I was an Elvis fanatic," admitted Green. "I had every Elvis record I could find, and I saw every movie." It was one more thing he felt his family just didn't understand. "Nine brothers and sisters, I'm upstairs in my room listening to 'Teddy Bear' and 'Love Me Tender.' Everybody's saying, 'This guy is tripped out.'" He's remained a lifelong fan. David Steele, who produced Green in the early nineties, witnessed Al warming up at the mic by singing a few lines of "Teddy Bear."*

Green "didn't make distinctions between spiritual and secular music to any great extent back then. If they sang with feeling, from their hearts, I loved their music." His father felt differently. Al would sneak records into the house,** and if Robert heard any secular sounds, he'd demand Al turn them off immediately. "When he'd leave again, I'd turn it back on," said Green. Cora, on the other hand, would whisper her encouragement. "My mother said, 'Play 'em.' I'd say, 'You sure?' She'd say, 'Play 'em!'" When they heard Robert coming in, Al would dive for the stereo controls.

❖

---

* Elvis and Al crossed paths only once during the early seventies—in a Memphis restroom "at a club over on Union Avenue," said Green. "Two men standin' up against some stalls, we both got it out and we are juicing the stall. I said, 'Man, I like your music.'" More pleasantries were exchanged. "I'd like to have shaken his hand, but it didn't seem like the right time," said Green.

** Green says the first one he actually bought was Solomon Burke's fabulous 1964 hit, "Cry to Me," which seems a little late compared to the other influences named here.

Even more sinful was the fact that Green had started singing R&B himself. Curtis Rodgers was a friend of Lee's who had a vocal group called the Enchanters that had lost its lead singer. Virgins told him about Al. They "asked me if I wouldn't sing with their rock group. I said, 'Man, my dad would hang me—literally *hang* me—do you hear me?'" The temptation proved too great, however. After he'd rehearse with his brothers, Green began sneaking over to 10 p.m. rehearsals with Lee Virgins, Curtis Rodgers, and another local teenager, Gene Mason. Blamed for leading Al astray, Lee Virgins wouldn't set foot in the apartment. Green would "always come out to the car. He'd get in, we'd take off." Even Cora was displeased with her son at the time.

From the get-go, Al "was really terrific," said Rodgers, and despite his churchy exterior "knew all the songs." The Creations wouldn't do any originals. Their material was the R&B of the day—"Please, Please, Please" by James Brown, "Knock on Wood" by Eddie Floyd, "My Girl" by the Temptations, Otis Redding. "Al did a lot of Jackie Wilson," said Curtis, and according to Lee, it was Curtis or Gene who came up with a name for their group: the Creations. From the beginning, Al was the main attraction. "He sung all of the leads," said Virgins. The Creations "rehearsed for a few weeks, until we sang at an American Legion club—our first public performance," said Rodgers. It was a local band talent contest, "twenty-five dollars for the winner," Curtis recalled. "We won the contest!" The next time they came back, they won again.*

Al's father soon caught wind that his son was singing the devil's music. Matters came to a head over a record Green had slipped into the house: Jackie Wilson's number one R&B smash, "Baby Workout," which had been released in March 1963, a month before Al turned seventeen. "Come out here on the floor, let's rock some more," wailed Jackie. The innuendos on parade were too much for Robert Greene. "He caught me playing it and broke it," said Al. "So I bought it again."**

---

* Note: According to my research, just about everything in Green's book concerning the Creations period and Al's first recordings in Grand Rapids is off the mark. It states that the group performed original material. Not so, say other members; nor was their first gig in Battle Creek, Michigan; nor did they ever record a single for Zodiac (actually another Detroit-based group also called the Creations), even though Al describes this event in some detail. And Lee Virgins's name is incorrectly stated as Virgis.

** In his book, Green says the record that got him ejected was Wilson's 1960 recording of "A Woman, a Lover, a Friend." In most other tellings of the incident during interviews it is "Baby Workout."

Before Al could manage that, though, he was thrown out of the house. This would mean the end of the Greene Brothers gospel group,* which only added to the guilt. "I was the terrible kid who broke up the good, old-fashioned family group," said Al. Lee recalled that Cora "didn't really care for it when Al left." Virgins maintained this was a very rough time for Green. "I told him, 'Al, don't let nobody stop you. You gonna make it.'"

At the moment, though, Al was homeless. "I left home at sixteen to take care of myself, and I've been alone ever since."

❖

Al turned to Lee Virgins for help. Lee, who was married with two kids, let him have an upstairs bedroom rent-free at his 1312 Prospect home. At first Al dropped out of school and looked for work. After the storm clouds passed, he returned to the family apartment for Sunday meals, and an uneasy truce was struck with his father, who snagged him a nine-to-five job at Kaminder's Car Wash as a detailer. Green would reenroll at age nineteen, graduating from South High School in 1966.

"I wanted to prove something to my father," maintained Green. One day before he left home, his father predicted Al would be a failure. "You're not gonna be worth a dime!" he told his son. "That's when I made up my mind—I'm gonna be all he said I'm *not* gonna be." According to Lee, not one member of Al's family was present at his graduation. "I was the only somebody there. That really bothered me. I was the onliest one."

As soon as Green moved in with Lee, the Creations took off. Virgins contacted a small-time promoter in nearby Battle Creek by the name of Big Jim Sweet. Following an audition at the local VFW hall, Sweet agreed to hire them for a Sunday matinee show at the El Grotto Club in Battle Creek. That day, the Creations rehearsed with the club's house band "until they got our songs right," said Virgins. "The band was fantastic."

That band was Jr. Walker and the All Stars. This was before they'd score big at Motown with "Shotgun," a song based on a dance Walker witnessed at the El Grotto. "They was nobody then, they was just like us," said Virgins. "They told us, 'You guys are going somewhere.'" Together the All Stars and the Creations proved to be a hot combination. Jr. Walker and the All Stars "rocked the house, the whole place just rocked!" said

---

* At least with Al. In 1971 Green would say the group was still going strong as the family had "brought in a guy from outside the family and changed the name to the Golden Harmonaires." I've never seen mention of this anywhere else.

Rodgers. The Creations wrecked the joint that Sunday at the El Grotto. When they returned the next Sunday "there was a line around the building," said Virgins. According to Curtis Rodgers, Big Jim Sweet then invited the Creations on the road. "He said, 'Whoa, man! I'd like for you guys to join my traveling road show and be the stars! That's how good I think you are.' He was quite a talker."

Big Jim Sweet not only promoted this ragtag revue, he was the emcee and comedian of the show. "He was like Redd Foxx," said Rodgers. "Real dark, fat, and ugly—and funny as all get out. Before the show he would come on the stage dressed like a lady." There were several other acts on the show, like Bobby 'Blue' Bland soundalike Lou Wilson and a "dancer that did a burlesque-type thing," Rodgers recalled. "We was the last act on the show, 'cause we were the main thing." Jr. Walker and the All Stars provided backup, and together they "really kept the places jam-packed," said Curtis.

Lee took care of bookings. "I was the spokesman for the group, we didn't have a manager. We voted on everything." They had choreographed dance moves to go with the songs, and Lee designed some snappy red shirts for the group to wear with their suits. "We dressed very conservative," said Virgins. The Creations drove to the gigs in Lee's '60 white-with-black-top Chevy convertible, until things got so busy Sweet provided a ride. "A large four-door Buick or Olds," recalled Rodgers. "The driver weighed about four hundred pounds. I never saw him out of the car once. He would come all the way to Grand Rapids to pick us up, we'd do all the shows, and he'd bring us back to Grand Rapids. Jim Sweet took care of us—we ate good, didn't drink or do drugs, I don't even think we smoked cigarettes. We'd hook up with different promoters and stay at their big, fancy homes. We felt like stars!" We didn't make a lotta money . . . it might've gone to Mr. Sweet."

Being underage, Green couldn't hang out at the bar. "I would go get a pop for him, no alcohol. Club owners were very strict then," said Virgins. Al was "nice, quiet, he wasn't a bar guy. Never was a big drinker. He wasn't loud. Al was shy until he got on the stage. When he got on there, he changed into the Wolf Man. A completely different person." Virgins particularly remembered Green tearing up James Brown's "Please, Please, Please." "He killed it, just *killed* it. 'Papa's Got a Brand New Bag,' 'Bewildered' . . . he sang all the James Brown songs."

Lee chuckled recalling a show the Creations did in Muskegon with another Arkansas-born singer, J. J. Jackson, then hot due to his 1966 hit "But It's Alright." Though they were only the opening act for Jackson, "Al just ripped him apart," said Lee, laughing. "When we got offstage, man, those people were still hollerin' for Al Green and the Creations." Green had burning ambition. "He called me Virge—he'd say, 'Virge, I know I can make it.' Al *knew* he had the talent. I told everybody here in town, 'Whether I'm singin' with him or not, Al Green's gonna be a superstar.' They laughed at me . . . they didn't know *Al.* I could see his drive. That song 'Driving Wheel'?* That was strictly him!"

Despite all the confidence, Green suffered from stage fright, a lifelong affliction. Recalled Virgins, "I used to talk to him—I said, 'Al, you don't need no stage fright. You got everything. All you got to do is play with the ladies. That's what this thing is all about—*you got to play with the ladies.*' Once he'd sing a couple songs he was at home." Even early on it was apparent that once onstage, Al Green knew a thing or two about playing with the ladies—and they liked it. "Oh man, I'm tellin' ya, it was fantastic," said Virgins. "I used to tell him, 'Al, when you get out there onstage, see the women out there shakin' their legs together? They're lookin' right at *you.*'"

The Creations were now the Fabulous Creations. "We became so powerful and popular onstage, we'd do five or six cities, and when we came around again, it was sold out," said Rodgers. "We were a total *hit.*" Again, contrary to what's been written in Green's book and elsewhere, the Creations never stepped into a recording studio. "Stars, but no recordings," maintained Curtis. "Just a traveling road show."

The original version of the Creations lasted a year and a half. Virgins found a guitar player to add to the group, Otis Webster, and he'd inadvertently break up the group one day at rehearsal when he suggested they change their billing to capitalize on Al's star power. "He wanted to name the group Al Greene and the Creations," said Lee. "It wasn't Al, it was Otis." An argument ensued. Curtis maintains Al wasn't happy because "his name wasn't on the front. We got upset about that—'Why do we have to change our name? We're doin' fine right now,'" recalled Rodgers. "That hurt." He and Gene walked out of the rehearsal. Virgins had been off picking up his wife, and when he returned, he asked where Curtis and

---

* Written by Roosevelt Sykes, "Driving Wheel" was best known through Little Junior Parker's 1961 hit cover. Green would record a fantastic version in 1971.

Gene were. "They quit," was the response. It was Tuesday, and they had a show booked for Sunday. Lee got ahold of two guys he'd sung with before, Palmer James and Johnny Curry. "They came to rehearsal, man, it just fit like a glove." According to Virgins, this version of the Creations would last for several years.*

❖

Green moved out of Lee's place and got an apartment on Sheldon Avenue. He stopped working full time at the car wash so he could return to South High School. A part-time job at Fat Man's Fish Fry augmented whatever he made with the Creations. Sometimes Green sat in solo at local jazz clubs and sang standards like "Willow Weep for Me." This part of his early life is an undocumented puzzler not really discussed in his book. Lee said that this was not a frequent occurrence and that "R&B was really his thing," but Al has claimed in a few interviews that as a "little kid" he "sang jazz on Rush Street in Chicago." It was there at age sixteen or so he heard Otis Redding at the Regal Theater by hanging out in back under the fire escape. "I had no money to get in. I was a nobody." Redding finally emerged from the stage door, and as he slipped through the big crowd before being whisked away in a limo, Al saw his first star up close, and was rendered speechless by Redding's fancy red and silver silk threads and shiny black shoes. "It was like God or something stepping out of heaven!"**

Around this time Al got involved with an older Grand Rapids prostitute named Juanita. If Green's book is to be believed, he first encountered her walking out of Mother Bates's House of Worship one Sunday. From the sacred to the profane in the blink of an eye—it seems befitting of the man who'd later follow up a raunchy number like "Sweet Sixteen" with "Jesus Is Waiting" in concert. Lee Virgins maintained that Green met her

---

* Despite the billing controversy, Virgins maintained Al was loyal to the Creations. "A lot of people wanted to hire him and didn't want the group, because they thought they could get him cheaper," said Lee, who fielded a call from a Kalamazoo club owner who wanted only Green. He told him he'd have to speak to Al. During that call the booker explained to Al that he wanted only him and not the group, and asked about his fee. "Well, the group is gonna cost four hundred dollars. But if you want me to come without the group, it'll be eight hundred."

** Later, in 1967, Green was represented briefly by Phil Walden, Redding's manager, and got to know Otis. "I spent the last week of Otis Redding's life with him," Al told Stanley Booth. "Watched him write and record 'Dock of the Bay.' Said goodbye to him on a Friday and Sunday night he was dead. Broke my heart." In 2003 he'd confess that Redding "was one of my favorites. Every now and then you can hear a little Otis Redding in Al Green."

during a rare trip to the Limelight Bar. "She hit on him, he didn't hit on her," said Virgins. "Juanita was crazy 'bout Al. Street women would say, "I choose this guy," and that's what she done—she chose Al."

Juanita "was a wild child, all the guys knew her," said George Lowe, another local singer. She was "not the best looking, but had a hot body—that's what all the guys were after." In Green's book there are melodramatic descriptions of life with Juanita, the couple functioning as "pimp and whore," with Green maintaining that "sex was sort of a distraction" and that the pair was more interested in the "flamboyant costumes" they sported on the street together. He boasts of an education in hard drugs and hanging out in basement transvestite clubs. "I learned more about the dark side of the human animal than I care to pass along." These shadowy experiences left "a scar upon my soul."

When I told Lowe that Green claimed to be Juanita's sometime pimp in his book, he burst out laughing. "That's fantasy! I don't remember any of that." According to Lowe, Al "didn't know what she was really like; he was smitten and I think she broke his heart." Lee Virgins insists that it was indeed true that Green was her sometime pimp, and he saw the couple in action at the Jim Williams Motel on Division. At the time, "Al didn't have a job—but *she* did," said Lee, chuckling. But Virgins admitted Green wasn't as streetwise as his brother Walter, a pimp deep into the life. "Al, he didn't hang out with Walt. He really didn't hang out in the streets like some guys did, in after-hours and gambling joints. He stayed at home."

❖

After he left the Creations, Curtis Rodgers put together another group with George Lowe called the People's Choice. Rodgers also began hanging around Palmer James, and they discovered they both had an interest in learning about the music industry. The pair started studying everything they could find on how record companies, publishing, and radio airplay worked. The real story of Al Green's first hit, "Back Up Train," has never been told, and what has been written is "all wrong," according to Rodgers. The record came about because of "Palmer and I only," said Rodgers, who maintained even "Al didn't really know the story. We never had time to sit and talk about what we did."

First came a label called Grand Land Records. "Palmer and I decided we'd put this record company together," said Rodgers. "The idea was, 'Hey, if Berry Gordy can do it in Detroit, we can do it in Grand Rapids."

Excited about this new enterprise, Rodgers "approached Al Green and I said, 'Al, Palmer and I have a record company—why don't you sign with us, man?' He said, 'Naw, I ain't signing with you guys. I wanna go with a big company.'" Giving up on Green, Curtis informed his own band, the People's Choice, about his new label. "They laughed at me . . . thought I was crazy." Rodgers explained that they'd record them and put out a single at no expense to the band. Thus Grand Land Records released "Hot Wire" by the People's Choice in 1966. The 45 featured a crude, hand-drawn logo with a little box exclaiming, "Hits Go Better With *Grand Land*!"

A silky up-tempo soul number, "Hot Wire" was a bit of a hit. "They started to play it on the radio like crazy," said Rodgers. "Night and day . . . you'd hear it in all the cars! That kind of made Al Green uptight—'Man, every time I turn on the radio, it's "The People's Choice on Grand Land Records!"'" Suddenly Green was interested in signing—but only for a year. Palmer and Rodgers talked him into a year and a half. "Now that I've signed with you, what do you want me to do?" asked Al. They presented him with a song, told him to learn it, show up at the studio, and they'd handle the rest. Unlike the rest of his recordings, Green had no involvement in the music other than overdubbing the vocal as Rodgers and James put the rest of it together. Palmer had dropped out of school to become a songwriter. According to their soon-to-be-partner, Larry Redd, James was the artistic one. "He was a genius, a Renaissance-type of person," said Redd. Curtis was "the nuts and bolts businessman. He knew how to sell. I thought they were a good team."

Curtis declared he was the main writer on "Back Up Train," although Palmer earned a cowriting credit by contributing background parts. The inspiration for the song came from continually being on the road with bands. "I had a girlfriend in Grand Rapids and I was always leaving her behind," said Rodgers. The song was cut at the same local studio where they'd recorded the People's Choice—Midwestern Sound Studios at 444 West Leonard, in a Polish neighborhood a block away from a hot dog stand favored by musicians on nonexistent budgets. The studio was run and co-owned by Phil Roberts, a bespectacled member of local garage rockers the Kingtones. It was a thirty-by-forty room in back of a music store with a cinder-block control room containing an Ampex eight-channel one-inch tube tape recorder bought at fire-sale prices when Ampex switched to solid state. The recorder also provided the studio's only warmth; when the tube-driven machine started to glow "the whole studio would heat up."

Roberts liked Rodgers and Palmer, finding the duo "very polished," but found they "had very limited budgets. One time we had a little scrap—they didn't have enough money to pay for the session. And they got upset with me 'cause I wouldn't let them walk out with a copy." In fact, the Al Green session might not have happened had it not been for the kindness of a stranger.

Rodgers was working two jobs to fund the label, which was short the $300 they needed to record Green. One day Curtis went down to the local Woolworth's he used to haunt as a kid, as it had "a fabulous record department. The manager was a tall white guy, John Vandervort. Mr. Vandervort said, 'How are you doing, young man? I remember you. You always seemed to be the nicest young man when you came in the store and went to the music department. What're you doing now that you all grown up?'" Curtis told him about the Al Green project and how he needed money to finish it. Vandervort told him to come upstairs to his office, where he promptly wrote him a check for $300. "Now go finish your recording session," he told a dumbfounded Rodgers, who admitted, "It blew my mind."

The "Back Up Train" session went quickly. Some members of Jr. Walker's band from the El Grotto days provided instrumentation, Curtis's sister Linda provided backing vocals alongside the Creations, and the small string section comprised the Indiana-based Mancini Strings augmented by members of the Grand Rapids Symphony. Local jingle creator Ted Maters was hired to write the arrangements. Phil Roberts admitted he found the People's Choice sessions more exciting. "I thought 'Back Up Train' was a reasonably good song, but not great. I didn't really like the strings. I thought they were scratchy . . . the arrangement isn't all that great." And as far as Al Green went, "I thought he was good but not big-time good. I gotta give Curt and Palmer credit, 'cause they spotted that talent."

Judging by the accounts of those present, Al Green had no problem rising to the occasion of his first real recording session.* He was a supremely confident individual. "I was such a cocky little dude," he said years later. "I was unsure, but I had to try and hide it." Larry Redd was present when he cut vocal tracks for the album that followed "Back Up Train." "Al comes in, he sits on a stool, there's a single mic he's singing into. First track plays,

---

* According to an online post by a former classmate, Green's high school choir recorded an album locally that features a vocal solo by Al. I've never seen a copy.

he records it. It's a keeper—one take. Second take gets played, he records that. Ten tracks—all of them done in one shot. The only artist I knew that could do that was Sinatra."

Al had a way of visualizing the end result in his mind. "I just wanted it so bad, I *desired* it. You got to meditate on it, dream it . . . you have to see what you want ahead of you as being already successful," he said in 2000, comparing himself to a ballplayer at bat or a golf pro on the green. "I picture the ball going right in the cup—I saw it in my innermost self." And when the results were more than he'd even dreamed of, he could only gaze heavenward. "Lord, you must be up there."

The talents of Al Green are certainly in evidence on his first single. He whispers, shouts, hits a bit of falsetto on the fade. It's all right there; the packaging's just a bit lacking. This is a seventies singer trapped in a sixties production—the arrangement is old-fashioned, the sound a bit sludgy, and the song, not one he'd written, is far from memorable. The home-made quality adds to its charm, the plunky xylophone a nice touch. Al does his best with what he's been given, and it's a respectable debut. "A plaintive blues ballad, with Al pouring his heart out—sometimes tenderly, sometimes almost viciously," the *New Musical Express* would declare in January 1968. "Gospel chanting enhances the authenticity." But if "Back Up Train" and the largely forgettable album to follow were the sum total of his career, all he'd have is a small cult in Europe and a poorly designed website by some forlorn fan in Dublin asking, "Whatever Happened to Al Green?" Greatness would only come with the addition of Willie Mitchell, and that was off in a distant future.

❖

What is amazing is what Rodgers, James, and Larry Redd did with Green's record once it was released in October 1967. "Back Up Train" did not come out on Grand Land Records. Once more inspired by the Detroit empire of Berry Gordy, who had other labels in addition to Motown, they created a new label for their new artist—the baroquely named Hot Line Music Journal. This time the 45 label was slightly less crude—a jumbled collage of destinations (New York! Chicago! Memphis!) that James and Rodgers had stayed up all night cutting out of magazines, pasting them together. They had a thousand copies pressed at the American Record Company plant in Owosso, Michigan, and then—sure they had a win-ner—proudly marched a few copies down to play for a deejay at WLAV in

Grand Rapids, a popular station that had jumped on the People's Choice record. The reaction was one of indifference. Leaving the station, James was crushed. "Palmer said, 'Man, I'm gonna give up,'" recalled Rodgers, who gave him a pep talk. "I said, 'I'm not letting these guys discourage me. Forget Grand Rapids. I'm going to Detroit!'"

Before that happened, a crucial player joined the enterprise—Larry Redd. A childhood friend of Rodgers and James, Redd was a schoolteacher who worked a night shift deejaying at WZZM, a "middle of the road" Grand Rapids station. He became Hot Line Music Journal's head of promotion and, despite the fact his wife threatened to leave him over such a gamble, also sank $400 of his own money into the company.

The first thing Larry did was to design a poster promoting the song, which only said "BACK UP TRAIN" IS COMING! in big red letters against a white background. "We didn't have enough money to be fancy," noted Redd, laughing. They posted the cryptic signs "in a three-block radius along major streets leading in four directions to the Top 40 radio stations." It had no effect, so Redd decided to take matters into his own hands. He was going to dare to play "Back Up Train" on his own MOR station after the news one night—but only once, and for a purpose.

He'd already organized a group of telephone callers, instructing them to listen in. Right after "Back Up Train" was broadcast, they were to bombard WLAV with calls demanding to hear the hot new song they'd just heard on WZZM. Thus Larry Redd was, as he pointed out, "the first person to play 'Back Up Train' in Grand Rapids." His crafty ploy worked. The fact that WZZM was an early FM station instead of the usual tinny mono AM only added magic to the sound of "Back Up Train." As far as Grand Rapids radio was concerned, "the ice was broken," said Redd, and the other white stations followed suit. He reported that "'Back Up Train' reached number three on local charts."

Now Hot Line Music Journal turned its attention to Detroit. In college, Redd had worked with two disc jockeys who were now important players in Motor City radio—Wash Allen and Jay Butler. First Rodgers and James went to Detroit and made contact with Allen, the program director for WJLB. When he heard Redd was involved with "Back Up Train," he agreed to listen and liked what he heard. Larry went along on the second Detroit trip, visiting a local distributor, Merit Music, that got behind the record. Then they paid a visit to WCHB, where Jay Butler was on the air. "We could see him through the glass," said Rodgers. Butler waved them in and listened to their single. There was no time for small talk as the dee-jay had to get back on the air, but he told them, "Don't worry, fellas, I'm gonna take care of you." With the trifecta of Allen, Merit, and Butler now behind "Back Up Train," Rodgers said it was only a matter of weeks before "our record was number one in Detroit."

In the meantime, Rodgers went to the pressing plant in Owosso to pick up more singles. The boss there said he had somebody who wanted to talk to him. Within minutes Curtis was on the phone with Irv Beagle, one of the vice presidents at Bell Records in New York City. Rodgers had actually worked with Beagle before on some People's Choice dealings in Detroit. "I've got your record right in front of me," he said to Curtis. "We're interested in a deal." Before he knew it, Larry Utall, the head of Bell Records, flew to Grand Rapids to sign the papers. Bell was now distributing Hot Line Music Journal.

"Back Up Train" would climb to number five on the R&B charts, and number forty-one on the pop, missing the Top 40 by a single digit. It also came out in England on the Stateside label. According to Redd, Bell "froze all local sales" from the original pressings, leaving them with nine hundred copies of the single they couldn't sell. The Vietnam War was on, and local TV station WOOD was asking people to send gifts to the troops overseas. Being "aware of Armed Forces Radio and its paucity of programmed black music," Redd donated seven hundred copies of "Back Up Train" to the effort. The result? "Al Green became a hit recording artist in Vietnam."

❖

With "Back Up Train" burning up the charts, Green appeared at New York City's fabled Apollo Theater for the first time. It was only his second gig as a solo act, and as he later admitted, it "scared me to death." Lee Virgins was the force that got them there. "I kept bugging this guy about booking us there and I wouldn't give up. One day they called me and told us to come." Green, Virgins, James, and Curry hopped into Lee's black-and-white Chevy convertible for the trek to New York City. Green and Virgins would pass the time on these long trips harmonizing on old gospel songs and talking religion. "We used to discuss the Bible all the time," said Virgins. "Other guys be sleepin', Al and I would be talkin' about the Bible at one o'clock in the morning."

Once they made it to the Apollo, Green was allotted only eight minutes total to do his thing. As he recalled, "four of those minutes it takes to get from the tenth-floor dressing room all the way down to the bottom, and by the time you're into the song, they're calling you from the side, ready for the next act." Al was allowed one number—his hit. "I tried to do some Sam and Dave tunes, but they'd only let me sing 'Back Up Train.'" Green claimed he received nine encores for the one song, and Lee Virgins said it was "not an exaggeration. That was fantastic. We talked about it all the way home." Before they left the Apollo, Al told the blasé floor manager that he'd be returning, the next time occupying "a dressing room on the first floor instead of the tenth." Al was on the money with that prediction, but it would take a few more years of struggling to get there.

The first deejay to play the song at Grand Rapids' WERX station was a popular personality named Lee Lyons. When Rodgers and James brought him a copy of the single, he asked if Green had a manager. Al signed his first management contract with Lyons over a steak dinner at John Brann's Steakhouse on Division. Lyons was a pilot, and flew Al to various appearances in his private plane. A new backup group was put together, the Soul Mates, which consisted only of Lee Virgins and Al's brother Bob. Now they all had the church in common—Virgins said they'd begin every rehearsal with Al singing "Keep Your Arms Around Me," a spine-tingling gospel ballad that had been recorded by a group from Flint, Michigan, called the Bright Stars.

Everything was heading in the right direction for Al. The *Back Up Train* album was released in March 1968. The cover is classic, showing a pompadoured, suit-and-tie Green looking backward as he mans a locomotive (according to local music historian Tom Shannon, photographer Jack Carter, who shot the cover in the Grand Rapids train yards, also took a sequence of photos illustrating the lyrics of the hit—which "featured Al's girlfriend crying as he left on the train"—that were put together in slide-show fashion and, accompanied by the song, shown on local TV as a sort of crude, very early music video).

❖

Hit single. New album. Manager. Booking agent. Al Green must've felt like he'd hit the big time. Unfortunately, his career promptly fizzled out fast. Once that first hit faded away, two more singles (credited only to "Al Greene," no Soul Mates) were released—"Don't Hurt Me No More" in April 1968 and "A Lover's Hideaway" in July—and neither charted. The rest of the *Back Up Train* album material is unmemorable, the only

standout being Green's first recorded original, "Stop and Check Myself."
Throughout, Al wears his influences on his sleeve—you can hear a lot of
Jackie Wilson in his strangled cries. The album went nowhere.

Only a few months earlier Al Green had been a hot commodity. Just
as suddenly no one cared. It was a grim lesson in show business brutality.
"The walls of Jericho came tumbling down," said Green. "I came with it."
Was his career to begin and end with "Back Up Train"? "I was a one-record
act, and everybody frowns on a one record-act," lamented Al, who continued to play dates around the country to scrape together a living. "I didn't
have any direction, no plan." Worse yet, Lee Virgins insists that Green saw
next to nothing in payment for his hit. "You know how much money we
got out of 'Back Up Train'? Thirty-five dollars apiece," said Virgins, adding
that he and Al talked to a local lawyer about suing Palmer James, but were
told there was no point as Hot Line was already going under and James
was broke. "He's getting ready to lose his house," informed the mouth-
piece (according to Virgins, Palmer later tried to sue Al, but "nothing ever
came of it").

For the next few months Green wandered the country singing his
one hit, supported by pickup bands, sometimes not even getting paid. In
many an interview later, Al would recall this difficult period and reference
the fact he "only weighed 155 pounds, a little, puny guy, and it was nothing
for the club owner to take my money." He gave pained examples, such as
the Ascot Room in Dallas, which was lorded over by a guy named Big Bo,
who'd proceed to tell Al how great he'd done onstage, then refuse to pay
him. "This guy would say, 'Man, I have no money, I have NO money' . . .
and he'd get in the car and leave."

Many people I interviewed were of the opinion that unknown events
occurring early in Al's life had wounded him deeply. Johnny Brown,
Green's later bandleader, felt his starting days as a solo act and the way
he'd been treated by older, streetwise musicians had created a festering
desire for payback. One night driving to a revival gig, Al revealed how
when he was starting out, musicians thought they could take advantage of
him because they perceived him as weak. There was that high falsetto, his
enigmatic ways. "People thought Al might be a little—what's the word?
Gay," said Johnny. "They would want to charge him a whole lot, and he
knew they were playin' for other people for cheaper. That's what he had
against musicians—'Okay, all y'all want to play for me now, but when I

was struggling, didn't nobody want to mess with me.'" Al would go to great lengths to even the score in the future.

Al Green was at a crossroads. His life had been far from easy thus far. He'd been laughed at by his brothers, his peers at school. His father had disowned him. Al had tasted a bit of success only to have it abruptly pulled away. Then, in the fall of 1968, he played a handful of dates in Texas, one of them in Midland. It was there he first encountered Willie Mitchell, whose band would back him for the gig.

When Green returned to Grand Rapids, Larry Redd ran into him at the Wolverine Market. He told Redd this Willie Mitchell guy had invited him to Memphis and to record. "Should I go?" he asked Larry. "I told him he should take it."

❖

There was one person Green intended to take with him. "Al wanted to take Juanita to Memphis," said Lee Virgins. "But she couldn't leave those streets alone."

In his book Green paints a dramatic picture of their relationship's demise. Al goes to visit Juanita and finds her in bed, bearing the marks of a beating by some unknown john or pimp. He leaves without saying good-bye.

There was an equally painful but different story. Al got into an unexpected and embarrassing altercation with one of Juanita's other paramours. "He got roughed up a bit," said George Lowe. "Al wasn't a fighter, he was an easygoing guy, so that added to his humiliation. People were snickering, they whispered about it. I doubt that Al would tell the truth about being tricked and deceived or hurt, you know. He was awfully young. When you're in love for the first time and you get your heart broke, it devastates you."

Lending credence to Lowe's story is a remarkable exchange in an interview with Juan Williams in 2000, during which Green—without being asked—lurches into a telling anecdote revealing how his relationship with Juanita ended. "My girlfriend is fooling around and I find out about it," said Green, who found her in a Grand Rapids bar with some other male. Al told her it was time to go. "So the guy says to me, 'Man, the lady ain't going nowhere.'" Green repeated the command, but Juanita just ignored him. A fight ensued, which Green pontificated on in the third person. "Al weighs a hundred and forty pounds, right? He's a skinny little kid, and he's trying to fight with some guy that's a construction worker." Denizens of the bar held back his attacker, who was flashing a blade. "The guy told me, 'Al, go home.'"

That was the end of the fight, his relationship with Juanita, and life in Grand Rapids. "I left that night, packed my clothes, went over to the U-Haul place, got me a hitch and put a little tiny trailer on the back of my Buick, and I came to Memphis."

Everything would change for Al Green in Memphis. There he'd meet Willie Mitchell and his genius crew of musicians—Hi Rhythm, a funky bunch that went by the nicknames Teenie, Flick, Do Funny, and Bulldog.

Al's gonna disappear into the night for a few chapters while we set the stage for his arrival. To understand the greatness of Al Green, you have to experience the unlikely early days of Hi as well as the intricate evolution Willie Mitchell went through to develop that precise and particular Hi sound. That began by producing such fantastic singers as Syl Johnson, Ann Peebles, and the mighty O. V. Wright.

You're not in a hurry, are you? Let's relax, take our time, and do this Memphis style. A little behind the beat.

HIT INSTRUMENTALS

*Stax had everything going for itself, and Hi Records, where I was,
was like the ugly duckling across town.*
—AL GREEN

Elvis Presley. Howlin' Wolf. Jerry Lee Lewis. Ike Turner. Johnny Cash.
B.B. King. Charlie Rich. Wilson Pickett. Charlie Feathers. Tina Turner.
Roy Orbison. Otis Redding. Dusty Springfield. Willie Mitchell. Al Green.
They all made the journey to mythical, mysterious Memphis, Tennessee.

Funny place, Memphis. Sun Records and soul music, barbecue, Beale
Street. Undeniably great, all of it, but nowadays it's all neatly wrapped up
as a fun, funky commodity to be fed the tourists. I've made the pilgrim-
age more than a few times; love the place, but you never feel like you're
getting the full story. A certain gothic quality hangs in the air; there are
whispers in the shadows. Memphis—it gave the world Elvis and denied it
Dr. Martin Luther King Jr.

"Memphis despised its African-American culture, was ashamed of exactly what the world loved us for, dismissive of what made us unique,"
writes Robert Gordon, supreme historian of this town's musical history.
"Oppression is not unique to Memphis, though it's neatly encapsulated
here." King was shot down as he stood on the balcony of the Lorraine
Motel, itself a hangout for many a local musician. Racism was a daily
reality, but when it came to blacks and whites making music, Memphis
was futuristic.

"Race didn't matter. Nobody ever even cared about that," said engineer extraordinaire Terry Manning, who mixed many a Memphis classic. "People who grew up in different cultures became best friends. In the middle of Memphis, which was really backwards socially, here were two places where the first real mixing of races in the South was happening and where blacks and whites came together to make music—Stax and Hi."

Unlike other music capitals like Nashville or Los Angeles, major labels did not divide and conquer here. "Memphis has never been a company town," writes Gordon. "The forces have all been independent, renegade." Sun Records inspired countless others to start labels, even if (like Scotty Moore's Fernwood) it was from their garages. For the purpose of this book, we're talking about two labels: Hi Records and Stax. If you count Stax's precursor, Satellite, Hi and Stax started around the same time, releasing their first singles in 1957. Both would inhabit former movie theaters, although Hi's Royal Studios started in one from the very beginning while Stax moved into it (only about a mile away from Royal) in 1960. Hi and Stax had very distinct and original house bands that shared a formidable drummer essential to both: Al Jackson Jr.

The similarities really end there. Stax was a mom-and-pop operation that exploded into a department store of producers, musicians, and executives. It ebbed and flowed with the times and wasn't afraid to make music that commented on politics and inequality. Stax was the first to hit it big with its incredible roster of artists: Otis Redding, Booker T. and the MG's, Sam and Dave and many others.

Hi Records became more of a one-man band that remained true to the vision of its auteur, Willie Mitchell. It took the label much longer to find its way, but as Mitchell gained control, Hi evolved into a hit factory dependent on a singular, very specific sound and groove, dominated by one artist: Al Green.

While Stax became a darker and darker place in the seventies, undone by success and excess and populated by gun-toting thugs, Hi would remain loose, laid back, and friendly. Martin Luther King's death changed Stax into an armed camp practically overnight. Hi's studio remained untouched, even by the riots. Mitchell just slipped a few winos booze money to guard the place. Like its sound, Hi seemed timeless, somehow exempt from the turbulence of the times.

These days the very notion of "Memphis soul" has degenerated into a kind of bland, lip-service cliché, with such masters of rock overstatement as Melissa Etheridge and Paul Rodgers descending on Royal Studios intent on sucking out any marrow left in the old bones. Desperate for career-resuscitating nutrients, such artists can only churn out dull, dutiful tributes to Memphis soul that somehow manage to be 100 percent soul-free. Off to the Americana cemetery, that catchall, Norman Rockwell–friendly category that to me only indicates a dilution and declawing of fiery past glories. The thrill, as they say, is definitely gone. But once this sound had a life outside of a museum exhibit. To cop a line from Jimmy Castor, let's go back—way, way back. To the dawn of Hi Records in Memphis, Tennessee, a place, as Robert Gordon points out, "where nothing ever happens but the impossible always does."

❖

Three white Southerners, frustrated by the music business: Ray Harris was thirty; Quinton Claunch and Bill Cantrell were six years older. All had connections to Sun Records and Sam Phillips.

A man who called everybody "Hoss," Homer Ray Harris left an impression. "Tall and imposing with sharp angular features, Ray Harris carries about him a frightening intensity, and speaks with an impenetrable accent that almost demands subtitles," wrote Colin Escott. No shit. As guitarist Reggie Young recalled of a Hi Records Christmas party at Ray's house, "he introduced his wife as Murnell." When Ray left the room, Mrs. Harris expressed her irritation. "She looked at me and said, 'I wish you guys would get my name right. It's not Murnell, it's Mary Nell.'"

Born dirt poor in Mantachie, Mississippi, Harris picked cotton to purchase his first guitar. He was working at the Firestone tire plant with bass player Bill Black when Black invited him to tag along for a recording session with "some boy named Presley." Watching Elvis cut "Good Rockin' Tonight" lit a match in the Harris mind. He'd grown up at the altar of Hank Williams, but this rockabilly sound was something new, wild. He wanted in. "I thought, 'Hell! He ain't doing anything I can't do.'"

Something glorious happened next, and not unlike Ed Wood Jr. picking up a movie camera after seeing *Citizen Kane*. Harris, who'd concocted a couple of crude, crazy numbers with his ace guitarist, Wayne Cogswell, "couldn't sing and he wasn't good to look at, but he didn't care," said friend Bill Cantrell, who could hear the racket Harris made rehearsing a block away as he approached Ray's home. There he was, standing before a recorder, belting out a tune, "wearing nothing but his overalls, dripping with sweat . . . singing and sweating."

"Come On, Little Mama," Sun single 254, October 1956: There are a thousand and one ways to say "Let's do the horizontal mambo," but Ray sounds on the verge of sexual assault. "Pull my britches down to my knees / Mama mama play house with me," he demands, that thick accent probably the only thing saving all involved from doing time in the slammer. You can taste the sweat and smell the overalls. At the time kids were enjoying the jaunty rhythms of Bill Haley, the baroque stylings of Elvis . . . this was something else—deep, dark Memphis. Music for those who don't walk upright. Harris "looked like he was going to have a heart attack every time he played," noted Sam Phillips, declaring him "intense." It is a filthy, magnificent record.

Ol' Ray was certain he was number one with a bullet. Hell, he even went out and bought himself a brand-new set of wheels—a persimmon-and-white '57 Mercury. But a hopped-up follow-up of "Greenback Dollar" ("The more we drank, the better it sounded") wilted in the shadow of Jerry Lee's "Whole Lotta Shakin' Going On," a song that Harris claimed to have demoed first. "Lonely Wolf," another masterpiece, went unreleased, and a squabble with Sam over material left Ray's big-time dreams in the dust. What a shame the world has only a handful of his recordings. On the prowl for a new career, the Lonely Wolf "finally decided that I was on the wrong side of the mic."

❖

Enter Quinton Claunch and Bill Cantrell. Fiddle player Cantrell was "a farm boy from Hackelburg, Alabama, population 300"; guitarist Claunch was born in Tishomingo, Mississippi, son of a sharecropper so poor he couldn't afford an outhouse. "We took a Sears and Roebuck catalogue to do our business behind the barn," Claunch informed David Whiteis. Together they were part of a country outfit called the Blue Seal Pals, appearing on radio for years, eventually with WSM in Nashville. Once the band broke up, both men turned to day jobs, but couldn't get the music bug out of their systems. They wrote a song called "Daydreamin'" and cut a demo with a singer named Bud Deckelman.

First they pitched it to Sun. Sam Phillips had put an earlier version of their band on the air in Muscle Shoals, Alabama, in the forties. He liked "Daydreamin'," but wanted to monkey with it, so they took the tape over to Lester Bihari's Meteor Records. Lester's tape recorder was on the fritz, but Deckelman managed to get it up and running before belting out the number in front of a five-piece band. "We cut the whole thing on one microphone," says Claunch. "That thing came out, man, shoot, it went to number one—Memphis, New Orleans, Cleveland, Des Moines." Then Cajun star Jimmy C. Newman covered the regional hit, but Deckelman blew a promising career ("Women and booze," says Claunch).

No doubt miffed over letting a hit slip through his fingers, Sam Phillips offered Claunch and Cantrell a spot at Sun. They'd produce, write, and play backup for upcoming unknowns for Sun's short-lived country subsidiary label, Flip. The duo worked with the Miller Sisters, Carl Perkins, and the future mad genius of rockabilly, Charlie Feathers. Charlie "had a head of his own," says Claunch. "He was kind of hard to get along with. He didn't have any education at all. He could hardly write his name." In mid-1955 Claunch and Cantrell wrote and played on the spare, stunning hardcore country numbers "Defrost Your Heart" and "I've Been Deceived" as well as Charlie's self-penned glimpse of his future sound, "Peepin' Eyes." Music for the ages, but at the time it didn't add up to hit records. Claunch's verdict: Sam Phillips "wasn't into country music too much."

Cantrell and Claunch's Sun deal was a meager one: they only got paid if Sam actually released whatever they worked on. A Cantrell and Claunch song, "Sure to Fall," was slotted as the B-side of the next Carl Perkins single, "Honey Don't." But Carl had a new song called "Blue Suede Shoes" that Phillips went with instead. "That little mistake cost me about $140,000 in royalties," a rueful Cantrell confessed to Escott, Hawkins, and Davis. "From that moment on Quinton and I decided we should put our songs on the back of every record we could. The only way to control this was to have our own record company."

❖

Which is where Ray Harris comes in. Cantrell and Claunch had made his acquaintance during his brief flare-up at Sun. Ray had this artist he wanted to record—Carl McVoy, who'd been taught boogie-woogie piano by his cousin, Jerry Lee Lewis. Harris happened to know an old lady who had a small record shop on Poplar Avenue with a tape recorder and an upright piano in the back room. Harris cut a demo of McVoy doing a rocked-up version of "You Are My Sunshine," plus a Claunch/Cantrell song, "Tootsie." The first investment in Hi Records was the fee Ray paid grandma: $3.50.

The trio of would-be potentates met up at Claunch's house to discuss their next move. They needed somebody with loot to back their plan. Madman local deejay Dewey Phillips was discussed and rejected before Joe Cuoghi's name was thrown in the hat.

"A cigar chewin' poppa," says drummer Hayward Bishop. Short, fat, gray-haired Joe Cuoghi "looked like an Italian bookie." He'd grown up in the Little Italy section of town. He and John Novarese, a buddy from high school, were trying to figure out a business to get into. First they tried importing bananas from New Orleans, but that ended fast when a crate arrived full of spiders feasting upon rotten fruit. On July 12, 1946, they bought Poplar Tunes, a small record shop at 306 Poplar.* "We took in exactly $5.63," said Cuoghi. "We didn't know Harry James from Tommy Dorsey." They learned fast. "I learned what the public wanted . . . I got a feel for what the demand was." Cuoghi oversaw a numbered list of the most popular records that they'd type up and mimeograph, their own version of the Top 40. Joe "just had a feel for it," said Novarese. Customers "took his word . . . we made charts right from the beginning." Meanwhile, Novarese mastered the soon-to-explode jukebox market.

Pop Tunes sold to everybody—other stores, disc jockeys, jukeboxes—becoming a powerful one-stop distributorship that, as *Billboard* reported in 1961, supplied product "to ninety-five percent of the operators in Memphis and a great deal in the Mid-South." By 1965 they'd be raking in a million a year from their combined music ventures.

The store itself stayed open until 9 p.m. and "was very unique, probably not more than forty-five feet square," said club owner Gene Mason. "They had about eight turntables—you could get the record, play it, see how you like it." People told Cuoghi this was a terrible idea—why lay down cash if you can hear it for free? "He'd say, 'No—if they'll listen, they'll buy,'" said Novarese.

Buy they did, including a young nobody named Elvis on lunch breaks from his day job. Along with Falstaff Beer, Poplar Tunes was a main advertiser on "Daddy-O" Dewey Phillips's *Red Hot and Blue* show on WHBQ, where he'd command everybody to "get yourself a load of goober dust, take it on down to Joe Cuoghi at Poplar Tunes and tell him Phillips sent you." Dewey's snappy "Poppa Joe" palaver made the low-key Cuoghi

---

* The store moved to 308 in 1960 and stayed open until 2009.

blush, but, as Pop Tunes worker Milton Pond recalled, it also made him "legendary, a household name."

According to Novarese, Joe Cuoghi was responsible for the first integrated rock and roll show in Memphis on September 13, 1954, at Ellis Auditorium. Cuoghi had put blues pianist Piano Red on the bill alongside the extremely pale Bill Haley and His Comets. Backstage, the chief of police tried to stop it. "You can't go on with this show with Piano Red," he told Cuoghi and Novarese. "He's black. You can't mix white and black on the same stage."

On the spot, Joe conjured up a dubious way out by saying, "Chief, look—do me a favor. He won't go on if you don't want him on. But don't call him black. . . . You might hurt his feelings." The chief responded, "You sure he's not black?" Cuoghi answered in the affirmative and sent Novarese to retrieve the now-nervous musician from his dressing room. Piano Red was an albino. After a visual inspection by a now-convinced chief, Red went on. (Not only that, said Novarese, after the Memphis show "the sales of his records doubled.")

Cuoghi and Novarese—together these two Italians wielded much clout in the Memphis music scene. When Joe was failing to get the right action on his 1964 single "Haunted House" by "Jumpin'" Gene Simmons, he rang up his powerful distributor, London Records, and barked, "I got a hit. If you don't show me some progress on 'Haunted House' in the next 48 hours, then don't bother sending me the next release by the Rolling Stones!" "Haunted House" shot to number eleven on the charts. Cuoghi was "like the Godfather," said producer Paul Zaleski. "He could determine who was gonna be on the radio—and who wasn't."

And so sometime in 1957 the trio of Harris, Claunch, and Cantrell marched into Pop Tunes with their three-and-a-half-buck demo. Cuoghi remembered Ray's tune "Greenback Dollar." Time for "You Are My Sunshine." "Joe played it and he liked it," said Claunch. "He said, 'What you guys got in mind?' We said, 'Well, we'd like to start our own label.'" Cuoghi was game, on one condition: he wanted to add more partners to finance it. "Beggars can't be choosers," says Claunch. Cuoghi, Novarese, their lawyer Nick Pesce, Jim Crudgington, Sam Esgro, and Bill Brown all ponied $500 a piece (Cuoghi quickly bought out the last three and became president). Harris, Cantrell, and Claunch invested their sweat and blood.

Cuoghi is credited with dubbing the company Hi Records—inspired by (depending on who you ask) (a) the last two letters of his name, (b) "high" on the charts, or (c) a reference to that new wonder, hi-fi. In time Hi would come to represent "Hit Instrumentals." The stark but arresting logo consisted of HI in festive red letters, a musical note on each side, all of it outlined in silver on a black background. Once it developed, Hi was one of those dependable independents—like Sun, King, Goldwax, Starday, and so many others—that had the heart of any self-respecting record hound skipping a beat. Chances were you'd find something to savor in those shiny grooves.

❖

Claunch wanted to record Carl McVoy a few hours away in Music City, USA. "Set it up and I'll handle the expenses," said Cuoghi. With Chet Atkins at the helm, they recut the two McVoy songs, and their very first single—"You Are My Sunshine," Hi 2001—was released December 9, 1957. At first it looked promising. A distributor on the East Coast ordered eight hundred copies. "That afternoon, he ordered eight hundred more," recalls Claunch. "Joe said, 'Man, looks like we got us a hit!' He jumps the gun, calls the pressing plant, presses up a few thousand—and it died on the vine." Cuoghi wound up with a mountain of unsold records—and a huge bill from a local pressing plant he couldn't pay.

Sam Phillips stepped in, engineering a deal to snatch up both the record and McVoy's contract for $2,600 (Carl never had another hit). Cuoghi used those funds to secure a recording location for the label—an abandoned movie theater at 1320 S. Lauderdale Street. Originally he rented it from a certain Mrs. Frisbee for fifty bucks a month. It was a funky location. "Bad neighborhood," says drummer Jerry Arnold. "We had an artist come down from Chicago and get accosted out there in the street." Horn player Jack Hale, veteran of many a Hi session, recalled showing up for a date, and as he was getting his trombone out, "I heard these sirens . . . I found out later a man was being killed right behind the studio there."

Built in 1915, the Shamrock Theater became the Royal when it converted to sound. It had been out of commission two years before Cuoghi and company took it over. Royal Studios was now in business. At the time Royal had only one door in and out; this humble, two-tone brick building's "lone architectural purpose was to barrier the outside world, no light, no sound," writes Preston Lauterbach. Inside "there was a magic there," says keyboard player James Hooker (aka James Brown).* "Usually the AC wouldn't work and it was hot as hell. You had to walk uphill to the control room and downhill to the instruments—your instrument was set on a slant a little bit." Something happened to the music due to that old theater-floor tilt. "As you go down that slope the music gets bigger, it separates," Willie Mitchell explained to Robert Palmer in 1975.

"The redneck electrician," as Hayward Bishop affectionately called him, Bill Cantrell oversaw all the Royal equipment for years to come. Ray Harris started the ball rolling by having a mono one-track Ampex recorder installed (they graduated to three-track in 1961). It is said the first record cut was an outside job for another independent Memphis label, Fernwood—Thomas Wayne's "Tragedy." This weepy ballad had only a pair of pickers present, Bill Black on bass and producer Scotty Moore on guitar. Author of the song, Fred Burch, noted that Ray Harris's brand-new Ampex deck wasn't working on Royal's very first session: "Finally somebody kicked it and got it going." In the beginning the studio "didn't even have an echo chamber," noted Moore, who had to take the track to a local radio station and add it there. Harris soon built an echo chamber—"a little concrete room with a door on it," said sax man Martin Willis. "We thought that was technology."

Royal was now in business, although Harris, Claunch, and Cantrell kept their day jobs. "I'd come in from doing construction work, be muddy up to here, and we'd just meet at the studio at whatever time we got off," said Harris. Hi released sixteen singles that went in all sorts of directions except up the charts. Pop, country, a singing dentist (even a female Elvis impersonator, whose recordings never got released)—they were the kind of curious but dull artifacts destined to be remembered only by sad old record collectors with questionable hygiene. The one early Hi single that clicked was that of a fifteen-year-old rockabilly singer by the name of Jay B. Loyd. "I'm So Lonely" / "I'll Be All Right" sold 40,000 copies, making enough noise to get Hi a national distribution deal with a major, London Records, but it had been hell to record. Wobbly delivery nearly derails the band

---

* One of the unsung studio musicians from the early Mitchell/Hi days, James Brown was on the road with his later band the Amazing Rhythm Aces and staying at the Hyatt House (aka "the Riot House") in Los Angeles when he received yet another phone call for "the real James Brown. I looked down the hall and there were two hookers getting on the elevator. I thought, 'OK—James Hooker!' That's how I changed my name."

toward the end of the A-side as Loyd "couldn't get his meter straight," says Jerry Arnold. "Never did. He would jump not only the chord changes, but he'd jump time. It made for a difficult situation." ("We couldn't bear to try another take," said an exasperated Harris, who played one writer the unedited session tape. "Hear that door slamming? That's McVoy walking out.")

Not an auspicious beginning, this aimless group of all-but-one nonhits. By 1959 Hi Records was hanging by a thread. "Joe began to get disgusted," says Quinton Claunch, who sold his shares in the company to Carl McVoy for seven grand, even though Cantrell tried to talk him out of it. Hi historian Colin Escott has written that Claunch was forced out for recording a Bill Black soundalike combo, but Quinton, who bristles at that idea, says he abandoned ship before Bill Black hit because the music they'd put out thus far had gone nowhere. Cantrell told Escott that Claunch was unhappy with Ray Harris taking over the production duties. "He and Ray Harris didn't get along very well at all," says Jerry Arnold. "I think they actually came to blows one day." Whatever the case, Claunch was gone. "I sold out. Sure did," admits a rueful Claunch, who went off to form the Goldwax label, recording some of the most compelling Memphis soul ever recorded.

It looked like curtains for Hi—and for Royal. That's when a young guitar slinger from Missouri saved the day with a pencil. About to turn twenty-three, Young had played guitar for Eddie Bond and Johnny Horton before following Bill Black to Hi. Black, the man on the stand-up bass behind Elvis at Sun, had left Presley due to the cheapness of his nefarious manager, the Colonel, and was now part of a loose band of musicians working at Hi. Black, Young, and drummer Jerry "Satch" Arnold had played on Jay B. Loyd's "mediocre hit," as Young described it. Credited as Bill Black's Combo, they were about to become a force to be reckoned with. According to singer Gene Simmons, Joe Cuoghi had told Black, "Why don't you pick some of the better musicians around town and cut some instrumental stuff?"

Reggie Young was the right man for the job. "Reggie was more than just a guitar player. He was just . . . *Reggie*," says drummer Arnold with admiration. "His ability and his creative sense was enough to lead the other instruments, primarily the rhythm section—he just made it gel." And Young kickstarted the song that would save Hi's ass: "Smokie—Part 2."

❖

That rubbery guitar, the toddlin' eighty-eights, a well-oiled sax—here was the secret sauce of so much Memphis music: a lazy, easy-on-the-ears groove that felt good. One can almost visualize Crazy Guggenheim face down at the bar (the faster "Part 1"—featuring clarinet by Willis and a toy piano belonging to Reggie's niece—has been forgotten).

A crucial moment in the history of Hi Records, the story behind Hi's first instrumental hit "Smokie—Part 2" has many layers. In more recent years Willie Mitchell—who maintained he was present when they cut it—claimed the song had emanated out of the rhythms of his own band, and that his piano player Joe Hall "gave" it to the other players. But Mitchell conceded what set it apart was the distinctive guitar. Reggie readily admits the influence Willie had on his music but says the idea was all his. "To be honest, the shuffle beat I came up with—the guitar-and-pencil rhythm. I tuned my guitar down two whole steps and instead of using a pick I used a pencil."

According to Ray Harris, who engineered the "Smokie" sessions, the group had been screwing around with a Hank Thompson tune and getting nowhere. So Reggie started in on this instrumental he'd been fooling around with. "Ray said, 'Hey, that's not bad—let's record this,'" recalled Young, who claims the record's release was practically an accident. A rep from London had come by to review the latest sessions with singers they'd cut, but "wasn't impressed," said Young, chuckling at the memory. "And he heard that wacky little instrumental and said, 'What's this?' I said, 'Well, we were just goofing off.' He said, 'Oh, I really like that.'" Intent on releasing it, the exec flew "Smokie—Part 2" back to New York.

Harris said they worked on the recording knowing they had a hit; Jerry Arnold also insists the song was not so impromptu. "Bill and Reggie and I worked on it first at Reggie's house. Our work was the rhythm part—the nucleus of the song was that rhythm." And they were already planning on recording it. "Bill had a mission. . . . He was tryin' to get himself a record cut," said Arnold. Of course, Bill Doggett's "Honky Tonk (Part 2)" had been a massively influential instrumental hit in '56, but Arnold states, "We weren't thinkin' too much about "'Honky Tonk.'" He pointed to a dance called the Slop, popular in black clubs at the time. "We were tryin' to cue this music to fit that."

Once they took it to Royal, the trio of Black, Young, and Arnold was augmented by sax player Martin Willis and piano player Joe Hall, the only African American in the band. For two weeks the band "just kept on cuttin' and cuttin' and cuttin' and developed a sound," said Ray. A former military drill instructor, Harris could be demanding. "We would do take after take before he was satisfied. Sometimes thirty or forty," testified bass player Mike Leech, who'd join the gang a bit later. Willis recalled playing a song "so many times that my jaws would give out and I couldn't play."

It should come as no surprise that the man responsible for "Come On Little Mama" preferred it frantic and crude. Harris was "crazy about rhythm . . . I always cut with all the VU meters in the red; I went to the point of distortion." Amusingly, Harris later found out that Cantrell set the VU meter so it would only appear to be overloaded just to placate Ray's need for noise. (When it came to mastering Hi singles, Joe Cuoghi "would want it cut so hot that the needle would skip down the record," says Jerry Arnold. This would ensure the Hi single "would be louder than the other songs on the jukebox.")

A subtle presence Ray wasn't. Years later he'd be first to record Dwight Twilley's power-pop band, barking at the intimidated youngsters, "Y'all sing like pussies. . . . Ya need some taters and gravy under your belt." When I asked Reggie Young if he thought Harris understood the finer points of R&B a la Willie Mitchell, he immediately responded in the negative, recalling a session where he and bass player Tommy Cogbill decided that they'd turn Tommy's amp off just to fuck with Ray. "We did a whole cut without bass on it," says Young. "He didn't notice." (Harris told them that was exactly the feel he was looking for.) Other artists—like Ace Cannon—swear by Ray. "He had a good sense of rhythm," says a diplomatic Jerry Arnold, chuckling. "Ray wasn't involved in the creative part. Best way I can say it—he wasn't a picker."

It was due to Harris that Joe Hall did not last long in the studio. Hall's piano provided "the melody line for 'Smokie,'" instructs Arnold, who says they were already planning on going out on the road with the musician, a daring concept in 1959. The plan screeched to a halt one night early into the recording of the song. Jerry Arnold tells a tale confirmed by Young. Ray was discussing the parties responsible for a nearby automobile accident. "Ray was sayin' 'this nigger this' and 'this nigger that' and he just kept on and on and on. And finally Joe said, 'I don't have to put up with this, man. I'm outta here.' And he left." Hall was immediately replaced by Carl McVoy, who jumped into the session, playing the part that Hall had designed (Arnold thinks he may even be the one on the record, although Harris might've used an earlier take with Hall). The day before "Smokie—Part

2" was released Hall showed up at Royal. He "needed twenty-seven dollars for the light bill," said Harris, who to my knowledge never acknowledged publicly what had happened with Hall.*

The rest of the band took over Joe's share—Cuoghi was so broke he couldn't pay the sidemen their fee and offered them a share of the proceeds instead (sax man Willis insisted on cash). Like most Hi instrumentals, "Smokie—Part 2" would be named by Cuoghi, but even though all the musicians participated in its creation, the only writer credited was Bill Black. According to Arnold, Cuoghi "didn't want all that clutter" on the record. "He wanted it simple—one person's name." Papers were drawn up dividing the group split equally. The same thing happened on Willie Mitchell's "Percolatin'" single—Arnold got sole authorship credit, but all the other players were silent partners in the writing.

❖

"Smokie—Part 2" was number one on the R&B charts four weeks in a row and made it to number seventeen on *Billboard*'s Hot 100. Hi Records was suddenly on the map. Bill Black's Combo would be named *Billboard*'s top instrumental group three years in a row. Their first album for Hi, 1963's *Saxy Jazz,* spent a year on the charts. Like all of their early Hi albums, the cover featured no pictures of the band, only art—a marketing decision by Cuoghi. When "Jumpin'" Gene Simmons, who later sang with the band, complained to Joe, he said, "About 90 percent of your sales are coming from black people . . . what do you think would happen if they saw your picture on those records?"

"We were a total funky R&B band for back then," says Young. "A lot of the gigs, they'd be black clubs. The five of us would show up and they'd say, 'Well, when's the band gonna get here? I don't see anybody but these white guys standin' around.'" Sax man Ace Cannon, who joined the band after their first two singles, adds, "Everybody thought we was black, and the name Bill Black Combo didn't help matters." According to Simmons, one pissed-off club owner—complaining, "'I put in an order for the Bill Black Combo,' just like he ordered ham and eggs"—refused to accept the white band until they played an impromptu medley of their hits. Said Simmons, "These were his very words, he said, 'Go ahead on,

---

* According to Bob Mehr, one day at Royal "Harris sent one of the African-American musicians out to his car to retrieve some equipment. There, nestled among the microphones and cables, was a Ku Klux Klan outfit."

motherfucker, you the Bill Black Combo, all right." The Combo opened for Ike and Tina and toured with Joe Tex and Brook Benton, everybody dancing the Slop to "Smokie—Part 2." Not that it was all fun and games in those segregated days. "There were a couple times we got very close to bein' arrested," says Arnold. One night in Louisiana their tour manager jumped onto the dance floor—the only white face in an audience of four hundred. "Someone called the police. Nothing ever came of it."

The secret of the Combo's sound? Nothing fancy. "I played the most simple solos I could think of," said sax player Willis, which meant aspiring musicians everywhere could latch onto the groove. "Our sound was very copyable." And sexy. "You could not go into a strip joint in America without a chick taking her clothes off to a Bill Black record," later member Bob Tucker told Griffin and Burke. Willis also revealed that while recording at Royal "they would plug the playback into a little tiny portable transistor radio" to check out how the recording would sound over the airwaves.

"White Silver Sands," the Combo's 1960 follow-up hit, illustrates the power of Cuoghi. "We already had what we thought was a cut on it," explains Arnold, who says the band had been playing it fast, not unlike Dave Gardner's 1957 version. "Cuoghi said, 'No, we're not gonna do that—I want it to sound like 'Smokie,'" says Arnold. They slowed the tempo down to a jaunty roller-rink beat, and their second record went to number one on the R&B charts. "Joe was the undisputed leader of Hi records," says Arnold. "What he said went. Joe was the kingpin."

❖

Hi Records was now the home of instrumentals. Next came Ace Cannon. The son of a country guitarist who also played fiddle, Mississippi sax man John Henry Cannon had grown up in the Hollywood section of Memphis (as a kid Cannon would tell people, "I live in Hollywood—I am doomed for stardom"). He'd played on the very first Hi Nashville session, gigged around town, and been one of Billy Lee Riley's Little Green Men at Sun, but he didn't quit his day job until he joined Bill Black's Combo to replace a too-busy-in-the-studio Martin Willis.

At the end of 1961 Cannon cut the incredible "Tuff" for Hi. Bill Justis had already cut an uptempo version of his tune called "Cattywampus" (itself based on the old "Columbus Stockade Blues"), but this time Cannon—the kind who can wring every drop of emotion out of a ballad—slowed the tempo way down. Minimal, hypnotic, the vibe is about three hours and four martinis past "Smokie—Part 2." Tiptoeing on the keyboard, producer Carl McVoy added perfectly cheesy accompaniment. "I'm not the greatest saxophone player in the world," admits Ace. "I'm a stylist. I play from my heart." And how. Fellow honker Martin Willis sums up Ace's sound in two words: "Barroom sax."

Ace would cut a slew of albums for Hi, including 1965's *Ace Cannon Live,* recorded not at a club but right inside Royal. "We invited fifty of our friends, set it up like a bar," says Cannon. "Put tables out in the studio, fed 'em drinks. . . . They couldn't dance, wasn't enough room with all of 'em sittin' there, but it was live, definitely."

Cuoghi, the man who'd named Cannon "Ace," took an intense interest in the sax player. "He'd be right there in that engineerin' room, and if I got off the track just a little bit, tryin' to play Earl Bostic, a little jazz, he'd say, 'Stop the tape, stop the tape—tell him to stick to the melody!' I was his favorite artist, and he wasn't afraid to tell nobody, either. He wanted to make me the Frank Sinatra of the saxophone."

Unfortunately, Cannon was a hellraiser. Unlike infamous boozer George "No Show" Jones, "I'd like to get there and *show* my ass," confesses Cannon, who might be so schnockered he'd "play the first note or two and fall back into the set of drums." One mob of fans was so angry at Ace for being too blotto to make a gig "they set fire underneath my truck." He says Cuoghi tried many times to talk him away from the bottle. "Oughta be a billionaire," Ace contends.

Cannon got tight with all the powers that be at Hi, his presence requested at the Italian-American Society and country club, where he'd bet on golf games with Cuoghi, Pesce, and Novarese. "Hell, before you know it, I was one of the mafia," he says, adding that he and a jukebox owner named Bill Dodson "sorta took a lot of their money." More gambling occurred right at Royal. "Man, we played more poker and throwed more dice than we played music," says Ace wistfully. "We were all so close, as close as could be."* Between 1962 and 1978 Ace cut a whopping thirty-eight singles and twenty-seven albums for Hi, staying nearly to the bitter end.

❖

---

* Jerry Arnold says the Royal crap games served to illustrate how low on the totem pole the musicians were at Hi. The label potentates "would bet fifty bucks on a quarter piece—we were pitchin' for quarters. There was quite a bit of difference, because we weren't makin' any money."

In 1962 Hi released the debut instrumental single by Willie Mitchell, "The Crawl." Here was the beginning of something new. The Ray Harris crew was a bunch of young white Southerners who'd happened into making instrumentals for a black R&B market. Willie Mitchell was interested in black music that appealed to whites. When it came to music, Harris was rock and roll crude; Mitchell was more experienced, more sophisticated, with roots in jazz.

"Willie wanted to do things his way," says Jerry Arnold. "He just came from a different background—big-band brass arrangements. We all came from string-guitar bands—country-flavored rock and roll."

Although it took eight years, Willie would take over Hi. He'd just do it at the Mitchell tempo. Laid back.

THE REDUCER

I know Al Green better than anybody else. I can read that man like a book. I created him.
—WILLIE MITCHELL

SCOTT BOMAR, producer, composer, musician: The first time I went to Royal, I just dropped in. I thought, "I wanna meet Willie Mitchell, one of the greatest producers of all time, who's made some of my favorite music of all time." Well, his studio was ten minutes from my house. You know—"I'm gonna go meet Willie." I went in, he was there by himself, his feet were propped up on a desk by the front door, and he was smoking Kools, drinkin' vodka, and listening to Clifford Jordan.

JOHN GARY WILLIAMS, singer: I learned so much from Pops about producing and singin'. I thought I knew it all, I didn't know nothin'. At Stax, didn't nobody take the time to teach anything, really. They just went on whatever raw talent you had.

Pops was very emotional, and mobile. He stayed on the floor and stayed involved in everything. Timing: he'd tell me, "Do it on the one, man, do it on the one. You're behind the beat—get ahead of the beat, get on top of the beat." And he'd say, "John, stop pattin' your feet. You can't get the groove if you pat your feet. You're disruptin' everything. You have to rock from side to side and feel the rhythm." It helped a lot.

WAYNE JACKSON, trumpet: Willie was an artist's dream. He loved us and we loved him. I always told him his playing influenced me. We had brotherly love. Willie loved to laugh and have a good time. He could share a joke with us and write a horn part at the same time. He was a charmer and he was a character.

I grew up in Arkansas where there was no style, so I really appreciate style. Willie could put on a suit and not look like he put on a suit.

JACK HALE JR., trumpet and French horn: Willie was always impeccably dressed.

GENE MASON, club owner: He was very suave, dapper, and—I hate to use this white-man word—debonair.

THOMAS BINGHAM, guitar: I saw Willie Mitchell on the cover of a magazine. His studio was a block from where I was born and raised. Knocked on the door and said, "I want to work in your studio." I was twenty-one. He asked, "You know all your chords?" I said, "Oh yeah, I know *all* of 'em." I whizzed off a solo for him and he went, "Wow. You work for me now. If you want somethin', boy, just ask. I'm gonna fill your ass-pockets full of money."

JACK HALE JR.: I had heard Al Green on the radio, I knew my dad was on a lot of records, and I knew who Willie Mitchell was. Every Christmas he would give all the musicians he used a couple bottles of excellent liquor—like scotch or vodka—and a ham or turkey. I thought that was really cool.

When I was about fourteen I started going with my dad to sessions and learned everything I could, both musically and technically. Now, I had been to other studios before I went to Royal—like Ardent Productions, a really high-end studio. Willie's studio had wrought-iron bars on the inside. The place was really funky, and Willie always had the guys play on one microphone. Also, Willie Mitchell was short, so they had a Coke bottle crate for him to stand on. I remember thinking, "Man, this is really weird." It didn't add up with the turkey, ham, and excellent liquor. Everything sounded great, though.

When I was twenty-four, we decided to put together a group of Memphis studio musicians. We came up with four rock songs, and they had difficult parts. I spent forever mixing this and I sweated the details. I want Willie to hear it, so I take it to his office and he pulls out this Radio Shack recorder, the AC adapter had frayed wires. It's monophonic, and looks like it was built in World War II. "That sounds real good," he says. "That's more rock than I can help you with, though. If there's more R&B, I can help you there." Here's this man who could afford any playback system in the world, but pulls out this Radio Shack recorder that cost, like, eight dollars.

TERRY MANNING, mixer: Royal Studio was not the world's greatest technically. I'm not at all putting it down. That wasn't their focus. Things could get a little funky. They might push microphones up into the red, but Willie got what he wanted.

When I'd mix for him, I'd start doing what I normally do, by the book, and then I would look at Willie, and he would say, "It doesn't quite move me." I would think *"Move* me?" He knew all the technical parts of the engineering and all the technical aspects of music, but he had that extra thing—I guess you'd call it soul . . .

As I watched him, I saw that certain things got him going when I put certain stuff in the mix. Finally he'd say, "That's kicking me, that's got it." It had more of the feel he wanted. And I remember thinking, "Either this is ridiculous—or maybe I should learn from this." Willie taught me the emotional side of music.

SCOTT BOMAR: Willie had incredible ears. Big ears.

CHARLES HODGES, keyboard: Not only an ear, he had a vision.

LEROY HODGES, bass: Willie, he could hear up the street. You could not fool him. If a guitar was out of tune, he could tell you which string.

TEENIE HODGES, guitar: Willie Mitchell, he know exactly what he want. He hear it before it's done. And until you do it the way he want it done, he'll keep you all day and all night—if you got a heart operation planned for yourself, it doesn't make any difference.

JACK HALE JR.: Willie was in the studio all the time. That really made an impression on me. He wasn't pretentious like the Nashville guys. Willie was there all day and all night.

SANDY RHODES, background singer, guitar player: He'd never go back and change something. I used to work with producers where you'd be singing backup and then they'd go, 'Oh, let's go back to what we did four hours ago, I don't like where we're headed.' That wasn't the way with Willie. If it took you thirty minutes and he got what he wanted, we were already done. He didn't belabor anything. Willie was the master of underproducing.

REUBEN "ROUBAIX" FAIRFAX JR., guitar and bass player, producer: Pops told me, "You spend most of the time pullin' shit out. We're not producers, we're reducers."

LAWRENCE "BOO" MITCHELL, studio manager, engineer, adopted son: Good music made him happy. He didn't care if he made it or not.

SANDY RHODES: If Willie told you, "That *sucks*!" well, you just thought, "Yeah, it really does kinda suck."

JACK HALE SR.: Willie never hesitated to let you know if something was wrong. One of his main phrases was, "Ya'll aren't drunk enough in there! You gotta slow down. Get drunk in there!" No matter how many times he said it, we were rushing.

CHARLES HODGES: Willie was *crucial* on a singer! He studied them, knew what was in them. And he knew how to get it *out* of them. He gonna get it—or else.

THOMAS BINGHAM: He would kick 'em in the ass. He'd say, "Well, that's pretty good. If we do it about ninety more times, we might have it." I'd look out there and think, "Oh God, they wanna kill him!"

SCOTT BOMAR: Willie would straight-up tell them, "You're not playing this shit right. If you can't do it right, I can get somebody else in here. I'm paying you, so you better do what I want you to do." I've seen that backfire in a really bad way, but Willie could get away with it!

THOMAS BINGHAM: To get a particular person to open up, he would kind of take a low-road approach and not be so talky—pretend to not be as deep as some people thought he was. Say somebody was talking to him about business. He'd just skim over the top to see what *you* know, then while that's goin' on, he's assessin' the situation.

BOO MITCHELL: I watched him with a lot of different singers. That's one of the things that was interesting about him, he'd get different stuff out of different people. He would read people really well and know what buttons to push. There was a psychological aspect to it, absolutely.

He'd get what he was hearing in his head. He never settled for less, no matter how long it took. Real disciplined. He would tell me, "You gotta make sure people are giving you a hundred and ten percent, 'cause they'll give you ninety if you let 'em." . . . He never settled. He'd say, "We'll try it again tomorrow."

CHARLES HODGES: He'd say, "Okay, girls, we're gonna call it a night. Come back in the morning." That was Willie's nickname for the band—girls.

JACK HALE SR., trombone: Willie had a dry sense of humor. He didn't stand there making jokes, but his sarcasm was really wild.

Willie's mouth was pretty . . . sometimes I'd take my wife down there and Willie would yell, "You motherfuckers!" And I'd say, "I'm sorry, baby . . . "

CHARLES HODGES: You know how Willie was. He would curse every other word.

SCOTT BOMAR: When the Bo-Keys were recording *The Royal Sessions*, it was Willie's birthday. And the keyboard player had a melodica. He came up behind Willie playing "Happy Birthday" on the melodica thinking it was cute and gonna impress him. Willie just deadpan says, "Muthafucka, *everything* you play is in the key of C!" I never really thought about it, but he was right. It was a true statement.

BOO MITCHELL: He had these great one-liners, Willieisms. We were recording Marti Pellow, from Wet Wet Wet. For some reason, we couldn't find the right strings. The players weren't right, a lot of older ladies. The wrong bunch. Me and Marti decided we gotta go to New York to do this, and we were gonna FedEx the tapes. Willie said, "You're gonna do *what*? Hold up, y'all got me nervous as a knocked-up nun!"

REUBEN FAIRFAX JR.: Pops wouldn't crack a smile; he'd look you right in the eye and tell you somethin' crazy. When Leon Thomas, a keyboard player, died, they played "Purple Rain" at his funeral. He and the bass player had a pact—"Whoever goes first, y'all get up and play 'Purple Rain.'" Me and Pops was at the funeral, sittin' together on a pew, and they start playin'. Pops leans over and say, "Hey, Roubaix, man—go up there and tune that nigger's guitar."

BOO MITCHELL: Pops and Ike Turner, that was the funniest shit. He'd tell Ike, "You can't play no guitar, put it down." I was sitting up front and I heard this Jerry Lee Lewis piano, I was like, what is that? Pops said, "That's Ike—he can't play guitar, but he can play the shit outta a piano."

REUBEN FAIRFAX JR.: Pops would tell me, "Get the money, get it honest. But if you *can't* get it honest, *get the money.*" His brother James found some money that fell out of a Brinks truck. And turned it in! Pops said, "You are a *stupid* motherfucker!"

JACK HALE JR.: I knew all the "hot" studios had twenty-four-track machines, and Willie was still using a sixteen-track. So he and I were in the control room and I asked, "Willie, when are you going to get a twenty-four-track machine?" He said, "Jack Jr., I already have the number one record in the world, how much higher would it go if I had eight more tracks?"

THOMAS BINGHAM: Pops hated the shit out of Pro Tools. I'd play him something and say, "We did that in Pro Tools. He'd go, "It sounds like SHIT! Take that shit outta my CD player."

BOO MITCHELL: He thought Pro Tools was the worst shit ever. He'd say, "*I'm* the fuckin' Pro Tool."

SCOTT BOMAR: Digital? Willie would say, "You can't beat that tape, man. Digital sounds like shit, ain't got no fuckin' bottom."

A lot of guys, all they talk about is equipment and gear. To him, they were just tools. At Royal, they never got rid of anything. It's like a museum, if you poke around in there you can pretty much see everything from when Bill Black had the studio. You can tell Willie knew his gear, but it wasn't nerdy. He got into it in the golden age and kept it up, kept it going. Once he got a studio up and running, he cut O. V. Wright and Al Green! Why change it? I wouldn't either.

The main thing about the Hi Sound is Willie Mitchell. It doesn't matter what equipment, what musicians, or what era, it sounds like Willie.

THOMAS BINGHAM: Willie was like this: if he liked you, he liked you. Once he didn't like you, he would say this: "I don't like him—and I don't like *nobody* to like him." It was like don't even mention his name. Permanent shit list.

He could be very intimidating. Even when he was cross with you, he didn't sound that way. He had these intense eyes and those big thick eyebrows, and when he got real intimidatin', those eyebrows would knit together and he's lookin' at you and you're sittin' there like, "Oh shit, I done fucked up."

SANDY RHODES: Everyone would call him Poppa Willie. He would take care of his own too, like if they needed twenty dollars or something. He really was the father.

REUBEN FAIRFAX JR.: If I was in trouble, he'd take care of it. I was at the age where I was no longer young and beautiful, and I had to adjust to real life. I had a marijuana bust. I'd never been arrested, that wasn't my character. He said, "How much money you need? Is that enough, do you need some more?" I've never met anybody who asks you, "Is that enough?" He never said, "You're stupid for doin' this" or asked why. Willie was not that way with me. He was always unconditional.

THOMAS BINGHAM: If you hung out with him a lot, he was generous to a fault. Paid a lot of people's bills. Matter of fact, Pops got about half of Memphis out of jail.

TEENIE HODGES: Willie was always fair. He'd tell you what he was gonna do, and he did it. He didn't lie 'bout nothin'. When we were in his band, if we drove hundreds of miles and he didn't get paid, he would still pay us. Exactly what he promised. Paid us himself.

JACK HALE JR.: Willie lived in a huge house, in a very prestigious area. I would pass it on the way to high school. Every now and then I'd see Willie drive by in one of his beaters. And I was in a hot sports car. Here comes a guy who is legend, driving a car with no air conditioning! It didn't matter to him.

SCOTT BOMAR: Willie was always so much fun. You didn't want it to stop.

I wouldn't have a career in music if I hadn't met and worked with Willie, that's for sure. He got a lot of people their start. I'm one of them.

THOMAS BINGHAM: If I turned in a song and he liked it, there were two words he'd always say: "That's clever." I never wanted to disappoint him. The reward was when he said those two words. "That's clever."

JACK HALE JR.: He wasn't a producer who isn't a musician. He was one of us.

LEROY HODGES: That man had done so much for me. Everything.

❖

Willie Lawrence "Poppa" Mitchell was born in Ashland, Mississippi, on March 1, 1928. His father, Willie Frank Mitchell, was a sharecropper, and mother, Ethel, a housecleaner and baker. "They were just hardworking people," says Willie Sr.'s son Pete. "I don't know if they ever went to see Willie play." There were nine kids. "We grew up with no money," noted Pete. "Never had a car until the late '40s, a station wagon. Their parents "bought it for Willie to travel with."

The Mitchells moved to Memphis in 1933; by 1940, they had moved to Orange Mound, the first neighborhood built by African Americans in the country. The tiny 720-square-foot house they lived in still stands at 1563 Hamilton. "All of us slept on two beds," Pete recalled. "We'd go to the cotton field on Friday and Saturday . . . Willie went too!" Preacher, a cousin from Detroit, played trumpet, and Willie became entranced watching him practice. His father had no money for an instrument, but somehow an older brother managed to finagle a trumpet for Willie when he was eight.

"It came hard," Willie said. "I would practice from three in the afternoon until midnight. Get up early and practice some more." Only two members of the Mitchell family were interested in music: Willie and his younger brother James. "Nobody in my family has rhythm," says Pete. "None of us can dance . . . Willie can't dance." Willie and James "were small guys . . . like my daddy. James was always tagging along after Willie, doing whatever Willie did." According to Reuben Fairfax Jr., not long after Willie got his trumpet, he "told James he had to learn to play the saxophone—because they had a gig in two weeks." Willie had started gigging right away—he'd tell one artist he recorded that his first gig was for blues great Ma Rainey.* Willie and James would have a lifelong partnership in music, although it was sometimes contentious.

A good student, Willie played first trumpet at Melrose High School. "At 14 I organized me a fourteen-piece band, a big band," he said. Mitchell was already leading things; when Willie went to Rust College, says Pete, "the whole band followed him." In the mid-1940s Willie moved in with Chicago Music Conservatory graduate Onzie Horne and started playing in his band. "He was a motherfucker of a piano player!" said Mitchell, who absorbed everything he could from Onzie, including the Schillinger System of Musical Composition, a comprehensive theory of music based on mathematical process rather than historical precedent. Willie would watch in awe as Horne whizzed through arrangements for a twenty-two-piece band. "He was so fast, within an hour he could have an arrangement that [would] scare you," said Mitchell, who gave Horne credit in interviews for the rest of his life. "He had his own thing, he was real melodic . . . no one ever knew how great he was."

In the fifties, Mitchell would join Horne in Al Jackson Sr.'s twelve-piece band and also did a stint with the Rocketeers, led by another Memphis heavyweight, Richard "Tuff" Green. "He was a motivator," said Mitchell. "He had some pride about his music and he had a heck of a band."

Pride in music: Willie oozed it. "If a guy come in here now to record and I'm producing it, if he bring plain chords I always add somethin' to it," said Mitchell, who'd credit the Schillinger System for showing him how. "I always found a way around the chords." A distinction of note:

---

* Rainey died in 1939 when Mitchell was only eleven, but as he told people he started playing live at age nine, it could be possible.

Willie's roots were not in gospel or blues. "I came up playing jazz," said Mitchell. "My chords were always different . . . a little more melody or harmony, but it still had that laid-back rhythm underneath it." How jazzy? Well, they were apparently too fancy for Howlin' Wolf. He hired young Willie and James for a gig at a nearby baseball stadium, then fired them on the spot once he'd heard them play. "I don't want no more of that blee-blop stuff," barked Wolf.

In September 1951 came what may have been Mitchell's first gig in a recording studio, B.B. King's first hit, "3 O'Clock Blues." Crudely recorded in a Memphis YMCA, Onzie Horne provided the arrangements, Tuff Green played bass, Ike Turner manned piano, and Willie was on trumpet. It's also said that he played on the Rufus Thomas recording "Bear Cat" at Sun Records.

❖

Willie was talented, charismatic, and "a nice-lookin' gentleman . . . them white women would go crazy over him," recalled Gene Mason, who'd met him in 1949. The fact that Willie was light-skinned gave him an advantage with ignorant Caucasians, claims Reuben Fairfax Jr: "They were the ones the white people would cosign and stand behind." Nightclub columnist John Knott would watch as Mitchell "tried to steer clear of racist police because, handsome as he was, plenty of white women came to fancy him," wrote Chris Davis. When it came to the opposite sex, Mitchell could be deprecating. "He talked about women bad, and then he talked about women badder," said Thomas Bingham. "He mostly thought they were walkin' around with a pussy for a brain."

Mitchell did a stint in the service, returning to work at an upholstery factory during the day while playing music at night. He got married and started a family. "Willie was always Willie, but he was a churchgoing man," revealed Charles Hodges. "He believed in prayer. Raised his children in Catholic school." Willie had two children with Anna, Yvonne and Lorrain. The couple remained together until Anna's death in 2001. People fondly recall visiting the Mitchell home, remembering the card games and good food. "Anna was genuine as she could be. She'd cook you some turnip greens, sweet potato pie, and cornbread, and I felt like she was my mother-in-law," said Sandy Rhodes. "Just a sweetheart of a lady." For a brief period Anna managed Hi singer Ann Peebles. "Everybody respected

Anna Barbara," said Charles Hodges. "She looked just like a little doll and dressed sharp."

Others, like Thomas Bingham, point out Anna was "a very, very aggressive person. When she came around, Willie was pretty much, 'Yes, dear.'" When Reuben Fairfax Jr. would visit, Anna would call him by his nickname. "She'd say, 'Come on in, Roubaix.' Then she'd go, '*Willie Mitchell* . . .' It used to crack me up because she called Pops by his whole name."

As in many a marriage, there were some dark shadows. Willie drank to excess early on. The daughter of one Hi Records partner, who wished to remain anonymous, remembered her father getting a hysterical call from Anna one night over Willie's drinking. There were other complications. One day Mitchell took Gene Mason aside. "He said, 'I want you to do some detective work for me. I want you to find out about Anna.' His wife. I said, 'Oh my God.'" But Mason did as requested. "I said, 'Well, I got some things to tell you.' I found out she was messin' around with this preacher. And I told him, 'One more thing—there's a white guy she's messin' around with, and he's a friend of mine and yours. It was this big Jew that owned a store. He said, 'Well, I already know about the nigger preacher, Gene.'" Not another word was spoken.

"Willie always kept his feelings really close inside—I never tried to ask him about shit he didn't want to talk about," said Mason. "If he wanted to talk about it, fine."

❖

In 1955 Willie put together his own band, Willie Mitchell and His Jumpin' Band. Vocals were handled by the Four Kings, which featured a handsome young R&B belter named Don Bryant who Willie had taken under his wing, the first of many. The rule for clubs: if it was on the radio, it came out of your instrument. "You had to know the hit songs," says Bryant, an R&B screamer of the highest order. "I was always trying to imitate whoever did the song—Little Richard, Howlin' Wolf." The band was smoking hot and extremely versatile. "We'd play pop music, R&B music, hillbilly music . . . polkas, we could play anything," said Mitchell. They were, boasted Willie, "the most popularest band you ever saw." Personally requested by Elvis, Mitchell's band played his Christmas parties seven years in a row.

There was a thriving music scene in town with some very popular and influential big bands led by Ben Branch, Tuff Green, Bowlegs Miller, and Phineas Newborn. Willie's band was known for its residence at the Manhattan Club, "a hole, a real dump, but it was open all night," said patron and club owner Ernie Barrasso. "You would go to the Manhattan Club and stay up drinking and dancing until five in the morning." Reggie Young would come by and play with the band all night. Mitchell "introduced me to a lot of soulful musicians," says Young. "I'll never forget it."

Across the Mississippi River bridge in Arkansas lurked West Memphis. Unlike Memphis itself, the clubs stayed open late and were easier for underage kids to slip into. It was a place where "law was a whimsy," writes Robert Gordon. "Everything was looser across the river." Mitchell had residences at two clubs there, the Plantation Inn and Danny's Club.

"A swing joint run by the Addams family," as Gordon puts it, the Plantation Inn was a big two-story house with a boxer for a bouncer. The PI, as it was known, "was really redneck," noted Wayne Jackson. "All the sailors went there." The future Memphis Horn was too young to legally enter, so he stood in the parking lot under the club's giant exhaust fan and struggled to decode the band's rhythms through the whoosh of the blades. "A lot of people say the origins of the 'Memphis Sound' began at the Plantation Inn, and I think there's a lot of truth to that," Jackson told Bob Mehr. "We dressed up and shined our shoes and did steps— we got that idea from the Four Kings, who were Willie Mitchell's band. We just learned about rhythm and blues, and what you had to do to make people dance."

At Danny's Club, Mitchell and his band played behind chicken wire to protect them from projectile bottles. "I used to go by there and listen to him—Al Jackson Jr. was the drummer," noted Reggie Young, who studied the band closely, although Arkansas segregation prevented him from sitting in. "They were just so tight. The tempos had to be funky and feel good—Willie wouldn't allow anything that didn't feel good. That's where I learned timing. And how to play a little bit behind the beat without rushing." It would be hard to underestimate the influence of Mitchell's band on many a young player who went on to impact the Memphis music scene. "We wanted to sound like Willie Mitchell's band," future Mar-Key Don Nix told Gordon.

❖

At the same time Mitchell began learning the ropes of the recording business. In 1957 came his first solo instrumental, "Coming Home Pt 1 &

2" on Chesney Sherod's House of Sound label, followed by a handful of singles for Stomper Time Records, a local label run by rockabilly singer Eddie Bond, infamous for advising a just-starting Elvis he should stick to driving trucks. The Stomper Time sessions were cut at Royal Studios, the recording base for Hi Records.

Mitchell's hip, jaunty cover of the Paul Williams instrumental "Thirty Five Thirty" came out in 1960 on Home of the Blues Records, a tiny label run by Reuben Cherry, who owned a record store of the same name on Beale. Even by Memphis standards, Reuben Cherry was an idiosyncratic character. "Cherry wore his pants high, parted his hair in the middle and wore a thin moustache," writes Pete Daniel. "When Cherry died his family tried to erase virtually all traces of his life, destroying nude photographs of women he had collected in various Memphis motel rooms and a thick, blank book titled 'The Sex Life of Reuben Cherry.'" Apparently Cherry held a grudge against Elvis for stealing a rubber snake from his store. It was Reuben who first hired Willie Mitchell as a producer, heading up sessions on the "5" Royales, Roy Brown, and Larry Birdsong for Cherry.

There are various versions of how Mitchell came to Hi. As mentioned, Willie maintained Joe Cuoghi came to him to ask to use his piano player, Joe Hall, on "Smokie," and although no one else recalled Willie being there, he claimed to be present for the session. Mitchell got directly involved in the wake of the single—when Cuoghi and Harris were "havin' problems" concocting a follow-up hit. "I became Bill Black's arranger. Then I began to record." Mitchell had grown tight with Cuoghi. He'd come out on the weekends to listen to Willie's band. "He used to say, "Willie, you're five years ahead of your time," said Mitchell. It would prove to be an astute observation. Willie always spoke highly of Cuoghi. "He respected musicians. He had a good ear. He knew when he heard a hit record."

Released February 5, 1962, Mitchell's first Hi instrumental was a revamping of a local hit he'd had on Stomper Time four years earlier—"The Crawl." ("I changed the rhythm," said Mitchell.) But it was the B-side of his fifth single in 1964, "20–75," that put him on the charts. According to Ray Harris, the song was practically an accident. He'd had a technician from a New York studio working on the board and asked Mitchell to play something so they could work on the sound. The more Harris heard, the more he liked it. He had the board patched back to working order, called Mitchell into the control room, and instructed him to "dig in hard." "20–75" (named by Cuoghi, who was out of ideas and just picked the actual release number on the single itself) hit number thirty-one on the pop charts and number thirty-two on the R&B.

Reggie Young was part of many Mitchell instrumentals during this time. "I was the white guitar player on Willie's records," he says proudly. Royal Studios "was a school, Willie Mitchell was a coach. I learned a lot. He was a teacher of soul music." Mitchell "told me I was his favorite guitar player," said Young, still moved by the compliment fifty years later.

Mitchell introduced a more sophisticated R&B sound at Royal, moving away from the (mostly) greasy-white-boy rocker sound. Out came the horns and the jazz chords, and a nearly maniacal obsession with a certain kind of stay-in-the-pocket groove was beginning to glimmer. "He would find that little magic sweet spot and he would not go to the left or right of it," Young told Roben Jones.

As great as making music was at Royal, Reggie was increasingly unhappy with other aspects of working there. The financial situation was "really funky." The union session standard at the time was sixty dollars for four songs, or fifteen a song. "Well, if we only cut two sides, you'd get paid sixty dollars, but you'd have to kick back thirty." Young says Cuoghi put their kickbacks in a safe, earmarked as "payola money for disc jockeys— I brought that up one time, "Why don't y'all pay us? Why give it away to disc jockeys that didn't earn it?" They laughed."*

Compounding the problem was the fact that unlike Nashville or New York, where you got paid for your time in a three-hour session no matter what, Memphis "had no time limit. It might take you all week to cut four songs—and then you got paid." (Not that Hi was different from any other studio in town. "Among players, Memphis had a reputation for tryin' to get you as cheap as they could," maintains Reggie, who says this was the reason many top Memphis pickers fled for Music City in the early seventies.)

At Royal, Ray Harris "would work us to death . . . he was always trying to get something for nothing," said Young. Harris eventually found Reggie's breaking point. "He called me one evening and said, "I'm gonna have to cut you down to ten dollars a side." Newly married, with a child on the way, Reggie wasn't having it. "I said, 'Okay—I quit.'"

---

* Some of the early Hi musicians I interviewed didn't recall this setup. But in an online interview, sax man Joe Arnold tells exactly the same story—you'd go to Pop Tunes, Cuoghi would pay you, you'd sign the union-rate check over to him, and if you cut fewer sides, he'd keep the difference. "I guess you could call it a kickback. If you wanted to play on recording sessions at Hi Records, that's the way it was."

Thirty minutes later Joe Cuoghi was on the phone "apologizin'—'Ray Harris is just an old horse trader.'" Young's rate was reinstated, but the damage had been done. "I thought, 'Okay, the first opportunity I get to get out of this studio, I'll take.' And it wasn't long after that Chips Moman called me." Lincoln Wayne "Chips" Moman, who had been around since the early days of Stax, ran American Sound Studio. Young became a central part of the band there, joining other Hi expatriates including Mike Leech, Tommy Cogbill, Bobby Emmons, and Gene Chrisman. At least 120 hit songs came out of American before it folded in 1971, including "Suspicious Minds" by Elvis, "Son of a Preacher Man" by Dusty Springfield, and "Sweet Caroline" by Neil Diamond. Hi Records must've seemed rinky-dink in comparison. Reggie Young says he never set foot in Royal again.

Hi had managed one other hit in 1964—an amusing rockabilly left-over written and sung by "Jumpin'" Gene Simmons, "Haunted House" (later a chaotic live favorite of Jerry Lee Lewis, who recorded it himself, complete with horn section)—but by the time Reggie left in 1967, Hi's hit instrumental period had run out of gas. The British Invasion had stormed America, and Stax and Atlantic were pumping out Memphis-recorded soul hits. Hi was looking like a relic of the past. And now it had no band. "When all the guys left and Hi was gonna continue makin' records, they had to have somebody there to do it," says Jerry Arnold. "That's when Willie made his move. He was tryin' to fill a void. Maintain some degree of success."

Looking back at the how the cards fell, it becomes clear that Mitchell was developing a plan to move Hi Records away from its instrumental/novelty record past. This primarily involved a band consisting of five African Americans: three young brothers nicknamed Teenie, Flick, and Do Funny, plus two monstrous drummers, Al Jackson Jr. and a man they called Bulldog. Jackson, who'd been there since the beginning of Hi, came first.

❖

Al Jackson Jr. had power. And command. Not just on the drums but in the world at large. In another life maybe he would've been a prizefighter, a matador, a Harlem numbers boss. Not a tall man, Jackson had a neat mustache, a bit of a goatee, and a flat nose that looked like it might've seen a punch or two. His peers talk about him with reverence. Jackson was "a gentleman," said Terry Manning, mixer of many a Stax/Hi hit. "A very, very smart, good-looking man who carried himself high. Proud. You didn't ever see him slouching, feeling bad, or mumbling. If he was angry, you'd know it. A straight-up kind of guy, larger than life." Al Jackson Jr. "knew how good he was," said Sam Moore of Sam and Dave. "He'd walk in with that head cocked to one side. He wasn't that tall, but he'd look at you. . . . Man, he was so cocky." But Moore had to admit once Jackson was through with a track, you saw it Al's way. "I'll tell it to you straight: he could make shit smell good." Willie Mitchell put it simply: "I think he's the greatest drummer that ever lived."

Jackson could propel a song with great force and at the same time lock it down to a particular groove. If, as Wayne Jackson told Robert Gordon, "Memphis is a tension that expresses itself in music," look no further than Al Jackson Jr. to experience it. There is a beautiful restraint you hear in Al Green's recordings for Hi. You can feel Al itching to jump off the canvas, yet the frame he's been put in is just too perfect to break out of. It feels too good. Al Jackson Jr. has a lot to do with that.

In a time when white prog rockers spun around on automated risers as they indulged in twenty-minute drum solos, "Al is remembered for what he *wouldn't* do," as T. Bruce Wittet wrote. "He avoided embellishments like the plague . . . rather than add inventive drum fills, he would just as soon work out some novel pattern that would interlock with the guitar and bass." No extra stuff for Jackson. Not that he wasn't capable—the man was versatile. Al knew jazz, loved big bands, and his hero was Sonny Payne in Count Basie's band. Jackson had "fast hands," said Mitchell. "He wasn't just a simple drummer, although he was simple on records."

Meaning Jackson knew what was best for the song. Al was maniacal when it came to percussion, a beat scientist. Jackson was known to disappear off to the Bahamas just so he could come back with a new rhythm he'd nabbed from the locals. His sense of time was unearthly. When the scourge of automated drums infected the studio, Steve Cropper would tell musicians, "Hell, I played with a drum machine 15 years ago; his name was Al Jackson Jr." Lengthy articles have been written attempting to decode Al's secrets. How he'd walk into a session and plop his fat wallet onto the snare so it wouldn't ring, or how breaking a snare head in Europe while playing "I Can't Turn You Loose" behind Otis somehow led to his trademark sound on many an Al Green record—hitting the snare and tom at the same time. "Al was the guy who played that tom-tom on the backbeats that everybody used to copy," said Cropper. Also: "Al had a way of putting the shuffle feel on the kick drum while playing the ride cymbal straight."

Jackson was the only musician allowed to halt a session at Stax. "We all lived in fear that he would stop the recording because of us," said Wayne Jackson. "So he made us play our asses off." Jackson was the boss. "You didn't play *with* Al Jackson Jr., you played *to* Al Jackson Jr.," said Steve Cropper. "*He* controlled the tempo, the flow, the mood and the dynamics." Lord forgive you if you were some youngster fumbling the beat. "If I would rush or slow down, he would yell and curse at me—onstage, in front of people," said Booker T. "He would hit you over the head with a drumstick if one eighth note or sixteenth note was off."

It was Willie Mitchell who gave Jackson his first break. Mitchell was playing in Al Jackson Sr.'s eighteen-piece band at the time. They had a prom gig in Little Rock, and Stokes, the drummer, had quit. Willie suggested Al Jr., an inexperienced teenager who'd been hanging around their rehearsals. "He can't play," Senior snorted. Mitchell vouched for him. When the band started the four-hour gig, Jackson was racing the tempo. "I told you he couldn't play," said Dad. "By the time they returned to play the final set, Jackson was swingin' that band all over the place," said Mitchell. "He stayed in the band—that's when he really learned."

Later Jackson joined Willie's band and started playing sessions for him at Royal. When Howard Grimes couldn't make a session at Stax, Jackson had been called to fill in. He was soon on salary at the studio, although his loyalty to Willie Mitchell was such that he tried to stay in the band and do sessions for a time. Sometimes Cropper would have to roust the overworked drummer out of bed. "Al was one of those sleepers that came up fighting . . . his wife would let me go in there and poke him with a broom handle so I could get him up."

It was Stax that unleashed the Al Jackson Jr. drum sound on the world. As drummer in its house band Booker T. and the MG's he played on all the hits—Otis, Sam and Dave, Eddie Floyd, Rufus Thomas. His style was powerful, minimal, and—when absolutely necessary—dramatic: check out his lone cymbal crash at the end of Otis's "I Can't Turn You Loose." "It was almost taboo to use a lot of cymbals," said Cropper, who shared a wild theory on the reason why: women record buyers "were offended by the high end." Personal research had shown when he climbed into their cars they'd "have the tone knob turned down so it was all bassy."

Despite the massive amount of work at Stax, Jackson remained loyal to Willie Mitchell. He'd sneak off and do sessions at Royal, particularly if Mitchell knew he had an Al Green hit to record. Not only would Jackson be summoned to play on that track, he'd be cut in on the writing. According to Teenie Hodges, Willie considered Al "an equal." Mitchell felt that Jackson "played a different style for me than over at Stax. I think he was a little more creative." Part of the secret, Willie maintained, was that—unlike at Stax—the drums weren't close-miked. He hung two RCA 77-DXs about four feet over Al's Rogers drum kit. "They have a pretty sound—not a hard sound." At Royal, Jackson "was hitting the drums different."

Mitchell had a genius drummer in his arsenal. Now he needed the rest of the band. Did he turn to seasoned Memphis professionals? No. Willie had a particular sound in his head, and to create it he took a group of young bucks and taught them to play every note to his exact specifications. He'd raid one family in particular to get them. "Willie taught *all* of us," said Leroy Hodges. "It's no secret."

❖

Leroy Hodges Sr. lived on a sprawling Germantown farm owned by his grandfather. A little over twenty miles from Memphis, Germantown was another world. "There wasn't nothing but cotton fields and corn liquor back in them days," said guitarist Earl "The Pearl" Banks. There were twelve children in the Hodges family, including three consecutive sets of twins. Leroy drove a cement truck during the day and played boogie-woogie piano in a band with Earl called Banks and the Blue Dots.* "Dad was the greatest piano player I ever heard in my life, and I've heard a-many of them," said son Charles. "Fingers, man, like you would not believe."

The Blue Dots played "blues, nothing but blues," said Charles. "B.B. King, Albert King–type blues." Howlin' Wolf's "Killing Floor" was a favorite number. The Blue Dots played "honky-tonk joints," said Banks. Places like the Top Hat Club in Blackfish Lake, Arkansas. "It was cold liquor, weenies, and hamburgers. We had a name out there. The ladies liked us!" Teenie, Leroy Jr., Charles—all three of the Hodges boys who wound up with Willie did time playing the blues in the Blue Dots.

Mitchell became aware of the brothers when they were still teenagers. Leroy and Teenie were in an R&B band called the Impalas with Willie's

---

* This band has been referred to as the Germantown Blue Dots. Incorrect, said Banks and others.

stepson Archie "Hubbie"* Turner and his brother Horace. They'd play James Brown and Hank Ballard, and singer Maurice Bowers would claim to be Major Lance, whose big hit was "Monkey Time." They got away with the ruse for years, even with Bowers "looking nothing like Major Lance, *nothing,*" said Leroy, chuckling.

The Impalas had the pleasure of backing Jimmy Reed when he blew through town. "When he came onstage, he had some scotch in one hand, a quart of beer in the other," Teenie Hodges recalled. "Jimmy only played for Caucasians. Everybody be screamin' for the hits—'Jimmy, play "Bright Lights Big City"!' Jimmy'd go up to the mic, he'd be wasted—'You want me to play every goddamn thing I ever played, but I tell you what, I ain't gonna play *a goddamn thing.*' He'd turn his back and tell the band 'Jimmy's Boogie,' in G—an instrumental! He wouldn't sing! We loved it."

Leroy, bass player in the Impalas, was the first Hodges that Willie Mitchell nabbed. Still in high school, the band was packing them in at a club called Danceland in Millington. Archie and his brother invited Willie Mitchell down to hear the group. "Next thing I know, he's callin' me to come to Royal and do sessions," said Leroy. "Here's Al Jackson, Joe Hall, Reggie Young." Hodges didn't know enough to be nervous. Leroy brought the Gibson bass his father had bought for him. Neither Willie nor Ray Harris liked the tone. Willie called his old bass player, Roy Strong, who lent Leroy a Fender. "Willie brought me a chord chart, just sat it in front of me—he'd never did that before—and he said, 'Go for it. Count yourself off.' And I pulled it off." His first session was a 1963 instrumental, "Sunrise Serenade."

Leroy "Flick" Hodges is the oldest of the Hodges trio within Hi Rhythm, yet magically looks the youngest. A smartly attired man of few words, Leroy is "so laid-back, when he talks, you have to get right up on him to hear what he's saying," said Thomas Bingham. "Even when he gets angry. I used to ride with Leroy and his girlfriend, and she'd say, 'Damn, why don't you ever holler? *Please* holler!'" The ladies love Leroy, including singer Denise LaSalle, who recorded several albums at Royal. She "liked the way he dominated that bass line," not to mention the fact that Leroy was "tall, dark, and handsome. I said, 'Wow, he's got the goods. All this talent—and handsome?' I thought he might become a superstar one day himself. He was so fine."

---

* On most albums the name is spelled "Hubby," but in a 2015 interview Turner states the correct spelling is "Hubbie," so that's what is used in this book.

Flick has a reputation as maybe the most versatile player in Hi Rhythm. His bass is "plain and simple—no tricks, no frills," said horn player Jack Hale Jr. "He just sits there and quietly plays the bass. You don't hear anything fast or funny." Leroy's big hero on the bass was Motown heavyweight James Jamerson. "Some guys influenced by Jamerson, it's just dumb impersonation, but with Leroy it comes out in this weird way where it doesn't sound like Jamerson—it sounds like Leroy," said musician Scott Bomar. "He's got a really unique touch." Like his brothers, Leroy gave Willie Mitchell all the credit. "He taught me everything—*everything*—about playing. How to not overplay, stay in your groove. Each member of a band, they got a lane to stay in. If you stay in your lane, everything else will come." That, he notes, is one of the secrets of Hi Rhythm. "We didn't try to outplay one another."

❖

Next Willie snatched guitarist Mabon "Teenie" Hodges, who was two years younger than Leroy. "I liked blues, country and western," said Teenie. The first song he could remember singing was the Ray Price country number "I'll Be There." "We picked cotton for white people. Their family would be out in the field and would start singin' country and western, and the blacks would start singin' along with them." Playing music began when his cousin Sammy Winfield gave him a black Stella guitar he'd won in a crap game on a two-dollar bet. Teenie loved baseball, but Sammy felt he was too little and might get hurt so he told him to take up guitar.

"I learned Teenie how to play a guitar," said Earl the Pearl. By the end of that first (and last) lesson Hodges could play Bill Doggett's "Honky Tonk" and B.B. King's "Woke Up This Morning (My Baby She Was Gone)." Soon he was playing guitar in Banks and the Blue Dots alongside his father. There was no bass in the group, just two guitars, and with Earl on lead, Teenie learned plenty about playing rhythm early.

Hodges switched to R&B when he joined the Impalas, and it was then he first encountered Willie Mitchell during a rehearsal at Willie's house. On the surface, this meeting was not an encouraging start. As Teenie recalled, "I asked him, 'How do you think I play? How do I sound?' He said, 'Like shit.'" All of sixteen, Hodges was crushed by the bad review. As he went to leave, Willie said, "Do you want to know why?" Teenie nodded. "You're playin' with a thumb pick. You need to play with a flat pick—like

Reggie Young." He also told Teenie to come to Royal. "Willie told me I needed to start hangin' out. Watch Reggie."

So Hodges started studying up on Reggie Young. He'd give this white guitar player much credit in influencing the Hi sound. When I asked Teenie if he looked up to Young, he responded, "I *still* do. He's the toughest guitar player I ever heard in my life. He plays so nonchalant. Reggie can play with all five of his fingers—five different melodies at one time." Teenie would even name a son after Reggie.

The admiration was mutual. During Young's last few years at Royal, "Teenie and I became really good friends and musician buddies," said Reggie. "When Teenie first started playin' I'd show him some stuff. Our styles were similar. He had his own style of playin'—with maybe a little bit of me thrown in there." Reggie laughed. "But Teenie held his own. He didn't try to be somebody that he wasn't. He played a certain style that he stuck with. He had the ability to know what to play that would be helpful to the record."

At sixteen Teenie started writing songs, but the motivation for that came by way of Stax. David Porter and Isaac Hayes were writing songs for a Sam and Dave album and were one song short. Steve Cropper was too busy to help them, so Isaac called on another guitar player that he'd played with—Teenie. "I can't write songs," Hodges insisted. They convinced him otherwise, telling him to just play the song as he would onstage. With Teenie supplying the riffs, they wrote the Sam and Dave 1965 single "I Take What I Want" in fifteen minutes. It was the first time any music he'd be part of was on the radio. "Wonderful. When I heard that, *whoooo*." Hodges would soon be cowriting many of Willie Mitchell's instrumentals and go on to collaborate on many an Al Green classic.

Two years after that first meeting with Willie, Hodges visited his house and found Pops out back replacing a window. Teenie tried to talk Mitchell into hiring him to fix it for a few bucks, but Willie said he could do it himself. "I went to walk off, and that's when Willie said, 'But I *will* hire you to play guitar.'" Having not forgotten Mitchell's stinging criticism of his fret work, Teenie, thinking it was a joke, said, "Yeah, right" and continued on his way. Willie said, "No, son, I'm not kidding. I'm serious."

Somehow Mitchell had spied on Teenie's progress, and he not only wanted him in the band, he wanted to adopt Teenie so he could teach him more. Leroy Sr. wouldn't sign adoption papers, but allowed his son to live at Mitchell's house, provided he made two promises: no drugs and no white women. Teenie agreed, but soon broke both rules.

Incredibly, Hodges was the very first guitar player Willie ever had in his band (and the first of the brothers to join; while Leroy had worked with Mitchell in the studio, he didn't join the band until after Teenie did). No one was more amazed than Teenie, because he remembered what Willie had told him when they'd first met. "I don't like guitar players no kind of way," Mitchell informed him. "They get in the way of the music." But he'd mold Teenie into a guitar player that not only stayed out of the way but complemented the ensemble around him.

Not that it came easy. "Teenie still had a long way to go skill-wise," maintained old-guard Hi drummer Jerry Arnold. "His talent was developed in the studio." And once he moved in with the Mitchells, Willie expected him to practice many hours a day. If Willie was away from home, the first thing he'd ask Teenie was "Have you done your exercises?" When he played with the band, Al Jackson Jr. would poke him in the back with a drumstick if his timing was off. "I'd either be playin' too fast or too slow," said Teenie. "Because I played next to him, he was the one who taught me timing."

The enforced discipline paid off. It was in Mitchell's band that Hodges's style began to evolve. He found just playing rote R&B chords dull. "I didn't want to play like that, so I started playing note by note." Sometimes he'd strum a chord. Teenie's approach was decidedly minimal. "Like the great Nashville pickers, Teenie never played the second note until the first note was done," wrote Colin Escott. Or as Hodges himself put it, "All the stuff I play, there's a trick in it, more or less. It's not just straight on. There are six notes on the guitar—but maybe just three or four notes the way *I* hear it."

It was an utterly original style. "Teenie sounds like Teenie, and that's what's so unique," said guitar player Thomas Bingham, who describes the Hodges style as "Curtis Mayfield and Ike Turner mixed together. He wasn't a technical guitar player—you aren't gonna see him rip off some big credenzas and superruns. His riffs are so unique and sometimes so odd, but he would make it work. Any time you hear it, you know: 'Hey, that's Teenie.'"

Teenie would later be the spokesperson for Hi Rhythm, and the rock star in the band. "I was—what did Flick like to call me?—the instigator," he said. "Anything to keep people laughing, keep 'em on their toes."

As Mitchell discovered early on. One night Willie's band was playing in Hattiesburg, Mississippi, and one of Teenie's white girlfriends came to the gig and to see him at the hotel afterward. Given the racial tensions of the time, such a liaison was definitely playing with fire. "Willie Mitchell was so scared," said Teenie, who noted Willie's relief when the band headed home and crossed the state line. Mitchell "stopped and took a big, deep breath. . . . He said, 'I'm out of Mississippi!'"

Teenie loved the ladies, and they loved him back. Before she hit big on the rock/pop charts, a young Rita Coolidge moved to Memphis in 1967 and had a torrid affair with Hodges, who was married at the time. "Dear, dear Teenie," she gushes in her memoir, noting his "really dark skin" and "a fabulous mop of hair." They were "absolutely crazy about each other." Hodges made sure she was included in everything, whether it was meeting Ike and Tina after a show, playing cards over at the Mitchells', or attending a session at Royal. "I would spend every minute I could with Teenie. He was pure sunshine."

There was something feline about Hodges. He could be finicky, unpredictable.* During an interview he might be utterly revealing one minute, only to clam up the next over some tiny detail he'd explained before. "Teenie was a very cool, funny, easygoing guy, but if somethin' ever raised his hackles, boy, he'd raise hell," said Thomas Bingham. "If he thought a song should go a certain way, him and Willie would have some words—'Well, goddamn it, I ain't gonna play it no mo'!' Lotta times Teenie was pretty much right."

A few words must be said about Teenie's sartorial style. Coolidge points out that Hodges didn't have to utter a word when he entered a party, as all eyes were already on him: "Teenie was a room rocker." Leroy, regarded as perhaps the sharpest dresser in Hi Rhythm, watched as the sixties turned to the seventies and Teenie's tastes got more and more out there. "I wore a suit," said Leroy. "Teenie just started putting on *anything*." Dashikis, capes, Hammer pants, lime-green socks. "In his mind, he was like a Jimi Hendrix," said Memphis Horn Jack Hale Jr. "If he went to Walmart, he

---

* Typical Teenie story: Hodges was to play a rare live date in England, and a well-known British musician (who wished to remain anonymous) was very excited. A big fan, he thought Teenie had "the greatest guitar tone of all time" and was looking forward to hearing it live. Hodges showed up playing a Flying V guitar with a flanger, a tasteless combination more suitable for a member of Spinal Tap than the great Teenie Hodges. "I didn't even get to hear his guitar," moaned the witness.

would have something on like he was gonna go onstage." Everybody re-members Ninja Teenie. "He went through several years where he loved that ninja outfit," said musician Joe Mulherin. "He'd show up on a gig in his ninja outfit, plug in, and play. Teenie was like a musical elf."

All of these qualities made Hodges a mythic character much sought after when superstars blew through town. As Memphis musical guru Jim Dickinson told Robert Gordon, when Dylan and the Band blew through town in January 1974, "There was one black person there, and that was Teenie. And he was wearing a dress. He was *that* cool."

❖

The next Hodges to join Mitchell was Charles, maybe the warmest of the brothers and certainly one of the deepest. He's lived through hair-raising periods of angel dust and cocaine. (One thing that kept him going: "I kept my radio on the gospel station. When I'd pick up people and we'd smoke, they'd want to change the station. I'd say, 'No. You wanna turn it off, turn it *off*—but don't change my radio station.'") Charles is a reverend these days, although he never rams it down your throat. Spirituality just oozes out of him, like the crazy runs from his keyboard.

Two years younger than Teenie, Charles had joined Banks and the Blue Dots at age fourteen, filling in for his father when he took a break. In sixth grade came his solo debut—playing "What'd I Say" for a gradua-tion ceremony at his Germantown school. "When I walked off they were still hollerin' and screamin'," said Charles." I knew right then without a shadow of a doubt that this was my callin'." By age sixteen he had joined the Memphis musician's union. "I don't read," said Hodges. "Teenie and Flick used to write down music. If you tell me something you want, I can play it." Charles was painfully shy when it came to live audiences. "I was thirty-three years old before I looked at the audience. I either had my head down or my eyes closed. It made me nervous."

Charles went on the road with soul singer O. V. Wright after O. V. heard him play on a beat-up piano in the locker room before a school talent show they both appeared on. Wright was worried his guitar player Melvin Carter wasn't going to show, and asked Charles if he knew his songs. "I know *all* your songs," said Charles. O. V. asked him what key his hit "You're Gonna Make Me Cry" was in. "C," Hodges told him. "What key is 'Poor Boy'"? "D." "Gone for Good"? "G." O. V. asked him to play a bit of the last tune on the battered piano, and with that Charles was in.

"I'm in the ninth grade, gonna play behind O. V. Wright!" enthused Hodges. "We got a standing ovation every song. This was on a Friday night. That Monday I went back to school, I was a star." O. V. told Charles he wanted to take him on the road once he was through with school.

Sure enough, a few years later the call came—O. V. had a gig in Macon, and if Charles wanted the job he had to leave that very night. Hodges wasn't sure if his parents would let him go. "*I'll* ask them," said Wright, and Charles hopped into the car next to O. V.'s wife, Norma, so they could zoom over to Germantown in O. V.'s sleek, powder-blue Brougham Fleetwood Caddy. "Blue top, blue interior," Charles recalled as he closed his eyes and smiled. "It was sharp, it was clean. Oh man, O. V. was tough. Good lookin' guy, kinda heavy. Wore dark, tinted shades."

Charles's parents, who were watching TV, were floored to see O. V. Wright suddenly standing in their living room. They happened to be fans of Wright's music, and cautiously gave their blessing. "I went and packed my bags up and I never stopped travelin'," said Charles.

It would be O. V. Wright—not one of the other Hodges brothers, as they were unaware of his musical progress—who informed Willie Mitchell of Charles's talent. Hodges said that once he joined Wright's band he did most of the arrangements. "O. V. would always come around me to sing the song, we would pick it out." This impressed Mitchell, who was having problems with Joe Hall, his erratic piano player, and the result was Teenie called Charles down to the Manhattan Club. "I changed the band," claimed Charles, who moved to revamp the standards like "Moon River." "I liked that kind of music, but I wanted to swing."

Charles played piano in Mitchell's band for a year, then switched to B3 organ. It's his wild runs and vibrating chords on the B3 that earned him his nickname from Willie: Do Funny. Those dramatic swells and exclamation points on the organ that you hear on Al Green's "Love and Happiness" and all the rest of the Hi records? That's Do Funny. As Thomas Bingham put it, Charles would "do those swoops and it's like, 'What planet is this guy from?'"

Now Mitchell had guitar, bass, and keyboard. The common ground with Stax was Al Jackson Jr. But the way the Hodges brothers saw it, they had an ace up their sleeve—three-quarters of the band was family. "We could do Booker T. and MG's better than Booker T. and the MG's, but they couldn't do *us*," said Leroy. Added Charles, "They couldn't gel the way we gelled. Because we were brothers. We felt each other. It got to the point when Teenie was playing, I knew where he was going, he knew where I was goin', and Flick knew where *we* were going. We got to the same place, because we were spiritually connected."

Unless they were heading in the wrong direction, Teenie maintained, Mitchell gave very little direction when they recorded. There were no rehearsals, no demos; Willie would sit down at the piano, teach them the song, and off they'd go. "We would play what we want. If he don't like it, he'll tell you and you have to change it. But very seldom did that happen. It might be played in a different key or played [with] a different feel or something. But he was very supportive of us."*

❖

A conundrum arose when Al Jackson Jr. proved too busy with his Stax commitments. Mitchell needed a second drummer on call, and that's where Howard "Bulldog" Grimes enters the picture. Like Jackson, he had roots in the old-school ways and knew how to drive a big band. "I liked the way he played—he was simple, straight to the beat. He was one of the best shuffle drummers," said Teenie, who was the one to approach Howard about joining Mitchell's band. This was in or around 1968, and Howard was the only African American member of the rock band Flash and the Board of Directors.

At first Grimes turned the offer down for a big tour with Flash and acts like Paul Revere and the Raiders, which Howard felt was his shot at the big time. The fact that Grimes was black did not sit well with a crowd in Montgomery, Alabama, and people in the balcony started pouring their drinks and dumping popcorn on his head. Shaken by the experience, he joined Willie's band on his return home, where, like the rest of Hi Rhythm, he'd remain until the end of the seventies.

While Jackson and Grimes had somewhat similar styles, musicians and fans love to pontificate on the differences between the two drummers. Howard has "just got a particular groove," Teenie pointed out, "whereas Al Jackson Jr., he's all over the place—he's on the top, he's on the bottom, he's in the middle . . . maybe because Al was more educated about the drums because his daddy was a music teacher, band director, he shined more than Howard—he was so diverse, could do more things." Grimes was more of a wild card. "When he was on, he was on, and when he was off, he was

---

* In addition to the Hodges brothers, Mitchell's stepson Archie "Hubbie" Turner would contribute (sometimes uncredited) piano to many a Hi session.

off," said Thomas Bingham. "He didn't interpret it like everyone else. He might roll in the middle of the beat and we'd stop and say, 'Goddamn it, Howard, no!'"

Mitchell summed it up this way: "There were times that Al Jackson Jr. couldn't get the feel I wanted, on songs like 'Take Me to the River' or 'Love and Happiness,' so I had Howard come in. Now, Al could actually play anything . . . but he couldn't play it *raggedy*." Mitchell would have some typically off-the-wall advice for Grimes, as he related to Andria Lisle. "He said, 'Howard, when you play drums think about your woman . . . think about when you take those titties when you're in the bed—play the goddamned drums that way!' It tripped me out! But it started soaking in."

Did it ever. Grimes "would get a hold of that beat and not let it go," said background singer Sandy Rhodes. "He wasn't fancy at all, but he would set that groove and wouldn't stop. Very few fills. How simple those drums are, but they hold the beat, the groove. Not too busy. An obvious, dominant beat that you can hook into. He never let you down." Howard's unrelenting tenacity for the groove would earn him a new title from Willie. "He said, 'You're not Howard no more, you're the Bulldog. When a bulldog gets mad, he gets something and just clamps down. When you play drums you lock into the tracks just like that!'"

There are those who feel Howard Grimes has spent too much time in Jackson's shadow. Al would "come up with stuff, but Howard was the master," says Leroy, who developed a particularly supernatural rhythmic bond with Bulldog. When it came to Hi Records, "Howard played most of the tracks. . . . He's the most creative drummer I've ever played with— Howard can create on the spot, come up with somethin' original." Flick points to a future Al Green classic—"I'm Glad You're Mine." That funky, drunken-telegraph opening drumbeat? Grimes "came up with that intro on his own."* (Willie would make the genius move of having Jackson and Grimes play together on tracks, but that wouldn't happen until Al Green.)

An unusual cat, Grimes. He could be moody, a little out there. "One of the oddest guys I've ever met in my life," said Thomas Bingham. "Howard would speak about religion a lot and it would be so contradictory, it was

---

* Grimes, who considers the track one of his best, revealed to Robert Gordon the inspiration for that intro came from Lee Dorsey's "Working in the Coal Mine." Another one Grimes is particularly proud of is Green's "Oh Me, Oh My (Dreams in My Arms)," the beat of which was inspired by old Popeye cartoons. "When you see Popeye skipping backwards like he'd do, that was that rhythm . . . when I did it, it blew Willie's mind. Willie told me, 'Boy, you are a crazy motherfucker.'"

hard not to burst out laughing. Once he said, 'As a Christian man with the things I'm studying in the Bible, I believe in peace. And I'll kill all those muthafuckas that don't.'"

❖

Teenie, Flick, Do Funny, Bulldog and/or Jackson—Mitchell had now assembled his band of doom. There is another ingredient we can't leave out: horns. They were closest to Willie's heart, being a trumpet player. On Al Green sessions the lineup would usually be Jack Hale Sr., Wayne Jackson, Andrew Love, Ed Logan (with Lewis Collins later replacing the hard-boozing Logan), and Willie's brother James.*

"Willie made up most of his horn lines," said Jack Hale Sr. They'd head into the control room with their horns, Willie would play the track, and if he "had something on his mind, he'd sing it to us." Occasionally there'd be written charts, but mostly it was "head arrangements" done on the fly. Sometimes Willie would join in on trumpet. "Having played together for so long, we all knew exactly what notes we were gonna play in the chord," Hale explained. "I would always take the five; Wayne, the one on top; James on the bottom; Andrew and Lewis on the hot notes, the third or sevenths. We never had to say, 'What note you gonna take on this chord?'" They'd go out in the room and stand around a single mic, with Willie mixing it as they laid down the parts together.

"His lines were really simple," said Jack Hale Jr., who remembered the day his father came home after cutting Al Green's "I'm Still in Love with You." "My dad said, 'You're not gonna believe this, it's like elementary-school simple—the horns go *da da da*. . . .' I'm thinking, 'This doesn't sound cool at all!' But when I heard it, it was *perfect*. It blew my mind. A lot of guys who don't know horns will have you play them all the time, but Willie never wasted horns on chords that would be better played on

---

* There is controversy when it comes to the players known collectively as "Memphis horns." In 1969 Wayne Jackson and Andrew Love were savvy enough to trademark the name Memphis Horns, and they have protected that property. (In 1996, they filed suit against Al Green, who had announced in the press he was touring with the Memphis Horns. When he refrained from using that particular assignation and publicly apologized for any confusion, the suit was dropped.) Some feel that the role of other players considered to be part of the group that played on so many historic sessions has been obscured in the process. This would include not only Jackson and Love, but at the very least Jack Hale Sr. and Jr., James Mitchell, Ed Logan, Lewis Collins, Ben Cauley, Roger Hopps, and Floyd Newman. (Others add early Hi player Joe Arnold.)

keyboards. Willie used them in a way that made them *integral to the song.* You couldn't really hear the song without those horns."

❖

There was one last thing Willie Mitchell needed for his music, and it had to do with the studio itself. "When I cut a record I could never hear what I wanted to hear," said Mitchell, who brought it up time and again with Joe Cuoghi. "I would always say to Joe, 'I don't like the sounds I'm getting out of this place. We can do better than this." Ray Harris had continued to engineer at Royal, and "everybody said he had a tin ear," said Teenie Hodges. "Everything was thin—no bass, no bottom." Mitchell had repeatedly complained to Joe Cuoghi, but Joe wouldn't overrule Harris. Finally, Willie had had enough.

"I told Joe Cuoghi, 'If I can't work the board, I'm going somewhere else.'" Cuoghi relented, and Harris no longer engineered sessions. Mitchell would soon buy out Ray's share in Hi. "When he left, I said, 'Ray, you really taught me a lot. I appreciate everything you taught me.'" Harris asked Willie what that was. "'You taught me *never* make a record like you make it!' And we had hits from then on."

Indeed. The very first single Mitchell engineered was a cover of "Soul Serenade" featuring the lineup of Teenie, Leroy, Charles, and Howard. With Willie manning the board, the sound, according to Teenie, "changed instantly." (Although once it played on the radio, Hodges wanted to re-record it because his guitar was slightly out of tune: "I couldn't stand to hear it.") The track went to number ten on the R&B charts and number twenty-three on the pop. "The biggest instrumental I had," said Mitchell, who would now engineer everything—even while playing on the record: "I would turn the board on, run out and play, then run in and check it."

"Soul Serenade" is a landmark recording in the history of Hi. One could say the Willie Mitchell sound begins here. The recordings that came before it sound rooted in the fifties, somewhat flat, with no one element particularly distinguishable from the whole. They were meant to be heard on a tinny mono AM station. "Soul Serenade" has depth and sounds three-dimensional. You can pick out all the instruments clearly. Other than the drums, the instruments sound close-miked, creating a very intimate sound. MG's bass player Donald "Duck" Dunn has said, "The Memphis sound was the rhythm section. It was good *separation:* if you like organ, you can hear organ, guitar, and so forth." With "Soul Serenade,"

Willie Mitchell was now on the way to taking this sound to its ultimate realization. You can practically imagine Al Green singing over the track.

All the dominoes were falling in line for Mitchell. He had his band, most of whom he'd taught exactly how to play, and now he was in control of recording their sound. Willie had big plans: "I wanted to cut a record that would sell black and white." That was a little ways off as of yet. He needed to cut a few vocalists first.

That part of the story blasts into gear with the arrival of one of the greatest deep-soul singers of all time: O. V. Wright.

I'VE BEEN SEARCHIN'

Sometimes I talk to an artist for hours about what the song means.
You can't just read lyrics off a piece of paper and have anyone
believe them.
—WILLIE MITCHELL

There's a song that I want you to hear. Not by Al Green, not even a hit—in fact, I've never heard anybody talk about it except Charles Hodges, one of the geniuses who plays on it. "You Must Believe in Yourself" is by O. V. Wright. It's on YouTube, so tap a few keys and live a little. Turn that crappy computer up so you can hear what everybody's doing.

My God, what a performance. Willie and Hi Rhythm at their absolute best. I actually have to stay away from listening to the song, because it can't be played only once. Hours disappear. As the title indicates, it's a motivational number. Now, if some namby-pamby folkie with an acoustic guitar were to unload such a sentiment, I'd reach for the vomit bag, but O. V. convinces you to *believe* in believing in yourself. He makes the idea sound necessary, noble, and even a little nasty—the kind of vocation best undertaken while flying down some nowhere highway with your hand on some paramour's leg. This is a rough, tough voice that knows a thing or two about pain—the kind one wants to hear in the wee hours when all the bridges have been burned. "O. V. was brought up in church, and he knew how to sing from his soul," said Charles Hodges. "It's something that can't be taught to you."

And Hi Rhythm supports O. V.'s every note. Bulldog pounds out that ironclad midtempo groove Hi's so famous for, the rest of the band locked in tight. Listen to Flick's bass pattern. It sounds like somebody sticking a plunger into a garbage disposal, but in perfect time. The horns kick in a ton of attitude. It reminds me of something Willie Mitchell once told Reuben Fairfax Jr.: "In order for us to record together, we got to be hearin' the same thing." Well, everybody is hearing the same thing on this one. Despite the phenomenal playing, nobody grandstands or sticks out. It's about the singer and the song.

❖

Mitchell and Hi Rhythm would soon be making history with Al Green, but O. V. Wright came first. Success with singers did not come right away for Mitchell. He cut a few vocalists at Hi, most notably Don Bryant, the fantastic R&B belter who'd sung with Willie's band. Between 1964 and 1969, Mitchell put out ten solo singles on Bryant, but despite Don's tremendous talents, they failed to click. "Willie admitted he just didn't know how to cut me," said Bryant. "I just never did find an identity. I would always kind of sound like somebody else. It wasn't a distinctive sound."

O. V. Wright came along in 1967. Born in Lenow, Tennessee, on October 9, 1939, Wright had grown up in Memphis and sung with a number of gospel groups, most notably the Sunset Travelers, who recorded for malevolent R&B/gospel potentate Don Robey, the gun-toting owner of Houston-based label Duke/Peacock Records. Wright's first secular recording was the magnificent "That's How Strong My Love Is" for Goldwax Records, a Memphis label run by ex-Hi partner Quinton Claunch.

Claunch signed O. V. to a five-year deal and had big plans. Unfortunately Don Robey claimed Wright was still under contract to Peacock. "He sued us," said Claunch. "As soon as the record started hittin'." Claunch and his partner "Doc" Russell bravely met Robey at the annual deejay convention in Nashville and tried to work out a compromise, but Robey insisted he'd have to okay everything they'd record on Wright. Claunch smelled a rat. "I said to Doc, 'Man, this guy here, he'll suck us dry, he's not gonna approve anything we send down.' I just didn't like his attitude." The end result was that Wright stayed put with Robey. "He did give us a nice little sum on the front end," admitted Claunch. But as far as O. V. went, Robey "just had him lock, stock, and barrel."

Robey began recording Wright solo for his R&B label, Duke. The haunting dirge "You're Gonna Make Me Cry" (that's O. V.'s wife, Norma, singing background alongside her sister) went to number six on the R&B charts in 1965. After a few more singles came and went, Willie Mitchell got a call from Robey, who wanted Wright back in the studio but "didn't want to fly O. V. to Houston to do it."

The first single recorded at Royal in April of 1967 was "Eight Men, Four Women," a tormented ballad in which Wright pleads to his woman that "the jury of love" had found him "guilty of loving you." The song went to number forty-four and would begin a run of classic singles, including such monsters as "Ace of Spades," "A Nickel and a Nail," "I'd Rather Be (Blind, Cripple and Crazy)," and "I've Been Searching."* These were hip, tough records, and some of the deepest soul music of all time. "You just close your eyes and sing what you feel," Wright said in 1967 in one of his only interviews. "Some people call it soul, but it's only the old blues."

Al Green may have been the most successful singer Mitchell ever recorded, but many of those close to Willie told me that O. V. was his favorite. "He's so emotional," said Mitchell, who admired "that hurtin' sound in his voice." Wright "could take a song and do anything he wanted with it . . . O. V. was a stylist." Mitchell produced all of Wright's secular records. "We worked real good together. O. V. stayed with me 13 years." Wright was the first singer to record a string of hits at Royal, but it took seven years to get Wright onto the Hi label itself and out of Robey's clutches. "Willie didn't like Don Robey," said Charles Hodges. "Willie didn't think he was doin' O. V. right, and that bothered him. O. V. wanted to get on the label, Robey wouldn't allow it. Finally, one day Robey sold him the contract."

It's not easy to convey how popular O. V. was in his prime. Soul fanatics rightly revere him, but he reminds me of another underrated, influential singer, Little Willie John, in that there exist no American TV performances, very little live footage, and a handful of photos. And as with John, there is an intensity to his singing some find hard to take. Back in the

---

* Many of the earlier O. V. Wright songs were credited to Don Robey's alias, Deadric Malone—when it came to songwriting he was famous for stealing the credits and the money that went with them. Mitchell and crew's contributions went unacknowledged. Take "A Nickel and a Nail." "If you had heard the demo that they sent us, it sounded like some ten-year-old across the street had recorded it," said Leroy Hodges. "There was no structure to the song, nothin'. We straightened that tune out. We should've gotten writers on that."

day Wright could whip African American audiences into a frenzy. "Man, we had women come up there, take their panties off, and throw 'em all on the stage," said George Journigan, who played bass for Wright. During one gig in Belle Glade, Florida, "they started throwin' money on the stage—twenty-dollar bills. I'd never seen anything like that in my life. I stopped playin', we started pickin' the money up! O. V. said, 'What are y'all *doin'*?'"

Charles Hodges remembered a gig at Mississippi State College. "We got down there to do a show, and there were ambulances lyin' outside the door," recalled Charles, who asked O. V. why they were there. "You'll see," said Wright, who demolished the audience that night. "They was bawlin', passin' out face first, just fallin' like flies! And they're takin' 'em out! I never saw anything like it before in my life." His brothers thought Charles was bullshitting until they saw it with their own eyes at the Paradise Club in Memphis. Once again people in the audience were "cryin' like babies, and just fallin' out." Into the ambulances they went.

O. V. was as streetwise as his songs suggest. "O. V. liked to gamble," said Gene Mason. "We'd go to these black pool halls and shoot pool and I used to win all O. V. Wright's money." Wright fared just as bad in tonk, a card game he'd play with Mitchell. "Willie would win *all* the fuckin' time." Mason maintained that when it came to gambling, "O. V. couldn't stick his finger in his ass." The singer loved the fast life. "He just wanted diamonds and fine cars," his brother Edward confessed to Peter Guralnick.

Wright became ensnared in narcotic addiction. Soon-to-be Hi artist Syl Johnson shared the bill with him out on the road and watched O. V. "shoot a needle in his hand. I was a square—he said, 'I'll show ya how to do it.'" Johnson passed on the offer. Charles Hodges saw things heading in a bad direction as early as 1967. "He started shootin' Dilaudid. I didn't want him to do it—I begged and pleaded with him, but he just wouldn't listen. Then he messed around and lost his wife." Norma filed for divorce first in 1967, then a final time in 1971. In court papers she alleged that Wright had "severely beat her about face and body" and "struck her in the eye with such force that it was necessary to seek medical attention." She claimed he'd dragged her into the bathroom of a beauty shop where she worked and knocked the hell out of her. O. V. would "frequently slap and beat the complaintant [*sic*] with great force and tremendous impact . . . the defendant acted at all times as if he were under the influence of some drug or medication." The divorce shattered Wright. "It just seemed like when he lost Norma, he just didn't care about nothin' anymore," said Hodges.

Wright drifted into a life of petty crime. O. V. once asked a band member to pull over to a liquor store. Wright casually walked in, but ran out: he'd held up the joint. O. V. was arrested for theft, forgery, stealing a woman's purse, yet throughout this mayhem continued to sing and perform. "Willie would get him out of jail to record," said Charles Chalmers. "Then he'd have to go back." On July 5, 1973, in a crime that shocked Memphis, Wright's manager, Arthur Brown, was found dead behind the wheel of his 1971 Cadillac in a desolate warehouse section of town. Brown and his female companion had been beaten, shot, and partially burned. On October 12 O. V. was convicted of "distributing a controlled substance"—heroin—and sentenced to five years in a Texas federal penitentiary, where he served twenty-seven months. Earlier that same year Wright had recorded his greatest album with Mitchell for ABC, *Memphis Unlimited*.

By the time Wright actually got on Hi Records, the chaos of his life had become audible in the vocal cords, even though there was still some gas in the engine on tracks like "Into Something (Can't Shake Loose)" and ballads like "I Don't Know Why." On one of the later Hi albums, Teenie Hodges confessed that O. V. "forgot to put in his false teeth."

After leaving Hi, Wright recorded just once more, an obscure gospel album cut in Nashville with the Luckett Brothers. "He really wanted to go back into gospel," said Charles Hodges. It was not to be. O. V. died after suffering a heart attack en route to a gig at Joe's Supper Club in Grand Bay, Alabama, on November 16, 1980. According to one source, Willie Mitchell and Al Green were pallbearers.* Green, not one to hand out compliments, said "OV was one of those phenomenal talents that never got the hit he needed . . . I'll never forget a concert I did with him in Flint, Michigan, where he sang 'You're Gonna Make Me Cry.' And I just stood there on stage watching him. He was incredible."

Wright was a rogue, a thief, a dope fiend (not to mention an alleged spouse abuser), but musicians were crazy about the guy. "I enjoyed working with O. V. more than all of them," said Charles Hodges. "He was one of a kind, down home. We had grown up in the same neighborhood and ate at each other's table. We'd hang out, did everything together. He was a comedian. He'd just have you laughing all the time." Musicians would not talk so fondly about Al Green.

---

* Wright's grave went without a headstone until 2008, when two writers, Red Kelly and Preston Lauterbach, initiated a campaign to raise the funds for one.

❖

After that first hit with O. V. in 1967, Don Robey sent another artist over to Royal to record with Willie Mitchell—Bobby "Blue" Bland. *Touch of the Blues* was a largely mediocre album (and the first session Teenie recalled playing on, alongside a quickly departing Reggie Young), but did well on the charts. At this point Mitchell knew he'd made it, because it was now that "everything exploded." A stream of artists showed up at Royal to work with Willie, including powerhouse duos Inez and Charlie Foxx and Ike and Tina Turner. The studio was becoming a hot, efficient assembly line, cranking out R&B hits like AMC cranked out Ramblers. Mitchell rarely cut singers live with the band, instead building the track first and overdubbing the vocals later. Yet the backing never sounded canned, fitting each singer like a glove. For these pros the identity of the artist was inspiration enough; as Bulldog told Bill Dahl, "We always used the vocalist as a ghost." And make no mistake, Willie was the boss, then and forever. Years later, when singer Willie Walker wanted to deviate from the Hi formula and try something new, Mitchell told him, "You sing it the way I say." Said Walker, "With Willie it was 'My way or the highway.'"

❖

The next singer to land at Royal was the man who could've been Al Green. Handsome, with a tight Afro and pencil mustache, both of which would expand with the seventies, Syl Johnson was a songwriter, producer, and guitar player cocky enough to wear a huge marijuana-leaf pendant in his publicity photos. Born near Lamar, Mississippi, on July 1, 1936 (Mitchell shaved eight years off his age when he signed to Hi), Johnson is different from many an artist that passed through Royal in the respect that he denies any gospel influence. (When asked if he started singing in church, his response was, "Hell, no.")

Syl grew up on the blues, and after moving to Chicago in 1950, he was soon playing guitar with the likes of Howlin' Wolf and Little Walter as well as recording with Billy Boy Arnold and Junior Wells. In the late sixties Johnson had some R&B hits on Twinight, an independent Chicago label he owned a sliver of. "Come On Sock It to Me" and (the much sampled) "Different Strokes" are tough, angular records driven by Johnson's high, reedy tenor, a voice sharp enough to cut a diamond from space. He first visited Royal in 1968 when tour buddy O. V. Wright invited him to check out one of his sessions.* Syl was knocked out by the Hi Rhythm band.

"They had a tremendous pocket, and their blend was so good," said Johnson, who proceeded to record a few singles there that year for Twinight, most notably miniskirt protest (and number thirty-six R&B hit) "Dresses Too Short." Johnson stressed that he produced his early Royal sessions himself, with Willie only engineering. In fact, they disagreed over some things, such as the ahead-of-its-time funky bass part on "Dresses." Mitchell "thought it was too hip-hoppish, too hi-step," said Johnson. "He wanted it in the pocket, laid-back. I said, 'Let me try it this way.'"

Syl insists that he contributed elements to the Royal sound that were later incorporated on Al Green records, and "Your Love Is Good for Me," an outtake cowritten by Johnson cut during this time, provides some embryonic evidence of the Mitchell-Green formula: double-tracked vocal, descending chord line, ad-libbed vocal asides. "I gave the band a type of uptown groove," said Syl. "That comes from *Chicago,* man."**

When Mitchell attempted to sign Syl to Hi, Johnson wanted fifty grand; they compromised at thirty-eight. Syl was all set to become the first solo star at Hi Records, and booked on a flight to Memphis to sign the papers. He never got on the plane. His wife, Hazel, was having difficulties at the time, so he blew off the trip and didn't even call Willie to tell him. "I drug my feet," confessed Syl. "I was ashamed to call 'em." Finally, while tooling around New Orleans in his Eldorado ("tomato red with a beige interior—beautiful car"), Syl rang Willie from a pay phone. "He said, 'We'll still sign you, but we just signed a young guy by the name of Al Green. We can't give the front money, but we still want you.' So I signed with Hi in 1971. I didn't get a dime to sign, but I cut some hits."

Johnson made some fabulous records for Hi during his four-album stretch, which ran from 1973 to 1978, among them "Back For a Taste of Your Love," "Anyway the Wind Blows," "Let Yourself Go" (cowritten by Charles Hodges, who plays both piano and B3), and his hit version of

---

* Syl wanted to point out that when it came to the reception both singers got from the ladies, he was more popular than O. V. Syl says he "was better lookin'," and not only that, physically Wright had "a big head."

** Howard Grimes was so excited when he learned Syl was coming into Royal he was determined to replicate the feel that he'd heard on "Different Strokes" and "Come On Sock It to Me"—as he told Bill Dahl, before he ever recorded with Johnson he was on a mission to "stay in focus and play whatever I heard on [those] first two records."

Green's "Take Me to the River." Hi Rhythm loved Syl, and he also introduced two important songwriters to the company, Earl Randle and Darryl Carter. But Johnson was one artist that wasn't completely suitable for Willie Mitchell's production. "I resented him, because I really didn't get to do my stuff, and I felt that I cut better songs when I was with Twinight than I was cutting with Hi." Johnson rarely played guitar on his Hi sessions and cowrote only three songs there. And he would not deal well with being in Al Green's shadow.

❖

The first singer signed to Hi that hit was female. Ann Peebles had a sleepy, sultry delivery that hid a restrained fury. Tales of romantic discord were her specialty at Hi. They often sound like they were recorded after a 3 a.m. motel-room fight and smoldered with weary ambience like an angry cigarette glowing in the dark. Listen and you're on her side. Ann's performances contain "vulnerability," said Jack Hale Jr., who played horn on her sessions. "Aretha Franklin hit you with horsepower, Ann got you with subtleties. She had a very sensitive delivery, a way of making you feel with each song that she wrote it, believed it, lived it."

One of nine children, Ann Peebles was born April 27, 1947, in Kinloch, Missouri. Her father directed the choir at a local Baptist church, and Ann started singing there at age nine. She'd fantasize about being an R&B singer before the mirror, using a broom as her mic. Her favorites ran to opposite ends of the spectrum—Mahalia Jackson and Tina Turner. On a trip to Memphis in 1969, she went to see the Bowlegs Miller band at the Club Rosewood. Getting up enough nerve to ask Bowlegs if she could sing a number, Ann did a rendition of "Steal Away," a scorching ballad of infidelity that had been a hit for Jimmy Hughes in 1964.

Peebles must've knocked it out of the park, because Miller immediately asked her if she wanted to record. "This is my whole life's dream," she told Bowlegs, and the next day she was at Royal meeting Willie Mitchell, who sat down at the piano and accompanied Ann as she belted out "Steal Away." She passed the audition. Her father had to sign the contract as Peebles was still underage. "When we first started recording, she weighed about eighty-nine pounds," said Charles Hodges. "But she had a big ol' voice. I said, 'How does all that voice come out of you, you're so little!' My favorite song she did was '(You Keep Me) Hangin' On.' Ooooh, when I hear that, I start fanning myself. Something just cuts in me real deep."

Ann's very first single, Hi 2157, went to number twenty-two on the R&B charts. "Walk Away" was a dirge of a ballad written by St. Louis bandleader Oliver Sain, a friend of the Peebles family who must've put on "Steal Away" for inspiration. The production, while also rooted in the sixties soul sound of Rick Hall at Muscle Shoals, hints at the new direction Mitchell was taking—listen to the in-your-face snare drum and the equally up-front distorted vocal (as Gregory Scott put it in an online forum, "Willie was one of the kings of artful distortion . . . the guy knew how to break shit up in the most musical ways.")*

You can hear Mitchell working out his approach to recording vocalists in these early Peebles singles (and having far more success at it than with Al Green, who'd arrived by this time). By Ann's fourth single, a tough cover of Little Johnny Taylor's "Part Time Love," the sound was locked in tight. Mitchell totally revamps the 1963 hit, changing the tempo to that chugging, midtempo Hi Rhythm groove (dig Teenie's two-second solo). "Part Time Love" hit number seven on the R&B charts and number forty-five on the pop. Hi Records finally had a bona fide singing star.

Peebles recorded a string of classic singles at Royal, among them "Slipped, Tripped and Fell in Love," "Somebody's on Your Case," "I'm Gonna Tear Your Playhouse Down," and "Breaking Up Somebody's Home," but she remains best known for her 1973 hit, "I Can't Stand the Rain," surely one of the greatest Hi tracks of all time. Inspired by an offhand remark Ann made at a party before heading off to a Bobby Bland concert, it is the song's striking electric timbale intro that grabs you. As Howard Grimes told Patrick Berkery, "Willie was looking for something." They tried bongos at first, but then Teenie suggested Bulldog pick up a set of electric timbales that had been lying around the studio. The drippity-drop rhythm Grimes plays was channeled from a Maxwell House coffee ad—"my favorite TV commercial," Howard noted. According to Teenie, it was Gene "Poo Poo Man" Anderson—later a Parliament-Funkadelic member, then a Hi recording

---

* Bowlegs Miller received a coproduction credit on "Walk Away," his first and last. "He and Willie got mad over Ann Peebles," said Charles Hodges. "Bowlegs felt like Ann was his artist and Willie stole her." A rude, crude character who yapped a mile a minute, Bowlegs was "a comedian—especially if you played in his band." When it came time to paying his musicians, Miller would throw each musician's loot behind their back, and invariably it would be short a few bucks. Jessie Butler, an albino keyboard player who'll enter the story later, had a particularly rough time in Bowleg's band. Miller would throw Butler's money, and when it came to finding it Jessie "couldn't see too good," said Hodges, laughing. "I loved Bowlegs Miller, man, but he was a crook."

artist—who suggested Mitchell ditch everything but the unorthodox percussion. "You're crazy," Willie told him, but once heard, the idea stuck (Peebles later maintained it was all Mitchell's idea).*

Many felt Peebles should've achieved far bigger stardom, including Willie Mitchell. "He was a little tough on Ann," said Leroy Hodges. "Willie said she was lazy." In a 1987 interview, Mitchell described Peebles as "the girl with the big voice who could have really gone further. I don't think she put as much energy into her career as a singer as some of the rest of these people!" People remember her back then as very shy, as well as "a very nervous person—nervous onstage," said Thomas Bingham, who toured with her. "Didn't like the spotlight."

Charles Hodges recalled an early gig at Disneyland where she appeared with the Willie Mitchell Band. "She started drinking a little bit. I knew it wasn't her. Ann and I dated for five years. That was my sweetheart. I was married too—God forgive us for what we were doing." James Mitchell told Charles to talk to her. When he told Ann to quit boozing, things escalated. "I went off—I slapped her. And she got mad. James said, 'I didn't want you to *hit* her—now she ain't gonna sing!' Willie said, 'Why'd you do that? Lord have mercy!' He was sitting there shaking—Willie was a real nervous guy. I said, 'Just give us a minute, y'all just leave.'" Charles, who then apologized to Ann, told her, "Ann, this is your big break. You don't need to drink, you're gonna mess up.'" According to Hodges, "She went out there, did the show of her life."

It was after an incident where Peebles fainted and he had to give her mouth-to-mouth resuscitation that he ended the affair. "It woke me up. God was telling me it was wrong." Charles called Don Bryant, who was heartbroken over a failed romance, and told Don he had to take him somewhere. That somewhere was Ann's apartment. "I said, 'Ann, Don, I want y'all to do this for me. Both of y'all sing, both of y'all write songs, y'all could be a great team. Why don't you try to work out your life together?' I put their hands together and I said, 'I'll see y'all later.' A few months later they called me and asked if I'd play at their wedding. They've been married ever since." Bryant, who admits he was initially jealous of Peebles as his own singing career never got off the ground at Hi, became

---

* The song was an all-time favorite of John Lennon, who infamously attended one of Ann's 1974 performances at the Troubadour in Los Angeles while on a degenerate drunken bender with Harry Nilsson. "I looked out in the audience and somebody kept screaming, 'I love you,'" said Peebles of Lennon. "I saw him, but he had a sanitary napkin on his head."

one of her primary songwriters and sang backup for her on the road. "When them women would hear 'Breaking Up Somebody's Home,' she'd have people crying," said Bryant. "They could relate to what she was singin' about."

❖

Artists were now flocking to Hi. Denise LaSalle was a Mississippi-born singer who'd been getting nowhere with singles on Chess and her own independent labels before landing at Royal. LaSalle, who was self-taught and didn't read or write music but composed her own lyrics, went into Royal with only one instrument—her voice—yet felt she could communicate her ideas to Hi Rhythm. "I'd sing the songs to them and they would pick up the sound of what I was doin' and go with it." One of her first singles with Mitchell was 1971's "Trapped by a Thing Called Love," which was recorded in one take. "I wanted to do it again, but Willie said, 'You're not touching that—you got a smash, Denise.'" "Trapped" not only gave LaSalle the confidence to quit her supermarket job, it went to number one on the R&B charts and number thirteen on pop. LaSalle recorded two albums at Royal (one of which includes the earthy, amusing single "Man Sized Job") and went on to a career as a down-home blues diva that continues to this day.

LaSalle recorded at Royal for the Detroit independent Westbound Records. When I asked Denise if Mitchell ever considered signing her to Hi, she let loose with a hearty laugh. "Actually, Willie Mitchell didn't think too much of my voice. Willie tried to buy one of my songs for Ann Peebles. He said, 'All you gonna do is screw that song up' . . . he used another word besides 'screw.'" After her initial recordings with Mitchell, he turned her over to Bowlegs Miller. She told me it was because Willie was just too busy, but Hi promotion man Willie Bean confided it was because the production credit on her first album went to her company, Crajon Enterprises (Willie Mitchell only got credit for arranging). "Willie got pissed off. It was a gold record. He wouldn't cut her again." LaSalle insisted she produced the sessions at Royal herself. Mitchell "would just sit back at the control and listen. Willie didn't have too much to say until you had somethin' he disliked."

❖

In the seventies, Hi expanded and the roster grew. Otis Clay was another gravel-voiced belter that came out of gospel. He'd record a 1972 hit with Willie, "Trying to Live My Life Without You," as well as superb sides like "The Woman Don't Live Here No More," but he'd be frustrated at Hi due to the fact that "everything was concentrated on Al Green." Non-Hi acts continued to record there as well. The Detroit Emeralds cut some great stuff at Royal, including "Feel the Need" and "Do Me Right." They were favorites of Leroy Hodges. "I used to love when they came to town. We'd cut the rhythm track here, but they took the tape back to Detroit, put the horns, voices, and strings on up there—that's how you got that different sound: Detroit-Memphis." Scores of other artists recorded singles at Hi that are cherished by soul fanatics, including Quiet Elegance, George Jackson, Erma Coffee, Jean Plum, and a favorite of mine, a scorching 1972 single by Joe L. (aka Joe E. Lee/John Lee Carter), "Let Me Know" / "I Can't Stand It."

But all this began happening after Al Green hit. On July 13, 1970, a tragedy occurred that put the final nail in the coffin for the old Hi era: Joe Cuoghi died suddenly at the Memphis airport. He was only forty-five years old. Cuoghi had accompanied Ace Cannon on a New Orleans concert trip and they were returning home. "We landed the plane in Memphis, he passed out getting off the plane, and never recuperated," said Cannon. "Had a heart attack. Fell dead." It was an unexpected blow. "Joe was like a father to me," said Mitchell. "I loved him and he loved me . . . Joe was just a wonderful man."

Back when it looked like the label was dying a slow death, Willie had considered leaving Hi—he'd gotten a healthy offer from Jerry Wexler at Atlantic. Cuoghi couldn't pay the money Wexler was offering, but he made Mitchell a vice president and gave him stock in the company. Now that Cuoghi was dead, John Novarese offered Willie the role of president. Mitchell turned it down because "that's the way Willie wanted it," said Teenie Hodges. "I was there when he told him—'I don't want to be no president. You be the president. Keep on doin' what you're doin'.'"

Mitchell had more important matters at hand. He first addressed Hi Rhythm. "I called all the guys in—everybody loved Joe—I said, 'Joe's gone.'" After that sad news had sunk in, he told them there was a new plan in effect. "I'll put you guys on salary. . . . Now, we're gonna be here nine o'clock in the morning and we're gonna work until five or six in the evening. Every day. Seven days a week." Mitchell then "called in the art-ists—Ann Peebles, everybody. I said, 'Look, it's time to cut records.'"

Willie had taken over Hi Records. He'd slowly assembled his band, overhauled the studio, and was on his way to perfecting the sound that would take him to the top of the charts. It was the perfect environment for creating Al Green, although it didn't come easy. By July 1970, Green had already been at Hi a year and a half, and nothing was really happen-ing. But that would all change a few months later with the release of his first hit, "I Can't Get Next to You." As great as they were, O. V. Wright and Ann Peebles (and even to some extent Syl Johnson) were rooted in an old-school bluesy R&B sound. With Al Green came something utterly new. Wildly idiosyncratic singing. Hypnotic love songs with open-ended, sometimes obtuse lyrics. Intimate, nakedly sexual performances. And it all came wrapped in a package that contained more than a bit of mystery. When Green finally connected with a mass audience, Hi Records would explode.

One man who'd been instrumental in starting the company didn't think much of Green's talent. Not long before Cuoghi died, Ray Harris had left Hi. Perhaps he felt out of place with the Willie Mitchell regime. He sold his shares in the company to Willie for $22,000 and returned to Mississippi, where he'd soon partner with Sam Phillips and build another studio. According to writer Colin Escott, before he walked out the door for good, the ever-blunt Harris informed Bill Cantrell their new singing sensation Al Green would get nowhere fast.

Ray, bless his heart, just didn't care for "that sissy voice."

SILKY ON TOP,
ROUGH ON THE BOTTOM

I'd rather be a singer with a future than a star with a past.
—AL GREEN

Midland, Texas. They all remember it differently. Name of the joint? Nobody knows. Held 2,500 people, said Mitchell. "Wasn't no huge club," insists Flick. They got paid for the gig; they got stiffed. Willie said it was hot that day, 112 degrees. Bulldog says it was night, and cold. The band was returning from a short California tour in support of "Soul Serenade." No, it was a one-off gig. Al was on the bill; Al begged to sing a few numbers for fifty bucks. He had a hole in his shoe, said Mitchell. "I heard that, I don't remember that," says Charles Hodges. (He says the band all knew "Back Up Train," and, in fact, Hodges was so moved by the tune he requested divine intervention. "When I heard that song, I prayed, I talked to God—'I would like to play behind that man.'")

Charles says the band learned Al was on the bill in the van ride down to the gig. Bulldog informed Robert Gordon they didn't know until they met Green backstage that night. "He took charge in the dressing room. He said, 'All I want you to do is vamp.'" Grimes noted Green's conk—his processed do—was wilting. "Al need his hair fixed." Green says he had three dates to play in Texas. "I was a lone singer . . . I didn't even have a road manager . . .

a guitar player, nuthin'." About Willie Mitchell, he told *Rolling Stone* in 1972, "I didn't know who he was. It was just another band to me."

The way Willie remembered it, the band had arrived at the club that afternoon to drop off their equipment. Green was there and wanted to rehearse a few numbers. In a hurry to get to the hotel, Mitchell dumped the singer on his brother James so he could down a beer. Willie, his back to the stage, snapped to attention when Green began singing "Your Precious Love." "Before he finished, I stopped the band," said Mitchell. "He had a perfect voice. I had been looking for a singer . . . when I heard Al Green in that club I knew I had found my man." He'd soon find out that Green "had mid-range, high range, low range, every kind of range. And he really sings on pitch . . . very unique," marveled Willie.

Teenie maintained Al put across nothing during the earlier rehearsal—"average" was his verdict—and he went as far as telling horn player J. P. Louper right before Green went on that it was going be "popcorn," meaning lightweight. Al then proceeded to kill it from the very first number.* Louper, a stutterer who'd nicknamed Teenie "Breeze," leaned over to the guitar player and muttered, "B-B-B-B-B-Breeze, what do you think of him now? He's a *bad* boy." Hodges couldn't wait to get off the bandstand. Willie had told him to find a young singer they could work with. He rushed over to Mitchell, sitting at a table with Green, and whispered to Willie, "This is the guy." Mitchell said, "What do you think I'm sittin' here with this pen for?" "He knew Al was the guy," said Teenie.

Whatever the particulars, Mitchell made his move. "I said, 'Come over here, kid. Man, you got a great voice. Why don't you go back to Memphis with me? We got a little label called Hi Records and we can cut some records.' And he said, 'Well, how long will it take for me to be a star?' I told him about 18 months. He said, 'I don't have that long.'"

This down-and-out singer "was real cocky, but I liked his attitude," said Mitchell.

According to Green, there was some back-and-forth on the idea of Memphis.

"I wouldn't like it," said Al.

"Well, you might," said Willie.

---

* Further muddying the waters, Green has also claimed that he "didn't know Willie Mitchell was there. During the show I started walking the tables: I got up on the tables singing to the people and they were applauding and screaming and singing along." None of the Hodges brothers recall any of this.

"I'm *sure* I wouldn't like it—I'll tell you, I wouldn't like it."

"Wanna try it?"

"Yup, but I wouldn't like it."

Yes, no, maybe so. Welcome to the finicky, oddball world of Al Green.

❖

With Al neither here nor there, the band went off to pack Willie's green GMC van, but as they were getting ready to step on the gas, an old jalopy blocked their exit.

Out popped Al. "Really, it would take 18 months for me to be a star?"

"Yeah," said Willie.

"Wait a minute, I'm goin' with ya!"

According to Mitchell, they talked future plans all the way back. "We are about ten minutes from Memphis, about to cross the bridge and he says, 'I have to go back to Grand Rapids, Michigan . . . I'm gonna need some money.'" Green needed fifteen hundred bucks to get things squared back home before the move to Memphis. This gave Mitchell pause. It was a sizable chunk of change in 1968. But he gave Al a tour of Royal and convinced Cuoghi to give Al the dough. Green might have been living on another plane, but he was still a shrewd customer. After his experience with "Back-Up Train" he'd maintain he didn't want to sign with a major—"Al Green might get lost," he said. He wanted a company that had big distribution, lots of money, and "no artists." He also caught on that "Joe Cuoghi owned half the durn town."

And so Al took his fifteen hundred and disappeared into the night. Mitchell had no address, no phone number, and wasn't sure if he'd ever see him again. Time passed. Mitchell claimed it was months; reality suggests a few weeks. Willie came in from a gig in the wee hours and crashed. 6:30 a.m. Somebody was banging on the door. Thinking it was a handyman coming to work on his house, a groggy Mitchell let the guy in. "Don't you remember me? I'm Albert Green," said the invader. Green was sporting longer hair, and Mitchell had forgotten his face, but came around quickly.

"You're the motherfucker who got my money," said Willie.

Thus it began.

❖

"We started working," said Willie Mitchell. "Eight o'clock in the morning 'til two in the morning."

December 3, 1968, is the date of the first Al Green session at Royal (he'd sign a contract with Cuoghi and company dated January 3, 1969). These first sessions, released in three 1969–1970 singles and on the 1969 *Green Is Blues* album, were a rather bare-bones beginning in terms of production. Teenie, Flick, Do Funny, Bulldog, the horn section, a few other players—no strings, no backup vocals, no double-tracked vocals by Al. The first single came out in April—"I Want to Hold Your Hand." Yes, *that* "I Want to Hold Your Hand." "A great song—for the Beatles," Al correctly noted. Oozing confidence, Green belts it out and sounds great, that effortless falsetto unleashed, but talk about the wrong choice of material. The flip—"What Am I Going to Do with Myself," a ballad (which Green has claimed was the first song he'd written in Grand Rapids but is credited to "Mitchell-Jones") that was far more in keeping with his talents.

The rest of *Green Is Blues* is a case of "let's throw everything against the wall and see if it sticks." A standard here, more covers of R&B and pop tunes there—Al sounds particularly uncomfortable on another Beatles number, "Get Back." Written by soon-to-be key background vocalists Charlie Chalmers and Sandy Rhodes, "One Woman"—the second single—was a leaden, ponderous misfire on infidelity guilt complete with flute that went nowhere and that, says Chalmers, was recorded first by Isaac Hayes for *Hot Buttered Soul*. "Willie just flipped over the song," and they gave him permission to cut it as well, much to the fury of the Hayes mafia. "We thought, 'What's it gonna hurt?' It was gonna be a single on Isaac, but they cancelled that idea . . . big mistake." *

The only song actually credited to Green was a vague, forgettable piece of funk of the James Brown variety complete with derivative grunting called "Get Back Baby." Already Green's starting to reference himself—"back up train" is tossed into the lyrics. Listen to the flashy drumming by Howard Grimes, because before very long you won't hear any of it. Willie "didn't like all that rolling on the drums. He'd say, 'Man, motherfucker, don't play that shit. I don't want that,'" said Bulldog. "Willie never liked [cymbal] crashes too much. He thought they interfere . . . I tried to play the ride cymbal. He thought the ride cymbal interfered too."

---

* Green has said he cut the song first and that Hayes had "come over to the studio and heard my rendition. . . . Isaac went back over to Stax and put a version on his LP *Hot Buttered Soul*—the first song on the album." It's actually the third. Whatever the case, it led to some rivalry between Al and the bald, chained one.

This was no casual matter of taste. Mitchell was "fixated on the sound of my drums," said Grimes. When Howard had been in Ben Branch's band, he'd been taught to tune his drums to the bass by Robert McGee. Willie would hear Howard do this and get ideas. "He'd call me in two hours before the session, he'd work with me. I'd be at the kit and he'd be at the board, getting the sound. He liked the snare real loose. He had a Telefunken mic on the snare. That's what he was most interested in—that snare, that foot and the hi-hat . . . whatever I was doing on the snare, he wanted it to spread. . . . Through the board, he could make it so big."

❖

Green sings hard on *Green Is Blues*—which he can excel at, don't get me wrong—but he doesn't feel quite at home yet. Those dreamy, relaxed vocals you can disappear into were still around the corner. "When he first came to town, he wasn't Al Green, you know?" says Charles Chalmers. "I know that a lotta times Willie would be frustrated. Willie would get down on him pretty hard sometimes. I think later on Al would kinda resent that. When Al wasn't singin' the way Willie was tellin' him to, he'd just tell him, 'Man, you ain't doin' it. Quit trying to sound like somebody else. I want to know what Al Green is. Find yourself.'" (Teenie Hodges cracked up quoting Mitchell's bluntness: "'You sound like *shit,* man.' Willie might say anything when doing a song—*anything.*")

Two cuts on *Green Is Blues* hint at the future, both of them slow, spartan covers—"Summertime" and a moody, slightly menacing version of local Box Tops hit "The Letter"—but it's a scattershot effort at best. The original album cover, with a sullen, unsmiling Al suited up, staring at the camera, says it all. You can practically hear Green muttering, "Willie thinks my singing ain't shit." As Mitchell himself admitted, "We was still lost at that time."

Time: that's what it took to unlock Green's true power. "The biggest thing I had to do with Al was soften him up, because he had so much Sam Cooke in him. He wanted to sound like Otis Redding, he wanted to sound like Sam and Dave. I said, 'We don't need that. You can't compare with these guys. You need to be smooth and sweet, you don't need to scream.'" Silky on top, rough on the bottom: that was Willie's mantra. He also knew that they had to be original, not a retread of Stax or Motown. "If you want to go somewhere, you can't want yesterday's dinner," noted

Mitchell. "You got to go forward, gotta do your own thing." What's impressive is the amount of energy Willie devoted to figuring out just the right approach for Al Green. He had a label to run, other artists. But he wasn't in quite the hurry Al was. "He was getting real frantic," said Mitchell. "I knew he was gonna get there."

As did Joe Cuoghi. "Al used to beg Mr. Cuoghi for money," said Hi employee Willie Bean. "He would sit around Pop Tunes goin', 'Mr. Cuoghi, I need two hundred dollars. I'll give it back to you.' Mr. Cuoghi would go, 'Look, Al, I can't keep givin' you money.' Al sat there all day. Finally Mr. Cuoghi let him have it. Mr. Cuoghi told me, 'He's worryin' the shit outta me now, but he's gonna be a star one day.'"

❖

Mitchell got Green a $70-a-month third-floor walk-up in an apartment building on Haynes Street that also housed Ann Peebles, O. V. Wright, and Leroy Hodges. Charles Hodges remembered hanging out there fondly. "I always liked singers. And he could *sing*. He was a really nice guy and he was in Memphis and didn't know anyone. I wanted to make sure that he felt comfortable, because we were on a mission.

"We'd sit on the floor on big ol' beanbag pillows," he says, and listen to Green's record collection. No doubt thinking of Willie's demands, Al stared into the abyss of The Big Three—Jackie Wilson, James Brown, and Sam Cooke. "I asked him, are these your favorite artists? 'Yeah,' he said, 'I'm just trying to find myself between all of them.'" Particular attention was paid to Wilson. His work reminded Green that "if you sing in a falsetto, you don't have to be feminine," says Charles.

Green grew particularly tight with Teenie. At that time, Green "was great. We'd hang out five, six nights a week with a sister of mine, Veniece Starks. We danced all night with girls, smoked plenty of reefer." There are those who say Teenie was more of an influence on Green than anyone realizes. "People have been telling me that since the early seventies. When Al first came here from Grand Rapids he kind of took on my dress—except I don't dress as wild as he do at times. A lotta people used to think I was him—and he was me."

Teenie became more involved in Green's sessions than he had been with other Hi artists, and they started writing songs together. "After that first album Al thought he couldn't write—Willie told him he couldn't," said Teenie. Mitchell told Green he was thinking of using Detroit writers like Motown's Norman Whitfield. Teenie told Al, "It ain't that you can't write—but you can't write no *music*. I can do the music and you do the lyrics." From here on Teenie "had one song on every album." Even so, it was usually the last song Willie agreed to do—and Teenie maintained he was sometimes screwed out of a credit—such as on "Call Me," "You Ought to Be with Me," and the first song he says they wrote together (but recorded later), "It Ain't No Fun to Me."

Even with all the work at Royal, Teenie had somehow managed to swing a deal working in the studio for Ike and Tina Turner out in Los Angeles. For over a decade Hodges would head off to Los Angeles every year and record with Ike for a few months. (Did Willie mind? I asked Teenie. "Oh, he minded." Mitchell on Hi Rhythm: "They don't work other sessions unless I let them—and that's not too often.") Once he even took Al along, the idea being that Green was going to collaborate with Ike on some songs. Apparently Turner was a multitasker, and as they tried to write, Ike rehearsed Tina and the backup singers on their dance routines.

"Ike was at the piano, and we sat for hours as he took these girls over their routines, right there on the floor. I'm going like, 'Couldn't they do that separately?' And Ike's like, 'Nah, while you write it, they can do it—now turn, turn.'" It threw Al. "I was still sitting there with a pencil and a blank sheet of paper, and Ike said, 'Man, get that guy out of here! That guy can't write no song!'" Once Green had a hit, "Ike called Teenie up and said, 'Hey man, bring him back! Bring him back!'"

❖

Al Green had not forgotten his gospel upbringing. Even this early in his career, spiritual forces were roiling within. "I have had a mystical, magical and electrifying experience with God," Green explained to *Ebony* in 1976, maintaining that it was in March 1969, during his "down and out" period on Haynes Street, that he communicated his desire for superstardom directly to God himself. "We got together, talked about it," said Al. "I made a deal . . . for everything I ever wanted." He'd later elaborate that "God told me I could have more clothes than I could ever possibly wear, and more food than I ever could eat, and more cars than I could ever drive—and all that money." There was one catch: "I'd get everything I ever wanted, but that someday I'd have to pay for it."

According to Green, God would not ask to collect on Al's debt until one night in Disneyland in the summer of 1973. By then he'd be a superstar at the height of his career.*

❖

The next two Hi singles were more hard-sung derivative funk songs written by Green. In his book he says he was now insisting his originals, not any covers, be released. As he was still a half-baked songwriter (at least by himself) it didn't help matters, although Mitchell said the tepid "You Say It" sold 100,000 copies. "I wasn't satisfied with that. I said, 'We're off on a Sly Stone groove and we've got to find our own thing.'"

May 1970 brought "Right Now, Right Now," another funky number indistinguishable from the last. Hard funk and Willie Mitchell were not peanut butter and jelly. Far better was the flip side, the first public offering written by Green-Hodges: "All Because (I'm a Foolish One)." Teenie's amusing wah-wah guitar intro, more of Charles on the B3, Al's ad-libbing and letting loose with a scream . . . and how about those doomy horns? Great opening lyric couplet: "In the morning, when I rise / Sweet teardrops drop from my eyes." Too many secondhand "huh"s and "good God"s, but things are starting to gel.

"Right Now" is notable for being the first time Al and Bulldog got into it. According to Teenie, they did twenty-eight takes of the song because Green was unhappy with the drums (at Teenie's insistence, they went back and listened to take three and used it: "He had us cut that motherfucker all this time?").

"Howard is a great drummer but he has a mind of his own," says Charles. "Al just wanted him to play some things, but he just wouldn't do it . . . it happened several times." Teenie said it got a little more personal than that. Some of Green's minions "heard Howard call him a motherfucker"; Teenie tried to explain that Howard wasn't being serious. "I told Al, 'We call each other motherfucker, you call me motherfucker . . . '" Green wasn't amused. He could "have a sense of humor, but if he thinks you're talking 'bout him—no, he ain't gonna have no sense of humor."

---

* Green spoke so obliquely to one reporter, he'd completely misunderstand just what entity Al had bargained with. "Did Al Green Make a Deal with the Devil?" screamed the cover of the April 1974 issue of *Sepia*. Green "is convinced some mysterious occult force is shaping his existence," wrote Paul Niemark. "He speaks eerily in low foreboding tones like the legendary Faust who sold his soul to Mephistopheles."

Plus Howard wasn't the pal-around type. "I did what I would have to do and I'd leave," said Grimes. Green "started nitpicking at me . . . Teenie and him and the rest of the guys, they was so friendly and I wasn't . . . I just did my job." But one day Green "shifted on me. He told Willie to call Al Jackson Jr. and it hurt me.

"Al Green had made this suggestion: 'Well, I don't want Howard to play no more.' He told me, 'You fired.' I told him, 'You can't fire me, man . . . I work for Willie Mitchell.' Willie heard this. I didn't know he had the control button on . . . he said, '*I* do the hiring and I do the firing.'"*

Nonetheless, the situation provoked an unusual resolution. Grimes would record the album tracks and Al Jackson Jr. would sneak off from Stax to record those particular songs Mitchell thought had the most potential to be hits (usually ones Jackson either shared or was given a writing credit for). And sometimes Willie used both drummers together—Jackson on the kit, Grimes on congas. "I had 'em runnin' against each other," said Mitchell with a laugh.

Grimes "was a forceful player, but Al was cockier in his playing," says James Hooker. "I guess that's why Willie put him on the kit and Howard on percussion. They'd play at the same time in the same booth, maybe a baffle to separate them a little bit. The rhythm changed ever so slightly. That was phenomenal, that switch. Willie *knew* to do that. I don't know what woke him up in the middle of the night, but it worked! Every jukebox on the planet lined up for that." Their style melded so well that it's hard for those involved to tell you who played what. Even Willie would admit, "There's two people you can put in a studio and I wouldn't know which of them is playing, that's Al Jackson Jr. and Howard Grimes."

❖

The ante was upped on Al Green single number five, a wild, inventive cover of the 1969 Temptations hit "I Can't Get Next to You." Willie and company slowed the song to an ominous grind and turned it into a threat. The drums are way up front—hi-hat locked in, a chisel in granite. Listen to Teenie's beautiful rhythm figure, pretty as ripples on a pond, and those

---

* From the darker recesses of the Grimes mind comes this: "I was kind of leery of Al Green because his voice would go up and down . . . like something else was inside that voice . . . you don't want to say, 'Is this a faggot?'" Howard went on to question Green's sexuality, saying that "somebody" told him "that I could get anything I want through him . . . I don't indulge in men, I like women."

swaggering horns. Al is starting to sound like Al. "He was still singing hard, but he had such command," said Mitchell. "You didn't have to lead Al to a chord," adds Charles Hodges. "He would lead you. Al had perfect control of his voice—*perfect control.* He would take you there." Versed in the harmony of his gospel-group family, Green is starting to overdub himself to provide his own Al Green choir. Many different Als will soon seep out of the tracks. At times even his lead vocals sound like a conflict between the Al Greens. "With a gospel singer's chutzpah, he would employ his voices—a limber falsetto, a breathless crooner, a growling preacher—in a three-way encounter," wrote Anthony Heilbut. It makes for thrilling listening.

A word about the guitar solo—yes, Teenie plays a guitar solo, however beautifully brief it is (the guitar is more prominent on the first two Green albums; the emphasis would soon switch to Charles on the B3). Mixer Terry Manning had introduced Hodges to the music of Jimi Hendrix after a session "and it completely blew his mind." Teenie went right out and got a fuzztone. The result was the gnarly, Link Wray–style stab of a solo on "I Can't Get Next to You," which ends before you can even think of reaching for a stopwatch.* "Of course, it sounds like Teenie, not Jimi Hendrix," Manning points out, and thank God for that—it feels a bit half-assed, spontaneous, a little wild, and provided just the right sandpaper for Willie's ultra-smooth sounds. (Otherworldly Teenie didn't even realize that it was a Temptations cover "until three months after [their version] was on the radio.")

"I Can't Get Next to You" hit number eleven on the R&B charts, number sixty on the pop, and according to Willie, sold about 700,000. Mitchell had Green to thank for the idea. Along with a singer named Laura Lee. Al and Laura had been tooling around Detroit one rainy night and started singing the song together. Lee was quite the catalyst in Green's life. "I wrote my first million seller because of her," admits Al. The intense search for the Al Green sound was about to come up aces. "It took a long time to find it," admitted Mitchell. "'Can't Get Next to You' was close, but 'Tired of Being Alone' was *it.*"

❖

---

* Teenie overdubbed the solo over his own rhythm parts, and he'd find playing solos a particular challenge. "I have to go in the control room and hear the music real loud in my ear to play lead. Otherwise I can't do it."

A tiny saucer-eyed fashion plate possessing a way-down-low contralto peppered with the sexiest bit of grit, Lee was a "skinny beanpole with lots of hair." A year older than Green, Lee had been born in Chicago, but raised in Detroit. Her adoptive mother, Ernestine Rundless, led a premier Detroit gospel group, the Meditation Singers, and Laura started singing with them as a teenager. Lee said they were "the first gospel group to sing in nightclubs" and it was during a Vegas engagement that Sinatra tried to sign her to a secular contract, dubbing her "the little girl with the big voice." Her parents nixed the idea, but "weary of being dominated," Laura was talked into it by a gravel-voiced Motor City club owner.

Eventually this led to Chess Records, but Lee didn't hit until she recorded at "a little shack with all these hillbilly musicians"—FAME Studios down in Muscle Shoals, Alabama. There she cut the slow and sublime "Dirty Man" in 1967, and her double-tracked vocals give one pause: Did they inspire Al Green to do something similar? Lee started racking up R&B hits, and right around the time Green landed in Memphis, she went to see his show (in his book Green puts it around the time of "Let's Stay Together," but this contradicts the many interviews he's mentioned her in).

"Al Green was actually a fan of mine," Lee told Colin Dilnot. "He had my records, 'Dirty Man' and 'Uptight Good Man.'" Green was informed she was there and sent word for her to come backstage. Lee: "My reply was this—'I don't go to men's dressing rooms. Tell him if he wants to see me he has to come up here.'" And he did.

"I was sitting in the bar. He said, 'Miss Lee, I'm a fan of yours and I have your records. Can I see you after the show?' I said, 'No.'" But she did come back the next night. "I kept telling the people that was around me, I said, 'That boy? That's gonna be a superstar, he's got superstar qualities' . . . they laughed at him."

Laura came back for a third night, and soon they were involved, splitting time between Memphis and a swanky, top-floor apartment at 1300 Lafayette in Detroit. The Temptations were downstairs neighbors. "We lived together," said Lee, who helped Green with his career. "I would actually get on the phone to book him myself—book him around Milwaukee, around the area." Musically "we would just create together." Lee is one of the only women Green mentions by name in his book, calling her a "soul mate."

Green and Lee would be off and on for the next few years. Sightings of the duo appeared in *Jet* magazine's gossip column: "Miss Lee, decked out in a black dress and a silver turban, wouldn't say if the pair are headed for the altar." They'd tour together, bringing down the house at the Apollo. Lee had a bunch of baroque seventies hits when she recorded for Holland-Dozier-Holland's Hot Wax label: "Women's Love Rights," "Crumbs Off the Table," "If You Can Beat Me Rockin' (You Can Have My Chair)."

Considered outspoken for the seventies, Lee's songs often incorporated long spoken raps that were ahead of their time. Despite this, one senses her vision of love is an old-fashioned one. "They tried to get me into a women's lib thing, like I was a man basher, but I refused to go there . . . I was not advocating women's lib but advocating women's love!" The agony and the ecstasy of her entanglement with Green would provide recording inspiration: in her covers of "Since I Fell for You" ("This shy guy from Memphis who hung around my house all the time . . . he'd speak to me and go in and talk to my mother . . . "), "At Last (My Love Has Come Along)," and "Every Little Bit Hurts," "I was singing about Mr. Green."

Like most of Green's relationships, it was deeply troubled. "That was early Al Green—during his pseudo-pimping years," says band member Buddy Jarrett. "He was actin' like he was all that . . . Laura Lee had her nose open, she bought him jewelry." Lee was "really a nice person but she always chose the wrong men," said Green's soon-to-be road manager/emcee Roland Jones. "She was a socialite in Detroit. In them days, black people wanted a Cadillac, and here come this girl in a Rolls-Royce—a blue Rolls-Royce—and she'd pick Al up in it. Laura was self-made . . . she had some money, some kind of success, so she didn't bow down to Al—she talked shit to Al. And that's where the conflict was."

Out of this came "Tired of Being Alone." "This lady used to leave me alone all the time," said Green. "She was the busiest woman I'd ever seen. Always had something to do—her nails, hair, shopping. Consequently I was alone a lot and that's why I wrote that song." Lee was working at Phelps Lounge, leaving Green to fend for himself at home. The bar closed at two, but she was coming home at three or four a.m. and Mr. Green wasn't happy about it. "I say, 'Man, this has got to stop.' So she says to me, 'Look, I'll tell you, I'll stay here and *you* pay the rent.'"

"I kicked him out of the bed—I got mad at him," said Lee. "He was hurt about it." Green drifted off to sleep on the couch or wherever he was. At about 5 a.m. he woke up. "I was dreamin' about me singin' this weird song. And I'd never heard that song before . . . it kind of frightened me, y'know." Green scribbled down some lyrics and fell back to sleep. When Lee woke up the next morning she found a brown paper bag. On it Al had "kept writing, 'I'm tired, I'm tired, I'm tired.'" Which became "Tired of Being Alone." The line "Help me, girl, just as soon as you can" came from a saying that Larry Lee, Green's new guitar player for live gigs, used on the road: "Larry would say, 'I don't give a damn when you help me, just as soon as possible,'" Green recalled. The song's subject was that of most of Green's songs: "love, emotional relationships . . . my songs deal with these basic relationships . . . I don't talk in symbols very much. I try to say whatever I mean without being phony about it."

❖

Spend time inspecting his lyrics, and it becomes apparent Al Green is an odd, idiosyncratic songwriter. "Needing you has proven to me to be my greatest dream"? Clunky and convoluted—until you listen to the way Al delivers it. The message here is I need, not even I need *you*. When Green is at his best—which for the most part means when Willie Mitchell was pushing him—he has an uncanny ability to tap into the universal.

His lyrics often sound conversational, simple. They can feel like haphazard, half-remembered dreams, stream of consciousness thoughts dashed off in a minute. But when they connect they have a peculiar ability to invade your brain. Robert Christgau charitably described Green as "a structurally unconventional composer whose lyrics veer savvily between stone-simple romantic views and tormented reveries on the heaven-and-earth split that infuses and haunts all soul music." Maybe. I don't know how savvy it all is. You never get the feeling Green labors over or even rewrites these things (and by that I mean the entire song) for longer than it takes to eat a ham sandwich. This is great when he's fully plugged into a moment that matters to him, and a vacuum of greeting-card clichés or sketchy nothingness when he isn't.

❖

The way Green tells it, Willie Mitchell was a bit resistant when he finally spoke up about his own material one night. "After we got done cutting all these other people's songs—the Beatles and all these blues songs and the Temptations—I says, 'I got a song, too.' So Willie says, 'Oh, please,' because he'd been cutting all day . . . it was one o'clock in the morning. I says, 'I got me a song and I wrote it on my own.'

"So Willie told one of the guys, 'Go out there and see what he's got, would you, please? I got to have a drink.' Willie had a little shot of vodka . . . after he went to feeling better, he says, 'All right, what we got out here?' And it was this song "Tired of Being Alone," and I had worked it up with the band." Mitchell: "When I heard the song, I knew that was gonna be it." Green: "Willie says, 'I'll tell you what. Don't sing with the rough voice . . . sing mellow. Don't sing hard. Sing mellow.'" The battle wasn't over yet—it would take one more single for that—but Al was starting to get the message. "Willie sat me down and showed me you don't have to use so much power in singing as conviction. He told me to use personality instead of raw vocal strength."

That personality arrives fully realized for the first time on "Tired of Being Alone." Green starts out big and churchy and then gets intimate as a confessional. Drama: Al squeals, screams, goes high, goes low, and throws in ad-libs on the spot. You listen, taking bets on where he might land next. When the band dips down and Al murmurs, "Sometimes I wonder"—oh baby, it feels Peaches-and-Herb so good. The vocal sounds very relaxed, off the cuff, but according to the song's mixer, Terry Manning,* the Al Green Hi vocals on the songs picked out for singles are "very heavily punched." In those days the vocals were on one, maybe two of Willie's eight tracks. After Al laid down a master take they'd go back and punch in the improvements Mitchell wanted to make, word by word. "That adds to the immediacy of 'Tired of Being Alone'—the vocals are punched in so much that you really don't ever hear a breath."

All that digging in the Royal mine had paid off with a big, fat diamond. The track is crisp, uncluttered. No extra stuff. There's Teenie's ripple-in-a-pond rhythm guitar and those exclamation-point horns, which provide a little grease to move the song along. You can close your eyes and see each instrument crystal clear—everything is perfectly defined, minimal yet complete. Its own little self-contained universe, like gazing into a George Herriman drawing: there's Krazy Kat, over there's Ignatz and Offissa Pupp, here's the jail cell and the brick. You can get lost in these Al Green records. Lost. Like *Krazy Kat,* it may be the same old story over and over, but it's those minute variations that capture the

---

* Manning would mix many of the Green singles sitting alongside Mitchell. "He does shit that no one else would do, his sound was impeccable," said producer Paul Zaleski of the countless hits Manning mixed. "He was the invisible genius of Memphis—you don't see him, but you hear him."

imagination. How many times did Al track his vocals? Does the hi-hat sound like a *whoosh* or a *dit*? How will Teenie gild the lily this time? Hi Rhythm is a sound—sublimely narrow in its design, impossible to duplicate, immediately recognizable.

According to Charles Hodges, that's Al Jackson Jr., the human metronome, the man who put the pow into Stax, on the kit. If so, Jackson set the standard for much that was to follow right here. That hi-hat's closed tight. Rhythm with delicious restraint: listen to Jackson let loose with a sly little cymbal bash—just one—ONE—in the whole goddamn song, wait for it. The "big" ending, haha! The song's an ascending whale, and when it finally meets water's surface, there's a tiny little spurt from the blowhole. Willie Mitchell, mad genius of drum production! (And, he insisted, recorded with "never more than two mics . . . it's the placement, tuning of the snares.")

Mitchell would liken the dynamics of recording a song to sex. Years later he'd explain to Reuben Fairfax Jr., "When you make a record, you build to the climax—if you jump on a woman, just go to humpin' her and get off in the first two minutes, she'll look at you like you're crazy. You got to set it up, you got to talk to her, play with the poochie, kiss her on the neck and build on that emotion 'til you get to the orgasm.

"Pops said, 'When you bust a nut, that's when you start fadin' it out.'" That lone cymbal? Al Jackson Jr. busting a nut.

❖

There was a new ingredient to the Al Green sound: the background trio vocals of Charles Chalmers and sisters Sandra and Donna Rhodes. The Rhodes sisters were white, Southern, and more than a bit country. "We grew up on television," explains Sandra Rhodes. She and her sister Donna had recorded for RCA as the Lonesome Rhodes and were just teenagers when Willie Mitchell first saw them singing on *The Rhodes Show,* a long-running Memphis TV broadcast that featured (among other family members) their fiddle-playing dad, Dusty, and his brother Speck, the latter most famous for being the plaid-suited, gap-toothed comedic foil to Porter Wagoner. Willie "liked our country harmony," says Donna. Mitchell called up their mother and asked "if she'd bring us over to the studio." According to Willie, she was doubtful at first, but relented. Sandra thinks the first thing they sang on for Hi was a 1966 Narvel Felts session. Later, when Willie was working on "Tired of Being Alone," the sisters were once more on his mind after he'd heard some demos Charlie Chalmers had recorded over at Sun featuring Sandra and Donna (Chalmers was married to Sandra at the time). Mitchell told Charlie, "Bring them over here, let's see what they sound like on some of this stuff of Al's."

As Donna and Sandra went to work recording background vocals, Chalmers was in the control room with Mitchell. "Willie turned and looked over at me and said, 'Charlie, they ain't got any meat'—in other words, they needed some balls." Mitchell commanded him to "get your ass out there and sing the next part with 'em.'"

Charlie was a sax player, an arranger, and a producer. One thing he wasn't was a singer. "I had never even thought of doing it before. I was a horn player!" But he did what Willie told him to do. "I approached it like the mix on a horn session—that kind of gave it that black feel—and it all blended so good together it was unbelievable."

Rhodes, Chalmers, Rhodes instantly became an essential element of the Al Green sound. And part of the Hi family. Since Royal was in a rough neighborhood, Mitchell worried over Donna and Sandy's welfare, so when they arrived either Willie or members of the Hi Rhythm "would be sitting in the parking lot waiting on us," says Chalmers. "They didn't let us stand out there beating on the door, ever."

As far as the vocal parts went, Mitchell "mostly just let us come up with our arrangements," Chalmers admitted. "He liked our fresh ears. He gave us a lotta room to do our thing." Willie "didn't belabor anything. He knew instantly what he wanted to hear, and if you threw him a few lines he'd like it—or not," says Sandra. "Another thing I learned from Willie Mitchell was not to overdo. We were full of ideas, sometimes too many—we'd have a tendency to want to do wall-to-wall oohs. He'd say, 'No, no, no! Let it breathe, give it some space!' I learned that lesson well—when in doubt, lay out!" They knew they'd struck gold when Willie would "clap, laugh, and say, 'God from glory—that's so *good*!'"

And if Willie liked what he heard, forget changing it. Much to her dismay, at the end of "Tired of Being Alone," Donna "hit a long sharp note and it should've been a flat. He wouldn't let me redo it. Willie was like a brick wall—'It's a feel thing. If it makes me feel good, you ain't messin' with it!'" Sometimes Charlie had the added advantage of playing horn on the song before they added the vocals, so he'd be "thinkin' about what we'd soon be doin' on the backup vocals so I could stay away from those parts. I'd put the horns in a different spot."

Chalmers says that just weeks after "Tired of Being Alone" was released, "everybody wanted to know who the backup singers were." Suddenly they were in demand to provide backing vocals for Frank Sinatra, Liza Minnelli, the Bee Gees, and KC and the Sunshine Band. Some were surprised when they entered the studio, "shocked that we were white people," said Sandra. One producer hid their identities from a well-known seventies black female vocalist at first because she "did not want to use any white people on her records . . . we sang on several of her albums."*

❖

Both "I Can't Get Next to You" and "Tired of Being Alone" were part of Green's next album, *Al Green Gets Next to You.* Overall it feels a bit schizophrenic, not fully formed—one foot in the past, one in the future. Even the mod-lettered cover, with a beatific Al swathed in a frilly blue suit with furry lapels and cuffs looking like a stoned Christmas elf, seemed to belong to the sixties, not 1971. There are two beautiful covers, Freddie Scott's "Are You Lonely for Me, Baby" and Johnny Taylor's "God Is Standing By," the latter initiating Green's practice of one outright gospel song on nearly every pop album. Lumped together, the funky stuff sounds too similar and a bit faceless, and worst of all Mitchell had forced Al into doing another rock cover, "Light My Fire." "Stick a match to my fire," warbles a woeful Al. What a miserable track. It sounds like the whole band's crying.

The Green-Hodges of-its-time astrological boast "I'm a Ram" was the best piece of funkiness thus far, however. (According to Teenie, Green "wanted to name it 'Scorpio' because I'm a Scorpio—I told him, 'No, the song is "I'm a Ram," write about yourself!'") The joys of "I'm a Ram" are many—the drum pattern! The organ! The guitar! Badass horns, badass! That breakdown! I'll be minding my own business, just walking along, or steaming a shirt, maybe eating a cheese puff, and suddenly there it will be, an old friend: "Drive on . . . 'til I get there." If this performance doesn't move your body, give up and crawl into a grave. Mitchell: "People dance by rhythm, so it's, 'How rhythm can you get?' How mean can you make it? Rhythm that make the walls shake, *excitin'*

---

* Sandra Rhodes was also renowned for her guitar playing. She'd been taught a thing or two by pedal steel great John Hughey, a member of the band on *The Rhodes Show.* Reggie Young was another influence. "Sandy and Reggie played a lot alike," said Chalmers. "She was a demon on guitar. All the guitar players repected her." Mitchell used her in the studio upon occasion—Rhodes plays rhythm guitar on Green's "How Do You Mend a Broken Heart?"

rhythm . . . I used to tell the band, the rhythm section, 'Make it thunder!'" Too bad that Mitchell would largely shy away from this heavier direction. I'm a Ram!

❖

No longer did Willie Mitchell have to worry about being yesterday's dinner. On the pop/R&B charts in 1971: "Joy to the World." "Indian Reservation." "Brown Sugar." "Mr. Big Stuff." "Family Affair." "Never Can Say Goodbye." In an era given to endless guitar solos, big production, and general pomposity, Mitchell shrewdly took it in the opposite direction. "Tired of Being Alone" didn't sound like anything on the radio. And despite sharing the same town and some of the same musicians, it sure didn't sound like Stax. (From Teenie's point of view, Hi was "pop R&B." Stax was "R&B pop.")

In its first few months, "Tired of Being Alone" looked like another dud—"We sold about 900 of 'em," said Willie. I said, 'I can't be *this* wrong. This song was gonna be a hit.'" He packed a suitcase with ten grand and hit the road, visiting radio stations across the South. In Atlanta, deejay Zilla "The Dream Girl" Mays ruled on WAOK-AM.

"Everybody was after her to play their records, Columbia, Atlantic, everybody," said Mitchell. "'Tired of Being Alone' had been out for six months, and it wasn't doing shit. I showed up with a big old thing of J&B. I said, 'Please play the record.' She refused." Mitchell hung around, "buying her drinks." Eventually, Mays relented "and the phones started ringing," said Mitchell. "We did 30,000 the first week . . . then I went to New York and all hell broke loose. It ended up doing 1.5 million." (Years later Mitchell told friend Gene Mason they had to lay another suitcase of dough on the mob to break the record on the East Coast.)*

On October 30, 1971, Al Green made his first known appearance on *Soul Train*. A lively oasis of African American culture that made much of the rest of TV seem even blander and paler than it was, this was very early in the national syndication of the show. Not worthy of a live band yet, Green appeared alone onstage, lip-synching "Tired of Being Alone." What is remarkable is his appearance. For those who know only his slick, suave,

---

* As far as Hi Records, Willie Mitchell, and organized crime, Charles Hodges told me this story, which I could find no one to verify. Some gangsters had been to visit Mitchell, and one night while Pops and Hi Rhythm were all in a session "they brought a cashier's check for a million dollars to give to Willie . . . the secretary came and said, 'Willie, some people came back and they brought you this check.' Looked at it and tore it up, put it in the garbage—'Tell them not to come back here.' Willie didn't wanna do that."

giver-of-roses persona it may come as a shock. Green is dressed in black hot pants and maroon muscle tee (both vinyl), gold swashbuckler boots, a fuzzy top hat festooned with a glittery band cocked to one side of his fro, not to mention a thick gold chain upon his chest and a leather man-bag slung over a bare shoulder. Pimp or ho? Why, there's something here for everybody. Al looks like a space-age buccaneer styled by Tom of Finland. Thank God for the shadow of that big hat, because he also lip-synchs very badly. Green is such an immediate, give-your-all performer, mouthing an already recorded performance seems to be a bewildering humiliation. He would soon give some of the most compelling live performances ever to be broadcast on this same show.

Green was also starting to get gigs. Willie Mitchell asked his friend Bettye Berger, who ran his former booking agency, Continental Artists, to represent Green. "He was a peculiar guy," said Berger. "He said, 'I need some bookings, I need some money.'" She booked him in "little clubs in Mississippi." Then she got a call from one of the club owners, who reported not only on Al's great performance but the fact that Green had gone behind her back and attempted to book himself there for another date. Furious, Berger summoned Green for a face-to-face. "I wasn't gonna book him anymore . . . I told him, 'You need to get your ass outta my office.' I thought he'd get up and walk out, but he just smiled and said, 'Miss Berger, you don't wanna do that . . . '" The Green charm—it worked every time. Al moved into a modest, 1,500-square-foot house at 920 Inman Road. And bought some new wheels. "He kept getting bigger and bigger," said Berger. "And we were making money."

❖

"Al will try and impress me. Because I'm hard to impress," said Willie Mitchell in 2003. This was never more true than in that fall of 1971. With "Tired of Being Alone" starting to happen, Mitchell wasted no time recording a follow-up.

Green entered Royal one day to find Willie and Al Jackson Jr. "going over some mellow changes." Mitchell was on piano and Jackson "was beating on the side of the wall, piano stools, everything else he could find to get a beat out of."* What's that song? Green asked. Nothing yet, said the duo. "They were just playing this particular melody," he recalled. Al

---

* Green recalled watching him sit in the corner for hours at Royal as he practiced new sounds. "I thought he was crazy at first—five or ten minutes, fine—but hours?"

took a pen and paper and disappeared into the back, locking himself in "where all the machines are, and I wouldn't answer the phone. They were calling back there—'Al, open up!'" He emerged fifteen minutes later with a song—"Let's Stay Together."

This classic ballad would be Green's second million-seller in a row and his only number one pop hit. When asked about the song in later years, Green maintained the inspiration for the song came not from a lover but out of the troubling events of recent times—the '68 riots, the assassination of Dr. Martin Luther King Jr., the Black Panthers falling apart. "I sat down and wrote it, 'Let's stay together. What you doing? If you burn up the town, we're going to have to build it again.'" From that beginning he turned personal and "just started writing about my baby." All of this in fifteen minutes.

Recording the song took considerably longer. Mitchell once likened his role as producer to that of a schoolteacher: "It makes it so much easier and so much better when the student likes to get his lesson." It appears that Albert was an unruly student. Green and Mitchell often clashed—over what songs to record, what choice of single, even over Al's appearance; he made Green cut his hair, bought him "some sharp suits." Most of all they fought over Al's vocals, and once again on "Let's Stay Together" Willie wanted him to tone down his delivery, telling Green "you got to whisper . . . you got to sing it soft." According to Mitchell, Al had had enough of this "soft" business. "He said, 'Man, I can't sing that way. That's *too* soft. That ain't gonna sound like no man singing.' We had the damnedest fights." They worked on the vocal for eight days straight. Green "just wouldn't listen. Finally, he started to cry. I told him, 'You sound like everybody out on the street. I want to hear Al Green.' He said, 'I don't know who Al Green is.'"

Exasperated, the singer tore off in his new wheels. "I got so upset I left the studio—squeaked the wheels of my Corvette just so he would hear me. I rode out to the country with the top down." When he returned, a sullen Green told Mitchell, "I'm not even gonna try to put no emphasis in it at all." Meaning he was going to sing it flat. Plain. No hollering, no fancy stuff. And that's what he did. "That's Al Green!" exclaimed Willie once it was over. Al "sang the shit out of that song. He said, 'I think I want to sing it again.' I told him, 'You can sing it all night if you want, but I got what I wanted.'" Not that there weren't endless vocal punch-ins still to do to render it perfect. Green would tell Syl Johnson they'd spent "a hundred hours on one vocal on one song. A word at a time."

Mitchell knew he had a smash: "I wanted 500,000 copies pressed on 'Let's Stay Together.'" London Records "thought I was crazy. The record came out on Monday and by Thursday it was gold." It would remain on the charts sixteen weeks.

What a vocal performance. Green sings with such feeling, yet he's in check—you can practically feel him chomping at the bit to cut loose. This is the tension you get by putting a somewhat crazy gospel-based singer in a jazzier setting and telling him to rein it in—but still demanding he deliver all the emotion necessary. Mitchell would speak with pride about sneaking some B-flats into the song. "When people used three chords we used ten. Big chords, fat chords . . . the chords were so weird, that's what made the music happen."

Compared to "Tired of Being Alone," the "Let's Stay Together" track sounds voluptuous. There's more going on, new ingredients in the stew. Now you've got Bulldog on congas alongside Jackson on drums, but don't expect "Bongo Rock." At first Grimes didn't know what Willie "was after. I thought the song was complete with Al playing the kit." Mitchell didn't want him to "pound on the conga drums—he always told me to use two fingers, index fingers, and play it soft. With me playing thataway, I didn't feel like I was really doing anything, but when I went in to hear the playback, it was *there*, man." Indeed. Together Jackson and Grimes provide that rolling, galloping rhythm so perfect for the song.

Once again the horns are used sparingly, little jabs of emphasis. Horns in seventies pop/rock usually meant busy, overwrought—go listen to some Chicago if you want to torture yourself.* That wasn't the Memphis way. "If you listen to 'Let's Stay Together,' we're only playing a little in the intro and those *ba-dop*s throughout," says trombone player Jack Hale Sr. "That's *it*. We were the accents, not super dominant. Lot of times we'd play an eight-bar solo ensemble thing in the middle—and that might be it until the fade. We did very little. Willie was the master of that." Volume among the horns was controlled by means of a wooden Coca-Cola case. "If Willie wanted more volume from Brother James' baritone, he would simply say, 'James, go get the Coke case,'" wrote Wayne Jackson. "James would be three or four inches closer to the mic. Voila . . . more volume."

---

* Speaking of the dreaded Chicago, there's a clip floating around YouTube of a (possibly unaired) 1973 TV appearance where Green joins Chicago at Caribou Studio for a rather understated version of "I'm So Tired of Being Alone." Watch how easily Al commands this rock band, who seem entranced by his every move. Pretty sure Willie Mitchell would've fired the drummer, though.

❖

And here begin the strings, the wonderfully strange Hi strings. They call like a drunken siren on the rocks. The string overdubs were often done right at Royal with occasionally crusty contractor Noel Gilbert in charge as Willie engineered. In Detroit you might have an orchestra of sixty on a session. At Hi you'd have eight players, maybe sixteen on a rare occasion. Sometimes Willie took the eight string players and double-tracked them to fatten the sound.

Never saccharine, rarely overdone, these were "not strings in the way people use strings, they were not symphonic," says Terry Manning admiringly, but done "the Memphis way . . . they sound weird—not Halloweeny or scary—but there's something . . . off." Drummer Hayward Bishop concurs, maintaining the Hi strings possess a "combination of perfection and imperfection that make them kind of squirm a little."

"We were definitely different from a lot of other string sounds comin' out around the country," says Bill Thurman, who played viola on many a Hi session. Compared to string sessions in New York, Los Angeles, or "all those slick recordings comin' from Motown," Thurman admits the Memphis strings came off sounding "funkier, just a little bit weird around the edges." Part of the reason for this is that a couple of the players used might have been "just a little bit out of tune . . . there was always one or two in there that didn't quite play as well as they possibly could." And then there were the arrangements themselves, which were "kind of unconventional, unorthodox, off the wall—some of the melodies almost sounded like horn or guitar licks."

The string arrangements—and the last surprise in Mitchell's bag of tricks—came from an unexpected source: brother James. For the *Let's Stay Together* album, "Willie was trying to get the violins out of New York and Detroit, and he couldn't get them, couldn't book them," Teenie told Robert Gordon. "So I said, 'Why not James?' And that's when James started writing and the Memphis Symphony started recording."*

Hi Rhythm had been after Willie to let James do string arrangements for a while. He'd been using his old mentor Onzie Horne for that task. Teenie says "the whole band" felt Horne was too old-fashioned. "James was more modern. He loved music—he *lived* music."

---

* It should be noted that Charles Chalmers also did string arrangements for Mitchell, but Teenie maintained "James was the best person for it. Once he did it, we used James ninety-five percent of the time." Bill Thurman found Chalmers's string work to be "real slick, real smooth—a lot of long notes."

It took a lot of convincing. The Mitchell brothers looked somewhat alike, but there the similarities ended. Willie was older, and they had clashed forever. Jack Hale Sr., who used to room with James on the road, recalled James telling of "one time when they were growing up he got so mad at Willie he almost killed him." Hale shuddered as he conjured up what Willie could've done to set off the perpetually laid-back James. "He was an angel," said Hi songwriter Earl Randle. "James was real serious about his work, but very mild-mannered, low-key." There are endless stories of his kindness. "James was real," said Randle. "If he could help you, he'd help you. He didn't have any airs about him." If you were on a session with James, he was liable to fix your car after the session ended. "He put a clutch in for me," said Hale.

Musically, James "was a bad man, he was a *bad* man," said an admiring Leroy Hodges, who watched James write a horn chart without any instrument in hand. "Tell you what he did—James Mitchell wrote the horn chart in the air—not on a piano, no nuthin'." James "had an ear so good, he could hear a rat pissin' on cotton," said Thomas Bingham, who worked with him in the nineties. "I can tell his arrangements immediately. It's how he used voicings and how he used his baritone horn." Bingham points out most people would have the bari flow along with the rest of the arrangement. James would use it "almost like counter—when the horns would go up, he'd take the baritone down. He'd call that 'makin' a daddyo.'" In 1997 Thomas and James worked together on an arrangement for the Boz Scaggs track "Ask Me 'Bout Nothin' (But the Blues)." "He did a 'daddyo' on that one," said Bingham. Not that anybody would know. When the album came out, Willie neglected to credit either of them. "James actually cried," said Thomas.

"I didn't agree with it—as a matter of fact, I had a word with Willie at the studio one day about it," Teenie reluctantly revealed. "I told him, 'You're a goddamn liar—I was there, I know who did the arrangement!'" James was not one to blow his own horn, except in the literal sense. Those around felt that James didn't get near enough credit for the work he did at Hi. It pained other musicians to see him struggling in his brother's very long shadow. "James felt deep, he had deep feelings," said Teenie. "His soul was very fragile. Willie wanted control."

Charles Hodges agrees. "That had to do with the brotherly thing . . . a little jealousy."

❖

The *Let's Stay Together* album was released January 31, 1972. Wearing a leather jacket and sporting a tall Afro on the cover, his image as slick soul man isn't quite complete, but this is the first fully realized Al Green album. Besides the title cut there are so many pleasures: "La-La for You" with that dynamic horn-piano-cymbal opening (that fabulous piano is played by Willie's stepson Hubbie Turner, uncredited on the album) and, in each channel, numerous call-and-response Als perfectly designed to be scrutinized on a headful of weed; "So You're Leaving," featuring that striking "If they'll lie on Jesus can't you see / They'll lie on you and me" couplet and that delirious bit of Bo Diddley's "Who Do You Love" tossed in just before the fade-out; the summer-afternoon lazy of "Old Time Lovin'," a choir of Al Greens lending vocal support; and that monster "Ain't No Fun to Me," which I could talk about all day long. There's Grimes opening the hi-hat a bit to lay down a beat that sounds like King Kong doing a two-step in a metal grass skirt, Leroy's irresistible bass pattern (for once clearly audible; he's the only element of Hi Rhythm that often remains a mysterious rumble in the background), and the foghorn note the horns hit that (for some reason) conjures up the opening madness of obscure noir *Blast of Silence*. The musical tension is such that when Green hits that bit of repeating falsetto near the end of the song—"sit down"—that release feels like a little balloon escaping into the night sky.

For an album of love songs, there sure is a lot of unhappiness lurking everywhere: the continual mentions of leaving, the casual dismissal on display in "La-La for You," the mixed messages of "What Is This Feeling?" (contrast the nearly mumbled delivery and the half-realized thoughts on this—groovy as they are—to any of Green's hits as evidence of how hard Mitchell worked this singer to wring out of him what he wanted). Most melancholy of all is Green's remarkable cover of "How Can You Mend a Broken Heart?" Already a number one hit just the year before for those titans of castrato-pop, the Bee Gees, the Barry and Robin Gibb song registered with Willie while out on the road in Detroit working the "Let's Stay Together" single. When he told Al he wanted him to cut the song, Green "laughed in my face and said, 'That shit is country, man!' I told him he didn't understand what we were gonna do with it."

And what they did with it! Here's the band instruction Willie gave Hi Rhythm: imagine you're sitting by a river, a forest across the water, with "all this music coming out of the forest and floating across the river, kind of delayed." Well, listen and you feel the mist. Slow, slow, slow, this one—at 6:22, Mitchell was adding nearly two and a half minutes to the song's original running time.* The Bee Gees version is a classic expression of angst-ridden youth; Green's is something deeper—he gives the lyric the weight, an ancient screed chiseled on tablets excavated deep within some pyramid. Hearing Al sing the line "I was never told about the sorrow" somehow alleviates all pain. The inescapable struggles of life that we all face—divorce, death, not having money to pay the rent—feel acknowledged in Green's delicate, reflective delivery of those seven little words.

❖

Let's Stay Together shows off a group of musicians at the top of their game. And it would only get better. "We've now gotten the sound I've wanted to hear since I got into music," Mitchell would say in 1973. This was one of those rare moments in pop culture history: the public was completely tuned into what Al Green and Hi Records were doing, and Green and Hi had a lot to give. "We were on a mission," said Charles Hodges. "I wanted Al's hit records as much as he did. We *all* wanted it bad. That's the reason we got 'em! Didn't nobody drag nobody down . . . you didn't have to hunt for nobody, everyone was there. What made it so good . . . we *loved* each other. And we were together. When we wasn't recording, we was together; when we was recording, we was together. Wasn't nothing fake about it."

The atmosphere at Hi was different from that of Stax, or anywhere else. Willie Mitchell liked to tell the story of how they invited a bunch of street people in while they were cutting *Let's Stay Together*. "There's a bunch of winos out there," he told Robert Mugge. "So Al says, 'Why don't you go and get four or five gallons of wine—let's bring these people in the studio.' So we brought about fifty people in here, all the winos, they're drinkin' wine, layin' on the floor while we were cutting the record . . . we'd all tell them to be quiet. If you'll notice on the *Let's Stay Together* album, you'll hear a lot of noise in the background . . . it's the winos."

Royal Studio was friendly, loose, open. The Hodges brothers palled around with players from local sports teams; they'd hang out and watch the sessions. At the center of it all was Willie, who remained remarkably

---

* Charles Hodges said it was on this session that he really earned his "Do Funny" moniker. Willie had heard Charles doing all sorts of wild turns on the B3 out on the road. Mitchell told him to stop imitating other players—"I don't want to hear no Jimmy Smith, I want to hear Charles." When Hodges cut loose on this track "everything changed."

accessible to people. "You could catch him every day at the studio," said songwriter Earl Randle. "People would ask, 'How can I get in contact with Willie?' I said, 'Go down to Hi and walk in.'"

It had been a long climb for Willie Mitchell. Since joining Hi in the early sixties, he'd fought to engineer his own records. Taught the band to play what he heard in his head. Happened onto such magical additions as Rhodes, Chalmers, Rhodes and—though he might've been loath to admit it—James Mitchell. Now that he'd unlocked Al Green, Willie had it all. "Once he got a hook on a song, it was hard to beat him. The song was dead," said Mitchell. "We had six years of nothing but gold and platinum records with Al."

Once the die was cast in the recording process, Mitchell changed nothing. He was particularly superstitious about the equipment (Green: "This man will not let you remove the cobwebs in the corner—'No, no, no, don't touch that, it adds to the sound.'"), such as the RCA 77-DX ribbon mic reserved for Al's use. "It has a real romantic sound, a soft, warm sound," said Mitchell, who admitted the day he absently marked it number nine "I was drinking vodka." Willie stood by Royal's tube deck, even when everybody else had turned to transistors: "As long as Al records for Hi Records he'll always record on the eight-track." And he refused to deviate from that signature sound. Later on, when Denise LaSalle would report to him that "everybody's sayin' all your stuff sounds the same," Willie shot right back: "I will ride this horse until it falls dead."

And while Al Green was the Hi supernova, other artists were happening there as well. According to Willie, by 1973 Otis Clay was selling 300,000 an album, Ann Peebles a little more. And Syl Johnson's "We Did It" sold over half a million. Royal was humming with activity around the clock. People were creating music "all the time, all the time," said Don Bryant, who had switched his career at Hi from artist to songwriter. "Somebody was always on the piano . . . you'd hear a couple of lines you like and before you know it, y'all writin' a song. Somebody would sing a few words, next thing you know the office was full and everybody's rappin' at each other." Those present for the glory days of Hi have not forgotten the experience. "It was a spiritual thing of coming together and being a part of something you believed in," said Bryant. "Every time you came in there it was a joy—a joy just to be there, man."

❖

In December 1971 Al Green flew to England to play his first overseas dates in tiny clubs like the Spennymoor Top Hat and Middlesbrough Excel Bowl. Backed by Larry Lee leading a limey band with a four-piece horn section called Smack, Al did two dates with Rufus Thomas and Tami Lynn, then packed the upstairs room at Ronnie Scott's Jazz Club in London, charging into "Driving Wheel" "dressed in an outrageous moon-and-star-spangled black and white hot pantsuit with matching boxing boots . . . mincing about with effeminate but highly entertaining head, hand and foot shaking," as Roger St. Pierre wrote in an *NME* review, the implications of which must've had Green cringing (the reporter wound up being friendly with Al afterward).

When Green came back to the States, things had changed. He opened a Washington, DC, show for one of his heroes—James Brown. Being overseas, he hadn't realized the frenzy "Let's Stay Together" had been inciting, particularly among women. "Then it started," said Al. Suddenly he "was running from the girls—they was running to feel me, hug me and kiss me . . . they were ripping my clothes off . . . Brown turned around and said, 'Man, they love you.'" Around this time, reporter Lee Hildebrand attended an Oakland Coliseum R&B show where Al Green shared the bill with Joe Simon, Etta James, and Harvey Mandel's Pure Food and Drug Act.

"That was the first time I saw women rush the stage," he recalled. Some women managed to get onstage, and "when they got up there, Al ran to the back of the stage to get away from them . . . he was afraid." That fear didn't last long, though. By the time Hildebrand saw the singer perform a year or two later at the Circle Star Theatre in San Carlos, Green "was encouraging them—and handing them roses."

Suddenly women everywhere wanted a piece of the Green Machine. "Oh man, once Al Green hit the stage and opened his mouth, they was through," said emcee Roland Jones. "His voice just captivated them." There would be truckloads of females. On the bus, in hotels, hiding in bushes. Later bandleader Johnny Brown said when they'd check into a hotel "the lobby was packed—women, women, women and some guys, too. Guys with drugs. Pimps. Fast hustlers. He was like a chick magnet. Everywhere you went, there were women."

And they were fanatical. In 1973, 208 Memphis women would sign a petition entitled "Al, Please Don't Get Married." One fan sent Green a poem called "Black Magic at a Microphone": "Your music makes my body smile . . . creates a thousand different orgasms on my brain." A reporter describing the frenzy of a 1974 show: "Hordes of female fans rush forward while three guards standing on their tiptoes push them back. 'Take off your pants!' screams an especially enthusiastic fan. 'I know how to create excitement,' says Al." During a Louisville show women actually pulled Green's knit pants off as he belted out "Tired of Being Alone": "The police had to get me, 'cause I was lying on the floor with fifteen girls on top of me."

Stardom was happening, and very quickly. Right now, though, Green needed his own band. Thus far he'd been playing gigs with a guitar player, Larry Lee, and using the headliner's band or whatever pickup musicians he could get. Green's studio outfit, Hi Rhythm, was nimble and precise. With it came perfection. His live band, a motley collection of ragtag characters he'd christen the Enterprise Orchestra, was anything but. When Al found them he said they "couldn't play dead. They were playing with worn-out instruments. Oh you should've seen those raggedy ass drums . . . when Willie first heard them he said, 'Good God, where did you get these cats from?'"

"When Al got big enough to get his own band, he got the worst band of all," Larry Lee used to joke. But that wasn't exactly true. The Enterprise Orchestra has never gotten its due as one of the great seventies bands, and that's a crying shame. Hi Rhythm was the perfect studio unit—they interlocked together clean and precise as an Escher drawing. Rude, crude, and not always in tune, the Enterprise Orchestra was more like a drunken explosion of Pollock. "They were just crazy," said Teenie Hodges.

Enterprise horn player Buddy Jarrett agreed. "We were outlaw. That's the thing that used to trip us up with Al, because we didn't give a fuck."

MASCULINE AL, FEMININE AL

I may not be from this place. I may not be from this planet.
—AL GREEN

Al Green and his band, another strange relationship. Back in the seventies and eighties you could almost call it adversarial. Al didn't hang out with his musicians, traveled separately, and didn't want the women he was involved with talking to them. "He and his band would always fight," said Green's latter-day producer Paul Zaleski. Bass player Jeff "Stick" Davis did a short stint with Green in the eighties and found him to be "strictly business . . . he had this wall around him. I would've loved to get to know him . . . I didn't even know if he was married—or anything. A very guarded person."

Early on, Teenie Hodges had gone out on the road with Green, first with pickup bands, then on a short stint with Aretha Franklin, with Teenie and three members of Franklin's band backing Al. But around the time of "I Can't Get Next to You," there was an incident at a Memphis club called the Showroom. The line had stretched around the corner, and the owner held Al over the next night and wanted the band to play an hour set before Green went on. Hodges asked what they were getting paid, and the owner said nothing, because he was only paying Green. Teenie told him to forget it. "The owner called Al, Al called me, and I told him the same thing—he's gonna have to pay me. He went to cursin' . . . 'I guess you want as much money as I do, you're a star now? *You're* a star?'"

Teenie, who just wanted to be paid for his time, said things got ugly: "I got really pissed off at him . . . that just changed everything." When Teenie showed up at the Showroom the next night, Al had already hired his replacement: Larry Lee. Hodges, who felt he'd done nothing but help Green, vowed to keep his distance from Al other than time spent in the studio. As far as Teenie doing anything else, "he's gonna piss me off," Teenie said in 2013. "So I just stay away." Many of Al Green's musicians would wind up feeling the same way.

❖

Larry Lee would become Green's bandleader for much of the next decade (he'd play with him sporadically after that, but only begrudgingly). Lee had written songs for Stax artists the Astors while still a teenager and in 1969—just back from a tour of duty in Vietnam—Jimi Hendrix, whom he'd joined on the chitlin' circuit backing artists like Curtis Mayfield and Aretha Franklin, asked him to play rhythm guitar at Woodstock. Next came Al Green. At first it was just the two of them working with whatever band they were opening for.

Then one night in Rome, Georgia, Green was backed up by a band called the Sounds of Friction, a five-piece band that had formed in Louisville, Kentucky. "We had a fat sound, but we was a small group when Al met us—two horns, guitar, bass, and drum," said sax player Buddy Jarrett. "We were mediocre musicians, but put us together, it was a powerful package, man. We'd go up against anybody." And that's how they got gigs. "We'd pull out a map, I'd stick my finger down, and we'd go to that town and find out where the best band was playin' and we'd go sit in, and consequently get a job," said emcee Roland Jones.

What a bunch they were. Buddy "Genius" Jarrett was a wild man known for his penchant for nudity. As later bandleader Johnny Brown recalls, "I'd tell him, 'Buddy, you gotta put some clothes on—I don't need no man walkin' around butt-nekkid like we was in the army.'" Buddy was also known to dye his hair blond—including his mustache, goatee, and eyelashes. "We called him 'Genius' because he knew everything," says later arrival Reuben Fairfax Jr.*

---

* Jarrett said the nickname came during a tour in Tokyo after the band went on a binge buying Seikos and boom boxes. One band member couldn't understand why Buddy's tiny boom box sounded so much better than his huge one. "I told him, 'Yours says seven watts per channel. Look at mine—twenty watts per channel, which means I have forty. Which sounds better?' They called me 'Genius' from that day on."

William McBroom played bass. A husky, dark-skinned fellow sporting glasses with thick, Coke-bottle lenses covered with clip-on shades, he wore neon-blue three-piece suits, white shoes with five-inch heels ("Miami stompers"), a mink coat and hat. He also glittered, due to "diamonds on every hand, on his wrist, round his neck," recalled Jarrett. Despite his dubious vision, McBroom drove a big blue Caddy kitted out with custom side-mount spares. (When a Memphis cop pulled him and Buddy over for speeding, he asked Mac, who also happened to be packing heat, about them. He responded, "What can I say, man—I'm a freak for wheels." Suitably impressed, the cop drove off without writing a ticket.) When Green and band performed on a TV show hosted by Sammy Davis Jr.— no slouch when it came to outlandish accessories—Davis took one look at Mac's bling and hurried back to his dressing room to load more on. There are a zillion stories about McBroom. Mac was tone-deaf and couldn't tune his bass (Larry Lee did it for him). Mac was a pimp. Mac passed counterfeit money. (Jarrett: "Mac said, 'Cuz, you want a few bucks?' 'No, man, I'm cool, I'm gonna pass on that one.'") "Mac was a motherfuckin' hustler," said Roland Jones. "Mac was cold, man—if there was a dollar, he was gonna get it."

Then you had the hermetically sealed James Bass on rhythm guitar. "People that would meet us would think James was gay," said Jarrett, who said that James had an airy way of closing his eyes and laughing in the middle of a conversation. "Guys would be—'Oh, shit—he gay.' Well, leave your woman in there, James'd tear their ass up *every* time. I was like, 'Damn, you'd think they'd learn after a while.' James went through so many women it was pitiful." Bass wasn't exactly renowned for his rhythm playing (although he'd sometimes morph into a character named Fenimore to bust out some beautiful fret work). In fact, on that first gig they played for Green, Bass had just been filling in. At the next show, when they had their real guitar player, who was "a hundred times better than James," Green wanted to know where the tall guy was. "Al told them, 'No James, no gig,'" said Roland Jones, who maintains Bass always managed somehow to stay buried in the mix. "Craziest thing about it—you could never hear James play onstage. He was able to stay with Al for years and years. Never been heard onstage."

A green South Carolina kid fresh out of college (the band had to talk his mother into letting him go on the road), drummer Aaron Purdie was "this tall, lanky dark guy, real nappy hair 'bout a quarter inch long," said

Jarrett. "His hair was so tight, it looked like mail-carryin' hair—each row had its own little route." (Purdie was "a prince, and the blackest guy I've ever seen," said James Hooker. "I told him, 'You're past black, you have a . . . purple radiance.'") The band took Purdie shopping for clothes in Chicago. "We went to Jewtown to buy him a suit real cheap," says Jarrett, who talked him into platform shoes as well. When they got back to the hotel Larry Lee took one look at the drummer and caused everybody to fall out by asking, "Damn, son—where'd you get that pressed cotton-candy suit and them smoked sausages on your feet?" Aaron was a monster on the drums—watch any of the vintage Al Green clips to see him pound that kit. "Purdie was the real musician out of the whole bunch. Everybody else was self-taught," says Roland Jones. "He was the baddest drummer out there, period. Everybody wanted him—everybody." (Purdie would eventually get fed up with Green and defect to James Brown's band.)

Roland Jones was the band's emcee and road manager. Inspired by the sartorial splendor that was Gorgeous George—not the wrestler but a legendary emcee and tailor who'd also cut the magnificent "Biggest Fool in Town" for Stax—Jones was a snappy dresser who "traveled with twelve suits and six pair shoes," said Jarrett. "He never wore denim." Jones would be another catalyst in Green's life, particularly when it came to his threads. At the time Green dressed like "a leprechaun. Roland helped him a lot," Jarrett explains. "Al was dressin' so country it used to tickle the shit out of us. Al's pants would be way down in the back and way up in the front. Man, it looked like he was goin' uphill. And he had folks *makin'* this stuff for him!"

"No disrespect, but Al dressed like he came from Forrest City, Arkansas," added Jones. "His hair was never right. Never. He was always scuffy like on the *Let's Stay Together* album. He was wearing stuff like hot pants, great big ol' hat, great big ol' Afro, half-naked top, carrying a bag . . . he started to get a little more finesse with it after bein' around us. Al started seein' me dress, then he started buyin' stuff. And I started pickin' out stuff for him, did a lot of shoppin' for Al. I taught him how to put together colors and shit . . . that's when he started wearin' nice-ass suits and ties—the white suit thing came from me."

As did Green's trademark of doling out long-stemmed roses to the ladies in the audience, according to Jones. He recalled the exact concert where it happened: the opening of the Omni Coliseum in Atlanta, Georgia, October 17, 1972. "Bobby Bland was the supporting act," recalled

Jones, who emceed the show. "Bobby Bland had it so goddamn hot on that fuckin' stage, Al didn't really want to go out there. They had two pots of roses, one on each side of the stage . . . when I went to bring Al on, I grabbed some roses. I told Al, 'Throw these motherfuckers out to the crowd.' He threw 'em out; all the women went crazy. They *forgot* Bobby Bland. From that day on, Al Green always had roses. That's the God's truth."

Later came horn players Darryl Neely and Ron Echols; and on keyboards James Hooker, Larry Robinson, Perry Michael Allen, and the only female member of the band, Lynda Harper (Jarrett: "We called her Ma Harper, 'cause she acted like everybody's mama"); and not forgetting "Bongo" Eddie Folk, known for the flashy outfits he designed for himself. (And who, Hooker recalls, "opened up a clothing shop in Memphis—the most god-awful stuff you ever saw, capes and stuff." Folk "played congas— we didn't even consider that a real instrument," said later arrival Ruben Fairfax Jr., who saw Eddie as table dressing for the Al Green show. "When you're getting real money you got to bring a bunch of people. You just can't just show up by yourself. So Eddie was beatin' on stuff.") Comedian Herb Jubirt, who'd cut comedy albums on Hi (*Plant the Corn* and *Laff Me into the Big Time*), was Green's opening act into the eighties.

When an Indianapolis promoter hired the Sounds of Friction to back Al for that very first Rome gig, they didn't really know who he was, although Buddy Jarrett had already been singing "Tired of Being Alone" in their set. Green "was astonished when the group backed him up in Rome, because Buddy could sound just like Al. Al could be hoarse, Buddy would sing and you would never know the difference." The other horn player, eighteen-year-old Michael Baker, was another badass singer. "Michael had a voice like Philip Bailey—the wider he opened his mouth, the higher the note went," said Jarrett. "All that high, pretty stuff—Michael would be all over top of Al," said Jones. They started backing him on the road.

Not long after, when Green had an important gig at New York City's Apollo Theater, he summoned Sounds of Friction to Memphis. Jones maintains that Green had only wanted to snatch drummer Aaron Purdie at first. "Al really and truly didn't plan on keeping the Sounds of Friction, okay? But he couldn't keep Purdie without keeping everybody else. That's how loyal Purdie was." Green took the band on, renaming them the Enterprise Orchestra.

❖

On January 5, 1972, Al Green played the Apollo. Filling out the bill were the Staple Singers, Freddie North, People's Choice, and on-again/off-again girlfriend Laura Lee. "Three shows a day for six days, and they held Al over by himself for another week," said Jones. "It was astonishing—the brother had people lined up four New York City blocks long to get into the Apollo." "Let's Stay Together" was a smash hit, and at that moment the Apollo belonged to Al Green. Stars came every night. Jarrett: "This little bitty guy walks onstage and says, 'Yeah, man, heard about you cats. You cats are fat, man. Fat.'" Trumpet player Michael Baker started trembling. "You know who that was?" he asked Buddy. "Miles Davis."

While Green and company stayed at the Gorham Hotel, the band's equipment was stolen from their van, and Al was forced to replace it all. Little did the band care. Women were everywhere. One has to have a band member tell the tale to get the full picture. "We got the whole floor of suites," recalled Buddy Jarrett. "I get up to the floor, there is a *line*—I don't mean one or two—I mean a line of women to each room. And there wasn't an ugly one in the group. They were all different shades—tall, short, big bones, small bones, medium-large . . . even the big ones were fine. I had like nine women sittin' around the room. Round the bed, three or four on the divan, one in the chair, one in the window. Nine gorgeous women."

Jarrett was dumbfounded. Overwhelmed, he headed over to Larry Lee's room (which was also packed with females) for advice. Jarrett said, "Larry, I got all these women in my room . . . one or two I got my eye on, but how am I gonna clear the rest?" Lee, the Yoda of the Enterprise Orchestra, leaned over and whispered the solution in Buddy's ear. "I said, 'For real?'" "For real," answered Lee.

Jarrett sauntered back to his room. "I rolled up three nice-ass joints, Panama Red—we called it 'Joe Simon' [not due to any weed intake on the singer's part, but because of his 1969 hit "The Choking Kind"], and I got my little two-by-four-inch mirror, got my razor out, made about eighteen lines.

"About forty-five minutes go by, everybody is really nice—smiling, talking. Larry told me what to do—I thought, 'Fuck, I might as well try it.'"

He addressed the harem.

"I said, 'Okay, let's start takin' our clothes off.' Larry told me when you do that, the ones that are not serious—that just want to be seen—will find an excuse to leave by the time you get your shoes off—'Uh, my cousin gonna be comin' to pick me up.' 'Uh, I gotta go to work tomorrow, here's my number.' I'm thinking, 'They all gonna leave, I'll get a good night's sleep.'" After escorting out those not interested in participating, Buddy "walked back in there with my shoes off . . . there were three fine naked women sayin', 'Welcome back.'"

And so it was in the world of Al. Night after night after night. "Only the *prettiest* women, wearin' the *prettiest* stuff, bringin' the *best* drugs, wearin' the *sweetest* colognes," said Buddy. "Yeah, we had women, but they never felt like they were bein' used—they always felt like they were the only one." Buddy smiled. "At least right then."

And he was just the sax player. One can only imagine what came Al Green's way.

❖

Larry Lee was the captain of the Enterprise. Everybody loved him. "Larry smoked plenty of weed," recalled Johnny Brown, who noted that once Lee returned from a trip to England with Green he only smoked a blend of tobacco and weed he called EJs—English joints. "He'd roll these big ol' fat EJs and bite on his lower lip while he'd roll 'em and look at you real straight sayin' the most craziest things, but even though they were crazy they all made sense. He'd say, 'This guitar has all the answers to everything in life.' A philosopher and comedian." Larry's deadpan delivery would have everybody howling with laughter.

Early on Green and Lee had shared a dressing room. "One day after Al got big, Al's got a few girls in the dressing room," said Brown. "Larry walked in with his clothes to change and Al looked up at Larry and said, 'Larry, y'know, the band's dressing room is right down the hall.' From that day forward it was Al's dressing room only." Slowly but surely, "Larry and Al were like oil and water."

Maybe the biggest challenge for Green's musicians was actually getting paid. "One thing about Al—I knew I was gonna get my money, it was just always gonna be late," said Brown.* "So it didn't bother me as much as it bothered everybody else." One of those frequently bothered was Larry

---

* Brown was the one member to speak of the bonuses Al could dole out on the road in those days. "He'd walk up and down the hallway, pick out different people, knock on your door, tell you how good you played, shake your hand, and there would be hundreds of dollars in your hand. Before Al went to gospel he was way more generous, because he made way more money."

Lee. And he dared to speak up. Out on the road one day the band was sitting around feeling angry because they hadn't gotten an expected payment before they left. "We got on the bus, drove all the way across the country, and we *still* ain't got no money. We're kinda pissed off," said Brown. "Al walked in there just smiling and laughin' like everything was fine—'Hey, Johnny, how you doin'?'" Everybody smiled for the boss. "Then he walks over to Larry—'Hey, Larry, wassup? How you doin'?' Larry said, 'How you expect me to be doin'? You ain't paid me.' Al stormed out of the room."

According to Jarrett, the band had decided there were at least two distinct Al Greens they had to deal with—the masculine Al and the feminine Al. Buddy recalled a band meeting at Green's old offices at 3208 Winchester Road in Memphis. "He was sittin' in his office in a big chair. He had his Bible on the desk. Larry was sittin' right next to the desk." They were doing a show in Chicago, Green explained, but he wanted them to arrive four days early. And he wanted them to pay for their own hotel rooms.

"Larry's sittin' there, and Larry had this habit—he would rub his teeth and rub his nuts at the same time. He said, 'Al, you crazy as hell. You think we gonna pay for our own rooms? You think we're gonna pay YOU to work for you? Man, you're crazy as hell.'" Green was furious. "Al said, 'You gonna go out there and do exactly as I say!' He slammed his hand down on that Bible. Larry didn't move a muscle. Didn't nobody move."

But Lee then resumed his nervous rubbing and charged right back. "Larry set there and said, 'Okay, goddamn it, do the gig a cappella! We ain't payin' for no goddamn room! You send us up there, you gonna pay for the motherfucking rooms.'"

Jarrett said that Green's voice suddenly hit a higher register and turned pliant, soft. "Al set there and said, 'Wellllll . . . Okay, Larry.' See, we noticed it right away—there are two separate personalities to Al Green: there's the masculine Al Green and there's the feminine Al Green. I'm not sayin' this man is gay—he's not gay—but he has two separate personalities workin'. Now, the masculine Al Green will try to assert himself. The female Al Green will make you think he's *allowin'* you to do somethin', but he's always got a devious thing runnin' behind it."

Apparently Green liked to see people fight; Roland Jones said he tried to pit "everybody against one another." Green "liked to butt heads," said Johnny Brown. "He liked commotion. When things seemed to be goin' too good he liked to see people goin' at each other in the band." Al encouraged members of his entourage to spy for him. "He always had informers on the bus," said Charles Hodges, who went on the road with him in the later seventies. "Al would have somebody come and play like they're your friend to get information to take back to him," said Jones. "That's the way he weaves his web. Divide and conquer. He couldn't get us band members to do that to each other."

The fact the Enterprise Orchestra didn't kiss Green's ass "would drive him crazy, because he wanted everybody to bow down to him," said Jones. "He didn't have to respect you because he was Al Green, and you would not be able to do what you're doin' if it had not been for him. That was the attitude he took. He felt the money he was payin' you was too much. Al was all about Al. Period. Al didn't do nothing for nobody. And that's the reason he never paid nobody the way he should've paid 'em. He wanted to keep 'em down."

Jarrett maintains Green's continual bad vibes didn't slow the Enterprise down. "That superstar ego thing meant nothing to us. We were a bunch of guys who bonded together like family that went around the world—and got gypped out of a lot—but we still got paid something for it. We were feelin' immortal!"

❖

In February 1972 came a new single, "Look What You Done for Me." Outside of the great title phrase, the lyrics don't amount to much more than "Lovin' you baby is where it's at"—but this was Willie Mitchell's most complex offering yet. The opening horn-string-drum interlude topped off by a little falsetto cry from Al repeats nowhere else in the song. The slow tempo gains speed as it goes along, and there's so much going on: Teenie's quick, xylophone-like guitar break; the Rhodes, Chalmers, Rhodes *ooooooh*s that sound not unlike the *Star Trek* theremin; little touches of B3 from Charles Hodges that add headlights-at-dusk color. It's a jigsaw puzzle of seemingly disparate elements, arranged with an exquisite attention to detail, with nothing sounding extraneous or overcooked. "Look What You Done for Me" went to number four on the charts.

And in June came a number-three hit: the incredible "I'm Still in Love with You." Al and Willie had worked on it during a vacation to a hot-springs resort in nearly Hamilton, Arkansas (Al Jackson Jr. also received credit). Willie, who had brought a piano and an amp, started tinkling, and the words poured out of Green. Not much of a song, really, even less of a melody, and—though the opening lines ("Spendin' my days / Thinkin' 'bout you, girl") pull you right in—the lyrics are inane and at times incomprehensible, a hair away from song-poem territory. None of it matters. As far as singles, this is one of Willie's most extreme creations. "Some of the chord changes we use, they're almost impossible," said Mitchell. This song in particular was "nothing but jazz changes." Willie "used a C-minor nine chord with a major seventh and Al sang it, he sang the B-natural." A tricky number for a singer to pull off. "It's very, very difficult to sing something like 'I'm Still in Love with You,'" Green admitted. "Those songs will fool you. They sound like they're sung real high and in fact they're really low."

Ascending strings . . . the sly, cavalry-marching-slowly-over-the-hill horn charts . . . Green's falsetto chorus and its wistful echo sung by Rhodes, Chalmers, Rhodes . . . all send the song to outer space. The deep emotion of Green's delivery provides the perfect counterpoint to the sophisticated, jazzy arrangement. One would never know Mitchell had trouble getting Al to rein it in a little over a year previous listening to this, his delivery is so perfectly controlled and I'm-talking-right-to-you-through-this-car-radio intimate. You can just picture some lonely young woman hearing this across the midnight airwaves, then packing her Dodge in the morning and moving to Memphis because she knows, just knows, that Al Green is singing directly to her.

❖

In February Green returned to *Soul Train*, lip-synching a few hits as before, but this time with a little more accuracy. Far more exciting was his first appearance on the legendary public TV show *Soul!*, broadcast February 16. A landmark not only in terms of African American culture but of live music on television, *Soul!* was the brainchild of Ellis Haizlip, the first black producer at WNET in New York City. "Part of what made *Soul!* great was Ellis' consciousness," said director Stan Lathan, who directed both of Green's appearances. "His intent was to put black American culture out there, and for an audience to see themselves and see their heroes . . . Ellis was a pioneer in that aspect." Taped live before a small studio audience, *Soul!* featured an eclectic lineup of guests from the arts as well as politics—Stokely Carmichael and Sidney Poitier to the Last Poets and Wilson Pickett. The show was done in a low-key style that emphasized realness and eschewed any of the glitzy phoniness of current TV variety shows, thereby infusing it with an individuality and class quite unlike anything else on then or since. Green recorded his segment during his stand at the Apollo. "We got him to come down and do a set for us," said Lathan. "It was amazing, and we were there remarking how this guy looks like he's gonna go somewhere." Only three songs were broadcast—"Can't Get Next to You," "Tired of Being Alone," and "Let's Stay Together." This is the first live Al Green footage I know of, and a rare window into the dawn of his success at Hi.

The Enterprise Orchestra, which had been playing with Green only a few months, seems stiff. The songs end abruptly; he's barely ad-libbing. Performing in front of a stark blast of color against a black backdrop that was a trademark of the show's distinctive visual style, Green is dressed in a vested suit with no shirt, still sporting a beard and well-oiled pompadour. His performance is raw, unpolished, and carries the power of a shy, introverted soul who simply has to let all that music inside him out. The awkwardness is appealing. There's no dancing, no snappy patter—it's all about the vocals, which are anguished and intense. In his heyday, Al was one of those rare performers where you didn't question the sounds coming out of his throat; they seemed instantly authentic and true. Nearly a decade later Green would admit to David Less that he suffered from terrible stage fright. "I'd be so scared. I'm talking about my flesh trembled, right? I'd say my prayers before every show, standing there backstage behind the curtain . . . I have the possibility of failing as well as succeeding . . . I'd sing the first song and then I'd be okay." Green would return to *Soul!* at the end of the year, and the difference would be striking.

❖

The Al Green entourage grew. On came the secretaries, as many as three at one time. "He always had a bunch of them. They came and went like night and day," said Roland Jones. "Until he found somebody else that he was interested in." More people joined the road crew. There was six-foot-six Oliver Ingram, who was "the other half of Roland Jones," said Buddy Jarrett. "These two guys were like escorts, bodyguards, the concierge . . . whatever Al needed, they took care of it." Ed Pogue, aka Tick, was the soundman. "He didn't have any teeth," said later bassist Jeff "Stick" Davis. Those roses Green threw to the audience? Tick's job "was to pick the thorns off."

Tick wasn't to be confused with Pick—Haywood Anderson, called Pick due to his toothpick frame. A controversial character in the history of Al Green, Pick "did a lotta things for Al that Al wouldn't do," said Jarrett. Was he a road manager? Bodyguard? Confidant? Perhaps all that and more. Anderson "was just a used car salesman," said Johnny Brown. "You couldn't believe nothin' he said . . . I love me some Haywood. I bought a few cars from him. He used to come repossess 'em, I'd go and get 'em back." To Reuben Fairfax, Pick was "just a comedian. If you can be around music and you don't have to play, that's the greatest job in the world. All you have to do is tell jokes and go get coffee. You get the best money, all the tips, first dibs on whatever . . . " Fairfax no longer goes on the road, but if he ever returned, he'd want a job like Pick's—"I don't want to be the Man—I want to be the man *next* to the Man."

Others found Anderson to be a rather formidable character who was fiercely protective of Green. "Haywood was an East Saint Louis cat, right?" said Roland Jones. "He acted like he was a mini street gangster." Fiercely protective of Al, Haywood had a succinct way of dealing with rabid fans intent on making contact with their idol. Charles Hodges: "Haywood didn't play. He didn't want you to touch Al. You wanna hit somebody, hit Haywood—don't hit Al, you're gonna get killed. Haywood was a deadly guy. He would kill for Al, he would *kill.* You hear what I'm saying?"*

❖

To cart this circus around Green bought a bus off R&B singer Buddy "The Silver Fox" Ace and painted AL GREEN AND THE ENTERPRISE ORCHESTRA down the side of it. "It was one of them old, old, old, *old* Greyhounds," said Jones. "First time out on that bus, it broke down." It was a rare and unwanted event when Green was aboard. "Al didn't want to be associated with the band, so Al would fly," said Jones. "And every time he did get on the bus, somethin' happened to the motherfuckin' bus—every time."

Buddy Jarrett agreed. "We were on our way out West. Al's on the bus, he gonna ride with the band, he ridin' in the front seat—everybody like, 'Man, why he ridin' with *us*?' We get halfway between here and nowhere, there was no compression. The bus just stopped runnin'. This car with three girls pulls up—'Oooh, is Al on the bus?' Al gets off. 'Hey ladies, how y'all doin'?' 'Oooh, it's Al Green!' He gets in the car and leaves us— 'I'll meet y'all at the hotel.'" As soon as Green departed, "the bus started

---

* Haywood "Pick" Anderson agreed to an interview for this book. We were scheduled to meet the next day at a Memphis Cracker Barrel restaurant. Pick was a no-show. Subsequent phone calls went unanswered.

up—the air was working." Jarrett recalled another time Green was a passenger when "the bus slid down an embankment, flipped over . . . we told him, 'Man, we know you don't like to ride the bus. *Please don't ride the bus!*'" Jarrett said a bit of Green's 1976 song "Keep Me Crying" is about just that. "He wrote, 'Well, I tried to run my business / But the band said I can't.'"

A lot of drama revolved around Green's bus—and whoever was driving it. (One musician bus driver, who shall remain nameless, stranded the band in Vegas when he hijacked the bus for a crack run.) Willie "Pop" Aiken was one of Al's drivers. Aiken, who'd been associated with the Soul Children, had some sort of role in the aftermath of the Martin Luther King assassination. Aiken "was just involved in the underworld," said later band member Reuben Fairfax Jr. "A gangster. *Definitely* a gangster" is how Johnny Brown described ol' Pop. Nobody wanted to supply any further details when pressed.

Being a driver for Green was a tough gig. The pay was far from great, and in order to save on accommodations you were expected to drive straight through—"No stopping, no showers, no nothing. If the bus driver got tired, instead of pulling over, he'd drink Dr Pepper, eat candy bars, and keep going," said producer Paul Zaleski, who had the misfortune to ride on one of Al's band vans (the bus had burned up by this point) in the eighties. "Because if he would pull over and get one of the band guys sleeping to drive, the guy would want part of the driver's money." In order to cover his losses, the driver would tell Green there was something wrong with the bus, then Al would send funds—and instead of fixing anything the driver would "pocket the money and then the bus would blow up. You think Al Green's gonna pay for them to get back? Hell, no." This happened over and over. Sometimes Al's brother Walter drove, a terrible driver. When he'd change gears "they would grind," said Fairfax. "And Buddy Jarrett would yell out, 'Ground down another pound, Count!'"

Walter was muscular, had blue fingernails, wore a suit coat with no shirt to show off his shaved chest, and sported "a 1967 pompadour," says Roland Jones, with a widow's peak that came to a point, earning him the nickname "Count," as in Dracula. A former pimp, "Walter always thought he was a gangster," said Buddy Jarrett, but was actually "just a dude with a process."

Walter "had white girls long before most black folks, right?" said Jones. "He thought he was God's gift to the world, but he wasn't too intelligent."

Walter was known for knocking his women around. As Jeff Davis recalled, one of Walter's paramours "was constantly heavily made up. She'd gotten the crap beat out of her on a daily basis . . . she never said boo to a goose."

Brother Robert sometimes sang backup ("out of tune," claims Jarrett) or collected the money; younger brother Lonel, a dead ringer for Al, could be used, said Jarrett, "as a decoy" when Green needed to make a fast getaway. Al's sisters were also around, as family members sold T-shirts and worked concessions. "He gave all of 'em a shot at goin' out on the road for a minute or two," said Jones.

Relatives were not exempt from the mean Green treatment, however. Green "didn't really like Walter at all," said Jones. "Al didn't like none of his brothers. Only one he was kinda favorable to was Lonel, but Lonel was the spittin' image of Al, right?" Green was closer to his sisters, particularly Maxine. Al's father also went on tour, but worked mostly as a caretaker on Green's country property. "Pop was dedicated to his wife," said Jones. "And Al kinda came in between them. Al would do stuff for his mama— and wouldn't let her do nuthin' for his daddy. Al was vicious, man. He dogged them out like he dogged the band members out."

Fellow performers were not exempt either. "Al did not befriend nobody else," maintained Jones. "I remember *all* of 'em tryin' to come around and talk to Al, wantin' to associate, but Al wouldn't even let you in the dressing room, I don't care who you were. It just didn't matter. As long as I knew him he never let more than two or three people in that dressing room. If Al let you in and you figured him out, I guess he thought you were gonna fuck him or somethin'. There's some insecurity there."

Early on the Enterprise Orchestra backed Green for a couple of dates opening for Tyrone Davis, who'd scored a big hit with "Turn Back the Hands of Time" in 1970. In what would become a pattern, Green didn't exactly befriend his fellow artist, even though Davis had sent his own bus to rescue Al's band when they were stranded due to a snowstorm. "We was opening, but Al's record was playing more than Tyrone. It made Al more smirky," says Jones. "Him and Tyrone got into it. Tyrone asked Green to get off his damn bus."

Jones recalled a similar situation when Stax singer Johnnie "God Is Standing By" Taylor tried to come into the dressing room in Chicago. Green had met Taylor on the chitlin' circuit, playing a Memphis joint called the Paradise Club. Johnnie "was just tryin' to be his friend," said Jones. "Al refused. Johnnie Taylor was about drunk and said, 'Nigger, who the fuck you think you are?' He was so pissed off at Al. Al refused to even acknowledge Johnnie Taylor." Johnnie was so furious he spent the rest of the night circling around the venue in his limo.*

❖

Roland Jones would be fired and rehired by Green so many times he lost count. Post-show during a European tour, Jones and Ingram had to sneak Al back to his room by cutting through their own suite. The singer noticed both of the hotel's luggage carts in their room. "Al was madder than a motherfucker—'This is the reason I ain't got no place to hang my clothes, because y'all got the shit!! That's the reason I can't get no damn carts!'" He stormed off to his room. Jones felt the real reason Al was angry was because they'd dressed up the suite with black lights and portraits of themselves over their bed. "He knew for a fact we was about ready to have a good time."

When they returned to Memphis, Green began to criticize Roland's job performance. "He was mad as hell. I said, 'Whenever I can't fulfill my responsibilities for my position, I'll terminate myself.' I believe that was the first time Al had really heard that word—'terminate.' His whole damn expression changed. From that point on, it was up and down with me and Al." Fired and rehired; it is the history of many who work for Green.

Yet Roland also lived at Green's Memphis home for six months or so. This even surprised Jones. "Al never let nobody stay at his house. That was a first. Everybody was astonished." At the time Roland was seeing Willie Mitchell's daughter Yvonne (aka Vonne). "He had to get mad, 'cause Yvonne showed up at his door for me. He was jealous that I could have one of Willie's daughters and he couldn't. He was the star, and I'm this little rooty-coot guy that he considered to be nothin'."

Jones felt Green was insecure when it came to the Mitchells. "Al never felt he was equal to them. Willie *made* Al Green. He was his boss. Al was tryin' to get at Yvonne, but Yvonne wouldn't let him in. He always wants every woman he's seen. Al wanted her and he couldn't have her. Yvonne, she was classy. Poppa Willie had money. Yvonne was dating a lawyer and a doctor. She didn't give a fuck how much fame Al had. She looked at Al like, 'Shit, you work for my daddy.'" One day at the house when Yvonne said something mean to Green, "Al was really hurt—I'm talking he was *hurt,* you hear me? Al was basically a sensitive, emotional kind of person."

---

* Green and Taylor presumably made up at some point, as Al referred to him as "a friend of mine" in a 1989 interview and attended his 2000 funeral.

At one point Jones was going through a rough time and went back to Columbus, Ohio, where his family was. Green came through on tour and "greeted me with open arms and he put money in my pocket." Roland laughed. "Al wanted me to get onstage and do background vocals to justify the money that he gave me." This was, said Jones, "the first time he ever really showed me any kindness. At times Al could be a really nice guy. He showed compassion. I think that Al really wanted to be that kind of person but he couldn't, based on his own insecurities. He'd go left and become vengeful and hateful and all that other shit."

What kind of person is Al Green? "Complicated. I don't know no-body—*I don't know nobody*—that likes Al's personality. You never really knew how he was gonna be, you never really knew what he was thinking. Al has never been happy. Al is one of them people who had all the fame and fortune and he was so miserable that he couldn't enjoy it."

Jones said he had no friends. "He didn't trust nobody. Al has always been isolated and alone. He actually had no fuckin' life, man. Al really was a genius; he mastered vocals. He was just a damn fool. That's Al."

❖

Perry Michael Allen worked with Green as a musician and songwriter as well as behind the scenes. He experienced similar ups and downs as the rest of those interviewed, yet came away with a rarer empathetic point of view. "Everybody wanted something from Al, everybody was tearing at him, and he didn't come up to their fantasy, he didn't save their lives. Al just didn't do what they wanted him to do . . .

"He was an innocent backwoods gospel guy who came from a strange backwoods family that wasn't supportive. And he made it. All the stuff that comes from that level of success he faced by himself. He was alone . . . crooks, women, drugs, stabs in the back, the guy survived all that shit. The guy *survived.*"

❖

When Green returned to *Soul!* for an October 22, 1972, broadcast, he was the only guest, performing a live, in-studio concert interrupted only by a short interview. Now a full-blown star, Green was in full command of the Enterprise Orchestra, directing the dynamics with a raise of the hand or a glance back at the drummer. Any signs of awkwardness were gone. The Afro was trimmed tight, the beard replaced by a carefully executed five o'clock shadow, and there were two outfit changes—first, a black silk jacket with reddish-orange shirt and pants, plus a black silk tie dotted with spots of yellow and red; second, a plaid suit, blue turtleneck, and large gold medallion.

The show opens dramatically with a close-up of Al doing a quiet solo acoustic version of "What a Wonderful Thing Love Is." It is riveting, and your eyes don't leave him for the rest of the show, which never lets up. He goes from the odd funkiness of "Look What You Done for Me" to the slow anguish of "How Can You Mend a Broken Heart?" without pause. His showbiz affectations are quirky, funny. Al sings a few lines of the verse of the Bee Gees song only to follow his breathtaking phrasing with a calculated look out into the audience as he asks, "Is there *anybody* in *New York City* that can *mend* a broken heart?" During "I'm Still in Love with You" he actually invites the audience to sing along, as if any mere mortal could navigate the vocal gymnastics of that particular number.

To preface "Let's Stay Together," Green sings a bit of the Carpenters' "We've Only Just Begun," and it is stunning. No doubt taken with the melody as well as the sentiment of the lyric, which reads like a more polished version of one of his own, Green takes this already fully realized pop confection by the whitest of groups and, as he did with his Bee Gees cover, invests it with an unexpected richness and deepness. Al seems determined to get to some other plane, some higher state, when he sings, taking us all with him. "I like to be free as the air when I get onstage, so I can say, be and do just what I want to." That in-the-moment approach is central to the magic of Green's live performances. "We seldom rehearse . . . it takes away from the show to plan everything . . . the show changes every night depending on how I feel." Not that Al finds any charm in imperfection. When displeasure registers on his face after the horns hit a few sour notes during the *Soul!* broadcast, you feel he hates being dragged back into a less-perfect reality.

The crowd is hushed while he sings, clearly transfixed by his every utterance and gesture. The women in particular seem to be collectively holding their breath. They sit frozen, staring, some absently mouthing the lyrics. Clearly they feel Al is singing directly to them, for them. One pair even high-fives each other after a particular couplet. Has any performer cast a spell over women like Al Green? My wife, Natalia, who's seen the footage from this show many, many times, was entranced watching it once again. When I asked what Al's particular appeal was to the ladies, she just said, "He's a man-child," as if that explained everything. Maybe it does.*

❖

"I live way out in the woods, where there are twisted roads that lead to my home," said Al Green. On October 10, 1972, Green spent $128,000 on a split-level house surrounded by forty acres about forty minutes away from Memphis in Millington, Tennessee. 1404 St. Paul Road was a remote hideaway situated next to a state forest. Green made it clear in the press that unlike many of his fly-by-night peers, he wasn't going to squander all his loot on flashy baubles: "I didn't want a Cadillac, I was just as satisfied with a Buick. That wasn't my great inspiration . . . I had a lot of friends over my shoulder sayin', 'Hey man, it's about time for that new hog, isn't it?' I said, 'Well, okay—I tell you what: you go spend yours on a hog, and I'll drive my old raggedy Buick—and I'll buy this crib, this house.'"

Built in 1963, the home had five bedrooms, four bathrooms, and a G-shaped swimming pool. The few reporters lucky enough to visit his lair have poked fun at Green's gaudy taste in furnishings: bronze cupids; round beds with furry covers; a leopard-skin recliner with matching phone; a huge art-deco urn whose artwork featured Christopher Columbus, American flag-waving angels floating above his head; and a room done all in red, down to the plastic-covered sofa and even the lightbulbs. Apparently the Green hacienda remains frozen in time. When Davin Seay interviewed Al there in the late nineties, he found it to be "a fantastic place . . . a split-level ranch with pink shag carpet. A lot of wrought iron, gnarled-oak furniture. It looked like nothing had changed from 1972 . . . it was like a seventies drug den."

❖

In December 1972, the *I'm Still in Love with You* album was released. The cover crystalized Green's image as smooth, sexy soul man—in white suit, turtleneck, and shoes (the socks are black), lounging in a white wicker chair on white shag carpeting. Behind him hangs a smattering of plants

---

* As far as Al's attractiveness to his own gender, Robert Christgau worked himself into a lather issuing this proclamation: "Green's sexiness is so pervasive that no male who responds to his singing can do so without feeling a jolt that transcends identification." Elsewhere in the piece he pants over Green's "lean body and a winsome face . . . the lithe eloquence of his body . . . his immense physical attractiveness . . . his savvy, diffident style of sexual confidence."

that match the green lettering of the title. The back cover is a close-up from the same session, Al leaning on a hand sporting a diamond pinkie ring, gazing thoughtfully into the camera. The message transmitted? Here, my dear. Join me in paradise. I'm waiting here just for *you*.

As good as *Let's Stay Together* was, this was a notch higher. Besides the title single and "Look What You Done for Me," it is an album full of riches: "So Glad Your Mine," with Bulldog's killer intro, Charles's slinky B3 swells, and the sighing strings; the sly, unexpected Orbison cover, "Oh, Pretty Woman"; and "What a Wonderful Thing Love Is," perhaps Green's most convincing expression of universal love, which he sings the hell out of. Just listen to the way Green phrases "I walk the floor when you're leavin'" over the strings. If you built a hotel where that little bit of the song played on a loop in every room, day and night, no one would ever check out. The bliss in Al's voice is that palpable.

"Simply Beautiful" is as intimate as music gets—if "I'm Still in Love with You" is a whisper in the ear, this is something a bit more moist. You can practically hear the crackling of the fire and taste the champagne as Al writhes around on that album-cover white-shag carpet, laying it on thick. He coos "baby" not once but three times in a row. Al's lips are right on top of mic number nine, and as he overdubs himself he's not always singing the same thing. It plays with your mind, and Willie had the good sense to leave it in. That's Green's acoustic guitar doing the midnight creep. Apparently Teenie had a little too much to drink—a lucky break, as the rest of the band has to play at Al's speed, which is slower than any in the world. He may be a primitive, unsophisticated guitarist, but his playing is idiosyncratic and hypnotic, and his singing tends to intensify even more when he's in charge of the tempo. A stunning performance. I cannot believe any other artist would dare to cover this (and of course they've tried—including a duet version with Queen Latifah and Al himself).

"For the Good Times" was Al's first foray into country music. Green was introduced to the idea of doing country by the infamous Audrey Williams, Hank's ex-wife, who was a friend of Green's booking agent, Bettye Berger. "She wanted to meet him. She wanted to play him Hank Williams," Berger recalled. "And I think she had a crush on him, that's my feeling." As Al recalled, "I met Miss Audrey, she was older than me. I said, 'Well, all right, waddya want to do?' 'First,' she says, 'I wanna get a bottle of champagne . . .' We stop and get a bottle of the best champagne because Audrey don't drink nuthin' else. She took me to her house."

While the connection may seem unlikely, it should be noted that Williams had also managed R&B singer Roy Gaines in the late sixties. "Audrey—she was wild," said Teenie. "She and Miss Otis, one of the people who own Otis Elevators, were good friends and had an all-girls group that did things together. Al would go to Nashville and see 'em. He asked me many times to go. I never went." Williams, in decline and drinking heavily, "used to have us over to her mansion," said Green. "And we'd be out around the pool and she said, 'You should sing some country music, too. Don't leave country out.'"

It was during that visit to Audrey's Nashville home that she first played Al some country music, including songs by Hank (according to Berger, the pair got into an accident on the way from Memphis; Williams was arrested for drunk driving twice in 1972). She "played so many I couldn't just pick one," said Green. "I waited until I got back to Memphis and I picked 'For the Good Times.'" Al takes the Kristofferson song at a deadly slow pace, enunciating it beautifully. It would be the first of a handful of country covers. "Every R&B record you hear is not necessarily an R&B song," said Green. "It might have derived from country music." A couple of years later when he was deep inside a spiritual crisis, Green would turn to Audrey Williams for help.

❖

There is one more track on *I'm Still in Love with You* that bears discussing: the outrageous, unforgettable just-over-five-minutes that is "Love and Happiness." It wasn't even a US single at the time (although one-hit wonder Earnest Jackson scored a number-twenty-two R&B [and number-fifty-eight pop] hit with a slavish cover version—Mitchell would report he knew "of instances where a husband and wife have almost come to blows" when it came to buying the right version). A song conceived and cowritten by Teenie Hodges, it is maybe the most compelling creation of all from Al Green/Willie Mitchell/Hi Rhythm.

As Teenie revealed to Robert Gordon, "Love and Happiness" first came about due to an intersection of sexual frustration and pro wrestling. Teenie wrote it "not for" Al Green, but "because of this girlfriend of mine." At the time, Hodges was in a marriage that was falling apart and was seeing another dame (also married) on the side. "I wanted to screw on Saturday morning, woke up, and I asked her, and she said, 'Yes, I want to too,' but first she said, 'We ain't got no food, we need to go to the grocery store.'"

Teenie pestered her again. Same answer. "We need to go to the grocery store—we'll do it when we come back." She got up and took a shower. Frustrated, Teenie clicked on the TV to watch wrestling, a favorite pastime. "Jerry Lawler was on. . . . Before she got out of the shower, I had written 'Love and Happiness.' Not all the lyrics—a verse of it and the whole chorus . . . the hook, for sure."

In order to finish the *I'm Still in Love with You* album "we needed one more song," Teenie recalled. "I said, 'Well, I got a song.'" They often got to his songs last, and neither Al nor Willie had heard "Love and Happiness" before. They liked what they heard of the unfinished song. Charles remembers messing around with a rough version at Royal. "That night it didn't happen. Al Jackson and Willie and Al were trying to get it." He says Willie told everybody to go home—'Okay, girls, we're gonna call it a night. Come back in the morning. . . . We'll get it tomorrow.'" Teenie said he got together with Green, who "finished it while I was there. We did it together. The lyrics, he did two-thirds at least." Teenie wanted the bluesy licks in the intro to go under the verses. Al had other ideas. "He said no, turn it around. Al has to turn it around." Teenie clarified: "I said, 'It'll make you do right' first. He turned it around—'make you do *wrong*.'"*

Teenie loved the intro they had concocted and had some instructions for Green. "I said, 'Look, when we get back to the studio, Willie's going to try to talk you out of putting that introduction on that the way we've got it. But *you're* the artist. You've got to tell him this is the way the song goes, that's the way it's got to be. Also, he's gonna be fussin' about us smoking reefer. You just tell him'—because Al smoked too—'that we gonna smoke.'" Teenie smiled at the memory. "That's the instigator in me." Up until this point they had to do it secretly, because Willie was against it.

That next day, it was apparent Teenie had predicted correctly: "Sure enough, we ran the song down one time, and Willie said, "Everything is fine except that introduction—take that out and just pick it up from the guitar bit." They took a break and Teenie reminded Al what had to be done. "I said, 'Just break it gently.'" Green went into the control room and

---

* Green tells the writing of "Love and Happiness" differently: he says he just blurted out the title as he packed up the car after a vacation break to Lake Hamilton, Arkansas, with Willie and Teenie (the same trip during which "I'm Still in Love with You" had been written). Al started to sing the words "love and happiness," and Teenie started to stomp out a beat. "We drove 160 miles back to Memphis, went straight to the studio that night and cut 'Love and Happiness,'" according to Al. Nobody else remembered it that way.

told Mitchell the song had to remain as it was. And not only that, they were going to take a reefer break.

Mitchell didn't like it, but from then on, he "put up with it," said Charles Hodges. They'd slip off to what Charles dubbed "the Hi Room" and smoke. (Flick and Bulldog didn't imbibe.) Which is what they did before cutting "Love and Happiness." "Al, Teenie, Hubbie, and myself . . . we were sitting up there, we had some good weed." And, Charles added, "a little cocaine." Before too long it was time to record. "We were going back and I said, 'Al! You know what's wrong with that song? I need to be playing organ.'"

Green told him to go for it. Back in the studio, Charles started to lift the organ top. "When Willie saw, he said, 'Turn that organ off! We're getting ready to cut this song. Get on piano.'" His allies spoke up. "Teenie and Al said, 'Let him try the organ' . . . so we started messing around." Charles did one of those chill-producing swells that earned him his nickname, and Mitchell seized on it. "Willie said, 'Wait a minute, wait a minute, what'd you do?' So I did it again, and he said, 'Okay, but do it right *here*.'" Once Charles was in the right spot it all fell together. "We'd been working on it forever, seemed like, couldn't get the feel on it. Put that organ on it, there it was."

There was one final detail to address—getting Bulldog* from Teenie's guitar intro to the song itself. Teenie: "I said, 'Howard's not gonna be able to keep that tempo right, so I need to count it off—I'll do it with my guitar, hittin' the strings.'" Willie instructed him to use an old Coca-Cola crate lying around the studio instead. They stuck it in front of Teenie's amp. You can hear him stomping on the wooden crate to count off the song. "That case is still at Hi Records," Teenie recalled. "We cut it in one take." How long it took to get to that take is a matter of debate; Mitchell said they spent ninety hours on the song while Green claimed they cut it in a night.

What a track! Can one even imagine the song without the crazy color Charles provides with his stabs of high-low organ? To say nothing of that wild breakdown, which goes from spare to skeletal. Tense, tight, yet every moment's full of surprises you can dance to. And just when you think

---

* Al Jackson Jr. had been replaced by Grimes, which Mitchell told Reuben Fairfax Jr. Jackson was forever pissed off about. Charles Hodges says that Jackson was present for the final recording and not angry at all.

things can't get any heavier, the horns drop that big fat low note. A work of genius, "Love and Happiness." And we haven't even gotten to Al.

❖

"Love and Happiness" has inspired much breathless pontification, much of which seems to dwell on the surface of the song. In their quaint book *Love & Happiness: Eros According to Dante, Shakespeare, Jane Austen, and the Rev. Al Green,* Craig Werner and Rhonda Mawhood Lee state the song "marks the place where gospel meets the blues." Well, it also marks the place where Al, Teenie, Hubbie, and Charles met a big fat joint. Add a pinch of Jerry Lawler as well. Green was steeped in gospel music; of course it was going to ooze out of him. And any notion of blues is supplied by Teenie's iconic guitar lick (B.B. King was the reference he mentioned discussing the song). Neither blues nor gospel nor rock, this recording is some odd, utterly original hybrid that only Al Green, Willie Mitchell, and Hi Rhythm could conjure up.

Werner and Mawhood go on to declare that "Love and Happiness" "boils the *Divine Comedy*'s vision down to five minutes and three seconds . . . [Green] pulls back from the abyss and points toward the path that Dante followed in." Where's paradise come in, then? This song is a stroll into utter darkness. With Al Green one has to look beyond the opaque lyrics and gaze into the dark, muddy water below. Forget the title. Ask yourself: How does this song make me feel? This song's about as "happy" as the music of Brian Wilson's Beach Boys. A nameless melancholy lurks.

Trapped inside "Love and Happiness" is a man yearning for something he's never going to get. Maybe he isn't even sure if he wants it. Love is a far-away abstract ideal, and Green seems to distrust the notion anyway. "Walk away with victory" rings as hollow as any campaign slogan. Al makes the simple actions of a couple ("walking together . . . talking together") seem completely unobtainable. Then there's that repetitious invocation of "the power of love." Green's delivery renders it voodoo.

I detect no pulling back from the void. On the contrary—when Green lets loose with that high-pitched squeal on the fade-out it sounds like he's falling right into the fiery pit. Most vivid is the opening verse, with its woman in the wee hours desperate to save a relationship by telephone. Nothing gets resolved in the song. The end vamp doesn't build to some big, triumphant return to a redemptive, happy chorus; it just snakes on and on, those evil Jack-in-the-box horns laughing away as Green and company chug off into the night on their midnight train. "Love and Happiness" just might be Al's most revealing work, the one closest to who Al Green really is.

❖

By 1973 Al Green was just about the hottest singer on the planet. He had his own business, Al Green Enterprises (that year *Ebony* would report he was "responsible for a payroll of nearly 40 people"), and, however wacky the public persona was, proved to be a shrewd operator. "There are really two men," he told *Ebony.* "Al Green the singer is a baby . . . his personality is soft . . . understanding and congenial. . . . Mr. Green the businessman has more drive and is more forceful. He goes to the office early and stays late." Al had his forty-acre estate, plus more farmland he bought near Oakland, Tennessee. The press noted his philanthropic endeavors: a benefit for a free medical clinic in Arkansas, a Memphis program for underprivileged children, and shows at various prisons. "I try to help others," he said. "If the Lord blesses you, you must try to help someone else."

Green and Mitchell made a trip to Hollywood, where they turned down the opportunity to score *Across 110th Street* and *Black Caesar.* Green did not approve of "all that killing, dope and girls" and wanted to be part of films that he could "take my family to." Awards rolled in. Green was declared "Outstanding Star of the Year" at the annual Memphis Music Awards. Jesse Jackson named the opening day of his PUSH Expo Al Green Day. *Rolling Stone* declared Green "Rock Star of the Year" and feted him with champagne.

Other artists were envious, awestruck. Even Syl Johnson—who found plenty to complain about when it came to Al Green—does not deny his talent. "Ain't no better singer than him. He wasn't just a singer, he was an instrument—he was like a Sonny Stitt or Miles Davis, but with his *voice.* Hit notes, made melody . . . nobody ever topped him. *No one.*" As if that weren't formidable enough, added Johnson, "ain't nobody ever sold records like Al Green—he sold albums like they were 45s."

In terms of popularity? Johnson evoked the name of a great white God, albeit one that was a primary inspiration to the man he was talking about: Al Green was "the black Elvis."

AL AND THE WOMEN

an interlude

I don't beat up women or throw them through windows . . .
I just want to write good songs.
—AL GREEN

No good can come from this chapter. Try interviewing any of Al Green's exes—I dare you. They all seem to be writing books. They want money. Or they are afraid of derailing a mythical reunion with Al in some misty, nonexistent future. You start digging into the women of this story, and you can get very depressed. Especially for them. "I had a woman in every corner, all around the whole suite, man, nothing but women," boasted Al. "My dad said, 'Al, why don't you just pick one and send the rest of them home? They all got the same thing.'"

Green is notoriously secretive about this part of his life. Publicists who have worked for him over the years found themselves unable to state if he was married or sometimes even where he lived at the time. Musicians who had been with Al for years were unsure how many times he's been married (four seems to be the general consensus: some say there's one more) or the names of all the parties involved. "You didn't know about most of the women, 'cause he wouldn't let them be around," said Roland Jones. Reporters who have asked Green his marital status point blank are deftly thwarted. When Karen Schoemer put the question to him during a 1995 interview for *Newsweek*, Green's reply was characteristically obtuse: "Well,

I am composed to answer that," said Al, buying a little time as the wheels turned in his head. "Let me just answer it like this: your heart's in good hands. "Your Heart's in Good Hands" happened to be the first song off the album Green was currently promoting. "That's it," he added, obviously satisfied that he'd provided a solid gold response to her inquiry.

❖

Al Green married Shirley Kyles in 1977, and they were divorced in 1983 (more about that later). As for the rest, Green married Clover Dixon in 1983 and Martha Gibson in 1987. Both were brief affairs. (I believe Al was referencing Martha in a 2005 interview when he said, "She's a wonderful girl," then offered a rare admission: "I blew it.") In a recent interview Green states he's been married "three times," yet press reports from 1995 and 2000 mention an unnamed wife. There's also what Green calls his "10,000 girlfriends": Gladys, Cheryl, Autry, Candy, Denise, Shirley . . . and the other 9,994. The minute Al kicks the bucket, they'll come crawling out of the woodwork. Margaret Foxworth thinks there should be a reality show starring "all of Al's women. It would make money."

Green had three children with his first wife—Alva, Rubi, and Kora (they've provided background vocals for their father in recent years). He had a son with Clover, Adam. There are three more children from the mysterious, possibly fourth marriage—Trevor (born approximately 1992), Al Jr., and Kala, born approximately 2001. (Anonymous posts online name a marriage with a Jackie Ware-Green, but list four children.)* Background singer Margaret Foxworth had a son in 1978—another Al Jr.—and says Green acknowledges the child is his. A 1985 article reports Al had just come from Gary, Indiana, visiting "his oldest daughter from a romance that didn't result in marriage." A YouTube video entitled "Is This Al Green's Son?" stars Shaun Neal, son of longtime Green backup singer Wanda Neal Bobo. Possessing that familiar incandescent smile, Shaun

---

* There have been many rumors concerning Green being bisexual or gay. I found zero evidence of this, although it would certainly make him more interesting. Al's sexuality provoked "some of the biggest arguments I ever had with people," said Johnny Brown. "They said he was gay. And I'm sayin', 'I traveled the world with him . . . he had more children than I ever seen!' However he might've acted, he did the manly thing with 'em." Although when it came to "manly" things, Johnny felt the need to point out something he noticed during activities at Green's church picnics. Al "couldn't run. He looked bad running."

sings a couple of Al's hits and does them reasonably well. "I just want to know if he's my father," asks Shaun.

Bandleader Johnny Brown claims there are more offspring—in total, "probably over fifteen." On the road they've popped up everywhere. "You'd be in a city somewhere—'This is Al's daughter. This is Al's son.'" Willie Bean named a singer who'd met Al at the Apollo and allegedly had his baby. "She upped and moved to Memphis, okay? Came down here thinking she was gonna marry Al. Crazy, man." Bean says they should "take a survey in Memphis: How many women are livin' in Memphis because they followed Al Green here?"

Bean recalled being on Green's bus at a gospel show Al did one Sunday in Biloxi. A young lady was standing outside the vehicle with her family, holding a one-year-old baby she claimed was his. According to Bean, Al told his bus driver not to open the door. "I sat there and watched that girl cry—'Please Al, don't do this in front of my mama, don't do me like this.'" said Bean. "She was begging him just to open the door and meet her kid. He wouldn't do it." (Perhaps the child wasn't his.)

Strangely, Green suggested in a 1993 interview that he liked his women the same way he likes his bands—a little on the unpredictable side, admitting that "the wonderful one, the girl I could trust even to send to the mailbox to get my mail, she'd do anything I ask her—I don't love her so much. But the girl that won't do *nuthin'* I say—oh man, I'm crazy about her!" In his book he says just the opposite: "I personally didn't go for the upfront and outspoken type of woman. I like my girlfriends meek, mild and obedient." (He mentions none of his wives; the only two women he deems worthy of consideration are his working-girl first love, Juanita, and Laura Lee, who's remained a close friend. "There was something pure about our love as it grew over the years," Green writes.)

❖

"There are thousands of groupies and some of them are so beautiful," said Green in 1974. "There are girls who will walk up to you and do anything!" He'd cross paths with one of the more famous ones early on—Miss Mercy Fontenot, aka Judith Edra Peters, groupie extraordinaire and member of Frank Zappa's chaotic all-groupie band the GTOs.

A knowledgeable connoisseur of R&B, Mercy was a rabid fan of Stax's psychedelic soul brothers the Bar-Kays. So sometime in 1971, "My girlfriend Marquise and I decided to hitchhike to Memphis. We end up at the Stax parking lot, not knowing anybody."

As luck would have it, the Bar-Kays were just leaving the studio along with another bunch of musicians. "They walked up to us and said, 'Hi, we're going over to another studio, do you want to come?' It was the Hodges boys." Teenie, who took the women under his wing, was highly attuned to the racial tensions in the city. When cops or someone suspicious drove by, he'd have them duck down in the car.*

Teenie drove them to Royal. Mercy hung out at both Stax and Hi and felt the difference. "Stax at that time was really overblown, overcorrupted. So much money, a lot of gangsters. It seemed to have lost the essence—and all the essence seemed to have relocated to Hi."

At some point Teenie said, "I want you to meet our lead singer" and took the girls to a modest stucco house. Al came to the door. "He was kind of conservative to me, like a Frank Sinatra—I was used to the Bar-Kays. I had gypsy eye-makeup on, I was a total freak." Right off the bat, Al asked her if she wanted to stay the night. "He kind of scared me, so Teenie put us up in the Lorraine Motel." On the next trip to Royal, they were recording Green, and Mercy changed her tune once she heard him in action. "I went, 'Oh my God, what have we here?!'"

Although she didn't connect with Green on that trip, a year or so later, when he was a full-blown star playing Los Angeles, she wrote him a letter with her number enclosed. Al called, ringing a pay phone somehow installed in her home. Mercy was out, but when she got back, her roommate told her, "Al Green called. He's at Disneyland." They didn't connect until Green returned to play the Forum. He called in the wee hours and invited her over. She spent the night.

"I thought, 'Well, this is the biggest sex god on the planet right now.' And then I thought, 'Really? Is that all there is?' That was my exact thought, the Peggy Lee song. His persona was a lot bigger than he was, and I'm not talking about size." Mercy claimed that Al's own music provided the soundtrack as they went at it. "At the time I thought, 'What an ego this one has.' Maybe he just loved to be with women with his own music playing."

---

* Another interesting tidbit from Miss Mercy that I heard from no one else: "Everybody was on angel dust when I was in Memphis. Everybody. Oh my God, they were smoking so much dust."

The next morning? "We wake up, we smoke pot, of course. Al was really funny, fun to be around. He had a briefcase full of the money they paid him. So he hands me five dollars to take a cab home. This briefcase full of money and he hands me five dollars!" A bit miffed, Mercy opened the hotel room door to leave, and "two ladies who were working for him fell at my feet. They were listening to everything we did. I just thought, 'Wow, that's weird.' Later I heard rumors that they blackmailed him."

Miss Mercy never saw Green again, although she remained friends with Teenie for the rest of his life. "He didn't have a lot of great things to say about Al." Many years later he asked her, "Why didn't you go out with me?"

❖

Here is where David Gest slithers into the story. This bearded, bejeweled, surgically enhanced ("No one has a lower opinion of my looks than myself") bottom-rung celebrity gnome was most infamous in the States for his unnerving 2002 marriage to Liza Minnelli, which culminated in a lawsuit: Gest suing Liza with a Z for ten million, claiming he was the victim of physical abuse (the suit was dismissed, and the chapter about Minnelli in his autobiography consists of two blank pages). Overseas Gest was a reality-show star whose credits include such crimes against humanity as *I'm a Celebrity . . . Get Me Out of Here!* and *Celebrity Big Brother.*

At nineteen, Gest was hired as Hi Records' West Coast publicist after London executives noticed a glowing review he'd written of Green's guest star performance on a Smokey Robinson and the Miracles show at the Los Angeles Forum. Gest, who was also tight with the Jackson family dynasty, would handle publicity for the whole Hi roster and grow close to all the artists, including Al Green, who'd snatch him away so Gest could open his own PR company and represent him (although according to David, Al tried to sidestep any legal obligation by having his secretary sign their contract until Gest pressed him).*

In his pungent 2007 autobiography, *Simply the Gest,* David declares Green his show-business "mentor." Concerning Al's love life, Gest notes that "Al did not always go for the most beautiful women." A former paramour of Green's who had asked Al why he didn't seem to care about

---

* Gest, a true fan of soul music, continued to promote concerts featuring aging soul stars. In 2004 Green filed a cease-and-desist order after Gest had erroneously listed him on the poster for an upcoming Memphis charity concert called "David Gest's All-Star Holiday Extravaganza."

looks shared his succinct reply with Gest: "Because my dick don't know no better." Gest would watch in amazement as mainly female fans tore down barricades at a Central Park concert, intent on making contact (and when they escaped the mob in a helicopter whose door flew open mid-air, he'd credit Green with literally saving his ass when he calmly reached out and shut the door). He'd be equally incredulous—not to mention angry—one night in Philadelphia where he witnessed Al juggling three different women the same night. Gest walked into his own hotel room only to find Green on the bed hovering over his girlfriend, "clearly trying to persuade her to become the fourth member of his harem." When it came to women, Al Green "was the only guy I ever met who could go ten hours and still keep going. Eventually, it was to cause him mayhem."

❖

Things cooled with Laura Lee. "We used to be involved," said Green in 1974. "Women are sometimes hard to trust!" Lee "didn't bow down to Al—she talked shit to Al, and that's where the conflict was," said Roland Jones.

Green became involved with Linda Wills. Wills first met Green after a show at the Loew's Palace Theater in Washington, DC. She was already obsessed: she'd made a prayer request to meet Al, and admitted that as she sat in the front row she "even wanted to catch the sweat from his brow." She was standing outside the theater when Green's valet, Oliver Ingram, invited her onto the bus and then backstage to meet Al. They clicked. Green hired her as a secretary for Al Green Enterprises for $500 a week.

Wills may be the only woman around Green who has actually written a book, albeit a slim one, and her description of their relationship could've been lifted from a romance novel. "It was a magical, romantic kind of passion that submerged us . . . the lovemaking between us was supernatural . . . he gently kissed me with his butter-soft full lips and the shock waves shot through my body . . . that night we made love like Romeo and Juliet and it was freaking fantastic."

Wills expounds on the sharp businessman Green (he fined Enterprise Orchestra members for playing bum notes or playing too loudly), the fact that he checked his horoscope religiously, and how she counted the piles of cash Al got paid out on the road. She admits Green was the jealous type, didn't want her talking to the band, and that he had a "stable of women." She shares details both mundane and amusing: Al's love of Kentucky Fried

Chicken and Sucrets lozenges, as well as the excitement of a 1973 visit to Elton John's Beverly Hills palace—Elton gifted them two Polaroid cameras as members of his band (who were, for some unknown reason, wearing multicolored Afro wigs) frolicked in the pool.

Linda lays claim to inspiring (or at least being in the vicinity of their creation) "Love and Happiness," "You Ought to Be with Me," and "Let's Get Married." During a live recording outtake from a 1984 Washington, DC, show recorded by Robert Mugge, Al himself credits her with cowriting "Free at Last" while they were in a New Orleans hotel room (and has her take a bow).

Wills doesn't dwell on the dark side. She refuses to reveal the details of an incident involving "devious people" who wanted to break up the couple, but admits it so upset her she "wanted to end my life." It was Green who took her to the hospital, where they pumped her stomach. Al passed her a note: "Nothing or nobody could ever change the way you feel about me," which is interesting in terms of its emphasis. Wills says that the turning point in their romance was a fight they had in the car on the way to Green's home. That night he put her out of the car somewhere "in the boondocks." Green came back for her, but the relationship began to head south.

"Sometimes Al was hard to get along with, but they say artistic people are unconventional and don't always do the norm" is her charitable way of putting things. "There were times when he had temperament issues and it wasn't a good look." The first time Green fired Linda, she went to work for his old nemesis, Isaac Hayes. Apparently that was too much to bear for Al, because he hired her back to work at his publishing company. As their relationship continued to fray, so did her employment. Green fired her again.

What Wills doesn't mention in her book are the assault charges and lawsuits she filed. In 1974 she filed a civil suit against Al, accusing him of assault and battery. According to *Jet* magazine, Green and Wills got into a fight over her abrupt termination and back payment owed to her. She claimed Al "beat her repeatedly and shoved her through a glass door in his office," wrote *Jet*. "Wills was allegedly taken to a hospital by Green's sister." There, according to her lawyer, she was "treated for contusions, bruises and bleeding from the head." (In another news report she claimed Green "struck her with a bottle and kicked her.") Al denied the charges, and the assault and battery charges were eventually dropped due to conflicting evidence.

In August *Jet* noted that the $100,000 suit was settled out of court. In a bizarre twist, Wills testified as to the reason behind her 1972 firing: Green had a pair of his own underpants returned to him by a Washington preacher who claimed Wills had requested that the man of God "pray over the garment." On the stand, Linda "vehemently denied" she'd done it. (Was this the plot of "devious people," or was she hoping divine intervention would seal that busy underwear shut?)

❖

Some were disgusted by the way Al treated women. "He did Linda real bad," said Roland Jones, who claimed he witnessed Green explode at another girlfriend while walking down a concrete ramp leaving a Detroit venue. Larry Lee's wife, Jackie, alleges she saw Green spit on a girlfriend backstage. Buddy Jarrett also claims he saw Green being abusive to a fiancée in Jamaica. "You gotta be cold-blooded to do some of the things he did," said Jarrett.

Background singer Margaret Foxworth, who was involved with Green on and off for decades, describes him as a "Dr. Jekyll and Mr. Hyde. Anything would set him off." Despite his reputation, she says Al never struck her. "Even his sister asked me, 'He ever touch you?' I said no." One time the pair "were arguing. He picked up the phone like he was gonna . . . and I told him, I said, 'You must be crazy. My daddy will kill you. Don't put your hands on me.'" (Foxworth's father, Johnnie Foxworth, was a Cleveland gangster who ran Johnnie's South of the Border lounge. "They called him Al Capone. He carried a .45 in his pocket every day.") Margaret was mystified by the slavish devotion other women had for Green. One female in particular "would pack all his bags, be on the road with him. Woman, slave, whatever. I never did those things." Al asked her to carry his luggage once. "I looked at the bag like, who are you talking to? You better hire somebody. *My* bags are right there too."

When I asked Roland Jones if he thought Green had any great loves among these paramours, he responded with an emphatic, "Hell, no! I don't think Al really liked women. He never *loved* no woman. A woman was there for Al to use in whatever kind of way he wanted. He wanted them to act like Al was God."

As for the women themselves, Jones felt they didn't love Al, they "loved the status. It's bein' able to say that your man is fame-and-fortune Al

Green. That's what they had to love, right? Because they couldn't love Al. How do you love somebody that's vicious like that?"

Yet many of these women stuck around for years. Once the romance was over, "his girlfriends would become friends," said Johnny Brown. "They was always there for Al. You'd see certain ones pop up all the time. We always felt that they came to get some money."

Women? "I haven't had the best of luck with them," says Al Green.

BLACK ELVIS

Women crave certain gestures I make with my body.
—AL GREEN

In April 1973 Al Green, Willie Mitchell, and Hi Rhythm released their masterpiece, *Call Me*. Everything about the album speaks of perfection, down to the neon-lettered album title on the cover. The striking images of Al were shot by Jim Cummings at an Oakland Coliseum show. (Cummings would later accompany Green to a New York City public appearance at the Harlem Record Shack, right across from the Apollo. The crowd swarmed around the limo when they arrived. You couldn't see out of the car "'cause people were pressed against the windows. The PR woman that was in the car was freaking out—'Lemme get outta here, I wanna get out!!!'" Green just sat there, "calm and collected.")

The first single from the album was the lilting "You Ought to Be with Me," released in October 1972. Al Jackson Jr. was once more a co-writer, and that now-trademark rolling Grimes/Jackson drums-and-conga rhythm was front and center. It went to number three. Green gave one of the most buoyant, ebullient performances of his career singing the song on a *Dick Clark's New Year's Rockin' Eve* TV special at the tail end of 1972.

"You Ought to Be with Me" stirred deep feelings in Green, beyond those of terrestrial love. When writing the song, Al explained that he was "playing with God . . . I was so arrogant at the time, not being born-again . . . I was saying: You"—Green pointed upward—"ought to be with

155

me." But Al's little joke on the Lord just served to remind him of inner struggles that would surface soon enough. While singing the song in Manchester, England, May 20, 1973, he'd be so overcome with the spirit that he had "tears runnin' down both sides of my face." Green's emotional performance ground the show to a halt. "Everybody on the floor stopped dancing and stared. This was serious: 'You ought to be with me until I die.' The place was in a trance." Green said this event "was a turning point for me in seeing the kind of effect this music could have on the performer and the audience." A bigger turning point was just down the road for Green, one that would also involve God.

❖

"Call Me (Come Back Home)" came out in February 1973. A surge of horns and strings signal a chorus primarily sung by Rhodes, Chalmers, Rhodes, not Al. This was a lusher sound. Teenie's jazzy guitar plays throughout the song, building to a nifty blast of double time near the end. The lyric is a typical muddle of mixed messages: Al gently chiding his woman for her juvenile ways, telling her she's losing him, but instructing her to pick up the phone if she needs him. Al remains unfazed: "It's all in a day's work." Green's delivery is so soft he practically disappears. Listen to how he sings against his own falsetto note, or the way he double-tracks one single word in the song—"somebody"—to great effect. One of the most striking Mitchell productions, the song hit number ten. It was to be the last single written by the Mitchell/Jackson/Green triumvirate.

"Here I Am (Come and Take Me)"—the third *Call Me* single—came out in June and also shot to number ten. Another cowrite with Teenie (and the one he'd understandably declare his favorite), this song was an absolute beast. No strings, no background or overdubbed vocals, just a grinding piece of slow funk that further mines the dark territory of "Love and Happiness." Al wants someone he can't have. Desire, aggression, and finally release: "I believe there's going to be an explosion." As well as the usual paranoia.

According to Hodges, the chunky, choppy rhythm of "Here I Am" was inspired by Native American rock band Redbone, at that time best known for their sweaty 1971 hit, "Witch Queen of New Orleans." "Here I Am" unleashed some of Green's most ferocious live performances with the Enterprise Orchestra, but Teenie wasn't impressed. "People don't play it like I do," he explained. Timewise, "it's not just straight on. I don't know why I feel it like that—I can write somethin' that has five beats in it instead of eight or four." He claimed Willie told him to take out the funny stuff. "No," said Teenie. "That's the way it feels, that's the way it's gonna be." Mitchell demands songs take you somewhere, and this is a magic carpet ride through the land of lust. The way the baritone sax comes in on the tail of the big fat horn riff only makes the song more foreboding.

❖

The *Call Me* album was released in April 1973, and every drop of the rest of the material matches the quality of the three singles released. "Have You Been Making Out O.K." is a nothing song, but Green sings the refrain so beautifully (and so softly his falsetto cracks) that you don't care. The chugging rhythms and old-school Stax horns of "Stand Up" introduce a motivational Al speaking to African Americans as a whole, although some were unimpressed. Critic Michael Awkward trashes the song as a "cliché-ridden foray into social commentary . . . piling trite phrase upon trite phrase in such rapid-fire succession" that the song succeeds "more as parody than as heartfelt engagement" with any issues. ("As far as racial problems, I haven't had any," said Green that same year. He felt compelled to add, "I've been getting a bigger white audience as time goes on because we've been going more pop.")

There are two more expertly performed country covers on *Call Me* that came by way of Audrey Williams—Willie Nelson's "Funny How Time Slips Away" and Hank's "I'm So Lonesome I Could Cry." (The "square" backing vocals on the latter seem like a hip nod to the Ray Charles early-sixties country landmarks, and the round-robin Al overdubs at the end are something to behold, although one wonders why he speeds up the tempo on this of all songs.)

The *Call Me* album is Green's most dimensional and provocative statement on love, primarily because he forgoes simple, sketchy clichés to evoke something weightier—raw and immediate feelings of fear, jealousy, and confusion, as well as an altogether convincing sense of bliss. Al not only seems unafraid of the impermanence of life, he seems to revel in it. The spectacular "Your Love Is Like the Morning Sun" epitomizes the feel of it all. Slow, dreamy, and delivered in the most shadowy vocal murmurings this side of JJ Cale, the song feels like the first rays of dawn hitting just as a connection is recognized with a partner in crime after a wild, half-remembered night. It's so good that Green's listing his past hit titles at the end of the lyric only elicits a laugh. There's an off-the-cuff beauty to this music. It feels honest and unguarded, an attitude that would only return in full force four years later on *The Belle Album*.

As noted previously, Teenie had insisted Willie pay no mind to their weed smoking at the tail end of the last album. Nobody ever mentions that *Call Me* is a very druggy album that fits right in with such blurry seventies works as *Exile on Main Street*, *Tonight's the Night*, or Sly and the Family Stone's cover of "Que Sera, Sera (Whatever Will Be, Will Be)." Most of the vocals on this album sound as if Al—well, several Als, actually—are whispering them in your ear, and not always intelligibly. Feeling trumps clarity here. The whole album hangs together in the same beautiful, foggy cloud.

The closer, however, indicates a search for something (even) higher: the unearthly "Jesus Is Waiting." Willie didn't know what to do with the song, so he stuck it at the end. Brother James would admit he had trouble figuring out where to place the strings. No wonder they were scratching their heads. This was the furthest out Green had gotten thus far, and it was the first explicit gospel song he'd written himself. What a doozy. Droning, hypnotic, this was five and a half minutes of Al, his acoustic guitar, and his many voices. It's the sort of call-and-response you'd hear at top volume in Sunday church, but delivered like it's four in the morning, the party's over, and the last denizens are minutes away from dreamland unconsciousness. "I like to record when I'm really tired," said Green. "I think it comes out best when you're worn down to the real you."

As Green repeatedly intones phrases like "help me," "sorry," and "thank you," monk-like wordless murmurings snake in and out of the track, up in the mix one minute, nearly inaudible the next. "Jesus Is Waiting" features the only guitar solo on the record, and it's Al himself plunking away. (One wonders how Teenie felt about that!) It's an ominous, murky song, not exactly inviting or uplifting. For Al Green it was a look into the future.

But Al wasn't quite there yet. One of the few revealing things he'd later state in his book was that looking back, Green felt he sang "Jesus Is Waiting" with a "fervor that I could only remember once knowing. I could recite the words of repentance, the formula for forgiveness, and the attitude of saving grace. But behind that knowledge was spiritual ignorance."

❖

Sometime in the summer of 1973* Green appeared at the Cow Palace in San Francisco with Smokey Robinson. That same night he played a midnight show at Disneyland, the Disney people providing a jet for a quick getaway to Anaheim. There was his entourage, "doing 525 miles per hour, on a Disney jet . . . drinking champagne, smoking a little jay." They played the show at Disneyland; everything was business as usual. Al had flown his paramour Laura Lee out from Detroit, but after the show he claimed fatigue and returned to his room at the Coach N' Four Motel alone. Green was a bit haunted by the sky-high party he'd enjoyed on the way down. "I got scared. We were up there . . . at night, drinking champagne, flying right across the Rocky Mountains. And if our little asses had hit one of those peaks, we would have been out of this world!" Somehow he drifted off to sleep.

At four-thirty that morning, Green awoke with a jolt. Suddenly he was a new and different man: "I was singing and rejoicing! I was changing my personality!" Feelings surged through him "like a charge of electricity." Alone in the room, he found himself testifying. "I'm saying, 'Thank you, Jesus! Hallelujah! Praise God!' I never said that before." The spirit had gotten its hooks into Al.

"Then I got embarrassed because my daddy came into the room, and I couldn't stop saying, 'Thank you, Jesus!'" Green ran into the bathroom and, in an attempt to silence the message, stuffed a wet towel into his mouth. "I heard this voice say, 'Are you ashamed of me?'" There, in a hotel bathroom, the words of God got to Al. "My daddy asked me what's the matter. I says, 'Look at my hands . . . look at my feet . . . they're *glowing*. Can't you see it?' That was amazing."

---

* Even though 1973 is the year Green always references when telling this story, I strongly suspect the date might have been a year earlier. The only Cow Palace date I could find with both Green and Robinson is June 16, 1972. (Ben Fong-Torres in *Rolling Stone* reported that Green was "still second-billed at the major big auditorium concerts" at the time and that he "casually stole the audience of 14,000 away from a retiring Smokey Robinson.") *The Disneyland Book of Lists* states that the only year Al Green played Disneyland was 1972. This would put his June 17 conversion happening right when "I'm Still in Love with You" was released. It should be noted that sometime before the Disneyland awakening, a mysterious entity had placed a Bible in Green's hands after one of his concerts. He told Robert Mugge that this person had told him, "I got a book I want you to read . . . it's a Bible." At the time, Al was a little "happy, a little high—joints. Kind of loose." This person made Green promise that he would read it. "I sat down, I started to read it . . . I read it all night. It was so interesting [that] from that day to this day, I'm still readin' it." Although Al had grown up steeped in religion, perhaps he'd never actually read the Bible.

By now Laura Lee was present, knocking on the bathroom door and asking him what was wrong. "I come out there cryin'—'No I am *not* ashamed. I'm not ashamed and I never *will* be ashamed!'" Overcome by what was happening to him, Green charged out into the hotel corridor. "I went to knocking on people's doors . . . some white people down the hall. I told 'em I was born again." The nonplussed guest who answered the door told his wife to call security. When they arrived, Al shook their hands and proudly told them that he'd been born-again. "I was feelin' so good, I tried to keep that feeling for as long as I could," Green said.

Amid all the euphoria, something was demanded of Al Green. Al was reminded that in March 1969 he'd asked the Lord to make him a superstar, and now "He said to me, 'I kept my side of the bargain—what about you?'" God was calling in his chits. This was an obligation Al would have to face or pay the price. Green claimed that three other soul music superstars had been asked to heed the call, and had met terrible fates once they refused (I believe two of them are Jackie Wilson, who collapsed onstage in 1975 and spent nine years in a coma before dying, and Philippe Wynne, lead singer of the Spinners, who died onstage of a heart attack in 1984). How exactly Al knew this, I do not know. Presumably the information came from above. The bottom line: God was asking Green to abandon his career and work for Him.

God on one side; weed, women, and song on the other. It was a dilemma that tormented Al. (Perhaps it still does.) Green had a meeting with his parents at his office on Winchester Road. "We sat down and talked about it . . . I said, 'I don't know what to do. I'm confused, I'm totally confused.'" When his father asked what was wrong, Al reiterated once more that he'd been born-again. This moved the man who'd once thrown his son out of the house for listening to Jackie Wilson. "He said, 'Well, thank God' . . . he went into tears. My mother says, 'Hallelujah! Thank God!'" Cora started crying too. "I said, 'Y'all are not much help. I gotta figure out what to do! I mean I've got a million dollar career goin' here—and I'm tellin' folks they need to be born again!'" Out of nowhere, Green would start quoting scriptures, talking in tongues. Impulses that would soon creep into his live performances, wreaking havoc with his career.

Being born-again was by far the biggest event of Al Green's existence. The fact that it occurred at Disneyland—well, that was no more outrageous than the rest of Green's life. There was Al before his conversion, and there was Al after. "I've never been the same since that night," he's said over and over. Yet he couldn't bring himself to fully commit to the spiritual realm. "I wasn't ready. I was a superstar, and I didn't want to change . . . drinking champagne, plenty of chicks, plenty of money, gold records on the wall." In his heart, however, Green realized "I was going back on my word." It certainly haunted him. "I ran for three years, trying to pretend, but I couldn't get away."

❖

The TV performances of Al Green and the Enterprise Orchestra from 1973 to 1974 (culminating in the wild *Midnight Special* appearance in early October 1974) are a thing to behold. His band is locked in tight (not to mention starting to show their sartorial flair), and they follow Al's every whimsical tangent. This bunch loved to play a hard, heavy groove, and it afforded Green the opportunity to unleash that grittier vocal style Willie had talked him out of. It's something to see. No wonder Al said in the press at the time that the Enterprise Orchestra "play my music perfectly." (Sadly, I know of no live recordings from this period, only a handful of TV appearances.)

Green performed a three-song set at Bananafish Garden in Queens, New York, on February 21, 1973, that was broadcast a month later on the *In Concert* TV show. Unfortunately, only audio has surfaced thus far, which is particularly disappointing as this features the only contemporaneous performance of "Simply Beautiful." Green manages to duplicate the intimacy of the studio recording right down to the "baby" repetitions. (Oddly, they also perform "Call Me" sans any backing vocals; thus it's practically chorusless.)

On March 17, 1973, Green returned to *Soul Train* to perform "You Ought to Be with Me," "For the Good Times," and "Love and Happiness," finally appearing on the show with a live band, and they are on fire. Host Don Cornelius sports a green suit to "show how much respect I have for the messiah," and during the requisite audience Q&A one of the *Soul Train* dancers is so transfixed by Al's presence she's rendered speechless. A slow-death "For the Good Times" is particularly riveting, with Green singing with utter conviction. (Al also hosted *Midnight Special* on August 3, 1973, singing five songs, but aside from a superb rendition of "Call Me," the rest has yet to resurface.)

Everywhere Al Green went, audiences came unglued. Industry veteran Bill Bentley saw Green in San Antonio in 1973 and watched as the crowd went "completely insane. The place exploded for an hour and a half, the energy never went down, every song killed. Women were running to the front of the stage in droves, throwing their panties onstage. They just couldn't help themselves."

August 31 was declared Al Green Day in Memphis. "Keys to city in pocket, Al Green signals from his Rolls-Royce for motorcade to begin," read the picture caption in the *Commercial Appeal*. The next day he headlined a benefit concert at Mid-South Coliseum for local police community centers that drew 10,000 people. Green, who came onstage to "screams and deafening applause . . . opened his set with a customary red rose in his hand." (The article also mentions that Laura Lee opened the show and sang one of her Al-inspired torch songs, "Since I Fell for You.")

Then–Pop Tunes employee David Less attended the show and reported that Green "had complete control of that audience. If he'd have told 'em to drink poison lemonade, they would've done it. He had that charisma. I've never seen anybody control an audience like he did, to this day. He'd point up to people in the rafters and they'd swoon, fallin' out of their seats."

At one point the crowd got so unruly house lights came up and four or five security cops tried to restore order. Al, who was singing "I Can't Get Next to You," told the crowd, "If I was you I would let *nothin'* stop you from getting next to me." At which point the audience surged to the front of the stage. To get Al out of there "they had to pick him up and carry him over the crowd," said Less.

❖

Released in November 1973, Green's next single, "Livin' for You," was a sign the formula was weakening. The trick here is withholding the chorus until the climax of the song; unfortunately the melody is weak and the sentiment banal. It was the first single since "Let's Stay Together" that didn't crack the Top Ten. "Let's Get Married" came next in March 1974 and was a far more memorable affair, particularly the off-the-cuff and highly amusing "might as well" aside Green tosses into the lyric—but this was the first time one of his songs was realized far better live by the Enterprise Orchestra.

The *Livin' for You* album appeared in December 1973. A graveyard-slow "Unchained Melody" astonishes in the way it expands and contracts— listen to the deft way Al dovetails with the background vocals on the chorus, and the polyrhythm Bulldog keeps on the hi-hat (which is as loud as

Al!). "Sweet Sixteen," Al's unashamed paean to underage love (as well as exploring the jealousies attached), is another number better heard live. The egregious "Beware" is nothing but a paranoid vamp that seems to suggest no one is to be trusted but King Al himself, particularly if you're sharing his bed. Green's crude acoustic might have driven "Jesus Is Waiting," but here it's just making a lackluster racket—for over eight minutes (a fifteen-minute-plus version also exists).

There is something soft around the edges about this particular collection of songs. A new seriousness has crept into the lyrics—Green is singing of God, marriage, and the simple love of "home"—yet there's a distinct lack of energy and excitement compared to what came before. Too often the strings are just slathered on without a care, and the arrangements seem hasty, relying on what were by now old tricks. Even the cover—a cartoonish drawing of a towering Al being offered a rose by an outstretched female hand—reveals a lapse in taste due to its thrift-store folk art execution (Green reportedly hated it).

The quality control would erode drastically on the next record as well. The reasons for this were easily understandable. Since 1971's "Tired of Being Alone" Green and company had put out nine singles and five albums in three years. They were exhausting a sound, and maybe their audience. And then there was Al. His inner conflicts were becoming a serious distraction. With the constant touring there wasn't the luxury of getting it just right. "We didn't really take enough time on the last two albums at all," Willie admitted in 1976. "We just had to catch Al whenever we could, and that meant doing just three or four takes on some of the tunes—whereas years ago we'd do eighty or ninety on one tune alone."

❖

On April 6, 1974, Green and the Enterprise Orchestra returned to *Soul Train*. Don Cornelius once more genuflected to the king in his introduction, raving about Green's record sales, proclaiming Al "the closest the music business has come to having its own messiah."

This was not the dapper, sexy star of the recent past, but an extremely tentative Al, his arm in a sling and wearing a yellow-pants/gray-vest ensemble that might not have made it to the dry cleaner.* Al looks like he just fell out of bed.

---

* Apparently paying tribute to this Al Green performance, in 1991 Big Daddy Kane wore an arm sling (despite having no injury) in Heavy D's video for "Don't Curse."

The band lurches right into a slinky "Sweet Sixteen," and without so much as blinking an eye, Green has the audacity to follow it with "Jesus Is Waiting." He introduces the latter with an impassioned reading of the Lord's Prayer. "Lead us not into temptation, but deliver us from evil," he intones, not wasting a chance to preach to the *Soul Train* dancers, who respond in kind. Later in the show, after a tepid "Livin' for You," Green and the band smoke "Here I Am." Al, singing with a single red rose clutched tight to his face, looks as crazed as a late-period Louis Wain cat. This was one of those performances where Green, as Robert Palmer has written, "commands a power so intense it can almost be frightening."

About that cast on Al's arm—that "deliver us from evil" plea might've been more heartfelt than usual. During the *Soul Train* Q&A he says he "fractured it in Milwaukee" getting in a car trying to escape fans. In her book Linda Wills says Green claimed he injured it going through a revolving door. Members of the band have a story about a broken arm—perhaps the same one or perhaps apocryphal—that is nevertheless familiar to most of the musicians who have played for him.

Green had been playing a string of theaters-in-the-round. He and the Enterprise Orchestra toured "a whole circuit of them for about two or three years," said Buddy Jarrett. The people who ran them were tough customers. "Gangsters," said Jarrett.

According to Jarrett, Green and company were in Fort Lauderdale, about to play one of these theaters, when "Al said, 'I don't feel good, I don't feel like singin' tonight.'" After hearing this, one of the thugs in charge waltzed Green into the dressing room. "Al got a little chesty," said Roland Jones. "They took somebody to see his ass."

As Jarrett recalled, "the largest human I've ever seen" came a-knocking on Al's dressing room door. The goon in question "had a suit on, he didn't smile or nothing. He looked so hard, man, like a walking gold ingot." This imposing individual—whom they'd never encountered before—entered the dressing room. After a bit of time, he came out and left.

"Ten minutes later, here comes a man with a little satchel," said Jarrett. "The doctor." He too knocked on the door and went in. Then he came out and left. "We're standing there goin', 'What the hell's goin' on?'" According to Jarrett, these gangsters "told us, 'Y'all WILL play tonight.'" They went to the stage to tune up. When Al arrived, "his arm was in a cast."

Jarrett was told that the first dressing-room visitor "went in there and broke Al's arm for him—'You don't wanna sing? Next it will be your fuckin' neck.'" After that came the doctor. "They set Al's arm," said Jarrett. Any ambivalence about performing was gone, for that night "Al sung like a bird." Roland Jones was there and corroborated the tale. "Those gangsters *made* him go onstage. They were badass guys." According to Jones, that's when Al "started carryin' a weapon."*

❖

On September 8, 1974, Tito Jackson and his wife hosted a star-studded party for Green, who was opening a five-night stand at the Universal Amphitheatre the next day. All the Jacksons were there, as were various luminaries from the music world. "Both Green and Michael Jackson were seen on the dance floor teaching rock superstar David Bowie how to do the robot," went the report in *Right On!* magazine. Photos were taken of Green and Bowie conversing together in their alien tongues (Al: "I just said, 'Hey, man, I like your music.' He said, 'I like yours, too.' We just kind of looked at each other like bandy deers. There wasn't really a whole lot to say").

That same month "Sha-La-La (Make Me Happy)" was released, Al's first Top 10 single in a year. One of the lightest, happiest performances in the Green canon, it begins with joyful, swirling strings, a smoky chuckle from Al embedded within. It's a beautiful melody, and the supergroove's lit up by Charles's shimmering organ, not to mention Bulldog's big-roll-into-a-cymbal-crash (practically unheard of thus far on an Al Green record) as well as the additional ratchet-like percussion provided by a Latin American instrument called a guiro, a hollowed-out gourd you rake with a wand, that is also heard on "Gimme Shelter" and Tone Loc's "Wild Thing." Oddly, the background parts in the song repeat twice on the verse and don't come back. Pop music may be built on repetition, but Willie loved to throw an occasional curveball.

The exquisitely titled *Al Green Explores Your Mind* came out that October. Attrition had begun to set in, because the album is for the most part forgettable filler. You know the barrel's being scraped when the that's-our-crazy-life-on-the-road song makes an appearance, although the slyly rhythmic "One Nite Stand" is amusing enough. "Hangin' On" almost

---

* According to Charles Hodges, Green put rumors of any organized crime connections to good use during a heated band meeting called because his band had threatened not to play a particular show unless they were paid first. Hodges claims Al told them, "My stuff is syndicated. My music is syndicated. You gonna play."

gets there but for the pluck-a-doodle-doo strings. One wonders if they double-timed the generic "Stay with Me Forever" merely out of boredom.

The first three songs, though, kill. There's "Sha-La-La (Make Me Happy)" and the beautifully sung "God Blessed Our Love," which adds ace Hi songwriter Earl Randle to Green's arsenal for the first time. The result is a gospel-tinged ballad "with the simplicity and feeling of a[n Otis] Redding ballad and an accompaniment which is understated and elegant in the best Memphis tradition," wrote Robert Palmer. Most electrifying of all was "Take Me to the River."

❖

Teenie had started the song during a chilly tour stop in Boston playing behind Ann Peebles. As he explained to Jason Gross, Hodges was gazing at the snow and "thinking about being baptized." According to Teenie, Ann contributed "the melody and the lines 'I don't know why I love you like I do / With all the changes you put me through.'" (She never got a credit on the finished song.) Teenie then turned to Syl Johnson. "He wanted me to help him write the song and I drug my feet," he recalled. "Al Green got with Teenie," who "put some beautiful lyrics to it."

Green maintains he came up with the chorus and that it was inspired by a minister who Al says had a major influence on his preaching style, Reverend James Turner. "He was a teacher of mine. He was just so phenomenal, man." Turner could get in front of his congregation, pick just about any subject, "and man, he could preach a whole sensible text . . . with the joy of the Lord in the room. I just thought that was amazing. That's why I wrote 'Take Me to the River.' Because I was going to see James Turner in a baptismal that he was having in Arkansas."

Al witnessed the preacher wade into the water of the Saint Francis River with members of his church. "And I'm goin', 'Oh God, there's bottles, there's trash, there's tin cans, there's turtles, there's snakes, there's everything in this water out here." Green watched from the bank amazed as Turner performed the baptism in water that was "chest-deep. . . . After seein' this and really enjoyin' it I wrote, 'Take me to the river, wash me down, cleanse my soul, put my feet on the ground.' And that's *all* I wrote. All this about the cigarettes and the sixteen candles? That's Teenie."

When it came to recording "Take Me to the River," it was first offered to Syl Johnson. He was in Europe when Willie Mitchell rang. "He said, 'Al wrote a song for you . . . it's a *bad* song, man.'" (Perhaps it was not the best time to be pitching Syl Johnson an Al Green song. That very day Syl had been interviewed by *Blues and Soul* editor John Abbey, who told Johnson not only that his previous work for Twinight was far better than his current Hi material, but that he'd now become "a poor man's Al Green.") Hi Rhythm had already cut a track, and when Johnson got back to Memphis a demo tape of the song was waiting. His then-wife, present when he listened to it, wrote across a piece of paper "total smash." Had it not been for that, Syl admits, "I might not have cut that one . . . I was a little jealous of Al Green at the time."*

Although Syl graciously acknowledges Green's talent, the singer was a source of torment for him. "I was always standing in the shadows of Al Green at Hi," a feeling other artists on the label may have been reluctant to express. For Johnson, things happened that served to salt the wound. When Syl was sent to New York City to do a showcase, Willie let him know at the last minute that Al would also be backed by his band ("I said, 'If they play for him, they get paid double'").

On that same trip Johnson saw a cassette of his 1975 *Total Explosion* album for the first time at the local office of his label. The crazy cover photograph shows a pile of smoking dynamite with a small picture of Syl strapped on top of it. It's starting to detonate as a white hand lurks in the background, fingers on the detonator, "ready to blow my damn head off," said Syl, still angry about it forty years later. "This is the motherfuckin' album cover?" he said to the art director who showed it to him. "I threw the cassette out the window." Even worse was the lettering of his name, done in bright . . . green. As in Al Green. This particular detail was too much for Johnson to bear. "It's the most despicable cover I've ever seen."

To this day Johnson doesn't own a copy. When a fan showed Syl the *Total Explosion* cover during a 2008 Australian tour he went off. "Fuck this album! The white man is blowing me up." He once more pointed out that suspicious green lettering. "Fuck Al Green . . . this was a conspiracy by *him*."

❖

Nonetheless, Syl Johnson recorded "Take Me to the River"—and had a hit with it (number twenty-six on the pop charts, number seven on R&B). Green's version was never a single yet has become one of the songs most

---

* According to Johnson, Green's song "Rhymes" (also cowritten with Teenie) was offered to him as well. It was a single for O. V. Wright in 1976, not long after Green himself cut it.

identified with him. I think this is due not only to the many cover versions but the anguished content, which crystallizes the conflicts within Al Green most artfully. Green's version is where the sexual and celestial collide head-on. That irresistible opening verse paints a portrait of a manipulative, indifferent (and, referencing his own song from the last album, apparently sixteen-year-old) paramour: "You stole my money and buy cigarettes / And I haven't seen hide nor hair of you yet." (Whenever I think of Al Green lyrics, that first sentence, full of dimestore tragedy and wry humor, pops into my head. Who hasn't been there?)

Turning heavenward, Green demands to know the worth of this love, then asks for deliverance. (God's name is never mentioned in the song; the description of baptism is indelible enough.) Back and forth the number lurches, from the flesh to church and back again. By the time he lets loose with some of the most agonized, painful screams he's ever unleashed in a studio, Al's torment is palpable; this is deathly serious business to him. "Wash me in the water" he pleads over and over, clearly desperate to be free. "It's almost a gospel song," was Willie's astute assessment. Yes—almost. Al would revisit the same subject in 1977 on the song "Belle," but by that time there's little conflict. Green knows where his heart (and soul) belongs.

It's interesting to compare Johnson's version (which came out in 1975) with Green's. Syl's version begins with a blast of harmonica ("I hadn't been playing long," said Johnson, who'd been listening to Junior Wells at the time) and charges out of the gate in hard 4/4 time that never relents. There are no strings, no touch of guiro percussion. Green's version benefits from a spookier, more mysterious feel. It begins with Howard doing that chugging train rhythm on the rim and snare as the guitar, bass, and strings sneak in.* Al does a classic, old-timey spoken intro dedicating the song to Little Junior Parker, the man who brought us "Mystery Train" (not to mention a version of "Funny How Time Slips Away" that predates Green's) and a distant cousin of Al's. All of this sets the stage for a subtler, more complex reading of the song.**

---

* Known to be a quick study, Leroy Hodges had trouble with the bass line. "All my parts I did by myself—all but one song: 'Take Me to the River.' I couldn't find the pattern. I was doin' somethin', but it wasn't fitting. Willie and Teenie, they showed me."

** According to what Teenie Hodges told Bill Dahl, the dedication came about due to he and Al bumping into Parker at Poplar Tunes. Hodges knew Parker, introduced him to Green—who'd never met him—and there at the record store the pair played him Al's cover of "Driving Wheel." "Junior listened to it, and he thanked us," said Teenie. "Take Me to the River" came shortly thereafter.

There's more variation in the drumming, and all sorts of deft touches on the guitar not present in Syl's, during which you only really hear those violent jerks on the guitar neck also present on Green's version. On his the horns play the melody, then hand it off to the strings as they in turn provide dramatic emphasis on top of the band. Once again, Willie doesn't follow expected pop logic—Al sings one line of the second chorus, one line and some ad-libbing on the third, the music reinforcing the unheard chorus in your head. And Al's singing goes from a whisper to a scream. While Syl's version packs a wallop, Green's is far more dynamic.

"Take Me to the River" inspired a legion of cover versions, the most familiar being the one by the Talking Heads, which hit number twenty-six on the pop charts in 1979. ("More money for Mr. Green's Full Gospel Tabernacle Church," said a mocking David Byrne. "All praise the mighty spurtin' Jesus.")

To paraphrase Syl, fuck the Talking Heads. Unlike, say, Devo's complete demolition of "(I Can't Get No) Satisfaction," I don't think this deconstruction has aged particularly well—aiming for the cranium, not the soul, its art-school pretension feels overthought, gimmicky, and trivial, resulting in a novelty not exactly worlds away from Pat Boone's flat-footed Little Richard covers. The groove's all right, but the singer sinks the ship, and watching contemporaneous live performances featuring Byrne's un-funky-white-man shtick makes me embarrassed for the race, and not in an ironic way. (Now, both Green and Teenie have expressed admiration for this interpretation. It also had to make them a pile of loot.)

More amusing (though equally annoying) is the cover by the animatronic wall-hanging fish star of 2000, Big Mouth Billy Bass, which itself was utilized for a recurring plot point on the episode *The Sopranos* where Big Pussy meets his demise. Teenie Hodges informed writer Andria Lisle that "his biggest payday hasn't come from an Al Green session but a singing plastic fish."

❖

On October 4 Al Green was the only guest on the *Midnight Special* TV show, and the result is a high-water mark in pop culture. Dressed all-white in a quilted tux jacket (sans tails) dotted with rhinestones, silk pants, glittery platforms, and no shirt, this is Green as sweaty sex God. Looking higher than a kite and feeling real, real, good, he dances, prances, and sings his ass off. This is the performance where he purrs "I want to get to *know* you" to the women pressed hungrily against the stage. The right whisper from Green and panties throughout the venue would've dropped.

Outrageous, this entire spectacle. Surrounded by bodyguards, Al charges through the crowd like a half-naked toreador entering the arena. What comes next is one long Dionysian ramble. A lurid, snaky "Sweet Sixteen" and an unbelievably intense rendition of "Here I Am," which offers proof that this song stirs up something unholy in Al. By the time he gets to the "dark-end street" passage, he seems on the verge of leaving reality altogether (and how about that funky, lowdown guitar riff Larry Lee tacks onto the end?). The performance of "Let's Get Married" kicks the studio version up the block, and Green slips a hip bit of JJ Cale's "After Midnight" into the groove (unfortunately—very unfortunately—the show cuts to commercial).*

These are long vampy versions of these songs, and boy, is the band on top of it. Everybody seems plugged into the same socket. (They couldn't look more formidable either—as if they'd just ridden into a Sergio Leone western.) Dancing, doing very little singing at times, Al's lost in the music, off in his own groovy world. There are moments where watching him seems almost an intrusion. "Sometimes onstage I forget I'm performing, and I get so hung up, I have to apologize to the audience," he's said. "I forget about the people, and get so much into the song I go much further ahead mentally than where I am vocally. I go down on my knees and just moan . . . I forget how good I'm supposed to look—I just get ugly and soulful. Sometimes I throw my coat on the floor. Singing just winds me up."

Green summed it all up during a ridiculous interview segment for the show done out in nature somewhere. Standing in front of the flowers, he actually explains his music—and rather succinctly, in a roundabout way (if you can live with that contradiction). "Cultivating something that's *real,*" muses Al. "In reference to my singing, that is the whole basis of conversation . . . what my thing is all about, because I am a believer in *photosynthesis*—the idea of projection, of things not yet seen, like a flower blooming." Al then picks a flower for emphasis.

❖

That fall of 1974 Al Green was at the top of his game. Perhaps the hits weren't quite as plentiful, but he could've gone on for years filling venues and cranking out records. He re-signed to London Records in a deal David

---

* *Al Green Sings the Best of JJ Cale* is an album I'd love to hear.

Gest told *Rolling Stone* was worth "millions upon millions." (Such was the interest in Al at the time, a blind item in the *Jet* gossip column claimed, that an unnamed party was attempting to "peddle tapes concerning the performer's sex life.") And Green was about to star in and score a movie to be shot in the French Quarter of New Orleans called *Mimi*. Based on the opera *La Bohème*, it was to tell the story of a young girl who wants to be a star but finds out she has sickle cell anemia. Melba Moore, Curtis Mayfield, and Linda Hopkins were to costar. "It's a very beautiful love story," Al explained. "It's not about *Superfly* characters, or any pimps, or people sticking needles in their arms . . . this is the kind of movie I'd be proud to take any of my family to see." There was also talk of Green playing Sam Cooke in a biopic. Green had conquered the music business, and Hollywood was next. "I thought my ass was made out of gold," said Al.

Then, just two weeks after his triumphant appearance on *Midnight Special*, a woman named Mary Woodson would die in Al Green's home. And death would be delivered by way of Al's gun.

STRONG AS DEATH

You don't know what it's like to love someone.
—MARY WOODSON TO AL GREEN, SUICIDE NOTE

A .38-caliber Smith & Wesson lay on a heart-shaped bed. Al Green somehow picked the gun up. Having been hit with a boiling pot of gruel, Green was in agony, suffering second-degree burns, which would require a lengthy hospital stay, and he was looking for the person who did this to him.

The Al Green "grits"* story is one of those tales that has bled into pop consciousness. R. Kelly, Wu-Tang Clan, and Usher have all referenced it in songs. Reporters invariably toss Al a question or two about it, which usually provokes some fairy-tale response of how he thought he and Woodson would be together forever: "I loved Mary then and I love Mary now. I'll always love Mary." This is one part of his past Al can't escape. In 1985 Bill Bentley saw Green perform at the Saenger Theatre in New Orleans. At one point in the show, Green left the stage and "walked up the aisle singing, and this woman in the audience just steps towards him and hands him a box of grits," he recalled. "What was she saying—kill her?"

---

* Again, in most press accounts, grits are the culprit, but Green usually insists (although not in his own book) it was Cream of Wheat. He has also said it was Malt-O-Meal, other times that it was just the boiling water used "to fix grits."

It is hard to unearth any concrete information on what exactly transpired between Green and Mary Woodson. The officers attached to the case—William Maley, Dan Jones, Roy C. Nixon, Gerald Proctor, Ben Whitney—are all dead. I had one ex-cop who was close to the players involved look into the matter; after a few e-mails I never heard from him again. When I asked one of the few officers still around, the terse reply was, "Everybody's dead and I wasn't a detective then." With that he hung up. The records department of Shelby County said that since Woodson's death was ruled a suicide, none of the sheriff's reports were kept, as per policy. Despite many inconsistencies, the accepted version of the story is the one told by the only known living participant, the survivor of the attack. As Aliya S. King pointed out in her masterful 2004 *Vibe* article, "Love and Unhappiness,"* what is often forgotten is that a woman lost her life that night—Mary Woodson.

❖

The oldest of seven children, Mary Elizabeth Evans was born August 6, 1945, in Oxford, North Carolina. At the time of her death she was living at 126 King Road in Madison, New Jersey. Married (although separated at the time) with three children, she was working as a dental assistant. She'd also been manager of a Beauty Charm Wigs store. Mary was five foot four, weighed 130 pounds, and loved to hit the Continental Ballroom in Newark to chase after artists. She was a bit of a wild child.

On December 15, 1973, Woodson was arrested in East Orange for "aggravated assault with gun, threat to take own life." She'd shot an unfaithful boyfriend in the foot, nearly overdosed on sleeping pills, and had been seeing a psychiatrist. According to what her sister told Aliya S. King, just months before her death she told family members she wanted to be decked out wearing her favorite red dress in an open casket should she die. Rather ominously, she added, "If I ever kill myself, it's going to be with a gun. And I'm going to put it in my mouth, 'cause I want to make sure there are no mistakes."

Green says he met her during a prison benefit concert in upstate New York. "Mary was there with a lot of other visitors. I said, 'Man, you're *very* beautiful.' She said, 'Thank you'—and walked off!" recalled Al, clearly

---

* The article won King the ASCAP Foundation's Deems Taylor Award for magazine journalism. It is the essential source on Mary Woodson.

taking her indifference as a challenge. (Woodson's relatives maintain he met Mary backstage at a New York City concert.*)

At the time of her death, Green claimed he'd only known Mary since June 1974. Yet pages from her personal date book** suggest she'd known Al since mid-1972. As he'd done with Linda Wills, Green spent hours romancing her on the phone and (much to the consternation of her husband, Raymond) sent roses to her home. Margaret Foxworth remembered Woodson showing up somewhere on the road after Margaret and Al had had a big fight. "She followed us through New Jersey," said Foxworth, who felt Mary was "a stalker."

In his book, Green—who wistfully notes that Woodson was "fond of wearing dusty colors like burnt orange"—says that he was intrigued by the fact that Mary played a bit hard to get and seemed a little strange. "The way she stared off in the distance like she was listening to someone else from very far away . . . added to the mystery."

❖

Mary had come to visit Green for a week ("unexpectedly," he'd tell the police). They had an outing to Overton Park. Mary knew Al had been born-again and predicted his future. "She was the first one who formulated and discussed my having a church and members," said Green, who has referenced this story over and over. "She told me how pleased the Lord would be by it and how wonderful it would be for the people . . . she wanted to be the first usher." Not only that, but Green says Mary made him promise to "dedicate" a seat in the first pew to her. As Green related to Sandra Pointer-Jones, "I kept telling her, 'You're crazy. I'm a rock & roll singer. I sing rhythm & blues! I ain't no preacher and I ain't never gonna be no preacher.'"*** It was at this point Woodson confessed her love for

---

* One of the stranger quotes on the subject came via Third-Person Al in 2009: "You have to be careful. You don't know who these people are. They could be in another relationship and you're just sitting there enjoying life, and there's someone standing at the back of your brain with a semi-automatic. They came to a concert, Al, when you were singing at a New York State prison . . . I met these people in the audience, and I don't know, man. Yeah." To my knowledge the only person in this tale with a gun to their head was Woodson, and, at least according to the law, she was pointing it at herself.

** These are part of the handwriting samples in Woodson's FBI file, which I obtained by a Freedom of Information Act request. The contents haven't been made public until now.

*** Green rarely refers to himself as an R&B singer. "He thinks he's a rock and roll star," said producer Paul Zaleski. "He doesn't call his music soul, he calls it rock and roll."

him. As Al told Robert Mugge, "I said, 'Well, okay, great, then—you love me—I like you, too!'"

Many times Green has professed ignorance that Woodson was married or that she had children. "I never knew any of these things until after the incident happened," he told Mugge. This is contradicted by a January 1975 *Rolling Stone* interview in which Green recounts talking to Mary about her marriage and children, as well as Woodson directly referencing both subjects in her suicide notes to Al in a manner that suggests neither was a secret to Green.

Despite her fortune-telling abilities, Green grew tired of Woodson after three or four days and gave her money for a flight home. Instead Mary checked into a $15-a-night room at the Admiral Benbow Inn at 2201 Winchester Road, not far from Green's office. Mary phoned Al repeatedly, trying to coax him over to room 25. Green didn't go, "because I am angry with her for not going home."

On the fourteenth of October, Woodson and Sue Franks—a twenty-year old secretary of Green's—were busted for marijuana possession for two joints found in Mary's motel room. Green says he was in the studio when the sheriff called, informing him of the arrest and that Mary had dropped Al's name. He bailed her out—$250 courtesy of Al Green Enterprises. He states that Mary came back to Royal with him, quite shaken up. To lift her spirits, Al says he wrote Mary a song—"Sha-La-La (Make Me Happy)." The only problem with this is that Woodson got arrested on October 14 and "Sha-La-La" had entered the charts on September 22.*

On Wednesday the sixteenth, despondent over Green, Woodson took an overdose of pills and had her stomach pumped. "She took twelve pills at her hotel and took a scalpel and split her wrist open," said Green later. Apparently he didn't rush to her side, preferring to have Lieutenant Whitney ("a friend of mine," as Al puts it) keep an eye on Mary.**

Green would spend the next day with Whitney doing promotion for a Memphis event in his honor. In a reprise of the previous year, Friday the eighteenth was to be declared Al Green Day, and Al was scheduled to receive an award from the mayor, attend a luncheon, and visit the Shrine School for Crippled Children. That night another benefit concert for the Memphis police was to take place. "Green had flown about the city

---

* Colin Escott dates the recording of the song as August 1, 1974.

** Green has stated that Woodson stayed with Whitney and his wife and son, Ben III, but his son points out his parents were divorced and he only met Mary once briefly, as described here.

accompanied by Lieutenant Whitney in the WDIA weather-traffic helicopter, setting down in a number of places to sign autographs," reported
the *Baltimore Afro-American.*

❖

That night, Thursday the seventeenth, Green was at Royal Studios with
Hi Rhythm cutting a new song called "Strong as Death (Sweet as Love),"
a haunting ballad with a touch of vibes that more than lived up to its unnerving title.* While Al was there, Officer Whitney called to report Mary
was doing fine but that she wanted to see him, so Green invited them
to the studio. Earlier that day, Whitney's son, Ben III, had come home
from school to find his father entertaining a visitor. "My dad was in the
den talking to this lady, and he introduced her as 'Mr. Green's friend'—I
said hello and went on doing my eleven-year-old kid stuff." His father
soon called him back in "and said, 'Son, I want you to go down to Top's
Bar-B-Q.' So I just got on my bike, rode down, came back, and I sat and
ate barbecue with my dad and this lady."

Charles Hodges remembered the moment Mary Woodson walked into
the studio. "For some reason, everybody stopped at my organ stoop. She
came in and sat down beside me. We just clicked for some reason. She'd
left her husband and kids to go with Al—stars in her eyes. When she told
me what she'd done, I said, 'Why did you do that? Al Green is *a star*! Girls
gonna be in Al's face as long as he's out there! Why would you leave your
family?'" Woodson started to cry. Mary "had made a mistake. She had got
with Al."

To make matters worse, Green's ex Laura Lee showed up at the studio
and didn't cotton to Mary's presence. "A big argument come up and we
couldn't get any work done," said Charles. "Willie finally comes back and
says, 'Girls, this ain't gonna happen. We're not gonna cut this tonight, we
gotta come back tomorrow.'" Hodges said good-bye to Mary on the way
out. "I hugged her and told her, 'I'll pray for you, God bless you, but you
need to go home.'"

Green said Woodson informed him "she had no money and no place
to go." (At that moment, Mary had a room at the Memphis Airport Sheraton Inn.) Al told her she could stay at his house that night—provided she

---

* Apparently this was recorded for the never-to-be-released movie *Mimi*, which Green was
supposed to start shooting in New Orleans the following week. David Gest remembers them
also cutting the mediocre Green-written title track that night. "Mimi" went unreleased until
Hi UK put it out in 1989.

didn't try "any of that stupid mess," that is, killing herself—and that he'd get her an airplane ticket home the next day. They got in the car to leave. In Green's entourage was yet another woman—a twenty-one-year-old Delta flight attendant named Carlotta Williams. Apparently she was the primary female on Al's mind at the time, at least as far as the ride home. "This put the first party in the back seat," Green recalled in an interview a few months later, coldly referring to Mary.

❖

Back at Green's house, Al and Mary sat down for a talk. In most reports he says Woodson asked to marry him; in his book he states that she only inquired if he'd ever thought of getting married. Al told her no. (Speaking to *Rolling Stone* in 1975, he added a devastating detail: Mary told him that if she couldn't have him, she'd take her life. Green said he didn't believe her, even though she'd just attempted it a day before.) While Woodson was heating some water on the stove, Al retired to his bedroom. Right before that, he says they embraced briefly. "I would never do anything to hurt you, Al," she told him.

Green was in his bathroom and, according to his statements to the police, "just getting out of the tub" (in his book he says he was brushing his teeth; elsewhere he says he was taking a shower) when Woodson barged in. Whatever the case, he was barely clothed. "All of a sudden here comes someone with a cooking pot, in a rage." It was Mary, a bubbling cauldron in her hand. She poured the steaming sludge over Green's bare back and arms, then fled to another part of the house. Al relived the moment for Mugge: "I'm in total pain. And shock . . . I reach back and I got two fingers full of skin . . . I've got these big boils on my skin."

Shrieking in agony, it was then that Green says he ran to another bedroom where Carlotta was staying. She helped him into the shower to wash the porridge off his back—a mistake, as his skin went with it. Green describes what happened next: "I'm screaming and the next thing I hear is a shot fired and someone hit the floor."* Afraid for their lives, the pair moved furniture in front of the door. "Green and Mrs. Williams said they barricaded themselves in a bedroom for 45 minutes after hearing the

---

* There is some confusion as to how many shots there were. In the first known newspaper report, Captain William Maley said the gun next to Woodson's body had been fired three times and that bullets were removed from "a wall and couch." Subsequent reports say Green and Williams heard two shots.

shots," said news reports. Carlotta gave Al some "nerve pills" to calm him down.

Finally, hearing nothing more, they ventured out of the room. Despite his serious condition, Green picked up his .38 and the pair "retraced Green's steps."

In a bedroom in the southwest corner of the house* they found Woodson's body. A second gun—a .38 Rossi also belonging to Green—lay on the floor. As Williams cautioned that Mary might be playing possum, Al threw the Rossi onto a nearby bed, then checked Woodson for a pulse. There wasn't any. Green put the gun back. "I'm sayin', 'Oh, my God, what in the world, call the police.' [Carlotta] said, 'But this is crazy.' I said, 'Call the police—*just call the police.*'" It was approximately 2:15 a.m. on Friday, October 18. "I felt betrayed," Green told Sandra Pointer-Jones in 2003. "She done tried to get out of it easy, and now I gotta deal with this! Not that I'm guilty about anything because I wasn't even in the room." Despite Green's supposed pleas, authorities would not be alerted to Mary Woodson's death for another hour and forty-two minutes.

In his book, Green also maintains that his bodyguards—who he says were there the entire time, although they are never mentioned in contemporaneous reports—were "pounding down the hall" as they found the body.** They hadn't heard Green's screams? Or the shots?

Green and Williams went downstairs, where Al got on the phone, calling his brother Bill and secretary Cheryl Hodges (no relation to the Hi Rhythm Hodges). Lieutenant Whitney was contacted by "Green's relatives" around 2:20 a.m. and arrived on the scene with Al's father. When Whitney realized that authorities had not been notified, a call was finally made at 3:57 a.m. "Sergeant J.R. Roberts said deputies received a call that Green was en route to the hospital and that a woman was dead in his plush home," went the news report.

A handwritten suicide note was found in Mary's purse. According to what Green had said to the authorities, Woodson had told him it was "him or nothing."

❖

---

* In some versions of the story Green appears to put her death in a different location. In his book, the caption for a photograph of himself taken in the living room of his house states that "in this very room a tragedy occurred that would change the direction of my life."

** According to Charles Hodges, when Green left the studio to go home, Haywood "Pick" Anderson was with him. "They left there together that night," he said.

Early that morning Green was admitted to Baptist Hospital with second-degree burns to his back and arms. There in the emergency room he spoke to police, and at 9 a.m. a sample was taken from his hands for a neutron activation test, which detects recent use of a gun (similar samples were taken from Woodson and Williams; all three—even Woodson's—would prove negative).*

Green called his publicist, David Gest, from the hospital. "His voice was shaking," wrote Gest. "All he kept saying was, 'I didn't kill her, I didn't kill her. David, you have to believe me.'" He said exactly the same to Willie Mitchell when he came to Al's hospital room. As Mitchell told Aliya S. King, Green "grabbed my hand. I said, 'Man, did you kill that girl?' He said, 'I didn't kill her.'"

Green said he was in shock at the time. "They tell me the only thing I said for hours was, 'I don't believe it.'" Al's burns were "gruesome," said Gest, who went to visit him in the hospital, found him lying on his stomach, and says, somewhat unbelievably, that Green still "had all these grits sticking to his back. I tried to pull some off and that pulled his skin off all the way to the bone." Green described it thusly: "I'm all burned up. I have egg-sized blisters full of water. . . . So I don't need to go to hell—man, I know what hot is."

Margaret Foxworth, who spent ten days visiting Al in the hospital, still remembers the terror in his eyes. Foxworth said she saw Green at his "most vulnerable" and that she "held him in my arms." Al, who said he lost three layers of skin in the attack, would have the epidermis of a pig grafted onto his body (he remembered saying the Lord's Prayer aloud as he went under the anesthetic for the surgery).

Those who have seen his scars say they are extreme. While in the hospital, Foxworth described his burned skin as "pork rinds. He was in so much pain." In regard to the incident itself, Foxworth says she was "glad I wasn't there because [Woodson] had it in for me. Only thing Al said was, 'Baby, I am so glad that you are here.' 'Cause she was after me too."**

What Woodson had done was "torment to me," said Green in 2016. "Now, I wasn't sad about anything except what she had done to *me*. My

---

* In his book, Green states he took a lie detector test. It is the only place I've seen this mentioned.

** When asked what she knew about what actually happened that night, Foxworth grew vague. "I can't say too much . . . I mean, I know stuff, but I can't say. And I'm only saying that because of the scenario and how I know people and circumstances and what a person is capable of and how a person is." Was she talking about Al or Mary? I can't tell you.

Dad came to the hospital. I said, 'Is this true? Is this whole happening true?' He says, 'Well, I'm afraid it is, Al.'

"I had to just try to go on. There's nothing that's gonna stop you or fail you, except when you decide, 'Hey, man, that's it. I can't do no more.'" That wasn't Al Green.

❖

Word traveled fast among Green's inner circle. Charles Hodges recalled that at "about three forty or four in the morning, Willie called me—'Hey Charles, man, sorry for waking you up, but you know the girl that come see Al tonight? That girl is dead and Al is in the hospital.' I said, '*What*? Oh, Lord have mercy.' I never asked Al about what happened or nothing." Band member Buddy Jarrett says that he got a call in the wee hours from Al's bodyguard Haywood "Pick" Anderson, who told him, "Man, that crazy bitch Al picked up? She done thrown some grits on him, scarred his back all up and he's gotta go to the hospital." (Strangely, Jarrett said Woodson's death was not mentioned in the call.) Hi background singer Donna Rhodes found out from hearing it on the news. "We never knew what to believe," she said. Once Green recovered and was back in the studio, "nothing was ever said about it."

The tragedy had made headlines all over the country by that Saturday. JILTED LOVER BURNS AL GREEN, KILLS SELF screamed the *Baltimore Afro-American*. WOMAN SHOT DEAD IN AL GREEN'S HOME; HE TELLS CONFLICTING STORIES; FACES FBI PROBE—NAKED STAR HIT WITH A POT OF GRITS blasted the *New York Amsterdam News*. Jim Cole wrote the first in-depth local account of what happened for the *Commercial Appeal* on the nineteenth. The story was so convoluted that Cole felt a graphic—showing the floor plan of the house and the who, what, when, and where—might help. "It became such a huge mess that we just scrapped the whole idea. The way it all unfolded was so confusing . . . there were so many conflicting and contradictory stories."

Reporters showing up at Green's home couldn't get past the electrified fence surrounding the place, although one noted seeing a dog "said to be Green's" that was "was running about the yards with what appeared to be bloodstains on its back and ears." Down in front of City Hall, the marching band from Booker T. Washington High School waited over an hour before learning that Al Green Day had been called off. No award from the mayor would be given to Green, although he went ahead and gave Susan Hudson, a country singer scheduled to perform alongside Green at the now-cancelled benefit that night, a key to the city.

Former professional baseball player Captain William Maley headed up the investigation for the Shelby County Sheriff's Department, which was now "solely in charge of the investigation," according to wire reports. "Evidence collected from the house included a toilet seat, a machete, the head of a hammer, a shotgun, and a bullet removed from a wall," said a wire report. "After we complete the investigation, the facts will be presented to the Shelby County attorney general, and he will decide then whether it will go before a grand jury," said Maley. On the nineteenth, a day after the incident, Inspector Dan Jones told the press, "We've got enough evidence to where we can call it a suicide." According to James Cole, "Both of these guys were old-school detectives," and, despite what was being said publicly, "from the get-go they were suspicious . . . the stories just didn't add up."

In addition to the bullet embedded within Mary, two others were found. Green told police that the slug found in the wall above a love seat in the room where she died came from another gun that accidently went off as he was cleaning it two weeks before (that slug did not match the others). Another copper-jacketed bullet was located lying in the hallway next to the room where Woodson was found. FBI tests would indicate it came from the same .38 that killed her). Captain Maley declared this the result of a "courage shot" by Mary. "Frequently suicide victims will fire off a round to build up their courage and see if the gun is working. The second shot is the one they mean for themselves."

At 8:25 a.m. on the nineteenth, County Medical Examiner Jerry T. Francisco performed an autopsy,* noting the "contact gunshot wound" above the right ear and the "multiple healing incision/lacerations, left and right wrists" from her suicide attempt that Wednesday. Medical Examiner James Bell—who assisted with the autopsy—notified the sheriff's office at 1 p.m. that day. Woodson's death was provisionally ruled a suicide (the final report, which offered the same conclusion, wasn't completed until November 4).

---

* Francisco also performed the autopsy on Martin Luther King Jr. and signed Elvis Presley's death certificate.

On the twentieth, Green released a "taped statement played on some radio stations": "I am deeply hurt because of Mary Woodson's disastrous action—not because of what she did to me, but of taking her own life. It is for that I am more concerned. I pray that God will forgive her and I find it difficult to sleep nights and remove this tragedy from my mind because it was like a nightmare.

"As a human being and as an entertainer, I only hope I can continue on conveying that God-sent message of love and happiness and peace and joy among men and women all over the world. I will never lose this dream because I was sent here to do so. I hope that no one ever has to go through the torment I've gone through. I love you all."

❖

SINGER'S SECRETARY GETS SUICIDE NOTE was the *Memphis Press-Scimitar* headline on October 22. Unbelievably, a *second* suicide note had arrived at the home of Sue Franks the day before.

"Apparently . . . delayed in the mail" and postmarked Tuesday the fifteenth—a day after Woodson and Franks had been arrested on the drug charge, and a day before her first suicide attempt in Memphis—two pages were addressed to Green and one to Franks, all written in red ink. Neither suicide note—nor an envelope with further writing found in Woodson's hotel room—have ever been made public, except for the excerpts from the first note released to the press. Along with the bullets and guns found at the scene, Sheriff Roy C. Nixon* sent the notes off to the FBI on October 31,** along with samples of Woodson's other writings to see if they all matched—which is understandable, as the first note, from the purse, is written in cursive, and the second is crudely printed. They are all written on stationery from the Memphis Airport Sheraton Inn, where Woodson was staying. "It was something very drastic to the mind, it was terrifying to know that someone would actually go to that extent to get a message to you," said Green.

Here for the first time are the complete contents of the notes—including misspellings and bad grammar—save for names that have been redacted by the FBI (if they were revealed via the press, I've included them).

---

* Nixon is the man who gave Elvis his honorary sheriff's badge.

** The subject heading of the sheriff's letter describes the matter this way: "Offense: Homicide," "Victim: Mary Woodson." The "Suspect" listing is blank. "Suicide" is notably absent.

NOTE NUMBER ONE (from purse)

Dear Al,

The more I trust you the more you let me down. I can't take it any more please forgive me I'm sorry [Name redacted] tryed to tell me I had everything to live for and I did as long as it was you. Even my kids wasn't enough because if I'm not happy I can't make anyone else happy. You don't know how deep my love is for you and when you turned your back on me without hereing the facks I just could[n't] take it any more. If you were in trouble I would never leave you no matter what

Please be Good to your self I love you

[Name redacted]* I want everything that belongs to me to go to [name redacted] except my diamond ring on my right hand my wedding band goes to [name redacted] see that she gets it for me.

I['m] not mad just unhappy because I can't be with you

NOTE NUMBER TWO (mailed)

[dated "Mon." on top right]
Dear Al,

I can't stand living without you. I'm sorry I cause you trouble but all I wanted to do was stay with you. I can't explain because you wouldn't beleive me. I love you and by the time you read this I will be dead. I can't live without you & I won't try. I asked [name redacted]** to keep me company because I couldn't get in touch with you. She doesn't [unintelligible] she kept me from doing it this weekend.

I wasn't just waiting for mon. so I could see you.

Forgive me, But you don't know what it's like to love some one &
I'm sorry
I love you
Mary Woodson
I didn't have the money to go & come back or stay and since you don't want me any more this is easier for every one

---

* I assume this is to Al. For images of the notes, see the appendix of this book.

** I assume this is Sue (as in Sue Franks).

NOTE TWO SEPARATE PAGE

Sue,
I'm sorry [name redacted] took our friendship the wrong way.
Thanks for being kind to me.
   Do one last thing for me give this letter to Al.
   When you read this I will be dead

NOTE THREE—ENVELOPE FOUND IN WOODSON'S
HOTEL ROOM

It's not that I'm running from court you said you don't want to see me any
more and I [can't] live with that
   I'm tired of being alone—I want to go back to your home
[other side of envelope]
& be with you
   Where ever you go

❖

What do the notes tell us? That this relationship wasn't such a casual arrangement, at least on Mary's part, and that she was devastated when he "turned his back" on her. It also suggests he was angry over the drug arrest involving his secretary and not a sympathetic, "Sha-La-La"-writing friend afterward. What's also interesting about the notes (and what wasn't pointed out in the news reports at the time) is that they were written before Woodson's suicide attempt on Wednesday.

Why is that important? Well, I hadn't noticed it myself until I found a column called "Recordings and Stuff" buried in the November 2, 1974, issue of the *Pittsburgh Courier,* written by longtime African American journalist and opera singer Earl Calloway (in a 2014 obituary, Jesse Jackson called Calloway "a brilliant writer").

In discussing the Woodson death Calloway quoted an unnamed source who said that Woodson "was treated like a dog, and because of the mental and physical cruelty on the part of Green, Mrs. Woodson was suffering unbearable mental stress and threatened suicide if the relationship didn't improve."

This is the only contemporaneous press report noting Mary's previous pill overdose (and the only one to assign it a date—October 16). The source goes on to say that "the note that Inspector Dan Jones found was not related to the incident that actually caused Mrs. Woodson's death, but was written several days earlier. A suicide attempt that she actually attempted Wednesday." This source hadn't seen the second note, but since it is dated "Mon."—as in Monday the fourteenth—it backs up that notion.*

Woodson's notes were written in advance of a suicide attempt that had already happened, not one that was about to occur, which is how they were described in the press. Was Mary hell-bent on destroying herself and did she just succeed one day later? Perhaps.

There are those—some around Green—who suspect some sort of foul play. Say Woodson did commit suicide, but the circumstances surrounding it might've been embarrassing to Al. Did Mary walk in on something that made her angry? Was Green naked (or close to it) for reasons other than a bath or shower? Why did it take so long to contact the authorities? If bodyguards were in the house, why didn't they hear anything, and why was this not mentioned in news reports? Was there someone else in the house that could've killed Woodson on Green's behalf?

❖

Before she was released from custody, Carlotta Williams gave a statement to the police the afternoon of the nineteenth. To my knowledge it was never quoted in the press, and she was never interviewed about the incident.** After some digging in 2013, I thought I'd found her in Colorado, only to be informed by her daughter Kimberly that she'd passed away in 1998. Thrown off guard, I managed to ask Kimberly if there was more to the story than had been made public. "That's correct," she said, and told me that I needed to speak to her aunts as Carlotta had confided the real details to them.***

---

* "The informer also revealed that while it is surmised Green's interest in women was not sincere, he had all kinds of women around him," wrote Calloway, who noted the source said of the parties involved that "at the time of the grits incident they were extremely high."

** Carlotta did see Green at least one more time in May 1977 when Green gave a concert in Irving, Texas (Williams was living there at the time). As discussed later, Al was arrested the morning after the show, and Carlotta is listed on the police report as a witness.

*** Although she couldn't remember where or when it was, Kimberly also mentioned an inaccurate online story concerning the matter. "My aunt sent them the accurate account and they recanted what they said and replaced it with the actual account of what happened." Despite many searches, I've never been able to find it.

I then spoke briefly to one aunt, who confirmed that there was indeed more to the tale. "I appreciate your interest in telling the truth and telling the whole story," she told me, but I never heard back from her.

Finally in 2016 I spoke to Kimberly once more. Her aunt didn't want to get involved, but she briefly discussed her mother and what her mother had related to her about the death. A single mother, Carlotta "was a very beautiful, classy, upstanding lady," said Kimberly. "Remember the show *Dynasty* and the character that Diahann Carroll played, Dominique? That was what my mom was like. She was a kind, loving person; everybody who met her loved her." Carlotta had first encountered Al shortly before her Memphis visit at a Denver department store, where he was shooting a commercial to promote a local concert.

What Kimberly related matched Green's version of the story. She said her mother was "shocked" by the arrival of Woodson as she was Green's "invited guest," and that Carlotta told her she'd received threats from someone connected to Woodson as they'd suspected Williams had killed Mary.

As far as the aftermath of the event, Kimberly said, "My mom went through a lot psychologically behind it. I know that Al never reached out to her to check on her as far as her well-being, even though she helped him out of a really serious situation."

❖

On October 24, back in Madison, New Jersey, Mary Woodson—despite her wishes—was buried in a closed casket and "a dress she wouldn't be caught dead in," as sister Jo James put it. Green claims Woodson's doctor and mother, Irene Evans, both called him after her death, telling him she'd been under psychiatric care and that he "wasn't to let this affect his career."

On December 17, 1974, the FBI wrote back to the sheriff's office. After studying all the writing samples and comparing them to the notes, "It could not be determined definitely whether Mary Elizabeth Woodson wrote" both suicide notes and the envelope. In particular they noted the envelope's writing as having "more than the usual variations," and due to the lack of cursive samples submitted, they suggested "numerous specimens should be obtained" of Woodson's writing.

"They are not saying she did write them, but they're not saying she didn't, either," Captain Maley told the press. "You got to consider that woman's emotional state before the incident probably distorted her handwriting."

As far as the bullets went, the FBI concluded the bullet in the wall did not come from the other gun Green was carrying after the assault—but it possessed marks similar to those produced by the Rossi .38 that killed Mary Woodson. Unfortunately, "due to mutilation, there are no marks of value remaining in this bullet to identify the weapon from which it was fired."

SUICIDE RULING CLOSES PROBE read the headline of a tiny article in the *Commercial Appeal* on January 24, 1975. "We're satisfied from the advice of the attorney general's office, which reviewed the case, and the medical officer, that the death was a suicide," said Captain Maley.

❖

"For a while I think the finger of suspicion hung over Al," wrote David Gest, who had the thankless task of handling Green's publicity at the time. "In the end it was accepted that Mary committed suicide."

As far as Al Green, Superstar, "the impact on his career was huge," wrote Gest. "His record sales dipped." Not long after Green got out of the hospital, he did his first live show on November 14.* It was the Mid-South Coliseum police benefit he was supposed to do on the day Woodson died. The year before, 10,000 people had attended. This time it was 2,850. BENEFIT SHOW BY AL GREEN PLAYS TO SMALL AUDIENCE, went the *Commercial Appeal* headline. After Woodson's death, "Al Green stopped bein' popular for a long time with black people," said Hi promotion man Willie Bean. "They felt like he did it."

❖

Sometime in the early eighties, bandleader Johnny Brown was alone in a car with Green, driving some desolate stretch of highway, heading home from some no-pay revival appearance. It was late at night. Dark.

"Do you think I killed that girl?" inquired Al.

"I don't know—but I would have," answered Johnny.

"Well, let me tell you something, John—if somebody threw hot grits on your back like what was done to me—the amount of pain I was in,

---

* It appears Al was let out of the hospital to do it. He told Robert Mugge he was released three days later. Syl Johnson tells a story concerning that exit. Mitchell was visiting Green at Baptist Memorial and showed him a Billboard ad for Johnson's new album, *Diamond in the Rough*. Apparently this triggered Al's competitive spirit, because Willie told Syl, "I showed him that ad and that motherfucker went out the back door of that hospital" to get back in the studio and finish his own album.

there was no way in the world I was thinkin' about shootin' or killin' anybody. I just wanted help." Green described how he'd gotten into the shower to cool his wounds, and how the water had washed away his skin.

"The way he described that story, I believed him," said Brown. "I accepted that story from that day forward."

"The Mary Woodson thing is a torment for him," said Margaret Foxworth. "A torment. He can't get over it."

Paul Zaleski, who'd produce Green's gospel records in the eighties, agrees. He says Al "was scared for his life." And that whatever actually happened, "he knew he did wrong."

I asked Charles Hodges if he thought the incident had changed Al. "Yeah, he started singing gospel more. That's the *only* thing it did." While conceding that Green has "showed nothing but love and kindness to me and my family," he added, "I can say this about him . . . he knows the Bible, but do he *go* by it? I doubt it very sincerely. I'm not calling him no devil . . . he's a selfish guy, he's a jealous-hearted guy, and I don't think he knows how to love. I really don't."

I asked Teenie the same question. "No, he would've been Al anyway," he said, laughing. "He was *already* Al."

Not long after Woodson died, Willie Mitchell paid a visit to his and Al's old booking agent, Bettye Berger. Mitchell was "devastated, he walked the floor," said Berger. "I remember him saying, 'I created a monster.'"

❖

And what does Albert Leorns Green think? Who knows. Does Al himself know—any of the Als? He brings up Woodson more frequently in interviews now than he did in the past. Despite his seemingly cavalier attitude toward the relationship when she was alive, as recently as 2016 he claimed that he "had fourteen, fifteen years of looking for Mary in everyone else I saw . . . tryin' to find Mary in everybody I met. Mary Woodson couldn't be found in nobody else. I ultimately moved on because I stopped lookin'. I had to come to the realization with some Christian and spiritual people— 'Al, Mary is gone.'"

One of the most riveting moments in Robert Mugge's 1984 documentary *Gospel According to Al Green* occurs after Al's talked about Mary Woodson and, reprising what he asked his father in the hospital, inquires to nobody in particular "if that actually happened . . . was that really true? . . . I'll sneak off and ask the chief of police today—who's a good friend of mine—I says, 'Did this actually—or was she fakin', was she jokin'?' That's unbelievable, see? . . . I don't believe it happened."

One thing Green has been quick to correct over the years: he didn't run to the Lord because Mary Elizabeth Woodson died.

"That wasn't a turning point in my life," he said in 2008. "I was born-again a year earlier, in Anaheim.

"It had nothing to do with no woman."

ON THE RUN

There were knocks on my door, for three days . . . I was scared to answer, because I knew what it meant.
—AL GREEN, 1975

The chaos in Al Green's life did not abate. GUN-TOTING SECOND COUSIN THREATENS AL GREEN read the headline of the November 23, 1974, *Indianapolis Recorder.* Just two days out of the hospital, Green had returned to his office to take care of payroll when "a woman employee held him at gun-point for two hours" over back pay she said was owed. Al declined to press charges against the unnamed relative and refused to talk to reporters about the incident.

After he had left the hospital, Green jumped in his car "and drove for three or four hundred miles . . . on the wrong side of the road . . . I was in a terrible state . . . I couldn't sleep nights without taking three or four pills."

Eventually he was holed up at some bland Holiday Inn, asking a friend by the name of Reverend Meadows for help. An angst-ridden Al pleaded, "Please lift this weight from me, this weight is killing me." Meadows told him to pray and just say yes to God. After twenty minutes of prayer, Green, tears streaming down his face, delivered an affirmative.

Even Audrey Williams reappeared to whisk Al away on a nature retreat. The odd couple jumped into a Cadillac and vroomed off to Gatlinburg. "She took me up in the mountains and rented a chalet," said Green, who thought Williams "was gonna stay, too. Audrey said, 'I brought you a case of water.' 'A case of water? I'm gonna need some *steaks* up here.'" Audrey started to laugh. "'You don't need no steaks—bye bye, I'm goin'.' 'Hey! *Hey!* You can't leave us out here!' This woman is gone, in a green Cadillac!" Stranded in a little cabin beside a stream, Al fasted, "sat on the back porch and watched a little old Mallard duck come down the stream every day," and reflected on his life. "No phone, no TV, no Coca Cola," recalled Green, who claimed rather impossibly that he "didn't eat for forty days." He was in such anguish he found himself asking, "Lord, what are you trying to do to me?"*

❖

For the first time, Green started getting criticism in the press over his live shows. In December 1974, he played the Mill Run Playhouse, a Niles, Illinois, theater-in-the-round. "Al Green performs with not one, two or three but *four* bodyguards, stationed scant feet away from him right on stage," wrote reviewer Lynn Van Matre in a concert review entitled "Green's on Guard in Nile." "There is something absolutely sinister about an artist going through his paces surrounded by grim-faced guards watching his and the audience's every move. Is Green the victim of threats?"

When asked about such notices, Al was unfazed. "I haven't reacted to that bad press at all, really. Why should I? If they don't like my act they should stay away." In a January story for *Rolling Stone,* Ben Fong-Torres also noted the threatening presence of Green's onstage bodyguards at the Circle Star Theatre in San Carlos, California. A growling Doberman pinscher on a taut leash beside him during the accompanying interview, Green casually mentioned the Memphis Sheriff's Department had made him a special deputy the previous year.

Al elaborated on his undercover role later that year in an interview with *Crawdaddy*'s Jim Trombetta. "I work on a very secretive basis for the sheriff's department," explained Green, who refused to divulge further information as it "would dilute my projects," although he felt compelled to add, "We do *own* the *rifle range* at the sheriff's department . . . Al Green is the police!"** One hopes none of this had any bearing on the Woodson investigation.

---

* At times Green has credited this trip with influencing him to sing secular music again in the nineties, but that had to be another foray into nature, as Audrey Williams died in 1975.

** One of the more out-there interviews, Green's crackpot ramblings are more incomprehensible than usual. "To live is to die is to live; to live a little and die means to live a lot, okay?" Al started talking about the life cycle of corn and humans. "This in turn will enlighten you that there are clouds that you can ride on, there are extremely beautiful places to go."

❖

In February Green's *Greatest Hits* was released, a killer compilation of ten of his best (and surely one of the all-time finest of such albums), featuring a wicked, iconic cover of a shirtless Al wearing white leather pants that sport a cross-stitched crotch held together by rope (on the back cover, four hamming-it-up Als are in a row, looking ready to supply overdubs). One wonders how Green must've felt looking at this image now that his physique was scarred forever and his mind was in a tangle.

That same month came "L-O-V-E (Love)," which had been recorded right before the Woodson affair and which became a number thirteen pop hit. Those majestic strings charge in, and there's the return of Green's careful diction, telling us we're back to serious business. A classic Willie Mitchell production, the song starts out sparingly but adds elements to build emotion, with Charles's keyboard and Leroy's guitar-like bass lines providing the color. This song is from the same batch as "Sha-La-La," but the big difference is announced in the very first line: Al's writing this not about any special someone but love itself, and there is no doubt this love is one from above. For once Green doesn't sounded conflicted at all, and I l-o-v-e to hear him perform the song live, because couplets such as "I would give my life for the glory / To be able to tell the story" never fail to wrench deep emotion out of him.

The song was written by Al, Willie, and Teenie, although Hodges was quick to point out "all the stuff I did with Al except 'L-O-V-E (Love)' were my ideas . . . the music was already there." Hodges had just written the middle eight bars and felt this was Green throwing him a bone for previous songs his credit had been left off of. "Finally Al said, 'Well, Teenie, we need to put your name on this song.'"

On April 5, 1975, a checkered-suited, hoarse Green and the Enterprise Orchestra were back on *Soul Train* to perform "Sha-La-La," "Livin' for You," and a sloppy "Take Me to the River." During the Q&A he was asked why the religious songs on every album, and Green, obviously pleased with the question, shouts, "Because I am a *believer* in the *power* that *be!*" He then instructs the band to take it way down for an exquisite "God Blessed Our Love" (check out the way he worries the word "halo" three times in a row) that's over nine minutes long (and God bless *Soul Train*, because you weren't going to see this anyplace else).

❖

Green's catchy if slight "Oh Me, Oh My (Dreams in My Arms)" arrived in June and only hit number forty-eight. This and "L-O-V-E (Love)" were from *Al Green Is Love,* one loopy, idiosyncratic album. "It's aimed at the 'third level'—an elevation of the mind I can't say too much about," confided Al not long before its release. Started in October 1974 before Mary's death, finished approximately in May, and released in September, a good deal of it is filler—and one cut, "Love Ritual," I find laughable due to Green's lazy, hazy attempt to Africanize the lyrics, which feels about as convincing as the tribal musical number from the cheapo 1958 film *She Demons* (there are many who disagree). In his book Green suggests that the album was Willie's answer to the heavily orchestrated Philadelphia-sound disco hits burning up the charts at the time, Gamble and Huff productions like "TSOP (The Sound of Philadelphia)" by MFSB (itself a revamping of the *Soul Train* theme) and "When Will I See You Again" by the Three Degrees. Mitchell, however, would state in 1978, "I really didn't want to compete in that market. Disco is basically all instrumental."

There is some great material on *Al Green Is Love,* suffused with that hemmed-in funk that this crew handles so adroitly: the irresistible "I Gotta Be More (Take Me Higher)," with Green on the prowl for life's deeper meaning among the "cigarette smokers, practical jokers" (that's Do Funny supplying the pinball-machine B3 fills), and the smoky, quizzical Green/ Hodges number "Rhymes," which Teenie told me was inspired by nursery rhymes but which Al (unsurprisingly) takes to a more haunted place.

"The Love Sermon" is plain wild, a third-level elevation of the Al Green mind, with its evocations of love, heaven, children, and carnivals. Dig Bulldog's stuttering, reverbed hi-hat, Al's sermon-like delivery and impromptu clapping, not to mention the stylish manner in which Teenie sneers by way of guitar as Green belts out, "If you won't go with me / Listen to my melody"—breathtaking. There's no doubt that we're in Al's church; he even proclaims making a donation on the fade-out. One can only imagine Willie's utter frustration at trying to pull commercial soul records out of his star artist when Al delivered crazy shit like this. The beautiful thing about that tension is that it provoked some unique, never-to-be-repeated music. God is smeared all over this album, down to the back cover, with a bleary Al sporting a Barry White do, his ass parked in front of a stained-glass window. This is what Al's about now, he's telling us. I can't hide it much longer . . .

On July 26, 1975, David Gest whipped up another Al Green Day at the Memphis Hilton. For some glorious reason Phyllis Diller was there to present Green with three more gold and platinum records. "Al Green is an acorn to a hungry squirrel," she mused. "A hollow log to a sleepy bear in the fall . . . " The dynamic duo even posed for pictures. That night Al performed with a symphony before a crowd of six thousand at Mid-South Coliseum. The Green Machine had not run out of steam just yet.

Al was no longer the *Midnight Special* wild man of months before. He'd told *Jet* back in December that "my act will take on a more refined, sophisticated look. There will now be strings . . . you won't see any more of my musicians wearing hats and big boots. Everyone will be wearing a suit and tie." Alongside the band was a trio of female backup singers, Quiet Elegance, who'd already been recording for Hi.

Green got paid in cash. "That was his thing, brother," said Roland Jones. "He got his money *before* he went onstage." According to Roland, this was due to a gig at San Francisco's Cow Palace. When it came time to be paid, the promoters disappeared. ("I eventually got the money, but I was scared," said Jones. "They were gangsters.") From that point on, Green refused to step onstage until he was paid in full. "Al was pullin' his card— they knew if he didn't go onstage, those people would tear that goddamn auditorium up."

Al carried a briefcase for the money. "He'd open it up and there'd be nothing in but his sunglasses," said Arthur Baker, who'd produce Green in the nineties. "That's where the cash would go." Very few women were trusted to carry the case, and it was never far from Al, even when he was onstage. "Sometimes he'd put it next to the organ—where he could see where it was," noted keyboard player Johnny Brown.*

Reuben Fairfax Jr. remembered a show where nobody could leave until after "the family counted the money—Count, Maxine, Al, they were all countin' the money." After a few hours somebody went in to see if they were done. "Count said, 'I'm on my seventies.'" Since Green was getting a hundred grand, the band had plenty of time left to kill. "We sat out in the parking lot until damn near five in the morning."

---

* In addition to the bank briefcase, Green traveled with a large, mysterious bag full of keys. "When you carried it, you could hear the keys jinglin' . . . there might have been other things in that bag that I didn't know about," said Johnny Brown. "That bag was heavy—if you carried it, you'd have to keep switchin' shoulders. One time I just got tired of carryin' them keys and didn't do it no more. Al said, 'Okay.'" Brown had been flying to shows with Green. "Next thing I knew, I was back on the bus."

"Full of Fire," another single written by Al, Willie, and Teenie, came out in October 1975 and was another mild hit—number twenty-eight. For better or worse, I'd say this was the first real taste of disco-fied Al. As he related in his only known interview to Robert Gordon, James Mitchell was particularly proud of his horn arrangements on the song. He and the rest of the horn section Willie used were out on the road with the Doobie Brothers at the time. Mitchell booked time at Curtom, Curtis Mayfield's Chicago studio, so they could overdub horns on the tracks.

They flew out after a Kentucky gig, James starting to figure out the arrangements in his head on the plane to the Windy City. He continued working there as Willie provided pots of coffee to keep him awake. "I was writing without a piano or anything," said James, who finished right before the session began. When they started cutting, some of the players were thrown by his fancy chords. "Andrew and Jack said, 'Man, you got me on the 9th!' I said, 'Don't worry about it, just play it.'"

Then his brother got nervous. "Willie said, 'Motherfucker, I spent all this goddamn money and you done fucked that thing up!' Boy, he cursed me out. I said, 'Listen to it one time, and if it have to be, I'll pay for the studio time my damn self.'" They started to record. "Man, when it got to the bridge . . . the harmony was moving all kinds of ways." His brother was pleased. "He complimented me afterward, but boy, he was on me before!" Still, James felt that as far as the arrangements went, aside from "Full of Fire," "Willie wouldn't let me venture out."*

"Let It Shine," a rhythmically interesting Al/Teenie song I find far more compelling than the preceding single, came out in April 1976 and was the first Green single since 1971's "Driving Wheel" not to crack the Top 100. The *Full of Fire* album came out that same month. "I love the cover," said Green. "It's me. It's Al Green staring right out at you with a mouthful of teeth, saying hello." *Full of Fire* is another mixed bag full of spiritual references, this one less rewarding than the last. A cover of Buck Owens's "Together Again" proves that slowing down a country ballad Al Green style can turn dull, as were more than a few songs on the album.

But then there's the malevolent "That's the Way It Is," one of the darker songs in the Green oeuvre. Featuring Al's most extreme vocal ever—the way he quietly pulls on every syllable here is a way-out style that can only be called "hard whispering"—Green takes us on a tour of open doors,

---

* James felt "Full of Fire" "sounded a little like Tex Ritter's band," although that comparison is lost on my ears. It isn't exactly "Hillbilly Heaven."

lying people, and the Heavenly Father. One thing he wants us to know: Al can see us, but we can't see him, or is it the Holy Ghost? He's like a crazed shaman at the state fair, reading off the scribbles on his cardboard sign: "People, don't you *understand* what I am *trying* to *tell* you?"

The track snakes along, a car in the night on some nowhere back road. Charles provides a moody, muddy B3 bottom; Teenie's flick-of-the-dragon's-tail guitar on the break is utterly perfect. Paranoia, fear—whatever's got a grip on Green in this song, it has him writhing. The feeling I get is that Al's trying to get through to someone he has damaged deeply who won't come near, and he is offering not an apology but an anguished plea to "forget the bad," because "that's the way it is." It's full of dread, this cryptic Hodges/Green number, and makes God sound scary. "That's the Way It Is" is one of the last great Willie Mitchell/Al Green recordings.

In discussing the song recently with Bob Mehr, Green said he wrote it with Teenie way back on the same 1972 session as "I'm Still in Love with You." Willie and Al Jackson were fooling around with a song, and Al told Al to "get a pencil." (When Green tried to inquire what exactly it was they were playing, Jackson said, "That's the way it is," inspiring the title.) Asked if the song was spiritually inspired, Green answered, "Absolutely," linking it to some other undocumented period where he went from being out on tour to hanging out with "these preachers, travelling down to Jackson, Mississippi, with white evangelists. I'm the only Oreo . . . for seven days we lived out in these little campers."

There he attended a revival, "sawdust on the floor. We'd go hear these people singing 'Amazing Grace,' preaching and ministering . . . went to Nashville one night at one in the morning, got some preacher out of bed in his pajamas . . . he prayed for us . . . we left there around three." Green said "a whole bunch of stuff" was happening at the time, and he was so confused it caused him to gaze heavenward and inquire, "What are you doing up there?" And God answered, "What are you doing down there?" Al felt compelled to add that during this period he didn't "have time to fall in love because I'm busy prayin'."

So Al wrote the song in 1972, finally recorded it in 1976 (Al Jackson had died the previous year), yet it was inspired by events that seem to come from around the same time as when it was cut. And that's what Al Green had to say about "That's the Way It Is" in the course of just a few minutes. You figure it out.

❖

"Being a millionaire doesn't mean anything . . . you have got to be able to feel free to enjoy life . . . I have been in an arena with 40,000 people, but I was the loneliest man there," a morose Green confessed to Lynn Norment in the October 1976 issue of *Ebony*. Al would not forget just how bad he felt in those days; he elaborated on his condition to Andria Lisle in 2004. "Psychologically I was a mess. I couldn't sleep, I couldn't think. I was out of it, and had no idea of what to do." To Chet Flippo he admitted suicidal despair: "I was in a trauma, man . . . I could've jumped off a building I was in such turmoil."

Religion was the one thing that offered some kind of solace. Despite all the touring and recording, "Every Sunday morning I'd get up and go to church," Green told Robert Mugge. "This guy would be preachin', he'd set your soul on fire. I'd drive all the way to Arkansas to hear that preacher. I'd take my girlfriend and everything . . . I had to go."

Other times Green would seek out "any Pentecostal, Holy Ghost feel church, any Holiness Church I could find," he told Sandra Pointer-Jones. In order to remain anonymous, Green would "dress up in these disguises," but he'd end up "so overcome with the spirit . . . my glasses would fly off, wig's flying! Man, my incognito'd be gone."*

Green would hide away on his Oakland, Tennessee, farm, sit by the lake, and quietly read Genesis. People trying to reach him on business would have to listen to Al's bodyguard Curtis Forte explain just what the boss was up to. "My man Curtis would say, 'Oh, he's readin' the Bible . . . oh, yeah, Al's out there readin' the Bible.' People thought I was *nuts*. I thought it was wonderful."

At the same time, strange things began to happen onstage. In New Orleans, Green sang "Free at Last." And kept singing it. "The spirit came and I went to rejoicing onstage, but people never knew," Green admitted to Robert Mugge. "Tears, y'know . . . the song went on and on, the band thought it was goin' on quite long—and I was down at the end of the

---

* When Al was growing up, Robert Greene disapproved of these fire-and-brimstone churches. "My father didn't want us to have much to do with the Holy Ghost people. He would speed up the car whenever he drove past their church." Which had created a burning desire in his son "to find out what my dad didn't want us to see." And as far as disguises go, Green has implied using them from time to time. "Fame can be a headache if you let it bother you. . . . You just need a disguise. Give me a wig, a moustache, a great big white beard, some long white robe and a white fuzzy cap—they'll forget I'm there." So study that hirsute man on the corner carefully—it may be Al Green.

concert hall singin', 'Free at last' and people were havin' a *fit* thinkin' that I'm, y'know, just singin' a *song*! I'm rejoicing."

Green would sing his hits, like he'd do night after night, but "then, when I'd get to the point of "You Ought to Be with Me" or . . . "For the Good Times," man, I don't know, somethin' started happenin' . . . I'd get these impulses—BrrrrOOOOoo . . . the concert would start goin' off, I couldn't help it . . . I'd start quotin' scriptures . . . 'That if a man would confess to Lord Jesus with his mouth, believe in his heart God has raised him from the dead, thou shall be saved.'"

It happened again one night when Al was playing "this weird little casino gig. I stood onstage and said, 'When you open the Bible to Deuteronomy' . . . I had never seen 3,000 people leaving out of a place so fast! All the pimps and their ladies . . . were gone." Lee Hildebrand attended a Circle Star Theatre show where Green started preaching between hits. "I remember a lady sitting behind me saying quite loudly, 'I didn't pay to hear no gospel shit!' She was upset." When the women rushed the stage to touch the hem of Al's garment, he recoiled: "No, no, no—I want you to accept *Jesus Christ* as your personal savior."

"And so the concerts started goin' crazy, record sales started goin' crazy, Al was most *certainly* goin' crazy, Willie was goin' crazy—*everybody* was goin' crazy," Green told Mugge. "Everything was in an uproar because we had all invested . . . Willie had, Hi had, too. Put their time and effort into this thing."

The pressure mounted. As Green recalled, "I had producers, promoters, record companies, booking agents, all these people saying, 'Al has got WHAT? Religion? Eighteen million dollars invested in this boy and he's got *religion*? . . . Everyone around me was saying, 'We don't need God right now—tell him to come back *later.*'"

Green's manager Bob Schwaid finally threw in the towel. "I had to walk away from it," he said, clearly pained. "As much of a loss that was to me financially—Al was making $50,000–$60,000 a night, and that's *still* a lot of money—I couldn't continue working with him." Reluctant to talk about the situation, Schwaid admitted the relationship with Al was "not a comfortable one . . . he could not relate to management well. Coming from a strong gospel background, he had a tremendous amount of inner turmoil about the kind of music he was making."*

---

* Schwaid, who also managed Van Morrison, Miriam Makeba, and Evelyn "Champagne" King, died in 2002. Cynthia Lane, who was his significant other for twenty-five years, said Bob refused to discuss Al Green or listen to his music. "It was, 'Please don't play that in the house and I'm not telling you anything about him.' It must've been very unpleasant."

As Green told Geoffrey Himes, "At every concert, at every gateway, every doorway, every time a stage light would come on, I had trouble delivering [a] message that was not about the transformation in my life."

❖

Have a Good Time came out at the very end of 1976. Other than the brooding "Something"—featuring Teenie on *sitar*—the album has little to recommend it. A reading of the Toussaint McCall hit "Nothing Takes the Place of You" is respectable enough, and the altogether square single "Keep Me Cryin'" is pleasant, even with its unexpected horn solo. Used to be Green, Mitchell, and Hi Rhythm could take one of Al's vamps and magically transform it into a song, and do it with taste and originality, which is why it's painful to hear them flail about on something like "The Truth Marches On," where everything but the kitchen sink is thrown onto the track, down to a "Dust My Broom" riff from Teenie. It also reveals how slight some of these songs are.

This was the first Al Green album that sounded like just another car on the Royal assembly line, and sadly, aside from *Al Green's Greatest Hits Volume II* (all previously released material and the final Hi record under the London Records imprint), *Have a Good Time* was to be the last of Green's Hi albums to be produced by Willie Mitchell.

He and Green had recorded about seven songs for a new record (another nondescript "happy for the Lord" number a la "Have a Good Time," "Sweet Song" from 1977 eventually saw release; I'm told a cover of the Bobby Hebb chestnut "Sunny" was also recorded) when Al showed up unexpectedly at Mitchell's home in the wee hours.

As Willie told Karen Schoemer, a visibly emotional Green "came to my house about one o'clock in the morning. He said, 'I'm goin' gospel,' and I said, 'Well, I don't know anything about gospel—and I don't *want* to know anything about it.'" And with those words, the Al Green–Willie Mitchell partnership was just about over.

During this same time Perry Michael Allen had designed an entire stage show for Green's next tour, complete with seven dancers that interpreted Al's songs. The show, said to be way ahead of its time and which was written up in *Jet*, was booked for Hawaii, Japan, and New York City. After three dates Al cancelled the entire production.

Green had become a minister. Since that fateful night in Disneyland, Green had struggled "to avoid it. I didn't *want* to be a preacher." He'd make that point over and over: "I was instructed to do this . . . I wouldn't do this if I were on my own. I'd be a rock star."

Eventually, he told Robert Mugge, word from above "got to me: 'Okay, Al Green, alright—you gonna take the call or you gonna pass it up? Simple yes or no.' I said, 'I'll take it. *I will take it.* I'll bite the bullet . . . I'll grit my teeth and bear it, I'll just have to take it.'"

In October Green paid $335,000 for a church just a stone's throw from Graceland at 787 Hale Road. At the time he boasted to the *Commercial Appeal* that the Al Green Full Baptist Tabernacle Church "will be the most phenomenal and sensational act of spiritualism ever seen in Memphis. It will be a center of divine power." On December 19, 1975, Al preached his first sermon to a packed congregation.

Al Green had big plans for the future. As he told Mugge, "I shall be one of the greatest evangelists in the world—*in the world*—and not only will we fill auditoriums and coliseums and stadiums, but we will *multiply* blessings to people around the world!"

One person who seemed rather blasé about all the brouhaha was Willie Mitchell. "I'm a religious person, personally, but I'm not a gospel person. I'm not impressed with preachers."*

❖

It had not been an easy few years for the executives at Hi Records. Recognizing what the company would lose if Al Green went gospel, they had looked to sell the label. When Atlantic Records had offered nine million in 1975, Nick Pesce and Bill Cantrell wanted to accept the offer, but Willie turned it down, certain they'd double their offer the next year. But Green's hits had dried up, and nothing else was charting. "I was under too much pressure," Mitchell said in 1978. "It got to the point where I started wondering if it was me who had gotten it all wrong, and every record that missed found me questioning myself."

Willie's band was unhappy as well. *On the Loose,* Hi Rhythm's one album, came out in 1976. This loopy wonder seems to have a polarizing effect on Hi fanatics due to Teenie's rather idiosyncratic singing (I think the album's fantastic, right down to the cover). Said to be inspired by Al Green's erratic behavior in the limelight, "Superstar" (with Teenie on banjo) was

---

* In fact, Reuben Fairfax Jr. said Mitchell had a rule when it came to ministers who recorded projects at Royal: "Don't ever take a check from a preacher." He had a drawerful of bad paper to back up his sentiments. "They ain't worth nothin'," he said with a snort.

the single. According to Hodges, Green liked the album ("For years he wanted to produce an album on me—*Al Green Presents Teenie Hodges*," he said, adding, "I don't think I can sing"). He wanted Hi Rhythm to come on the road as his opening act, but Mitchell and company nixed that idea and, as Hi Rhythm saw it, intentionally buried the record.

In May 1977 Al Bennett of Cream Records bought Hi. Alvin Silas Bennett, who had been born in Joiner, Arkansas, had made a name for himself in the fifties rescuing Liberty Records from insolvency by discovering the likes of Julie London and unleashing novelty records such as "The Chipmunk Song" on the world (the Chipmunks were all named for Liberty executives; leader of the bunch Alvin was named for Bennett).

"Al Bennett was the last of the great independents—a big, impressive guy who spoke in all these wonderful Southern clichés," said Lee Housekeeper, who was briefly head of A&R at Cream. According to Housekeeper, Bennett had made a fortune selling Liberty. "He had pulled a great pump-and-dump—this was a time when all these megaconglomerates were trying to get into the recording business." Before putting it on the block, Bennett churned out scores of albums that were "shipped platinum and returned with an anchor . . . he put 'em in warehouses where he had pals and it showed on the books as all these gold records." Bennett made out like a bandit before anyone caught on. "Al had the charisma to sell anything to anybody," said Housekeeper. "There's no question in my mind that if you were on the other side of the deal, you got skinned."

In the beginning, Cream claimed to have big plans for Hi. Sales of 3.5 million by the end of 1977 was a "conservative projection," Bennett told *Billboard*. But it was all air guitar. "They came in here and said, 'Sessions gonna be greater than ever,'" said Leroy Hodges. "Never happened." Teenie felt Bennett was more interested in farming than music. "He owned all this cotton land over in Arkansas—55,000 acres." According to Housekeeper, the label was merely a lark for Bennett. "It was a funny hobby, an old-time music guys' version of the Friars Club. It was *McHale's Navy, Barney Miller* . . . these guys were at the tail end of their careers. He'd hold court in his office; we had bookies coming in. They were just sittin' there havin' a good time."

The move to Cream proved to be disastrous for Hi Records—and for Hi Rhythm in particular. The band who'd created the Hi sound had practically lived at Royal to record all that material. "Man, we were working hard," said Charles Hodges. "We didn't know what vacation was. We worked, we worked. Happily, eagerly, wanting to do it, thinking there was gonna be a payday. Lawyer, manager—we didn't do any of that stuff because we loved what we were doing." He says Willie looked after them "in the beginning, but then he stopped . . . there was a lotta things that we was promised that we never did receive."

When Cream entered the picture, Mitchell started employing other musicians. After more than a decade, Hi Rhythm was out of a job. The man who had told Denise LaSalle he'd ride the Hi horse until it dropped had blinked. It was clear that he'd exhausted the formula, and the fickle pop audience had moved on. "We've basically kept the same sound—the drum sound—for six or seven years now," Willie said in 1976. "It's time for a change."

"It was quite a letdown for me," said Teenie, who maintained when Cream came in they hired everybody back, "including the janitor—except the band. I thought that was mighty strange, and I was pissed off at Willie Mitchell . . . I didn't like the way they handled it . . . it was just crazy."

Promotion man Willie Bean had known Bennett since the dawn of Hi and liked him, although Bean felt compelled to add the opinion that Al was likely "a crook" who had been fired from Dot Records early in his career "to get him out of there." Bean felt a major part of the problem was that all the way back to Joe Cuoghi, Hi's executives "weren't record people," and "didn't understand the business side of it." Willie Mitchell was no exception.

"Willie was a producer; he never was a record executive who knew how to handle and maneuver the business . . . Al Bennett did. Let me tell you the truth: Al knew what he was doin'. When he got that company he collected overseas royalties—there was money owed and they didn't know how to collect it. Bennett knew how to collect." The first thing Bennett did was sell Hi's publishing.

When asked if Al Bennett was good for Hi, Bean answered with a resounding "*no*! He was just there for what he could get outta the thing for his own personal gain." Teenie agreed. "It wasn't about music; it was about makin' money on the publishing." Hi Records "was just somethin' to work to make money." It all boiled down to "greed, money," said Charles Hodges. As far as taking care of the musicians, "Bennett didn't care."

O. V. Wright's 1977 album *Into Something (Can't Shake Loose)* was the first Hi release under Bennett's rule. Nothing hit, not even the self-produced albums Al Green made next. There would only be eleven more releases before Hi went under. "Al Bennett was someone with power," said Cream publicist Howard Bloom. "He came from this elite Memphis world . . . what Al Bennett was good at was working with Union Planters Bank and getting funding.* Unfortunately, he wasn't capable of making hits. The records didn't go anywhere."** After Bennett died in 1989, as Harvey Kubernik points out, the once-great Hi records had "moved to a squalid little cubbyhole in a Hollywood office block."

Luckily Mitchell didn't lose Royal Studios, although he came close. As Teenie remembers, "Willie was getting ready to put padlocks on the studio because Al [Bennett] had said he was going to buy the studio, but he didn't pay any money down . . . Willie told me he was going to put a padlock on it that Monday . . . I asked him, 'Did he pay you any money?' And he said no. I said, 'What are you going to put the padlock on it for?'" Willie wound up keeping Royal, and, after a brief, unrewarding stint with Bearsville Records, Mitchell started another independent label in the early eighties called Waylo, recording Billy Always, Lynn White, and Ann Peebles. Eventually, though, according to Peebles, "the people that were funding him went bankrupt."

Although Royal Studios continued on, Hi Records was no more. For years the building had been humming with activity, full of singers, songwriters, and musicians doing their thing. Now it was over. "Sometimes it makes you a little teary—hey, we went through all of this, and a lot of people that we went through it with are gone," said Don Bryant. Hi was so open he could remember strangers coming in off the street to pitch a song. "I was always willing to listen to anybody who brought a song in . . . we had a lot of fun, a lot of joy . . . there was a lot created in that place that still stands."

Once the great Hi Rhythm disbanded, Teenie headed for Los Angeles, Leroy stayed on at Hi working as an engineer, and Charles went through a very bad run with drugs before becoming a minister. Howard Grimes lost everything. He was on his way to homelessness when Al Green paid an unexpected visit. As mentioned before, Green and Grimes had butted

---

* In 1986 Union Planters Bank sued Bennett and his wife, Cathleen, over $200,000 owed on a 1981 loan. The court ruled in the bank's favor for the full amount plus attorney's fees.

** During this time Bloom handled Al Green's publicity and flew to Memphis to meet him. Picked up at the airport by one of Green's sisters—"a very tall, black Amazon figure in almost combat gear"—Bloom was taken to American Studios. "Al decided to take me on a tour of Memphis," which included driving by a then-closed Graceland. "He was so down to earth. I remember how he dropped these amazing aphorisms, but not preachy at all. One was, 'Anything you seize, you can believe and achieve.'"

heads at Royal, and they weren't exactly bosom buddies. But there was Al at Howard's place not long before Grimes lost his home.

"I hadn't had no money in so long or nothing, and I hadn't got put out the house yet, because the people were so nice to me," Grimes told David Less. "They had let me stay. They were hoping I was going to get the job back or something was going to happen, but it never did."

Howard couldn't afford to pay his bills, and "everything was turned off . . . I was in this house, it was in the winter time . . . I had nothing but the Bible that was given to me. One night, it stormed real bad and I heard a knock at the door." The powerless house illuminated only by candle-light, Howard went to see who was there. "It was Al Green. He came in a white suit." Green, who'd arrived in a white Eldorado convertible, had a black briefcase in his hand.

"Al came and Al gave me $500. I hadn't seen no money in over two months . . . he was a little kind of leery about being out in the storm. But when he saw me, he had this wonderful smile on his face. He said, 'I've never been out in a storm for nobody, but everything will be all right for you.'"

Al told him to take what he was giving. "I said, 'Al, who told you to give me this money?'" He said, "I'm only following instructions; my instruction was to bring you this money." Green "laid the money on the table, and he said, 'You go tomorrow and have your utilities and things turned on.' I was afraid to take the money, because there was no way I could pay him back."

Al did something else. He asked Grimes if he'd ever considered work-ing on projects of his own. "He said, 'Howard, have you ever thought about recording for yourself?' And I said, 'Man, I'm a drummer. Who would be interested in me . . . I just play behind other people . . . nobody's going to help me.'" You never know, Al told him, then added, "I'll tell you what. Come over the studio . . . you've got the studio as long as you want it. See what you can come up with."

Although it would be a long road back, Howard Grimes would once more make a living as a professional musician. And he has not forgotten Al Green sitting out there in his white Eldorado during a raging storm, coming to give him five hundred dollars when he needed it most.

HAND LOTION AND DEAD DOGS

I was a fornicator, an adulterer. The celestial will not mix
with the terrestrial.
—AL GREEN

AL GREEN BUYS CHURCH, PREACHES HIS FIRST SERMON proclaimed the
January 20, 1977, cover of *Jet* magazine. The Reverend Al Green had arrived, and he wasn't shy about expressing his love for the Heavenly Father.
"He took *the rock & roll* and *the twisting the night away* from me and gave
me a *new* song, a song *the angels* can sing, and I want you to know his name
is *Jesus,*" he'd preach.

The Full Gospel Tabernacle Church is a "somewhat dilapidated . . .
low-slung, space-age structure not far from Graceland," as Gene Santoro described it (another scribe savored the seventies-vintage "parallelogram-obsessed architecture"). Other visitors note the painting depicting
the Rapture with its souls flying out of crashed cars, as well as the one
of an African American Jesus. And the life-sized cardboard Al suitable
for selfies (I think it's still there). It should come as no surprise that this
modest, five-hundred-or-so-capacity sanctuary is "totally different" from
other houses of worship, said Johnny Brown, who grew up in the church
world. "To this day, his church is not packed with people from Memphis.
Tourists go to Graceland and Al Green's church, so you had busloads of
people from all over the world coming into the service."

According to Full Gospel's corporation filing from October 20, 1976,* the church's mission is "to promote the interest of religion in our midst, the spread of spiritual holiness through the world . . . carry on educational and charitable work." Although the style of worship at Full Gospel is Baptist Pentecostal, their mission statement noted that "the corporation shall not be affiliated with any denominational body or missionary organization or branch thereof but shall have an entirely independent status."

Everybody is welcome.** "We have some Catholics, Baptists and there are even some Jewish kids that go," said Green in 1982. "It's a free-for-all church especially for a sinner." For all the fire and brimstone, Al's approach to religion seems to have remained down-home, somewhat open-minded, and free of sanctimony: "I think it's the commitment, more so than being . . . a goody two-shoes." The world of TV evangelism (and its scandals) held no interest for Green. "I felt, I must say, embarrassed by it." When Full Gospel opened, he had plans for including the arts. "It's not always going to be the regular service—there will be some drama, interpretive dances, a play every now and then."

Green has kept the church running since it opened, and when in Memphis he rarely misses a Sunday service (and has taught a midweek Bible study), although even here he can throw the wild card—one 2009 report had his mother, Cora, showing up to cover for an Al no-show and admitting she was worried about her son, whom she felt was "in league with the devil." Such bumps in the road aside, Full Gospel has been the one constant in an erratic life. "If I'm totally honest, I would have to say that my religion is more important to me than my music," he said in 1979. Paul Zaleski, who worked with Green for years, says, "The only time he was free was when he was preaching."

"I feel at home in that pulpit," said Green in 1992. "I'm at home there, son. I can do a concert in the Taj Mahal and I don't feel the same as I

---

* Just three trustees for the church were listed at the time: Al; his mother, Cora; and his brother William. Cora was at the church daily. Said Johnny Brown, "She just had to sit there and do whatever she was doin', read her Bible, laugh and talk with people—'Mama, answer the phone!' If it was my mama, she wouldn't have had to been there at all."

** Except anyone who's gay, according to online reports. A May 2016 TripAdvisor review described Green going into "an all out and extensive homophobic rant." A Yelp reviewer summed up Al's viewpoint this way: "If you're gay, you go to hell and Al Green wasn't shy in letting you know that."

feel at plain-Jane Full Gospel Tabernacle . . . in those moments, I'm il-luminated, I'm enlightened." Although singing is a major element of the church service, this is certainly not the Al that you might encounter at a Reno casino racing through the hits. "There's a tremendous difference performing a song on stage and singing it in church. We want you to have a good time, sure, but also want you to be fed from the Word." Another bonus: "In church I don't have to sing anything I don't want to." Some of the best performances I've heard Green give have come out of that church. He's liable to sing anything he feels—"Too Close to Heaven" followed by a snatch of Hank Williams's "I Saw the Light."

Michael McDonald, Mary Wilson, the Grateful Dead, and Michael Jackson have all visited Al's church. David Gest, who brought Jackson by, reported that as they sat in the audience a woman next to them was so overcome by the spirit she passed out and "fell right into Michael Jackson's crotch," wrote Gest. "I will never forget the look on Michael's face. It was pure horror. He just sat there, frozen, obviously in terrible pain, whisper-ing, 'Help me, help me.'" Green rescued the Gloved One by calling him up to the pulpit to join in on a version of "People Get Ready."

❖

The stars might pay their respects at Full Gospel, but the Memphis church crowd was a tougher bunch to convince. "Boy, you haven't seen no hatred 'til you get in the church," Green told Stanley Booth in 1986. Elsewhere he'd add, "There seem to be a lot of judgmental folks in the church world." Particularly in Memphis, where Al felt like "a prophet without honor in his own hometown. People here are naïve, slow . . . they watch me out of the corner of their eyes." The crux of the matter remained: Al was singing both gospel and secular. "Al Green . . . there's nothing to it. It's a front," said the Reverend Willie Morganfield, an old-school luminary in the gos-pel world. "Because if he was really truly centered on right and righteous-ness, he would leave that other stuff alone. But he mixes it. And that's not good. That's wrong."

Green was viewed as a Johnny-come-lately who only turned to gospel when the hits dried up. It would take "years before they finally accepted me, and they still ponder about it . . . I stayed, and one of the reasons I did was to show them." Johnny Brown felt that members of the Church of God in Christ were particularly hard on Green. "They'd be saying, 'He's singin' for the devil, and now he's tryin' to be there for the Lord.'"

But every year when they'd have their convocation in Memphis, "all the COGIC people would all be over at Al's church—because they were Al Green fans."

Those involved with the church experienced a different Al Green. This Al had "a heart of gold," said Paul Zaleski, who taped many a sermon for radio broadcasts. Zaleski said Green always wore "a money belt—he kept that money right by his balls" and that on Sunday "you'd have ten people lined up after the service. He knew the people, he knew who was broke. I'm talkin' about every fuckin' Sunday. Those people who didn't have any money, they had chicken dinners at his church and he paid for it all." Green didn't advertise doing it, and the press "didn't care about a black person doin' nice things for black people, so you never heard that publicity."

In April 1978 Green started a beauty salon called Al Green International Hair. "I had always believed in looking my best, so it only seemed natural to encourage others to let their own God-given beauty shine," explained entrepreneurial Al. Zaleski noted that Green "took four homeless girls that didn't have a future, sent 'em to hair school, made a salon for 'em, gave 'em a life. He's done a lot of things to give people a life that they never would've had without him."

It was just another side to a very complicated being. "Yes, he'll fuck you out of money," Paul added. "But yes, he'll give that money to somebody else."

❖

Unfortunately, Full Gospel Tabernacle was also a magnet for crazy female fans. "You had all these women that were showin' up from all over the world," said Johnny Brown. "God sent them there to marry Al." As Green put it, these were "women who come to the Tabernacle without avid Christian thoughts in mind."

One woman in particular was a thorn in Green's side. He and the band returned from the road to find an unexpected visitor at Al's home. "She'd jumped over the fence, went to the pool and was layin' out there naked." This same dame showed up at the service wanting to say a few words about what the Almighty had done for her. "The Lord turned out to be Al Green, and she was dreaming of having sex with him right there in the middle of the service," said Johnny Brown, who claims Al "knocked her cold."

One time "the wife of a deacon offered Al a gift to the church," said Brown. "He opened it up, and there was some bloody underwear, grits—voodoo-type stuff. Right in front of the church!"

Then there was the woman who managed to hide in the church once the service was over. "She would disappear and you couldn't find her," said Brown. "They'd lock the doors to the church and she'd be standin' there inside waving at everybody! They could never find where she was hidin'. She lived in the church for a good little while. It got to be folks would bring her food and toiletries."

Perhaps most memorable of all was the crotch sniffer. "One day Al had all these dignitaries at the church," recalled Brown, who watched as Green came in to greet them. A woman ran up to Al, got on her knees, "grabbed Al and said, 'Just let me smell it!' Al was so embarrassed."

❖

"A lot of my people found it difficult to stay on the ship," said Green of his new gospel persona. "There was a real division with the musicians." Spiritual matters aside, one reason for this was that the Enterprise Orchestra got paid a retainer during their time off, and now Al expected them to play at his church services for that money. He also wanted them to record their own music in a new studio he'd just built. "They didn't go for it," said Johnny Brown. "They said, 'You don't see the trick—we're getting paid to be off, this is the way it's been. All of a sudden he's gonna make us work for the little money?'" All Brown saw was opportunity: "I was the new kid on the block."

At this juncture, two young musicians would enter Green's life who would stick around for years as his bandleaders—Johnny Brown and Reuben Fairfax Jr. Both were outspoken Northerners. Fairfax was a rocker who knew nothing about Green's music or gospel; Brown was a preacher's kid from Chicago who knew everything about gospel. Fairfax was deadly serious when it came to playing and presenting Green's music. Mustachioed, with a mop of curly black hair, Brown was a flamboyant character who was fun to watch on stage.

There was a healthy rivalry between the two. Ask Johnny about Reuben and he'll tell you Fairfax was a strict bandleader and a "very controlling person." After a show, Brown and drummer Tim Dancy liked to walk out and mingle with the crowd in the post-show glow—until Reuben, who thought it was unprofessional, "passed a rule: no more walkin' into the audience after a show. We didn't pay no attention to him."

When I asked Fairfax about Brown, he laughed. "Johnny Brown, pardon my French, was just a fuckup. He couldn't follow rules."

❖

Johnny Brown had been living in Memphis for about a year in December 1975. He had a wife and a new baby, and was struggling to make ends meet. His pastor father told him to get his ass in church. That's when his wife, Susan, said, "Well, Al Green's opened up a church—why don't you go there?"

As luck would have it, church administrator (and future Green wife) Shirley Kyles had known Johnny in Chicago. "She saw me and asked would I play. I sat down at the piano and played from that day forward." Johnny started helping out with the choir, and Al began picking his brain. "He was an avid churchgoer at a younger age, so he knew a lot about church, but there were some inside things about church that he didn't know about. Since I was the son of a pastor, he'd ask me questions." In addition to having Johnny play at the church, Al began taking him on the road. "I owe a lot to Al," said Brown. "There were a lot of musicians at the time that were far better than I was. I wasn't that good. After five years or so I went from bein' the guy who couldn't play to bein' the bandleader and music director."

Johnny was uncontrollable. "I was young, wild, I was way out there. Al used to fly me around with the entourage just so he could watch me do crazy things. The band thought that I was snitchin'—'He's ridin' around with Al, he *must* be tellin' him what's goin' on.'"

Although Brown would be hired and fired many times, he had an ace in the hole when it came to Green. "Because I came out of the church, I was the one person in the band who knew a lot of gospel. Whenever I'd fall out with Al, I'd always end up goin' back to playin' the organ at the church. Whoever was on organ had to move over to the piano, because I just knew Al backwards and forwards—I know *all* of Al's music, whether its gospel or R&B. I might be playing there a couple of months, and Al would make his little cracks—'See that guy—Johnny? I can't get rid of him.' Then one day he'd come up to me, 'Hey, Johnny, you ready to go back to work? 'Yes, *SIR*!' 'Go get some clothes, be at the airport at five o'clock.' Al could even hold up the plane for you."

When the band was waiting to get paid, and contacting the elusive boss seemed impossible, Johnny "would go and jump his fence, walk past his dogs, cows, horses, and stand at his front door yellin' and talkin' crazy— 'Oh boss, oh Mighty One, will thou please come and open thy door? Your humble servant needs you.'"

Al knew how to zing Johnny too. "I had this girl, she was like a female pimp," said Johnny. "Every time I'd come to LA, she'd bring all her girl-friends. There would be so many beautiful women in my room . . . too many for one person."

One particular morning after a Miss Pimp visit, Brown and the boss had to leave for Memphis on the first flight. "Al had to be in church. All these females were comin' outta my room, I ain't had no sleep, we get down to the limo, and here's this flock of girls waving good-bye. There's nobody waving good-bye to Al.

"We get on the plane, fly to Memphis. We're in church. Al asks the congregation a question: 'How many of you men really trust your wives?' Of course, every man in the church puts his hand up. 'How many women really trust their husbands?'

"And every woman in the church—including my wife—puts their hand up. Al looks right out at Susan and says, 'Awww, Susan, you don't *really* trust Johnny, do you?' Right in front of the whole church. I was sittin' at the organ, wantin' to crawl under it. Al just passed it off like he was just jokin'—'I'm just playin'.'"

❖

An All-American triple jumper in track and field, Reuben Fairfax Jr. was still in college when he first encountered Al Green. In March 1977 he'd gone back home to Saint Louis on spring break to do a few shows with his Top 40 rock band, Grand Slam. On his way to a gig in Tupelo, he stopped in Memphis to use the restroom at his friend Darryl Neely's house. Neely was looking for a guitar player for the Enterprise Orchestra as Larry Lee, who was fed up over the money Al was paying him, had just quit the band.

"Darryl said, 'Hey, man, you think you'd want to play with us?' I asked him, 'Well, who is "us"?'" Neely told him. "I said, 'Man, I don't even *like* Al Green.' I grew up as a black guy playin' guitar in rock bands with a stack of Marshalls." Reuben gave Darryl a ride over to rehearsal. He'd never played with horns before, so for the hell of it he took his guitar and sat in. Since "Larry Lee had a rock style of guitar, that was a big part of their show"; Fairfax fit right in.

Green suddenly appeared. He must've liked what he heard, because Al "had some olive oil in his hand. He said, 'We are warriors and warriors must be *anointed*. If you're going with us, you're gonna be a warrior,' and he rubbed some oil on my head and spoke in tongues." Reuben was unfazed. "All I wanted to do was get back to my car." Green wanted him to start that night. "I told him, 'I'm with this group; we've signed contracts to do these shows.' He said, 'Well, son, contracts are made to broken.'" Unconvinced, Fairfax stuck with Grand Slam.

After a few weeks of thinking it over—his scholarship running out and money getting tight—Reuben called Green's new bandleader, Fred Jordan. "I joined the band in April of '77. We went up to White Plains, New York. Vicki Sue Robinson was the opening act." As Reuben sees it, he didn't get the gig because he was the best—he was just the guy who could supply some rock attitude. "I was hired to play the solos," said Fairfax, who at first just stepped out to take a flashy solo and nothing more. "The first year Al said, 'Don't even learn the songs, just play free.' I was not the best at playing black music; playing rock music is what I did . . . it was just a fluke, the big fluke of history. I started at the top. And I didn't pay any dues to get there."

Then Green heard him play bass in the studio. Fairfax played in the dynamic style of Larry Graham, who was having hits like "Your Love" with his band Graham Central Station. "Al just went crazy over Reuben poppin' the bass," said Buddy Jarrett. "That was the end of McBroom's job."

William McBroom, perhaps the most colorful character in the Enterprise Orchestra, was shown the door. "He took it with class," said Johnny Brown. "McBroom walked in and Reuben was on bass. He said to Al, 'So you fired me, motherfucker? You couldn't tell me yourself?' He turned around and left."

Fairfax pumped some new blood into the Enterprise Orchestra. "All these guys were Southern musicians," said Reuben. "All of them were older than me. I was green, a college boy from the North with cornrows. Definitely the odd man out." His arrival signified changes for the band. "They knew I was the guy comin' to take their jobs—but *I* didn't." By the end of 1979, the Enterprise Orchestra would be no more and Fairfax would become Green's bandleader.

❖

One of the earliest gigs Reuben Fairfax Jr. was on for Al Green led to a surreal summit meeting in the studio. They had played the Latin Casino in Cherry Hill, New Jersey, April 5–10, 1977. Deniece Williams was the opening act, and brought her old boss Stevie Wonder backstage to meet Al. Stevie was after Al to record a song he'd written, "I Love You Too Much." Fairfax was summoned to bring his guitar up to their hotel's penthouse, where Wonder and Williams were parked on a couch with Michael Jackson. "I remember Michael's hand was light as a feather," said Fairfax. Wonder showed him the song, and it was agreed that after checking out of their hotel Green and the band were to head over to Philadelphia to meet Wonder at Gamble and Huff's Sigma Sound Studios.*

As Buddy Jarrett vividly recounted, certain members of the Enterprise Orchestra could not contain their excitement over meeting Stevie. Trumpet player Darryl Neely thought he was an aspiring guitar player and vocalist, although he "couldn't sing *or* play—every time he played guitar, Larry Lee said it sounded like a bear clawin' at the guitar." Neely had secretly slipped Fairfax's guitar off the bus, and when Jarrett walked into the studio "my jaw just hit the floor." There was Darryl Neely, "standin' in the middle of the room with this guitar, singin' away." He was not the only band member who thought this was a golden opportunity. Sax player Ron Echols was "goin' through the room singing opera," Jarrett noted. Matters reached an absurd crescendo when soundman Ed "Tick" Pogue waltzed in doing the old soft shoe for Stevie's benefit. Jarrett told him, "Tick, the man is *blind*. He can't see you."

After things calmed down, Wonder showed the band the song. "He expected everybody to be able to play it right away, which people weren't able to do," said Johnny Brown, who felt this was deliberate so the old master could show them how it's done—by going instrument to instrument, overdubbing each part (except for the guitar, leaving Reuben, his first time in a recording studio, the only member of the band to play on the track).

At some point Wonder asked Charles Hodges to demonstrate just how he did his trademark B3 runs. And so Hodges revealed his little secret—by reaching into his leather bag, pulling out a bottle of Jergens lotion, and

---

* On the way, Green stopped at a Cherry Hill facility to visit Jackie Wilson, then in a comatose state, the aftermath of an onstage heart attack. Brown says one of the few times he saw Green cry was over Wilson's death.

promptly pouring it all over the keys. "Of course, Stevie didn't see what he was doin'," noted Brown, who watched in amusement as Charles "took Stevie Wonder's hand and plopped it down in the baby lotion." Said Buddy Jarrett, "That's the first time I ever seen Stevie's head stop moving."

Wonder called for his minions to clean up the mess, but once that was done, he "played the organ—and sounded *just like* Charles," said Brown. Emboldened with a new understanding of the Enterprise Orchestra, Stevie asked one of his producers to "go and get some wine—some wino wine," said Fairfax. "Because we were just crazy."

Once the track was built, Stevie, Deniece, and Al worked on the vocals. Green did not deliver. Al "could not sing—he could not sing the part," said Jarrett, amazed. "He could not articulate this song in his head to get it to come out his mouth . . . it had to be a mental thing, it wouldn't come out."* After a while Stevie said, 'Well, that's all right, I'll figure somethin' else out.'" (While Brown just thought he didn't know the song, Fairfax felt Green just bunted intentionally due to the fact he was under contract to Hi. Wonder later released a solo version of "I Love You Too Much" in 1985.)**

❖

Not long after this, Charles Hodges, who'd been touring with Green some in the past few years, was shown the door. On the road in Chicago he'd met a beautiful girl, a professional model who wanted to meet his boss. "That let me down, 'cause I wanted her myself." Nevertheless, Hodges introduced her to Al. "He was kissing her hand—'I'll see you when I get off,' Al said." After the show, she appeared. "Al said, 'You goin' with me?' She said, 'No, I'm going with *him*.' That was me and that was *it*." Green's feelings toward him "changed from that day."

To make matters worse, Hodges had gotten friendly with Green's main squeeze, background singer Margaret Foxworth. "Oooh, man, Margaret . . .

---

* As I was finishing this book I finally heard the (unremarkable) recording, and Buddy may be on to something. Green only adds harmony vocals, some falsetto whoops, and the occasional "I love you."

** Although Green is complimentary toward Wonder in the press, privately he's expressed other emotions. He told his producer Paul Zaleski he wasn't to let Stevie in should he show up. According to Zaleski, "He said, "If Stevie Wonder walks into the studio, shut it off. Because he'll steal everything."

Early Al Green publicity shots. Green was so new at Hi Records in the bearded shot that it was initially identified as a picture of labelmate Don Bryant. The slick, silky Al Green had yet to appear. "No disrespect, but Al dressed like he came from Forrest City, Arkansas," said road manager/emcee Roland Jones.
(Author's collection)

Ray Harris, the controversial, intense ex-rockabilly singer who was a founding member of Hi Records. Harris was "just an old horse trader," said partner Joe Cuoghi. Portrait by Ken Christian. (Courtesy Ken Christian)

Hi president Joe Cuoghi filing records at his highly influential Memphis record store, Poplar Tunes. "Joe was like a father to me," said Willie Mitchell. (Courtesy *The Commercial Appeal*)

1962 ad for Bill Black's Combo, the band behind Hi's first big hit, the instrumental "Smokie—Part 2." "Everybody thought we was black," said sometime member Ace Cannon. (Author's collection)

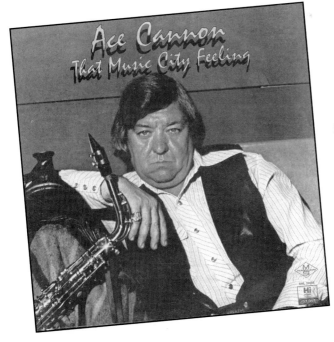

Boozy sax man Ace Cannon recorded twenty-seven albums for Hi, staying until the bitter end. (Author's collection)

Willie at work. "You spend most of the time pullin' shit out," he'd say. "We're not producers, we're reducers." **(Courtesy University of Memphis Libraries/ Preservation & Special Collections Department)**

The Manhattan Club and Danny's Club, two of the joints where Willie Mitchell's influential band played. Future super-star Memphis musicians came night after night to study the band's sound.

(Thanks to Sherman Wilmott for the ad; photo courtesy University of Memphis Libraries/Preservation & Special Collections Department)

Willie at his front gates. Mitchell "paid a lot of people's bills," said musician
Thomas Bingham. "Matter of fact, he bailed half of Memphis out of jail."
(Courtesy University of Memphis Libraries/Preservation & Special Collections Department)

Hi Studios, 2013. "It was a spiritual thing . . . being a part of something you believed in," said Hi songwriter and singer Don Bryant.
(Courtesy Jimmy Vapor)

Hi Rhythm, the band that played on all the Hi Records hits and surely one of the greatest outfits to ever enter a recording studio. "We felt each other," said Charles Hodges. "We were spiritually connected." Back row, from left to right: Leroy "Flick" Hodges, Charles "Do-Funny" Hodges, Archie "Hubbie" Turner, and Mabon "Teenie" Hodges. Howard "Bullog" Grimes in the hat. (Author's collection)

O. V. Wright. "O. V. was brought up in church, and he knew how to sing from his soul," said musician Charles Hodges.

(Courtesy University of Memphis Libraries/ Preservation & Special Collections Department)

Early publicity shot of Ann Peebles and a Rick Ivy portrait of Ann and Willie in the studio. Willie "was a little tough on Ann," said Leroy Hodges.

(Publicity shot courtesy University of Memphis Libraries/Preservation & Special Collections Department; Ann & Willie portrait courtesy Carol Ivy-Givens)

The mighty Syl Johnson. During his tenure at Hi, Johnson was the man who would've been king. "I was always standing in the shadows of Al Green," he said.

(Thanks to Rob Hatch-Miller)

Al and Willie at work at Royal Studios sometime in the 1970s. "I know Al Green better than anybody else. I created him," said Willie. (Courtesy *The Commercial Appeal*)

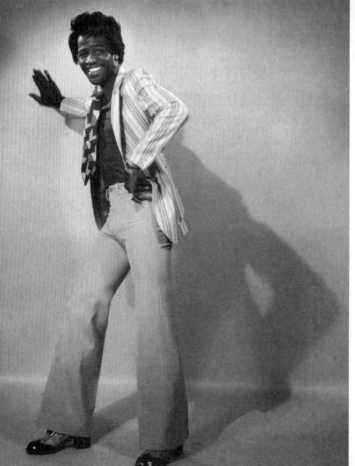

Al. No caption necessary. (Courtesy *The Commercial Appeal*)

Sandra Rhodes, Charles Chalmers, and Donna Rhodes—aka Rhodes, Chalmers, Rhodes. Their soulful backing vocals on nearly all of Al Green's hits led to work for Frank Sinatra, Liza Minnelli, the Bee Gees, and KC and the Sunshine Band. When they walked into the studio some were "shocked that we were white people," said Sandra. (Courtesy Donna Rhodes)

Laura Lee in an early publicity shot and on a 1974 album cover. "Laura was self-made . . . she had some money, some kind of success, so she didn't bow down to Al," said Roland Jones. (Author's collection)

Horn player Buddy Jarrett, 2013. "We called him 'Genius' because he knew everything," said a fellow band member. (Author's collection)

A 1973 publicity shot. (Author's collection)

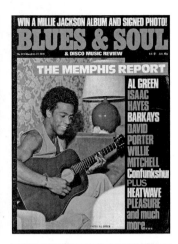

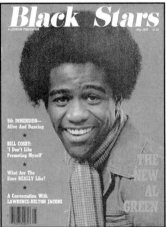

The many faces of Al. (Author's collection)

Al in June 1974. Mary Woodson would be found dead in his home four months later. (Fred Griffith/ Courtesy *The Commercial Appeal*)

Woodson's death made front-page headlines throughout the country. "Al Green stopped bein' popular for a long time with black people," said Hi promotion man Willie Bean. "They felt like he did it." (Author's collection)

Mary Woodson, taken from an employee ID card found with her body. "I can't stand living without you," wrote Woodson to Green in a note written four days before her death. (Courtesy *The Commercial Appeal*)

Green in 1975 at the podium of Full Gospel Tabernacle, his new church, which he declared "will be the most phenomenal and sensational act of spiritualism ever seen in Memphis. It will be a center of divine power." (Barney Sellers/Courtesy *The Commercial Appeal*)

Shirley Green ambushed by a newspaper photographer in 1977. Her marriage to Al would be a turbulent one. "Al wanted what Shirley had, and Shirley wanted Al," said band member Johnny Brown. (Fred Griffith/Courtesy *The Commercial Appeal*)

A space-age Al during an interview for *Downbeat* circa the release of *Truth n' Time*. He told them, "There are things done by the old Al Green that the new Al Green most certainly cannot do. . . . The new Al Green is a *free-expression* Al Green—the Believer." Portraits by Rick Ivy. (Courtesy Carol Ivy-Givens)

1977 mug shot of Al Green. "The complainant stated that he had been assaulted by Albert 'Al' Green," said the police report, in which it was also alleged that "Green struck him in the face and head several times with his fists." Nothing ever came of the charges. (Courtesy Irving, Texas, Police Department)

Al and members of his band during the *Truth n' Time* period, April 1, 1978. Left to right: Margaret Foxworth, Green, Carol Staton, Bernard Staton, and Ardis Hardin. **(Courtesy Bernard Staton)**

Green reunited with Hi founders Quentin Claunch (left) and Bill Cantrell (right) for the 1982 Grammy winner *Precious Lord*, only to follow it with an album of invitational hymns featuring Jim Walker (front) on piano that never saw release. Claunch and Cantrell wound up taking Al to court. According to Claunch, Al "didn't want to pay anybody . . . he was kind of a con man." **(Courtesy Nikki Walker)**

Robert Mugge and Green at a showing of *Gospel According to Al Green*, the definitive Green documentary. Al didn't make it easy for Mugge. "I had to chase him for thirteen months before he said yes," said Mugge. **(Courtesy Justin Freed)**

Paul Zaleski at the board while Al shakes hands with engineer Pat Taylor at Ardent Studios, Memphis, in the mideighties. Zaleski produced some of Green's most interesting gospel records and got him back on the charts. "I said, 'Look, you're not mouthing this shit.' Because Al, he will do that to you." **(Courtesy Paul Zaleski)**

A publicity photo from recent years.
(Author's collection)

"Al does what God tells him to do." Bishop Al Green preaching at Full Gospel Tabernacle in March 2016. Portrait by David Julian Leonard.
(Courtesy David Julian Leonard)

I wanted to sing some melodies in her ear!" admitted Charles. "That girl had a body on her. My, my, my."*

One night out on the road Hodges says Foxworth "wanted me to come in and put some oil on her back." Who should knock on the door but Al. "I said, 'I just brought Margaret's purse that she left on the bus,' and I slipped on out," said Charles, who was sent home the next day.

"He was talking to me," said Foxworth. "And the next day he was fired!"**

❖

On May 30, 1977, Al Green was arrested in Irving, Texas. Sometime keyboard player Larry Robinson had flown out from the East Coast to play a few shows and pick up money he was owed. "Al was supposed to give Larry a round-trip ticket," said Johnny Brown. "They gave him a one-way ticket. And they didn't pay him." After the concert, Green and company retreated to the Irving Holiday Inn across the highway, and a pissed-off Larry "beat on Al's door all night long." Finally Count, aka Walter, Green's brother, and John, husband of their sister Maxine, worked Robinson over.

Larry called the police, claiming in the report that the Reverend did the beating himself. "The complainant stated that he had been assaulted by Albert 'Al' Green. Robinson stated that he had gone to Green's room #215 to discuss financial business with him" went the report.*** "Robinson stated that upon arriving at Green's room Green invited him in and an argument ensued. Robinson advised that Green struck him in the face and head several times with his fists." The police report noted that Larry's "eye was puffed up and swollen shut."

---

* Irked by Green's unending string of women, Foxworth had a long affair with one of Al's roadies right under his nose. "'OK, if you can do it, I can do it,'" she reasoned. "He would react crazy." Apparently everybody was after "The Fox." "James Brown followed me around," she boasted. And Muhammad Ali. "To tell you the truth, Muhammad Ali had the worst halitosis. I couldn't take it."

** Hodges said it was a blessing in disguise as he was unsettled by the manner in which Green brought together the sacred and profane. "I got scared. He started mixing the songs up, R&B and gospel." While out on the road Charles literally started praying to be free of Green's world. "I can understand if he do a show and then maybe a few gospel songs at the end." But going from "Sweet Sixteen" to "Jesus Is Waiting"? "No, I couldn't handle that . . . I don't know how he can do it now."

*** It appears arresting officer Hutchison wasn't much of a soul fan. The first draft of the report refers to Green as "the actor Al Green."

"I was a rookie, I hadn't been out of the police academy three months," said arresting officer D. E. "Hutch" Hutchison. "Had it not been Al Green, it probably would've been just another call." Robinson "was pretty wound up and demanding that something be done. Of course, Al downplayed it." Hutchison said Green claimed Robinson had moved toward him and "took it as an aggressive act and he popped him."

At 12:05 Green was arrested; he paid $102.50 in bail. "He was good about the whole thing," Hutchison recalled. "I vaguely remember him saying something about being kind of claustrophobic about the cuffs or being confined in a small cell. He was booked in, processed, posted bond, and out the door he went." Nothing ever became of the charges.

But this was not the last of Larry Robinson. When Green played Radio City Music Hall in January 1978, Robinson was waiting inside the lobby when the star's limo pulled up.* As Johnny Brown recalled, "Al walked in, saw him, and said, 'Hey, Larry, nice to see you—you wanna come upstairs to the dressing room?'" Up in the dressing room there was a grand piano, which Brown played as the two men talked. Larry mentioned it was hot in the room and instructed one of Al's bodyguards to open the window.

As soon as he turned away, Larry, who had a black belt in karate, "walked over to Al and knocked the hell out of him, busted his lip," claimed Brown, who witnessed it. Green's bodyguards swarmed Robinson. "Boy, all you could see were the fists goin' into him and the blood splatterin' all over the place," said Brown. "I remember when they pushed him out of the dressing room all bloody. Pops and them got him down, bust his head with a pistol . . . just really violent stuff," said Reuben Fairfax Jr., shaken by what he had witnessed.

Local authorities were notified. "The police—and this is the truth—the police told Al that they would get rid of him, that Al would never see him again, that they would find him at the bottom of the river," claimed Brown. "Al told them, 'No, just put him in jail. My flight leaves at such-and-such a time, let him out when I leave. I'm not pressing any charges.' That's the last time I ever saw Larry Robinson."

---

* Opening for Green at Radio City was Patti LaBelle. "It was basically his audience—I didn't go out there to steal them, just to let them see and hear me," she said coyly. Patti "actually succeeded in getting far more response than the headliner on that particular occasion!" wrote soul music reporter David Nathan. Green and LaBelle would meet again in New York City five years later, and it would be a clash of the titans.

Fairfax said when they stepped onstage at Radio City, the mood was rather grave, with everybody in the band "just lookin' at each other." Green "told the audience, 'Man, I was feelin' so good, and a few minutes ago somebody just bust me in my jaw.' We went on and did a show . . . a good show." Nobody blamed Robinson for what he'd allegedly done. "You can only take bein' screwed so long, then you gonna screw back," said Buddy Jarrett. "Man, jump a dude because he don't want to pay him? They always did shit like that."

The ways of their leader were wearing on the Enterprise Orchestra. Jarrett realized Al Green "could do whatever the hell he pleased. He either knew or had access to pull all the strings to do whatever he wanted. I don't want to be around people like that. It's scary—real scary."

❖

On June 15, 1977, Reverend Al Green did a most unexpected thing—he got married for the first time. Born in Chicago and just about a month younger than Green, Shirley Anne Kyles Green is a formidable gospel singer, as the few clips of her on YouTube attest. She's also, as Al put it, "a church bird."

Shirley and her band, the Revelations, had opened two shows for Green at the Memphis Mid-South Coliseum—the first one being the November 1974 rescheduled police benefit concert, the second in July 1975. Having no interest in secular music, Kyles left both shows before the headliner (and future husband) appeared. "I saw her perform, but I didn't meet her then—it was almost a year before I got to shake her hand," Green gushed. Kyles had been married previously to a church organ player and had two young children.

No doubt Shirley's intensity as a singer appealed to Al. "She's incredible," said Ralph T. Lofton, a former member of the Revelations. Kyles was "one of those singers that every time you hear her she makes the hair stand up on your arms and brings chills to your body. She's always been that way." Kyles was a choir director at Mt. Vernon Baptist Church in Memphis. Jimmy Netters, the Revelations' guitarist, was the son of the pastor there, Dr. James LaVirt Netters Sr., an influential preacher who'd been at the church since 1955 and had been very active in civil rights. "Mt. Vernon was considered a megachurch."

The Revelations were ahead of their time and somewhat controversial. "Churches back then were not ready," said Lofton. "This was during the time when a lot of churches did not have instrumentation for church service. Jimmy had to convince his pastor—also his dad—we should do this, we needed this kind of music in the church. He was against it at first.

"We just took a spiritual approach to music and we made it our own. We would take old hymns the choirs would sing and redo 'em as instrumentals . . . it was mind blowing." Add Shirley to the package, and it became "very explosive. She was very dynamic, she knew how to deliver music and it touched people's hearts and souls."

This sort of adventurous gospel had to appeal to Green, welcomed into the church world by the pastor of Mt. Vernon, who "opened up an avenue where a lot of preachers did not want to deal with Al Green, but Reverend Netters was the one who stretched his hands out." Lofton claims that before he'd opened his own church, Green had "preached his first sermon" at Mt. Vernon.

"People say when Al came in the church, Al sang and Shirley turned around to the choir members and said, 'I'm gonna marry him,'" said Johnny Brown. She joined Green's church, organizing the church's business and starting its day-care center. "She's a business lady," Al would tell the press. Kyles "sang with us," conceded Margaret Foxworth. "She wasn't really into R&B, but she went along with it for a minute to trick him." (Foxworth claims Al's family "hated" Kyles.)

Unhappy with Green's blend of secular and gospel, Shirley quit his church altogether in April 1977. Out of nowhere Al showed up at her Memphis apartment telling her he needed her to "complete God's work." The way Green told it to *People* magazine: "I asked, 'What are you doing the rest of your life?' and she said, 'Helping you.' I took her hand and slipped the ring on and said, 'How 'bout it?'"

On June 15 at 9 p.m. the couple, dressed all in white, was secretly married in a ten-minute ceremony at the home of Elder Blair T. Hunt at 731 Hastings Street (they'd attempted it three times previously that day, but the minister, a friend of Green's, wasn't home). Al signed the register as "Leorns Green" and listed his previous address of 920 Inman (his brother Walter lived there now). By the twenty-fourth it was in the local paper. Green had been "determined to get married," said the only witness, Miss Harry Rae Simons. "He just wanted a quiet ceremony . . . she was very quiet and shy looking and he gave her a beautiful ring. They seemed very much in love."

But by the time the *Commercial Appeal* called to confirm the story, secretary Evelyn Alexander had apparently been instructed by Green to call the paper "and kill the story" as "it wasn't true." That day, when the couple arrived in New York for a concert, he introduced Shirley as his sister.

People were shocked by the news. "When she got with Al Green, a lotta people couldn't believe it," said Charles Hodges. "She had no business marrying him . . . she was anointed, she loved God, she was a gospel girl. She was naïve. Al had a knack to pick people he could manipulate." Margaret Foxworth had a more cynical view. "The thing with her was the church thing. Her brother and father were preachers." And Al "was trying to break into the church."

"Al wanted what Shirley had, and Shirley wanted Al" is how Johnny Brown saw it. "She's a strong person, a very dominant female. She was a PK—preacher's kid, one of them holier-than-thou folks, and it was a match made in hell. Al had to be in full control of everything and so did she. It was like two bulls in pasture."

Brown first saw the dynamic in action when he started playing organ at the church—and wasn't that good a musician yet. Shirley "was tryin' to get rid of me, even though we were cool. She was used to havin' the very best play behind her, and she figured she should have the very best. All these big-time organ players would come in the church and they would tear my butt up. But I didn't sulk or nothing. I'd just stand there, watch 'em, and then go home and practice all night long. Al kept tellin' her, 'One day he's gonna be good, you just watch him.' It did become quite frustrating to her . . . she could not get rid of me.

"The more Shirley tried to get him to hire really great musicians, the more he dug in and said no. According to Al, that was one of the things that went wrong in his marriage—the argument over me."

The marriage would get off to a somber start. The day after the wedding, Green got word in New York that his father had died of a heart attack back on Al's farm. Green didn't cancel the show. "He went onstage," said Brown. "That's the kind of person Al is."*

That December, *People* would feature the Green lovebirds in an upbeat article. There was a picture of the cheery couple, making the sign of the cross with their two index fingers combined. Al told the magazine he was producing an album on his wife, which might contain a duet. "We sing great together," said the Reverend. Nothing ever came of the album, although both Johnny Brown and Reuben Fairfax Jr. recall cutting a few

---

* In a 2016 interview, Green claimed he was on his honeymoon when his father passed.

tracks on her in Green's studio. "Shirley didn't come across in the studio like she came across live," said Brown. "I felt Al was intimidating to her."

❖

Around this time Al and the band booked a date in Hawaii, a trip that apparently had a dual purpose. According to Reuben Fairfax Jr., band gossip had it that Green's relatives felt certain a sinister curse had been placed upon Al. "The family believed in voodoo, and Al was under a spell. If he crossed an ocean, that would've broken the spell." They never made the trip, due to an attack by (and the demise of) one of Al's dogs. Once again, Green found himself involved in a mysterious death, only this life had walked on four legs.

"My dogs are my friends," he'd tell the press. "They're big and muscular. They're like men . . . they talked to me and listened to me." Green even took one dog onstage during a show. "He was terrified," said dog-lover Al. When his staff told him one particular pooch had passed on, Green "just went out of my mind . . . crying . . . breaking everything I could find in the room . . . even the strings on my guitar."

Al met his match in a particular Doberman. It was a fearsome animal. "I hated that dog," said Margaret Foxworth. "The dog would be sitting there, watching me. I could not move until he came and removed the dog."

Buddy Jarrett said that Green intended to train the animal as an attack dog, but since "that took too much time," Al took certain shortcuts. As Buddy put it, "he gonna microwave this dog to be his attack dog. The dog bit the shit out of Al. Chewed his arm all up." What happened next? "Al shot him," claimed Margaret Foxworth. "Al shot the dog."

Green told Reuben that after the dog had clamped onto his arm, he somehow managed to trap the canine in his car, leaving it locked inside— the vehicle still running—as he went off to the hospital for treatment. Mysteriously, Green told Fairfax, when he returned from the hospital "the dog was dead and the car wasn't running." Reuben didn't buy that story. Neither did anyone else.

When Jarrett asked Haywood "Pick" Anderson what had happened, he told him, "Well, the dog bit Al and felt so bad he went out to the car and killed itself . . . committed suicide because he bit Al."

"The dog killed itself?" asked an incredulous Buddy.

"Yeah, with a pistol," drawled Pick.

HIM THAT I NEED

If the wages of sin are death, I can't afford it.
—AL GREEN

"It's you that I want, but Him that I need," sings Al Green on "Belle," a succinct, oft-quoted summation that has served to symbolize his inner conflict over hot pants and the heavenly gates.* "With the *Belle* album I knew I had to move on. I felt a change coming on so strong . . . I could hear all this beautiful music. I had to take it upon myself to work up the sounds I was hearing in *my* studio with *my* band."

Green had quietly put half a million dollars into setting up American Music Recording Studios (not to be confused with Chip Moman's American Studios, also in Memphis) at 3208 Winchester Road. He'd snatched Hi founding member Bill Cantrell away from Royal to build a studio out of a former rehearsal hall and run the eight-track *The Belle Album* was recorded on.

"Nobody knew Al Green personally like Bill Cantrell," claimed Green's later producer Paul Zaleski. "Bill was Al's surrogate father. Al Green would confide in Bill . . . they knew each other on a spiritual basis." Deaf in one ear, "Uncle" Bill also liked his fishing. "We'd try to set up a session, he'd say, 'Well, I tell ya, Al, I'm gonna be up at the lake . . . ','" Reuben Fairfax Jr. recalled. "We had to do a lot of the record around Cantrell's fishing."

---

* According to Green, the song was written for Woodson. "'Belle' was Mary," he'd tell reporters.

That gives you an idea of how funky things were at Green's studio. For that extra Arkansas touch, Al adorned the vocal booth with cotton bolls, corn shucks, and, he noted, "an old straw hat somebody wore while they were picking cotton." A solo producer for the first time, Green was looking for something different from Mitchell's particular, precise ways. "Willie has everything pre-set . . . when you go in the studio *this* one has to be set on six, and *that* one on three," said Green. "That's too confining for me."

Green assembled a new team of musicians around him: Fred Jordan, who'd worked for Johnny Nash, was musical director, wrote arrangements, and played keyboards and synthetic strings (that grating sheet of sound you hear on "Belle" is a crude early synth called the Polyphonic Orchestron); Leon Thomas,* a pal of Reuben's, also played keyboards, as did Johnny Brown; John Toney, Ardis Hardin, and Rob Payne played drums (as well as the Syndrum, the first commercially available electronic drum); the horn section came from the Enterprise Orchestra—Ron Echols, Darryl Neely, and Buddy Jarrett (the Enterprise's James Bass also contributed guitar). For the first time Green played guitar throughout one of his albums, and Reuben switched to bass (he also contributed beautiful percussion color via a bell lyre, a type of glockenspiel). Rhodes, Chalmers, Rhodes had been replaced by three African Americans who provided the striking background vocals: Harvey and Linda Jones, plus Margaret Foxworth, who was also credited with the vocal arranging alongside Green; all three of these singers would stay with Al for years.

With *Belle,* Green recorded a brand-new lineup in a new studio with new songs, to capture "the spontaneity of the music that came out. I just let the tapes roll and the band soar." When they began recording, nobody had an idea it was an album, and some of the songs were recorded just as they were learning them. "Since Al was playin' guitar, I played bass . . . we just sat down and started—it was impromptu," explained Fairfax, who wrote the music with Jordan as Green supplied lyrics.** "We did a lot of it

---

* The way Leon Thomas got hired was typical Green. A friend of Reuben's, he tagged along for a rehearsal. As Fairfax recalled, "His hand just landed on the keyboard and Al said, 'That's it! That's what I need right there.'" "You didn't apply for a job with Al," said Johnny Brown. "You just happened to be in the right place at the right time. You'd walk in there with a friend—'Oh, who is that?' If he heard you and he liked you, you was hired."

** The *Belle* songs were credited to all three. Since Green was still bound by his London contract, which stipulated Willie Mitchell as the producer, Fairfax suspects that this wasn't just benevolence on Al's part—he named his coconspirators so they could be blamed later if things didn't work out. Fairfax and Jordan received no writer's credit on Green's next album, even though they did the same kind of work.

pretty much live," he said, with no song requiring more than two or three takes. "We had kind of sketched it—lyrics, melody, chord changes . . . once you have that, you start playin' the end vamp, you start playin' what you wanna play." Fairfax laughed at how loose it all was. "To be honest, I never knew how we were gonna get out of those songs . . . I never knew how those songs were gonna end!"

As far as recording the song "Belle," "We were just feelin' our way," said Reuben. "It was just magic. We just sat down and played the darn thing. I don't remember many overdubs. Al was in incredible form back then."

If some of the album sounds crude, nearly amateur, it was. Buddy Jarrett wrote the horn coda for "Feels Like Summer" while making a sandwich back at home. He returned to hum it for the other players. "You had to hold the first note for eight beats," said Jarrett, who claims he wasn't paid for his work on *Belle*. "They couldn't play it—they were too short-winded to hold the first note. It was comical. But Al said, 'C'mon, let's put it on tape.' They played it back, I almost cried. Al says, 'I think it's fine.'" Buddy said they ducked the volume on the horn part so "it's more of a suggestion." Fred Jordan recorded the sessions, and it was "on-the-job training," said Johnny Brown. "Fred wasn't that good an engineer." Al's vocals in particular sound buried at times, like on "Dream."*

"The sound is homemade and eccentric," wrote Robert Palmer of Green's gospel garage band, and therein lies a large part of *Belle*'s charm. Even the cover—a "now" shot of Al saying hey to the camera—has a Walmart vibe (the pictures were taken by WHBQ staff photographer Jim Shackleford in a "mom-and-pop studio" across from the station at Webb Studios. Jim wanted everybody to know Al was "a delight to work with.")

"The *Belle* album really came from within," said Green. "That album is different from any I ever had. There's a seriousness about it." From the sad opening notes of Johnny Brown's Fender Rhodes on the title cut, you know you're out in left field with *Belle*. Al wasn't kidding—this is an Al Green album like no other. The wistful backing track is delicate, gentle—pretty, even—and enlivened by touches of color from the bell lyre as well as the weird, low-note men's-choir murmur that comes in halfway through. Even that sheet-metal synth adds a certain flair.

---

* According to Paul Zaleski, part of the problem was that Green used some of Willie's tricks at American, but incorrectly. "Al sat down at the console and he had it in his head the only way that a mix could happen was if all of the faders were all across in a line," said Zaleski, but in order for it to work the machine had to be calibrated to zero. "They never did that." It was the first thing Paul did once he started working there.

In a slightly microphonic vocal that seems to come via a megaphone in outer space, Al sings plaintively of the wandering through "many drunken country bars" that has led him to Jesus. Green wants the woman but knows he needs God, and the conflict is over. He sounds humbled, even at peace, and listening to Al hit that falsetto ending, you can practically see him ascending to the heavens, at least in song. The message being delivered gains added power from the understated way it's expressed, and this subtle approach extends throughout the entire *Belle* album. As Greil Marcus noted, "There's no ad for Green's ministry on the back cover."

Green's exhortations of faith were already feeling clichéd and tired on *Have a Good Time,* but here they're fresh, immediate, provocative. There are many joys to be found on *Belle.* Reuben's snappy bass licks, an inventive alternative to the usual electric guitar . . . the warmly human handclaps darting in and out of the songs . . . the way Green intertwines with the backing vocals on "Loving You," the manner in which he sings "snow" over and over in "Feels Like Summer" . . . the long, funky bass intro to "Georgia Boy," not to mention Al's oddball whistling and the tossed-off "South's gonna do it again" nearly six minutes later . . . the clavinet/horn kookiness of "I Feel Good" and Al's crazy bell-like acoustic "solo" at the end of the song . . . the palpable anguish of "I've cried some tears / For years and years and years" in "All N All" . . . the lost-in-a-snowglobe feeling of "Dream" . . . this collection of songs hang together like no other Green album except *Call Me.* Aside from the attempt to update Al's sound with disco effects and those unnerving moments of unrestrained synth, *The Belle Album* is some kind of masterpiece. "I think *Belle* was the kind of record it was because it channeled both—religion and rock & roll—and it channeled them so well," Green rightly declared.

Released in December 1977, *Belle* was dedicated to both his late father and Dewitt Jordan, a renowned local artist who'd been murdered before he could finish a painting for Al entitled *The Harvest,* which pictured mules hitched to a wagon of freshly picked cotton, although the artist hadn't filled in the weighing scales before his demise. "I thought that was significant," said Green, pointing out Jordan had been killed "drinking . . . arguing with some guy about some girl that's irrelevant."*

---

* The "Delta Fox," Dewitt Jordan was one of those Memphis characters deserving of his own book. He painted portraits for Sammy Davis Jr., Charlie Pride, and Tennessee Ernie Ford, as well as vivid and sometimes controversial depictions of Southern black life. In 1977 he was shot in the forehead by the brother of his fiancée "under circumstances never fully established." He was forty-four years old. Dewitt was a cousin of *Belle* coproducer/cowriter Fred Jordan.

Belle was not a hit. The title single crawled to number eighty-three on the pop charts. "I can understand why," Green admitted. "People were confused—-they expected me to continue singing about girls and feeling good, and suddenly I wanted to sing about glory to God." Green fans swooned, however, among them many a white critic and rocker. "We may someday look back on *Belle* as Al Green's best," wrote Greil Marcus in *Rolling Stone,* comparing the title track to the Band's *Music from Big Pink.* No less than Lou Reed would name the tracks "Belle" and "Georgia Boy" as all-time favorites on more than one list. *Belle*'s biggest fan, however, might've been Cora Greene. "Mama Green[e] had the *Belle* album up on her wall," said Reuben Fairfax Jr.

❖

More than one musician of Green's has pointed out that the mention of a "bright morning star" in "Belle" is not just a biblical reference but a nod to the secret society of the Freemasons. Along with such notables as Jesse Jackson, Al Sharpton, and the late Richard Pryor, Al is a member of the Prince Hall Masons, the African American wing of Freemasonry, which dates back to 1776.

A 1983 issue of *Jet* has a photo of a beaming Green attending a group gathering in Little Rock where they'd been welcomed by then-Governor Bill Clinton. Al's shown wearing the ornate cap signifying he'd reached the Thirty-Third Degree—the highest station one can reach within Freemasonry. "I played for him several times at the Masonic Temple," said Johnny Brown, who remembered the Masonic regalia—black suit, white apron, ornate medallions and hats. "It was weird—you got these two guys sittin' over in the corner, lookin' like the joker on the playing card. Either they was brand new or in trouble."

As usual, Green played by his own rules. Brown said there were times when Al "would throw signs while he was singing." At first Johnny thought they were gang signs, but his Masonic friends pointed out otherwise. "They'd say, 'Do you know what Al just did?! He threw the Mason sign. He's gonna get in trouble!'"

❖

AL GREEN'S WIFE SEEKS DIVORCE, ran the headline of a tiny article in the *Commercial Appeal.* Shirley Green had filed on May 4, 1978. The couple hadn't even been married a year. The papers state that Shirley, five months pregnant, had left their home "because of fear" on April 23. She accused

Green of "cruel and inhuman treatment" as he has "on numerous occasions been guilty of physical cruelty to her, that he has made numerous threats to her and her minor children from a prior marriage, and that the Plaintiff is sincerely afraid of the Defendant." A protection order barring Green from having contact with her and her children was granted the next day.

Shirley Green did not provide details until a shocking article entitled "Silent No Longer" appeared in the January 3, 1995, edition of the *Chicago Tribune,* written by John W. Fountain, a reporter for the paper's church beat.* (Al agreed to talk to Fountain, but backed out a day later.) In the article she claims the abuse started the day after they got married June 15, 1977. Returning to Memphis due to the death of Al's father, they were driving home from the airport in Green's Cadillac when Shirley said something that "set him off." She alleged Al slapped her repeatedly.

Green apologized, but two days later she claimed Al woke her in the middle of the night, an argument ensued over sex, and he beat her severely with a guitar. Later in August when they were on the road, Al got mad because she did not know the details concerning where they were staying. She alleged he beat her in the face until "my eyes were black." She claimed it happened again the next morning when she wasn't on time. Shortly thereafter she miscarried and fled to Chicago. She'd return to him in September, but lived in a separate house at 4671 Hancock because she was "afraid."

In April 1978, when Shirley was five months pregnant, she met Al out on the road in Philadelphia. Another argument ensued over sex, and she claimed Green beat her with a boot and tore up her clothes. According to the *Tribune* article, the wound in her head required ten stitches. It was then that she filed for divorce.

In August, Shirley was back in court as Green had failed to keep up with alimony payments. "Defendant did indeed furnish to her a Pontiac automobile which became inoperable after 2 or 3 days," stated court documents. On August 21 her first child with Al was born, Alva Lei Green.

Mistakenly listing June 21 as their wedding day, Green's attorney would enter into evidence a badly photocopied "pre-marital agreement" he claimed Shirley had signed a day before the marriage in which she agreed to

---

* In a brief e-mail, Shirley said she was not happy with the article. "I detest what the writer did," she wrote, not explaining why, and in response to a request for an interview informed me that she was "in the process of selecting a writer for my own personal story . . . my story is one built on Faith in God, nothing else." Further inquiries went unanswered. According to David Gest's book, Shirley appeared on *The Oprah Winfrey Show* around the same time as the *Tribune* article making similar claims, but I have not been able to locate a copy.

"release all her marital rights in and to the property of the Defendant." This crude document, hand-dated June 24, which has blanks throughout to allow for any current wife-to-be's signature, was also signed by a pair of witnesses, Green's sister Maxine and his secretary Hattie Angel.*

As Shirley's lawyer pointed out, there was just one problem with the document: the date signified she signed it after they were married on the fifteenth, and she signed it with her married name. Nor were any of the blanks filled in with her name.

On December 15 Shirley would drop a bombshell in a new filing: "Defendant has been guilty of adultery with one Margaret Foxworth . . . said Margaret Foxworth gave birth to male child on approximately August 11, 1978, in Cleveland, Ohio . . . this child is named Albert Leorns Green II and the Defendant has admitted being the father of said child." It notes that at "approximately the end of September, 1978" Foxworth "lived with the Defendant at his home in Millington, Tennessee until mid-October 1978, openly and notoriously in an adulterous relationship."**

Incredibly, Shirley and Al reconciled in April 1979, and divorce proceedings were dropped. It was all "a misunderstanding," Green told *Jet*. "Shirley can't stay away from Al and Al can't stay away from Shirley." A truce, however temporary.

❖

In February 1978, Green and the band went to Skokie, Illinois, to tape a set for the public television show *Soundstage*. Every bootleg copy I've seen of this show appears to be taken from the same mediocre-quality VHS, which is a shame as this is one of the all-time classic Al Green performances.

Wearing a light plaid suit spiced up with a flouncy cravat that adds a crazed, Elizabethan touch, Green sports shades and a fluffy Afro, as well as an egregious amount of lip gloss. This is a new, goofy Al, full of manic energy, a rubbery cartoon nerd with a whiff of *Nutty Professor* Jerry Lewis. Green cannot wait to unveil his new purpose to the world, and his enthusiasm is infectious.

Charging into "L-O-V-E (Love)," with nearly all the band in suits and the backup singers in long white dresses, the feeling is one of a cosmic

---

* The Green "pre-marital agreement" is shown in the appendix of this book.

** "She hates my guts," said Margaret Foxworth of Shirley. "And she should! They were married and I was living with him."

church service. After a slightly perfunctory reading of a few hits (with that inimitable Al version of Vegas banter: he prefaces "How Can You Mend a Broken Heart?" as "something with a whole lot of love wrapped up inside" written by the Bee Gees, "some wonderful friends of mine and a beautiful group"), things get heavier as Al turns introspective on a deep, roller-coaster version of "You Ought to Be with Me."

Then comes the first live performance of "Belle." It's a stunner. The way he sings "the laughter of the sound has quieted down" evokes that decisive turning away from the pop life, and the manner in which he worries the word "no" several times in a row just leaves you shaking your head in wonder. The ensemble rips through "I Feel Good," "Dream," and "All N All," ending with a version of "Love and Happiness" that for once evokes what the title describes. It's a powerhouse performance—Al dances, jumps, preaches, talks in tongues, and loses his glasses, all the while singing with a nimble dexterity that is as thrillingly unpredictable as the ball on a roulette wheel, except that Green never seems to land on a losing note.

As Al bounds across the stage, leaping into the audience, the camera crew struggles to keep him in frame. Green knew the value of spontaneity and refused to be tamed by the bland constraints of television. Johnny Brown recalled how Green, taping a guest spot for a TV show with a bunch of other acts, was told not to step out of the circle marked on the stage floor due to the camera setup. "First thing Al did was go runnin' out of the circle," said Johnny, laughing. When he asked him why he'd disobeyed, Green said, "You've seen about five people on stage—all five of those people that stood in that circle got the same camera shots. Did you see all the camera folks scrambling when I ran out of the circle? They got shots of me they ain't got of *nobody* else."

Shortly after the *Soundstage* taping Green played the Dorothy Chandler Pavilion in Los Angeles on February 13 (the city had declared it Al Green Day). According to Fairfax, there was a near mutiny by the band, who hadn't gotten paid for the *Soundstage* appearance; Green claimed that "the union was gonna pay us—he wasn't," said Reuben, who was sent to discuss it with Al. "The whole band was sayin' it, but they kind of put it on me."

Meanwhile the Reverend got wind of the dissent via one of his snitches and laid down the law: either the band was with Al or against him. He also informed them that without Al, they were nothing: "You gotta find somebody that looks like *Al Green,* sounds like *Al Green,* and who can convince the people that he's *Al Green.*" Unable to locate a Green doppelganger at that particular moment, the band "went on and did the show," Fairfax admitted. "We didn't know nobody like that."

Due to the pay situation, Reuben had tried to back out of the California trek entirely, but Green's road-manager "gangster," Willie "Pop" Aiken, paid him a visit a la *The Godfather,* inferring that Fairfax would meet a bad end if he didn't make the trip. Pop "came by and said, 'If you stay in Memphis, I can't protect you.'" An unfazed Fairfax decided to go anyway. As far as *Soundstage,* Reuben claims, "We never did get paid for that."

In June 1978 Green performed in the Tokyo Music Festival. Looking beyond groovy in dark shades, gold chains, and a white suit with a pink rose tucked in the lapel, Al, accompanied by a full orchestra, delivered a masterful, transcendent "Belle" that slayed all competition. On the twenty-third and twenty-fourth, he'd record a live album at the Nakano Sun Plaza that wouldn't see release until 1981 (it would be the last Hi release on Cream Records). From the man who'd set stages afire on *Soul!, Midnight Special,* and *Soul Train,* it was a lackluster affair. One problem was the bass playing of sometime band member James Hunter, which was later replaced by Reuben Fairfax Jr.'s overdubs. "Al Green's show is not an easy show to play," said Fairfax. "You actually have to know the songs."*

❖

November 1978 saw the release of *Truth n' Time,* which was a real letdown after *Belle.* There were two covers—Lulu's hit "To Sir with Love," with Reverend Al obviously addressing a different "sir"; and the Bacharach-David staple "I Say a Little Prayer." The former had been on Green's mind since the Hi days, but Mitchell hadn't been interested; as Al told Terry Gross, "I'd start singing it and Willie would say, 'Everyone break.'"

The fact that Green had recast both covers with gospel intent wasn't enough to overcome the lackluster arrangements (clever backing vocals at the end of "Sir," though). "Wait Here," based on the book of Job, was a tough piece of funk left over from the *Belle* sessions. "When Job was sick . . . he said, 'I believe I'll wait until my change comes.' But if you didn't know that, it would slip right by you," said Al, who obviously delighted in sneaking a bit of the Lord's work into his pop songs. Most

---

* On the subject of Hunter's playing, Green told Johnny Brown, "If he played bass for the rest of his life and practiced every day for ten hours, he might become a good bass player by the time he's 70."

interesting is the title track, an underdeveloped, nebulous six-minute-plus musing on time.* The entire album is a little less than twenty-seven minutes long, with nary a hit to be found. It feels unfocused, dashed off.

One glaring problem with *Truth n' Time* is the fact that there are only three songs written by Green himself. Excusing some major potholes, I find the period from *Call Me* through *Belle* to be Al's most interesting period as a lyricist, but the well abruptly runs dry at this point. He's written very sporadically since then, and little of it rises above the kind of clichéd, generic love songs he thinks are expected from him. That idiosyncratic vision that makes his previous work so compelling seems to have vanished. Perhaps baring his soul is reserved for the pulpit these days.

Discussing the *Truth n' Time* period in 1979, Green admitted that he "was still in conflict with myself. I didn't want to be nobody's preacher. I had already said yeah but I was trying to back out . . . I wasn't together." During a *Downbeat* interview, Green proved once more that he could reference himself like no other, anxious to tell the world he had straightened up and was on the right path. As he explained to David Less, "There are things done by the old Al Green that the new Al Green most certainly cannot do . . . " Yes, world, there was a New Al Green, and we all had to "give him a chance to grow. Give him a chance to *wean hisself* from the bottle. He's *fresh*: he's *brand new*. He don't know *anything*. Really, he's just a kid . . .

"The new Al Green is a *free-expression* Al Green—the Believer. Al Green, the guy that *wants* to go by Mama and Daddy's rules, not by what I had thought of previously to go by—do my own thing, play with women and Cadillac cars. *No.*"

❖

No less than three songs on *Truth n' Time* bore the writing credit of Bernard Staton. "Six-foot-six with a perm and a guitar," Staton was another young rookie Green had plucked from out of nowhere (Bernard "was kind of invading my turf," Reuben Fairfax Jr. conceded). Staton, who hailed from Philadelphia, was out on the road with another band when his wife called in the wee hours. Carol had managed to meet Al Green "and he wanted to meet *me* . . . some kind of way she got backstage," said

---

* Like many Green songs, the lyrics you find online for *Truth n' Time* are wrong and some of what he says is very hard to deduce. An authorized, accurate book of Green's lyrics would be a valuable resource.

a still-amazed Bernard. "She was very pretty, and the same way she got my attention, she got Al's attention."

Carol had played Green some cassettes of her husband's music, and he immediately instructed her to summon him. To say the least, Bernard was stunned. "I had studied him for years," boasted Staton, who can sound remarkably like Al. Bernard quit his group that night. "I spent my last $33 on a taxicab to the airport."

When he arrived in Cleveland, where Al was performing, Carol took him to meet Green. "I'm sitting in his room and over in the corner was an acoustic—'Do you play guitar?' I couldn't wait. He gave me his guitar, and I started playing a song I had written for Bobby Womack—but I never got to sing it. Al said, 'STOP! *Stop singing.* You sound like *Al Green*! I'll be in touch with you.'"

Within a week the Statons were in Memphis, and for the next year and a half they'd tour and record with Green. "Carol and I were the only staff writers he ever hired," said Bernard, who maintains there is a mountain of unreleased material in Al's vault. "Hundreds and hundreds of songs," he said. "We sat down and wrote songs on brown paper bags." Johnny Brown agreed. "Al must have hundreds of recordings that have been sitting around for years."

The most interesting story concerning Staton comes from the tail end of his time in Green's world. Carol had taken him to a Memphis church, and he'd been born-again, which led him to quit the band. About to be evicted, Staton was desperate and hadn't eaten for days. "I was lying on my carpet, I had no food, and I called Al Green and told him I was hungry. He said he'd come by to get me. I waited and waited and waited. Every time I heard a car outside my apartment complex, I'd jump up and push the curtain aside on the window, but no Al."

The next morning he heard a car horn beeping and voices telling him to come out. "It was Al and some of his guys. He took me around the corner to Denny's. Al sat there and he was making small talk, cracking jokes . . . all I knew was that I was hungry." The waitress brought Bernard a salad. A famished Staton was about to dig in when "Al pulled the salad from my side to his. I'm sitting there with a fork and knife, but no salad. He said, 'We need to talk, you can eat later.'"

Green announced he had plans to make them both rich. There under the harsh Denny's light, Al "took his briefcase from under the table and pulled out a recording contract." Enthusing over how Bernard sounded exactly like him, Green wanted Bernard "to sing love songs while he sang gospel, so we could make money. He offered me a quarter of a million."

"You'll make so much money, you'll never need anything," Al promised. Al wanted Bernard to sign it on the spot, but Bernard refused, which had his boss flummoxed. "I'm *Al Green*!" said Al Green.

Staton had a lawyer look it over, minor changes were made, and everybody was in agreement. Bernard got back together with Carol, they moved into a townhouse, and the future looked very bright. But there was still that pesky contract. "Al came by the next week. And I still hadn't signed it."

Carol asked him why. "I told her I needed to ask God about it. She said, 'Okay, let's pray about it.' We sat on the bed and I asked God—'God, Al offered me this contract, I can help people, I can feed the homeless, clothe the naked . . . '"

The Lord wasn't impressed, and decreed that Bernard get on a bus, go to Nashville, get a job, and move his family there—right away. "Same way God spoke to Paul on the road to Damascus, God spoke to me." Staton was in shock, but he acquiesced. "I had to do what God told me to do!" And so Bernard "got a Greyhound bus to Nashville, not knowing where I was going."

At 5 a.m. the bus arrived in Music City. Staton got off the Greyhound at a stop near a dirt road lined with factories. Bernard picked one, went inside, and spoke to the first person he ran into. "I introduced myself and said, 'I wrote songs for Al Green, and God told me to come here for a job.' He looked at me and he said, 'You're hired.'"

That job somehow led to working for Little Richard, who was preaching in prisons at the time. Eventually Bernard wound up in Miami, where he established his own ministry.

Staton never signed the deal with Al, nor has he spoken to Green, whom he admires a great deal, since. "The last time I saw him, I said, 'I have to go. I have to serve God.' That wasn't something he could deny."

❖

By the end of 1979 the Enterprise Orchestra was no more. Johnny Brown says they just left one after another, pissed off by the new duties and lower wages that came with the new Reverend Al; Reuben Fairfax maintains he fired what was left of them after a trip to the Bahamas. While Aaron Purdie went on to play for James Brown, the rest of the band didn't fare so well. "I don't think Buddy's picked up his goddamn horn since he left Al," said Roland Jones, but when asked, Buddy had no regrets. "I have done everything on my list," said Jarrett, who is very active in the church these days. "I had been playin' twenty years. I don't wanna be a sideman all my life."

Some years ago Larry Lee called Jarrett to inform him a rumor was going around that Green was going to put the original band back together. "I wouldn't play with Al for all the tea in China," said Buddy.

"He dogged me once. I'm gonna go back for a *re*-dogging?"

❖

Something would happen to Al in September of 1979 that would ensure there would be no more secular shows, however gospel-infused they'd become. Green had gone off to play two sold-out shows in Ohio. It appears he'd done some sort of gospel-only appearance there in the recent past, because later he'd say his "inner self" had told him "not to go to Cincinnati to sing rhythm and blues after you've gone there to do a revival." Despite the warnings, Green "went anyway . . . I was kind of steppin' out on faith."

Fairfax was onstage that night. "It was a really good show—a *great* show," he recalled. "Al was in the spirit—actin' crazy, bumpin' into the speakers. I'll never forget it—he looked at me and said, 'The race is not given to the swift, son.'" That meant Reuben should "quit playin' so much and slow down." He went back and decreased the volume on his amp. When he turned around, "Al was gone . . . I didn't know what had happened to him."

As Johnny Brown remembered it, they were playing "Let's Stay Together," and there were no footlights at the edge of the stage. "Al danced right off the end of the stage," said Brown. "He was there . . . then he was gone."

Now minus a singer, the band kept on playing. "Reuben's cord was long enough to get to the edge of the stage, he walked over and looked down." Al had fallen into the orchestra pit. Luckily a steel instrument case had broken the twelve-foot fall. Soundman Ed Pogue helped Green crawl out of the pit. "Al finished the show," said Fairfax. After a short visit to a nearby hospital Green managed to come back and soldier through a few more songs for the second show.

The weirdest part of it was that drummer John Toney had dreamed the whole thing after a gig in London. Toney told Reuben, "Man, I had a dream we were playing like we had never played before and Al just jumped off in the audience and never came back."

Green, who later said he'd spent fifteen days in the hospital due to the fall, took the incident as a warning. "That was the final awakening. I could have been killed or crippled in that fall." There would be no more mixing secular and gospel music. Green would dedicate himself to the latter from now on.

"I was being disobedient to my calling. I was moving towards God, but I wasn't moving fast enough. The fall was God's way of saying I had to hurry up."

TOO CLOSE

We're all pulled and tugged on by God and the devil. We're in a constant battle between good and evil.
—AL GREEN

"I don't care about being in the Top 10," insisted Al Green in January 1981. "I care about being pleasing in the sight of the Lord." Following the stage accident, Al disappeared from public view. He played no concerts, gave no interviews. At the end of 1980 Green released his first actual gospel record, *The Lord Will Make a Way.* Just a glance at the cover told you how seriously he was taking this. No shades, no bling, just Al in a suit and tie, gazing heavenward on the back cover. It looks just as bland and inoffensive as any other gospel album of the time.

Green recorded *The Lord Will Make a Way* at his studio with a small band consisting of Al on acoustic guitar; Reuben Fairfax Jr. on bass; drummer John Toney; keyboard players Fred Jordan, Johnny Brown, and Jesse Butler; plus a four-piece horn section consisting of Hi/Stax regulars Jack Hale Sr., Andrew Love, Ben Cauley, and Edgar Matthews. There were no originals by Al on the album, just covers of traditional gospel songs such as "Pass Me Not," "Too Close," "None but the Righteous," and the title cut. "Saved" and "In the Holy Name of Jesus" were two of the most striking performances present and the only originals, written by former Enterprise Orchestra drummer Aaron Purdie.

The jazz chords and artfully built dramas of Willie Mitchell were a thing of the past. Aside from Fred Jordan's sometimes overwrought synthetic strings and an inane version of "Highway to Heaven" that's on the album twice, complete with children's choir and banjo, this was no-frills, straight-ahead gospel delivered by a fierce band and a singer who meant every word. "*The Lord Will Make a Way* was just magic, we just sat down and did it," said Fairfax.

The title cut, a smoky, serpentine cover of an old Thomas A. Dorsey hymn, is one of Al's best. Fairfax explained that the band played it in C-sharp, the key favored for many of Green's gospel recordings. "'Lord Will Make a Way,' 'Higher Plane,' 'I Feel Good'—that's what our trick was, to do major over minor in C-sharp," said Fairfax. The song became a staple of Green's live shows, but it's never sounded better than when Reuben was playing on it. (Fairfax finally admitted there's a secret to his bass part: "I play a low E note in there, nobody else seems to play it. Same on "I Feel Good.") "There's never gonna be another bass player like him," enthused Paul Zaleski. "Reuben played the bass like it could talk. You wanna hear some good gospel with a bass line? Listen to Reuben. That SOB played bass on 'Lord Will Make a Way'!"

Fairfax had to learn not to let any flash get in Green's way. "One day he told me, 'Look, I don't need your million-dollar bass playing. All I need is for you to play *boop boop de boop*. I'm gonna pay you your money.' So he'd sing, and I'd just play the changes and give him a foundation. He didn't need a whole bunch of bass up his ass while he was singin'. I never took it as derogatory—I had to learn that playin' with him."*

Another standout track is Al's impassioned cover of the 1954 Alex Bradford standard "Too Close." "That's my favorite Al song," said Reuben. "I have to pull over when that comes on the radio. I can't drive. It's a guy tellin' you he's getting ready to die—'Too close to heaven, I can almost see my journey's end.'** Al was goin' through somethin' at that time, I don't know exactly what it was. There's a lot of emotion in that whole album."

❖

---

* Some say Fairfax was just too good at his job. Paul Zaleski maintained that "Al was extremely jealous of the way this guy played the bass and the guitar. Al felt threatened by it."

** One who didn't care for "Too Close" was esteemed gospel authority Anthony Heilbut, who wrote that Green "treats gospel standards as vehicles for his eccentric musings." "Too Close" was "a virtually fail-safe song," but he felt that as Green "begins to achieve a more authentic groove, he lets it dissipate in mid-spirit."

While Al was still under contract to Hi, *Lord Will Make a Way* was the first of six albums to be manufactured and released by Myrrh Records, a Contemporary Christian label (a division of Word Records) based in Waco, Texas, that was home to such artists as Amy Grant, B. J. Thomas, and Billy Preston.

Then-general manager James Bullard was Al Green's man at Myrrh. When Word executive Stan Moser gave Bullard a cassette of the as-yet-unreleased Green album, he was unmoved. "Al Green—he ain't no gospel singer." Moser urged him to listen again. Bullard took the cassette, "put it in a little boom box, and God had arranged it to start on the downbeat of 'The Lord Will Make a Way.'" This time it sunk in. He told Moser, "I made a mistake about Al Green . . . I need to sign him."

Bullard went to Memphis and the two men met for lunch. "You're thinkin', 'Well, Al Green—you're goin' top lunch, an exclusive place," said Bullard. Instead Al took him to Picadilly, a no-frills cafeteria about a mile from his church. The two men hit it off instantly, although Green would later confess that he'd been warned not to sign with Bullard by a close friend who claimed that James knew nothing about the music industry and that he was like two left shoes. "I did my own research and I wanna be with the two left shoes," Green told Bullard.

Other companies were after Al—including Savoy Records—but Green went with Myrrh, taking ten thousand less than a competing offer because he believed in Bullard. From then on, anything to do with Green's gospel career went through James Bullard. "It was the most unusual situation that I had ever been in," said James, who'd worked with other performers "but never with an artist this big. Now, I heard a lotta horror stories, but I had come to understand that God put Al Green and I together." Although Bullard had been warned that Al might not show up for interviews or TV tapings, Green "never disappointed me," said James. "Al was a pop star, but the most humble person that I had ever worked with."

Green and Bullard definitely did things their way. In January 1981 James got Al back on *Soul Train,* the first of many gospel-only appearances. When they ran through the number, Bullard advised a *Soul Train* potentate that their dancers couldn't shake a tail feather during this particular performance like they normally did. "Sir, you can't dance to this, this is gospel," insisted James, who was informed that the *Soul Train* dancers were going to do their thing. "I said, 'Well, we walk.'" You can't do that, said Mr. *Soul Train.* "I said, 'Watch me.'"

Al, who was onstage, came up with a solution. "Come up to the stage, come close," he told the dancers. "Just do what I do . . . I just want you to sway back and forth, back and forth." That's exactly how it was shot—Green onstage, the dancers gathered before him rocking side to side and clapping, nary a bouncing booty in sight. Bullard contacted all the gospel radio stations to inform them of Green's appearance. "When Al appeared on that show, we got hundreds of phone calls—'Oh, Al Green had *church* on *Soul Train!*'"*

The Lord Will Make a Way earned Al his first of eleven Grammys. Bullard recalled Green accepted the award with a wide-eyed innocence—"like a child would when you give them something. Very appreciative but gracious." He'd been nominated before for some of his records with Willie Mitchell, and they'd even attended the awards show three times but had never won, something that obviously tickled Third-Person Al pink. "After seven years of R&B, the guy wins his first Grammy for a gospel song," he said. "After *40 million records*." (Considering how mediocre some of Al's gospel records are that won, it seems more of a knee-jerk reaction to Green's celebrity by Grammy insiders than any power exercised by the Almighty.)

In terms of sales, *The Lord Will Make a Way* "did a huge number," said Bullard, who'd been given a three-year sales projection by his bosses at Word. "I made it in eight months," said James (a court document indicates the album sold 400,000 copies). Bullard maintained that Green had "a tremendous impact" on the gospel industry. Before that they "didn't have anyone of Al Green's caliber. He definitely raised the bar of gospel music so it became more commercial." Bullard felt that Green being so open about his commitment made it easier for other artists to do the same. "When Al came in, Phillip Bailey followed, Leon Patillo, Candi Staton, Deniece Williams . . . he opened the door, it was okay." Not to mention the secular fans he brought in. "I don't know how many people came to Christ because of Al Green."

Reuben Fairfax Jr. maintained Green also raised standards when it came to road expenses. "The gospel people would stay in somebody's home, they'd have a chicken dinner, pass the plate for the money. We had an ironclad contract—hotel rooms, per diems." Upon occasion Al was known to cut a deal for an inexperienced gospel promoter, something that he would've never done in the secular days. Bullard remembered a show at the Cow Palace in San Francisco where the promoter lost his shirt. "He says,

---

* There are two of the early gospel *Soul Train* performances currently on YouTube, "Amazing Grace" from 1982 and "I Know It Was the Blood" from a year later, and they are certainly out of character for the show at that time.

'Reverend Green, I didn't raise the amount of money I committed to pay you. I can't pay you.' Al says, 'Let me say this . . . number one, your ticket price was too high and you probably didn't promote it in the area you should have. But you gave it a good effort. You owe me another $7,500, but you know what? It's paid in full.' This adult man started crying!"

Not that any of this meant that old-school gospel artists accepted Green. "There was some resistance," admitted James Bullard, who said only one group came forward and offered to open for Al—Willie Neal Johnson and the Gospel Keynotes (to Bullard's knowledge, they never did). "They felt he was taking advantage," said Johnny Brown. "Thing I couldn't understand, they had never did no gigs like they were doin' when they were tourin' with Al, so why would you dislike him? He opened doors for the gospel people." (One exception: the Mighty Clouds of Joy. "They loved Al," said Johnny.)

Chicago-born gospel titan James Cleveland "didn't like the fact he had to come on before Al," said Brown, who happened to share an elevator with Cleveland and a couple of his musicians. "They were talkin' like girls and they were talkin' about Al—'You know, baby, he ain't *nuthin'*. We gonna show him *tonight*.' When we got to the show, James was onstage and he wouldn't stop. It was time for Al, he was cutting into Al's time. They kept signaling and sendin' word out there—'You need to stop.' But James refused. They turned the sound system off on him."

Gospel queen Shirley Caesar also played a bill with Green, and even cut a duet with an overdubbed Al, "Sailin' on the Sea of Your Love," which won a Grammy in 1984. "One time Shirley got really pissed off with him because she called him out to do the song and he said to the audience, 'Yeah, we cut this song together—'Sailin' on the Sea of His *cotton-pickin'* Love'! She didn't like that at all."

Little Richard was active in gospel at the time, and he was a Green fan. As he was another secular artist to cross into gospel, one would think they might have something to talk about, but Green wanted nothing to do with him. "Little Richard came and sat in the hotel all day long tryin' to meet Al," said Brown. "Reuben grabs me and says, 'C'mon, let's take Little Richard up to Al's room.' So when Al looks out the little peephole, he sees Reuben. He opens the door and there's us with Little Richard. Reuben says, 'Richard wants to meet you.'" Fairfax and Brown left them alone, much to the fury of their boss, as they found out later. According to Johnny, Green was keenly aware of the rumors concerning his own sexuality, and this was the last person the Reverend wanted around. "Al was hot with Reuben for that," said Brown. "He didn't want Little Richard in his room . . . he didn't want to be *seen* with Little Richard."*

❖

There was a new cast of characters as far as the musicians went. The very first gospel performance Fairfax remembers Al doing was "The Lord Will Make a Way" on the *Bobby Jones Gospel* TV show in Nashville. It was there they met Moses Dillard, a guitar player extraordinaire who'd worked for Loretta Lynn and played sessions for Mighty Sam and Oscar Toney Jr.

Although Dillard would stick around for a few years, Moses was highly religious and perhaps a little too classy for the Green crowd. Dillard "was part of that Negro elite," said Reuben. "We were down-home black folk. He was shocked by us." Fairfax claimed that most of the musicians in Green's gospel bands weren't there for spiritual reasons. As for Reuben, "It didn't matter to me. I'm not a religious person, but I was into the music. That was what was important." Reuben said this was fine with Green "once he understood that I was a heathen . . . he was the one that found spirituality, I didn't. I'm twenty-four years old and out on the road—I was gon' get me some *women*."

Green had a couple of powerful drummers join him, first John Toney, then Tim Dancy, joined by Ardis Hardin on congas. Fairfax explained that Green's gospel music put unique demands on a drummer. They had to bring the beat way low when Al broke the band down, tap the rim when he danced or preached. "You'd have to play like the vaudeville days, the way the drummers would accent the women when they'd throw their butt. A schoolboy perfect-timing drummer would never make it because there's so much other stuff that you had to be able to do."**

---

* During a trip to Miami, Green bumped into Tom Jones, who informed Al he was contemplating going gospel. "He said, 'I'm gonna do what you do.' I said, 'Tom, you have to have a *divine calling* to do that.'"

** Out on the road John Toney had a trick where'd he play his drums with flaming sticks. On his very first show with Green his sticks had been soaked too long in alcohol. When Tick the soundman gave John the sticks "they were just drippin'," said Reuben, and when Toney started playing "his drums caught fire. John played the greatest drum solo ever that night, because he was tryin' to beat the fire out of 'em." The flames were so high fire marshals wouldn't let Toney do it on the second set. "It traumatized him so much he wouldn't come out and play," said Reuben. Ardis Hardin switched from congas to drums that night.

Toney was a powerhouse, a heavy hitter, but his sense of time was rather unwieldy. "The hardest thing to get Memphis musicians to do is play in time," notes Fairfax. "They grew up playin' in church, and that's based on the notion you might speed up in this part, slow down in that part, get loud over there, get soft over here. They don't really play consistently and they hate using a click track. These guys play some great stuff, but they don't play it in perfect time."

The one musician everybody remembers is Jesse "Spooky" Butler. An oversized albino who looked a bit like Oddjob from *Goldfinger,* Butler was a whiz on the B3. "He had a little trick," said Fairfax. "He'd put a matchbook in between the keys and let the note ring as he danced around the keyboard." Butler, who had grown up with Isaac Hayes, had even cut an obscure solo instrumental album in 1967 for Philips, *Memphis Soul.*

Stories about Spooky are legion. How Jesse passed for white in South Africa due to his lack of pigmentation, or the way he got fired by sad-sack televangelist Jim Bakker at his *PTL Club* after running up thousands of dollars in phone calls to Africa. There's the way Jesse drove cars up on the sidewalk due to his poor eyesight, or the magical ability he had to get you an airline ticket to anywhere in the world. And once you were at the airport, Butler would snatch a fellow traveler's suitcase and sell whatever happened to be inside to the rest of the band. "I got my first tux that way," said Fairfax, who can still remember what Jesse would order when they'd eat—"Baby, you got apple pie? Here's what I want you to do: warm up the pie on the grill, then put me a scoop of vanilla ice cream on top." Not that he ever paid for it.

Spooky was "a con man," said Paul Zaleski. "He'd con you outta your shorts if you didn't have 'em on. He took me for $30,000 *and* he stole my car. He took the sheriff's daughter for $750 . . . he beat Al out of a lot of money—twenty or thirty grand." Zaleski said the way Al handled that was to have Butler play a bunch of sessions and gigs "for free." Butler played on all the Al Green Myrrh albums save for one done in Nashville with white pickers. "Jesse would just show up and play," said Reuben. "I never paid him, I never sent him a ticket, I don't know how he got to where we were all the time."

Until he was snuffed out, that is. On June 7, 1985, Spooky had spent the day with Willie Mitchell over at Royal. He'd just gotten out of the slammer due to credit card fraud and had "conned this woman into marrying him," said Fairfax. He was living in a hotel across from the Peabody and that night "he went to beatin' on the woman and the woman's daughter stabbed him to death."

"No charges were pressed," claimed Zaleski. "The police told the daughter, 'Thank you.'"

❖

In February 1981 Green released *Higher Plane*. As *Truth n' Time* is to *Belle*, *Higher Plane* is a shadow of *The Lord Will Make a Way*. It turns out Al Green is far from the best producer for Al Green. If the setting is fresh and new like *Belle*, Al rises to the occasion; if he's bored, he can be utterly lazy, relying on pedestrian material and a familiar bag of vocal tricks. Over time it became apparent that Green needs a Willie Mitchell to kick him in the ass, provoke him.

The title track is a worthy addition to the gospel funk sound of "Lord Will Make a Way," and "The Spirit Might Come—On and On" might've passed as a lesser track on *Belle*, but the rest of this album fails to deliver much of anything. There's a respectable if unexciting cover of "People Get Ready" sung with underrated soul singer Margie Joseph, and a surprisingly pedestrian reading of a song Green often tears up live, "Amazing Grace."

It's all so predictable, and the production sounds chintzy and shrill, particularly the cloying, hyperactive strings, which sound like lost traces of some seventies disco nightmare. If you've ever wanted to hear Green sing "Battle Hymn of the Republic," well, here it is, complete with (more) bad banjo, flaccid steel guitar, and a saccharine vanilla chorus. It's clear from Al's jaunty performance that he digs patriotic schlock like this, but Eccentric Al doesn't guarantee greatness, and this is about as compelling as your drunk uncle in a funny hat. Needless to say, this mediocre mess of an album won Green Grammy number two.

"You take all of this that you learn in pop, R&B, and you use it to your best advantage, but it doesn't give you *the fire*," Green told Robert Mugge. "Either you have the fire or you don't have the fire—the spiritual fire." I feel next to no heat on most of these recordings, nor many that followed. You want the fire, search out the live performances of Al's gospel band, like the public television special *I'll Fly Away: A Gospel Celebration* broadcast in December 1983, which includes storming versions of "None but the Righteous" and "Lord Will Make a Way," as well as impassioned, inventive performances of "People Get Ready" and "I'll Fly Away" that demonstrate how Green could jolt such old chestnuts to life. ("I'll Fly Away" is particularly noteworthy as the band didn't know the number before Al slid into it that night.)

Gospel band members were hard-pressed to remember a night where Green put on anything less than a fantastic performance. "When I first joined the band, he'd pretty much do the same set," said Fairfax. "Later on, he was free to be the great singer that he was. A lot of times, he'd just pull whatever he wanted to sing out of his ass and the Al Green band better know how to play it. You had to follow him. He might start it a cappella, like he does in church." One night out of nowhere, Green reached way back to his very first hit. "He went to singin' 'Back Up Train' a cappella, and we had to catch it."

"Our band was so cold-blooded, we were so good," said Johnny Brown, who related what would occur when other gospel groups like the Winans or the Clark Sisters would be on the bill and ask to go on last, just because they had a current hit and Al didn't. Green would agree, but the other act didn't know what they were in for. Backstage he'd tell the band, "You know most of these people are here to see *Al*. Now, when we get finished playin', all of Al's folks might as well leave, 'cause the show's gonna be over." He stared a hole into the band. "And if that *don't* happen, there might need to be a few pink slips at the office." With that, he smiled and walked out.

Green and the band would then go out and burn the place down. "And just like he said, half the people would walk out," said Brown. If others on the bill were playing more than one show with Green, by the second night they'd be begging Al to go back to closing the show "because they didn't want everybody to walk out before they went on," said Johnny, laughing. When Green decided to give his all, no one could follow him. "Al used to come offstage, his clothes wringing-wet with sweat. Sometimes he'd be layin' down on the table, tryin' to catch a breath."

❖

On March 26, 1981, Al Green was arrested at the Memphis airport. According to press reports, he'd gone there to retrieve his car, which had been towed from a no-parking zone. It turned out there'd been an outstanding warrant for his arrest since July 26, 1979. According to the police report, on June 8 of that year at his offices at 3208 Winchester, Green had gotten into a physical altercation with one Lovie Smith.* According to the police report, "The defendant did strike the affiant about the body with a tree limb, knocking the affiant to the ground, at which time the defendant proceeded to kick the affiant about the body." Smith was taken to the hospital where "she received surgery on her right hand (finger)" and was

---

* On the arrest record she is incorrectly identified as Lovie Green, Green's "common-law" wife. Band members recall a Lovie Hill who hung around the church. I do not know if Lovie Smith/Hill are the same person. Nothing ever came of the charges.

"treated for severe bruises to the body." Green paid fifty dollars bond and was released.

That wasn't the end of his woes, however. There was another outstanding warrant on Al as Shirley had accused him of assault and battery. "After being released from the city jail, Green walked over to the Shelby County Sheriff's office detective division and surrendered himself on the warrant obtained by his wife." He paid another $250 there and walked out the door.

On April Fool's Day 1981 Shirley Green filed for divorce once more. This time it would stick. By now she'd had two kids with Al, Alva and Rubi, and a third, Kora, was on the way. According to court records, she'd left with a hundred dollars in her pocket. She owned three dresses and two pairs of shoes. Her complaint stated that "throughout the marriage the defendant has on numerous occasions been guilty of physical cruelty . . . the defendant is possessed with a violent temper and had inflicted upon the plaintiff brutal beatings, some of which required medical attention and treatment, including hospitalization."

The most recent alleged incident had occurred in March 1981, "when the plaintiff requested money from the defendant to buy milk for the baby, at which time the defendant became violent and began beating the plaintiff about the face as well as other parts of her body, knowing that she was six months pregnant." Another order of protection was granted.

Green's lawyer, Charles W. Burson,* filed a countercomplaint on June 8, 1981. Al denied all Shirley's claims except that he "admits that he struck the plaintiff in March of 1981 but would show that said action was provoked by harassment on the part of the plaintiff." In the 1995 *Tribune* article, a deposition of Green's is quoted in which—despite the objections of his lawyer—Al admits to physically abusing his wife, once again insisting it was only because he was provoked.

"I was raised for the street, called for the ministry . . . I had no other way to respond . . . other than to retaliate to my manhood being belittled." He also states that while he doesn't think physical abuse is "justifiable under any circumstances," he seems to downplay Shirley's: "The beating of the wife, I kind of reject that because 'beating' is a cruel word to me . . . it's more scars on the mind than it is on the surface." (In a May 2, 1981,

---

* Charles W. Burson went on to become attorney general of Tennessee, legal counsel to Al Gore during his tenure as vice president, and a vice president at Monsanto. According to Burson, he was Al's lawyer from 1973 to 1988. Citing attorney-client privilege, he declined to be interviewed unless permission was granted by Green.

newspaper article entitled "Reverend Al Green Denies Beating," Green told a reporter that "there was literally no beating, but I don't even fault her for that" and goes on to call Shirley "a wonderful, wonderful person," hinting at darker forces behind it all: "The devil will try to stop you from doing good work."

I know of only two reporters who asked Al about Shirley's allegations of physical abuse when they surfaced again in the *Tribune* article, and only one got a quotable response—Karen Schoemer during an interview for *Newsweek*. "You're talking about 15, 16, 17 years ago . . . [Shirley] might have experienced many things that were unpleasant. The way I saw it, it was just hopping in the car and going to the next gig. But I'm not a supporter of abusive families and abusive relationships."

In that *Tribune* article, Shirley also claimed that Al isolated her from her family, hid her Bibles, and chastised her for singing out during service. In November 1979 Shirley admitted to being so desperate that she shot at her husband with a .30-30 rifle but missed. She was pregnant with their second child at the time. Despite all of this, Shirley said during the deposition hearing that she'd still get back together with her husband if their problems could be rectified. This time Al insisted on ending their union.

Divorce was finally granted in 1983. In a settlement document dated December 29, 1982, Green agreed to pay Shirley a lump sum of $432,800.15 in alimony payments, take out a $250,000 life insurance policy, and put $15,000 into a fund for his children's college educations. She also got a 1981 Monte Carlo.

Shirley was back in court in May 1983, claiming Green had failed to honor the agreement. In February 1987 the court ordered Al to fulfill any obligations within thirty days.

❖

One thing you come away with in studying the divorce filing is how thoroughly Green had decimated his pop career. For producing two gospel albums a year Al was receiving a $28,000 advance. He claimed he was only netting $3,000–4,000 per concert, which he'd only started doing sporadically starting in March 1981. Green owed the IRS back taxes for 1973 and 1974 and had taken out a $500,000 bank loan to pay them.* His Hi royalties were tied up in litigation, no doubt due to the Cream

---

* According to Reuben Fairfax Jr., "Pops had written [Green] a million dollar check. For some reason Al didn't pay taxes on a million dollars. The I.R.S. came to Pops and made a copy of the check."

deal (his last royalty payment had been $600 early in 1981). Al claimed to have no savings account, no CDs, no funds in trust. He owned 1974 and 1964 Rolls-Royces, a '71 Eldorado, a '73 Caprice, a '76 Corvette, and a few other vehicles used by the church. In an affidavit he stated that he'd made $195,327 in 1980 and had $187,000 in expenses. His beauty shop netted $9,250 that year, and at his church day-care center twenty-six kids were paying $35 each. The church took in $500–$650 in collections on the Sundays when he was present. "I anticipate earning as a Gospel entertainer approximately $8,000 net," it said. This was hardly the life of a millionaire pop singer.

"I watched a guy who was the top superstar in R&B throw the whole thing away to go sing 'Pass Me Not, O Gentle Savior,'" said Reuben Fairfax Jr.

❖

On June 26, 1981, Green's dilapidated tour bus caught fire near Senatobia, Mississippi. As usual, Al wasn't traveling on the bus, but his band was. "The bus needed a new turbo—or covering for the turbo," said Fairfax. "Instead of getting one, they just cleaned the bus up and routed the exhaust out through the bathroom. Somebody went and opened the bathroom door and smoke filled the bus." Everybody got off the smoldering vehicle.

When the bus driver went back in to retrieve a smoking blanket, "it burst into flame and the bus was soon gutted from the inside," said Reuben. The band lost all their instruments, clothes, and personal effects. Green appeared on the scene the next morning. "Everybody was complainin', standin' there facin' Al," said Brown. "He said, 'I'll tell you what: the show must go on. There's two big vans. All that's goin' *with* me, come over behind me. All that's stayin', *stay*.'" (As Reuben put it, Green acted "kinda like George Bush—'You either with us or with the terrorists.'")

Soundman Ed Pogue and his wife, Jennie, refused to join the boss and his entourage. They later sued Green and the Easley Equipment Company for $10,000, although it appears the suit went nowhere. "We were not able to make a proper settlement with Al," said Reuben. "It was a situation of negligence; the bus shouldn't have been on the road."

❖

Off in the gospel wilderness, Al Green was more on his own than ever. "He was really in charge of himself," said Fairfax. "He really didn't have managers around. Whatever he said we were gonna do, we just did it. We had the freedom."

Finances being what they were at the time, Green would sometimes do gigs with just one other musician in tow. In April 1981 Fairfax accompanied Green to Seoul, South Korea, for another song contest. This had been the idea of Bob White, Al Bennett's assistant at Cream. They needed an R&B song to sing in the competition, and since Al was singing gospel, Reuben unearthed a song of his that Al had recorded around the time of *Belle*, "(No No) You'll Never Hurt Me Again." Fairfax had been recording some solo material when Green came in and said, "You're no singer—let me do that." (The song was finally released on the *Belle* expanded edition in 2006 along with another Fairfax number Al cut, "Running Out of Time." A third outtake on the CD, "Right on Time," was a Green song cut early in the *Belle* sessions.)

They performed the number at the festival, the only time Green has ever performed the song. "I really wasn't supposed to play," said Fairfax. "Before we did the final performance Al said, 'I done sang the song, now what you gonna do to get your money, sit around here in a tuxedo?'" And so Reuben attempted to sit in with the Korean orchestra. "They couldn't speak English," he recalled.

Green took second prize and split the $10,000 prize money with Fairfax—after expenses (which is interesting in itself because in divorce documents it states Cream Records paid all the expenses for the trip. "These guys can't split fifty-fifty with you on anything," notes Reuben). Fairfax bought a set of wheels off Al with the proceeds: "I bought the 'Tired of Being Alone' car." Willie Mitchell had bought Green a 1971 Cadillac Eldorado as a reward for that first hit. White with a red interior, it was in beautiful shape. Unfortunately Shirley was on paper for the car, and Reuben sold it cheap. "I could never transfer the title," he said.

Occasionally Green would appear at a revival. Al "actually wanted to preach and he was getting invitations to do things, so you had to have some kind of con game to get the money—you ain't gonna do a contract with a church." Meaning there was no payment for his appearance, just whatever he could cadge out of the attendees in terms of offerings. It was a situation where Al would bring an abbreviated version of the band (and sometimes just Johnny Brown).

One of these revivals took place in March 1982 in Philadelphia. "This white guy had a church," said Reuben. "He said he found God in the back of an old Chevy." There, Reuben saw all sorts of cons in the name of Christ. A plant in the audience would talk in tongues while another would translate. There was a man in a wheelchair suddenly empowered by the Lord to get up and walk. This particular revival was "like the carnival," said Reuben. "They had a hell of a game."*

Fairfax called the game that Green came up with "The Hem of the Master's Garment." This Philadelphia revival "was the only time we did that," Fairfax said, laughing. "Look, whatever happened, you'd just go with it. It was just spontaneous—if Al took the lead, I followed.

"Al started hustling the people for money; he gonna give 'em a touch from God. He said, 'This ain't no voodoo or nothing, it's the anointing of God.' I had a big ol' pair of scissors, and I would cut a piece out of Al's shirt. He put olive oil on his hand and rubbed it on his head. He'd put the piece of his shirt to his forehead and touch 'em with it. They'd fall out on the floor, then take the piece with 'em." The catch? "You had to put some money up there to get that touch."

First Green informed the audience that the Lord had told him one hundred people were going to give him a hundred dollars. That failed to open many purses. "Al didn't get a big line," said Reuben. "Then he said, 'The Lord say *two hundred* people gonna give me *twenty* dollars.' He got a line for the twenty dollars.

"That was crazy as hell. They lined up, I cut the shirt, he'd put oil on it, touch 'em, and they were fallin' out on the floor. Al didn't have nothing but the wrists of his shirt left at the end of that service. They had a little piece of Al Green for twenty dollars."

---

* According to Fairfax, Green attempted to get a disabled man to walk during a Chattanooga revival. "Al wasn't playin' a game, he was serious—he was tryin' to get the guy to walk out of faith. I think the guy had been paralyzed all his life, and when Al was tryin' to get him up outta the chair he couldn't get out. It was like Al had to wrestle him back into the chair." Reverend Green informed the fellow that his faith hadn't become strong enough yet.

BOXING WITH GOD

I'm here to do a job, to lift up the name of Jesus among the
gentiles . . . I'm called to do this, whether it's Broadway,
Las Vegas or Palestine.
—AL GREEN

Deep in the bowels of Broadway's Alvin Theatre, Patti LaBelle was about
to murder Al Green. "I had broken my glass of Courvoisier and I was moving towards Al with blood in my eye and a jagged edge in my hand," she
wrote in her autobiography. "I was going for the jugular."

The two singers were appearing together in the gospel musical *Your
Arms Too Short to Box with God.* Patti's sister Barbara was dying of cancer,
and in order to see her, Patti'd have to miss a matinee. A cast meeting took
place in the basement of the theater, during which Green's erratic onstage
behavior was also addressed. "It was intense," said a member of the cast
who declined to be identified. This witness claimed that Al alluded to
LaBelle "being tipsy from drinking" during the show. And when it came
to her dying sister, he had no sympathy.

"Everyone understood. Everyone except the one person I expected to
be the most understanding: the Reverend Al Green," wrote LaBelle. "He
was annoyed because he would have to sing some of my numbers, and, if
he had to sing my numbers he wanted top billing—his name in front of
mine on the marquee. I didn't give a damn about whose name came first
and that's what I told Al. They could put his picture up in lights for all

I cared." According to Patti, Green refused to relent. "He demanded to know what was so critical about my sister that I had to go home when we had a show to do and leave him carrying the burden."

According to the cast member present, Al then said to her, "Well, Ms. LaBelle, *we* didn't make your sister sick." His fellow performers were outraged. "That was just the most unforgivable thing he could possibly say," said the source. "And one of the guys in the show, Michael Gray, he was shaking, he was so mad. He told Al, 'You're an insult to Broadway and you're an insult to God.'"

Green's callous remark sent Patti into a fury. "I couldn't believe my ears. My sister was lying in a hospital bed fighting for her life and this ordained minister, a man who had pledged his life to God, only seemed to care about how many new songs he had to sing for a single matinee."

It was at that moment LaBelle went on the attack. Her hairdresser, Norma Harris, pulled her away, telling her the important thing was seeing her sister. But she'd never feel the same way about Al Green. "If you don't keep all the acclaim and recognition in perspective anyone—even a man of the cloth—can go to Hollywood." As for Al, he stormed out of the meeting—for the second time, according to my source. "The first time he said, 'I have forty million dollars, I don't need this.'"

❖

It was on September 2, 1982, that Al Green made his debut in *Your Arms Too Short to Box with God.* Directed by Vinette Carroll, the first African American woman to direct on Broadway, this landmark gospel musical was on its third revival at this point. The sketchy story (loosely based on the book of Matthew) was just an excuse for gospel singing and dancing, and it would prove to be a perfect vehicle for Al. I saw him in the show, and he was mesmerizing. Running through the aisles singing, Green seemed to do whatever struck his fancy at the moment, and it was exciting to witness.

For this limited run, the show's producers were looking for some new blood. Music publishing veteran Richie Becker, who'd been intertwined with the career of the great Arthur Alexander, owned the rights and suggested Green. The call was made; no answer. At this point Becker happened to pick up *Jet* magazine "and who do I see on the cover but Al Green and his brand new church?" Not only that, but one of the photo captions mentioned the song he was singing was Alex Bradford's "Too

Close." Bradford was the author of many of the numbers in *Arms*. This was pointed out to Al, he saw the show, and "that's how we got Al Green," said Becker, Bradford's partner at the time. "It was a one and a billion shot." Patti LaBelle, who'd already appeared in a previous run, was Al's costar in the show. It would prove to be a match made in hell.

"In the beginning he was fine, soft-spoken, happy to be there with Patti," said the member of the cast. "We would have prayer circles before the start of the show . . . and then he'd go out and do these crazy things! It was turbulent with a capital *T*." Green played a preacher in the show and during one performance "took off his top robe, threw it on the ground, and danced all over it. Broadway costumes cost a lot of money, thousands of dollars. We were horrified."

LaBelle and Green soon clashed. "Patti is one of the nicest, most giving people you will ever know," said the source. Green "wouldn't relate to her. He wouldn't look at her . . . it wasn't a duet." This sent LaBelle over the edge. "Patti's way of fixing things is to sing louder and harder. The louder she would sing, the softer Al would sing. She didn't realize it was working against her . . . the sound got so loud it was piercing. Al would just sing softer and softer." There was a moment in the show when LaBelle, who wore ultrahigh heels, had to descend a staircase, and Al was supposed to take her hand in his. He didn't. Richard Brown, another member of the cast, finally "put his hand out, 'cause Al Green just wasn't gonna do it."

There are those in Green's circle who take LaBelle's complaints with a grain of salt, chalking it up to diva behavior. "They'll sing all on top of you, holler louder than you, and jump in and interrupt you, that kinda old stuff," said Reuben Fairfax, who accused Laura Lee and Shirley Green of similar antics. "Al couldn't really sing with them bitches." Misogyny perhaps, but even the unnamed source said that LaBelle sang at such volume they had to wear earplugs onstage.

Al's behavior didn't just bedevil LaBelle; he drove the rest of the cast crazy as well. During one performance Green "didn't show up for the entire second act," said the source. Al was supposed to enter from the back of the audience, singing as he made his way through the theater. "He never came down the aisle." Luckily another cast member, Richard Brown, had done Green's role and started singing the song.

The gossip among the cast was that Al had gotten into it with his security team. "Al Green had two bodyguards," said the source. "One was a nice guy, the other one was a straight-up thug." One night at the theater

Thug Bodyguard's suit jacket "flew open and he was carrying, he was packin'! I was like, 'Oh my God!'" Clearly Broadway was not ready for the wild world of Al Green.

The bodyguards "were always with him, and one had a briefcase. The rumor was he had an altercation with the thuggish bodyguard—that bodyguard had taken the briefcase—and they were out running around New York City looking for him. That's why Al didn't show up." (Adds the source, "We were always speculating about what was in the briefcase—drugs, cocaine, gold . . . Al wore a lot of gold.")

The cast repeatedly complained, to no avail. "The producers just gave him free rein," said the source. "Michael Powell, the musical director, was no longer allowed to give him notes. He could do no wrong." In interviews, Green admitted he had trouble sticking to the script. "The first preview week I would vary off the script and go into Romans 9 and 10 . . . some people cursed and yelled and said, 'If he can't stick with the script, fire him.'"

Al's performance decimated any arguments. "The producers finally said, 'Leave him alone, throw away the script.' I'm being Al Green. Who else could I be? Bing Crosby? Bob Hope?" Whatever the complaints, Al was a hit. The limited four-week run turned into ten. "He really was a box office draw. I think he surprised the producers," said my source. "Broadway producers don't know much about the R&B world. Women really turned out to see him, yes they did."

Green received stellar notices in the press. "Mr. Green transforms the stage into a pulpit and the play into a revival meeting," wrote Robert Palmer in the *New York Times*. "And he proves once again after seven years in the ministry and away from the pop limelight, that he is the consummate soul singer of our time." Patti LaBelle fared less well. "Too often she falls back on mannerisms . . . and sheer overkill," wrote Palmer, accusing the singer of "glitzy showboating."

No matter what torture Green had put the cast and crew through, he'd triumphed once again. His work in *Your Arms Too Short to Box with God* got Al nominated for Broadway's highest honor. "The first and only gospel singer *and* preacher that has ever been nominated for a Tony," notes Richie Becker.

❖

For Green's next record, he reunited two of the original Hi Records partners, Bill Cantrell and Quinton Claunch, as executive producers. "We asked Al, 'How would you like to go over to Nashville and do a first-class session?'" recalled Claunch. Released in October 1982, *Precious Lord* was an album of classic gospel standards (excepting "Morningstar," a mediocre number cowritten by Moses Dillard, who accompanied Green to Nashville. "Moses was probably the only black person to play on that album," Johnny Brown pointed out, adding that Cantrell seemed "upset" that Green brought him).

In theory this could've been a rewarding idea: unite Green with top-echelon Music City pickers playing top-flight white gospel arrangements. In reality it was just Al lazily overdubbing a bunch of cut-rate tracks with pedestrian arrangements. Compared to previous efforts from Green's studio, the recording sounds technically better, but the music itself is by-the-numbers blandness, with tepid backing vocals and guitar solos that sound like they came out of a vending machine. With someone like an in-his-prime Billy Sherrill* in charge, maybe the album could've amounted to more. Sessions were done quickly, with the tracks recorded before Al's contributions. "We went and did all the tracks, took him over there, and overdubbed his voice on them," said Claunch. "It took two or three days to lay down."

When Al puts a little more into it, like on "In the Garden," the results are marvelous, but once again it feels like no one bothered to push him. You can't judge Green by the standards of mere mortal singers—even his weaker vocals eclipse most others. Al's always capable of greatness; this isn't it, however. He'd win another Grammy for *Precious Lord*, his second that year alongside *Higher Plane*.

Green, Claunch, and Cantrell also worked on another project together, an album of invitational hymns. "Bill picked all these songs, invitational hymns they used in services," said Claunch. It was another case of pre-recorded tracks that Green overdubbed onto. The piano was played by Jim Walker. "He was in a plane crash," said Claunch. "He had both legs off, one arm. His face was really disfigured. But boy, he had the talent. Damn near a genius."

Despite that, the album to be called *Invitation* never really came off. "The sound, the production, wasn't up to snuff and I didn't much like it," Claunch admitted. "It cost about five to twenty grand to cut that thing. Nobody would touch it with a ten-foot pole. Al kind of fell out with

---

* *Precious Lord* was actually engineered by another Nashville Billy Sherrill unrelated to the famed producer.

Bill." Cantrell and Claunch wound up taking Green to court over their payment for *Precious Lord*. Al "didn't want to pay anybody," said Claunch, who said they eventually settled with Word, Myrrh's parent company. "They ended up takin' money out of his royalties and payin' us." As far as Green, "he had a really good personality, couldn't help but like him," said Claunch. But by the end Quinton felt "he was kind of a con man, I guess you'd call it."

❖

I'll Rise Again, Green's next gospel album, came out in February 1983. It is another mishmash, this time mostly substandard originals, some by old Enterprise Orchestra member Michael Baker and others by one Emmett Wilson, which I believe is Green. Most promising of all was the return of Teenie Hodges on guitar and as cowriter of "Ocean Blue (I'll Rise Again)." Unfortunately the heavy-handed production—complete with farting synthesizers, tacky wind effects, and strings of molasses—sink the song, although the funky chorus is unmistakably Teenie. Other than a hypnotic "Leaning on the Everlasting Arms" with a return of the all-Al chorus, *I'll Rise Again* is one more underwhelming effort. It earned Green yet another Grammy.

"Straighten Out Your Life," a rather obvious message song on the album, was contributed by Green's old guitar player and bandleader Larry Lee. Larry would come back out on the road now and then, but it never lasted long. "Him and Al were like oil and water," said Johnny Brown. Whenever they'd lose a guitar player, Brown would head over to Larry's and beg him to fill in. Then it would start. "How I know Al gonna pay me?" Larry would ask. Johnny would respond with "Has Al ever *not* paid you?" "Eventually he'd say, 'Okay, Johnny, I'm gonna do this for you—but if Al don't pay me, you're gonna give me your check.' I'd take him out there, Al and him would act like they're happy to see each other. That would last two or three weeks. Then him and Al would fall out, because payday was Thursday but Larry didn't get paid until Monday."

It seems that sooner or later nearly every musician has had a falling out with Al over the long green stuff. How often, exactly? "Always. A-l-w-a-y-s," stressed Paul Zaleski. When asked about Al's philosophy when it comes to money, Paul simply replied, "It's mine. It's *all* mine." Green's parsimonious nature is somewhat legendary. "The first nickel Al ever made, he's got it somewhere," said Reuben Fairfax Jr.

"One thing about Al—I knew I was gonna get my money, it was just gonna be late," said Johnny Brown. "So it didn't bother me as much as it bothered everybody else." Sometimes you'd have to wait in his office for hours if you were to see the boss. "He wouldn't come out, and wasn't nobody allowed to come back past the double doors," said Brown. "He knew you was there, and you're waiting and you're waiting . . . all of a sudden you'd be sittin' there and you'd look up and see his car come from behind the building and drive off!"

It wasn't just lowly musicians Green treated this way; it was everybody. "Al did it to Michael Jackson one time," said Brown, who recalled Jackson had just played Memphis as part of the Jacksons' 1981 tour. "Michael was sittin' up there at the office, sat there for hours waitin' to see Al. Al finally showed up.*

"Al didn't care who you were. If he didn't want to come, he didn't come. And he didn't call you to tell you. Al did what Al wanted to do when Al wanted to do it.

"He was a very moody guy. So if Al was in a bad mood, you stayed away. Maddest I ever saw him was probably around Shirley. If we was gonna get some money from Al that Sunday and we saw Shirley show up, we didn't even bother to go to his office—'Won't be gettin' no money today. Shirley's here, you can forget anything you was gonna ask for.' For the next week he'd be really agitated and hard to talk to." Out on the road the musicians felt the girlfriends were another obstacle. "The thing the band used to hate—the girls could get money out of him that we couldn't," said Johnny. "We were the ones that just got through playin', doin' this, that, and the other, and this girl walked away with a diamond ring. We can't even get our pay."

There were also the fierce office matriarchs Green had in place to run interference—women like Renee Kirk, Hattie Angel, and Caroline Robinson, each one tougher than the last. Angel worked for Green off and on for years and was a formidable roadblock when it came to the boss. "I love me some Hattie Angel, but Hattie Angel was totally for Al, whether right or wrong," said Brown. "She'd come right out and tell me, 'John, I don't agree with it, I'm sorry, but this is just the way it is and there ain't

---

* Paul Zaleski maintained that Michael wanted to record a version of "Here I Am (Come and Take Me)"—odd in itself as Jackson had already recorded a limp cover of the song back in 1973—but it never came together. Paul Zaleski claims Al "wouldn't let him do it."

no sense in you standin' here arguing with me.' She did not take no stuff off of nobody."

Even if a band member had the chance to approach Green directly, they'd have to suss out exactly which Al they were talking to. "There was so many personalities in him," said Brown. "If you were talking to the holy Reverend Al Green, you didn't even want to touch him." And if it was the personality the band referred to as Albert, look out. "He could be quite uppity. You knew you weren't gonna get anything positive, so it was, 'Don't even talk to this guy. Come back later and ask Al.'"

❖

At times it seemed Green resented the obligations that came with keeping his band afloat. "There were times he really didn't want to work," said Brown. "But in order to keep his band together, he had to do somethin'. He used to say to me, 'Everybody depends on me. *Everybody.* You just don't know what it's like.' I used to tell him about my little problems—'Boss, I have a financial problem, we ain't workin'.'" Al's response was to inquire of Johnny how much his gas bill was. When Johnny would say a couple of hundred, Al would inform him the same bill for the church would be two thousand—"the more money you got, the more worries you got" went his logic. "That didn't satisfy me," said Johnny. "We'd go out and do shows, we were the star act, and we was not getting paid as much as the opening acts."

At one point Johnny bought a house out in the country. "Kind of like Al's house," he noted. "Larry Lee came out to my house and said, 'Johnny, whatever you do, do *not* invite Al out to see your house.'" Johnny asked why. "It looks too much like *his* house," said Lee. Johnny threw a party to show off the place, which he named Johnny's Ponderosa.

Brown sent out invitations and, despite Larry's warning, he sent one to Green. "Al showed up at the party. Told me how much he loved my house." And then the work abruptly stopped. "There was no more studio work, no more gigs, no more nuthin'," said Brown. "For a whole year." Johnny told Al the lack of work meant he was going to lose his house. "Can't help you, Johnny," said Al. The day Brown lost his home he went to Green and informed him. Suddenly there was work. "Everything Al could do to make money, he did. And I got paid real, real good. But I lost my house. Nothing happened until *after* I lost it.

"There are people that say to this day that Al did not go to work until I lost that house. That he could not stand for me to be in that house. Now whether that is true or not, I don't know. But I know I didn't make a dime with Al, except at the church. 'Course, Larry was standin' there tellin' me, 'Johnny, I told you not to let Al see that house.' I should've listened."

And yet, said Johnny, "it would be hard to stay mad at Al, no matter what. He was the most personable guy in the world—even when he didn't pay you. He'd be sittin' there laughin' and tellin' jokes. It was funny, but you'd be pissed off. Eventually you knew if you sat there and acted too mad, you'd probably wait another few days for your pay. So you'd laugh at his jokes."

Reuben Fairfax Jr. felt there was no point discussing anything potentially troublesome with Green. "Al's family grew up on plantations, so they have a certain mentality." He maintained there was no way to work your way up the ladder with Green to earn his respect. It was his way or the highway. It was Fairfax's opinion that Al respected white people more than his own. "Anybody black working for him, he's The Boss. It wasn't like you could reason. Al's not somebody you could reason with."

So when Reuben had had enough, he wouldn't quit, nor would he say anything to Al. He'd just disappear for a while.

❖

GUN CONFISCATED FROM ENTERTAINER, went the headline in the *Memphis Press-Scimitar* on April 7, 1983. Green had been stopped at the Memphis airport for carrying a weapon, but once they saw his Shelby County special deputy badge all was forgiven. Johnny Brown recalled coming back from an overseas tour and going through customs. "The lady let all the band members go by, and when she got to Al, she told Al to open up his luggage." Irritated, Green whipped out his badge. The customs agent told him, "That ain't got nuthin' to do with it. My daddy got one of them. Open up your luggage."

❖

In December of 1983, Green celebrated the seventh anniversary of his Full Gospel Tabernacle Church. This was a big deal, and a film crew was there to document it. A longtime admirer of Green's work, director Robert Mugge had been commissioned to do a documentary on Al for Channel 4. It had not been easy to get Green to commit.

As Mugge told Terry Gross, "I had to chase him for thirteen months before he said yes." Robert went to Memphis, New York, and New Orleans.

Sometimes he saw Green; sometimes he didn't. Mugge's friend David Appleby was there for the first meeting with Al at Green's church. "The service went on forever and ever," said Appleby. The guest preacher that day was "all about hell and brimstone." When Green hit the pulpit, "he was all about love and mercy and forgiveness. Al was playin' the good cop."

After the service one of his minions "led us to his back sanctuary," David recalled. "Al was sitting in a big chair at one end of the table, and behind him were all these women in white robes. The women were fawning over Green, tending to his every need. "Their eyes just seemed to be staring into me like, 'Here's this impostor who comes to speak to our leader.'"

One of the women brought out a can of Coke for the Reverend, who had a little test for his guests. Green had "two glasses in front of him, and he looks at me—not at Bob—and he says, 'One of these glasses is clean and one is unclean. And only someone who has been washed in the blood of *Jesus,* whose sins have been *cleansed,* can tell the difference.' And Al's staring at me and I'm thinking, "I'm Jewish, what do I know about this stuff? I hope Bob's film does not rest on the answer to this question.'"

No one said a word as Green sat there holding the shiny can, waiting for a reply. Appleby was about to tell him he had no idea when "Al just starts laughing, pours the Coke, and says, 'I'm just kidding,'" Appleby recalled. "It was funny later."

Green was amenable to the documentary—for a price, which turned out to be a large chunk of the budget as salary, plus Mugge's share of the profits. When the filmmaker told Green his cut was 30 percent of future profits, Al said that's what he wanted. "I said, 'Al! That won't give me anything.'" Mugge went back to Channel 4 and told them Green's demands, asking them to increase his end so he'd at least make something on the film. Luckily they upped it another 10 percent. "Al Green finally said yes, only when I agreed to give him three-fourths of my share of future profits of the film."

Mugge was cottoning on to how shrewd a character Green could be. "As I saw firsthand, if you really, really, really want to work with Al, he thinks nothing of taking advantage of that fact for his own betterment— as in taking all my salary for making the film. That was very clever of Al, and it gave him satisfaction to get my percentage . . . he was not gonna split that with me fifty-fifty. I was frustrated, but I didn't begrudge it. Because I certainly knew that Al deserved it—as *he* felt he did."

Green had agreed to the film only three days before the first shoot at Full Gospel Tabernacle on December 18, and Mugge had to scramble to get a crew together. Al takes the Monday off after church, so once filming the service was done, Mugge and his crew shot an interview with Willie Mitchell over at Royal. One of the many evocative moments in the film takes place as "Let's Stay Together" plays on the turntable in Mitchell's cluttered, unassuming office, Willie sitting silently as he listens to their now-past musical glory.

Mugge had asked Al to do some of his secular tunes for the film "over and over and over," he told Terry Gross. "I sort of had to trick him into 'Let's Stay Together.'" Tuesday the crew shot Green rehearsing the band doing their gospel numbers, and Mugge gently prodded the one secular song out of him. Al did an impromptu version on the spot—in the film you can see him teaching it to his backup singers—which was a bassless one, due to the fact Reuben's instrument was in the pawn shop as they'd been playing so little (Green "was supposed to give me the money to go get it," said Fairfax).

Then Al sat down and did a few acoustic numbers. Mugge had been asking for an interview for the film, and after the songs Green caught him off guard by suggesting they do it on the spot. Al spent the next few hours giving a rambling but fascinating interview—the only one I know of (other than a few contemporaneous print interviews) where Green discusses Mary Woodson's death at length.* It makes for riveting viewing. Mugge's director of photography, Erich Roland, was "a really interesting cameraman with a great photographic eye. I told him, 'I want a moody, noirish look for the interview, church service, and concert.'" The look suits Green's intensity well. During the interview you can hear Teenie Hodges, who was working on Green's next gospel album, noodling on Al's acoustic in the background. The third and final shoot was of a raucous gospel show Green gave with his band at the NCO Club at Bolling Air Force Base in Washington, DC, on February 12, 1984.

Mugge first showed the documentary at a Munich film festival and then on July 13, 1984, at its American premiere at the Filmex festival in Los Angeles. The original cut was substantially longer—Andy Bloch, the Channel 4 executive who'd underwritten the film, wanted Mugge to show

---

* Green was the one to bring Woodson up. He started telling the story of that night when the camera suddenly ran out of film and had to be reloaded. "Thank God Al picked up right where he left off and we got the whole thing," said Mugge.

"how Al's gospel music fit into the history of Christian art," so a few academic types pontificating on the subject were included in the film. At the Los Angeles showing "the audience got restless when the experts came on. All they wanted to hear was Al talking about being Al," said Mugge, who wisely jettisoned the footage. (Green told him he preferred the longer version. Robert felt the academic validation appealed to him.)

Mugge's finished film is regarded as a classic music documentary, all the more remarkable for being shot in 16mm on the fly for a very low budget. If you want to experience Al in all his glory, chaos, and mystery, then *Gospel According to Al Green* is the film to peruse. Unpretentious, executed in a disarmingly simple manner that only heightens the complexity of its subject, this is the definitive document of Al's early gospel years, and the song Green sings with his acoustic guitar at both ends of the film, "I Love You" (the final version referencing the Lord, fittingly enough), I would include on any Al Green best-of. It distills his charisma and otherworldly talent into a few very potent minutes, and he made it up on the spot.

When it came to showing up for screenings of the film, Green was as erratic as ever. Mugge had him booked for the New York opening, but as Al was heading to the Memphis airport he changed his mind. Green "just decided he needed to preach," said Mugge.

Most memorable of all was the Brookline, Massachusetts, premiere at the Coolidge Corner Theatre, where Green not only answered questions from the audience but did a set of songs solo on an electric guitar. "He was doing all the old hits he didn't do for me," said Mugge. At one point in the film where Mugge asks Green what he thinks of singing about young love, he responds, "I think of a person that has not yet grown up . . . he's still chasin' young girls at forty-five. See, there's a time when a man have to put away some of the childish things." Mugge, sitting in the audience next to Green as they watched that moment in the film, noted with irony that Al's date that night was approximately twenty-one to Green's fifty.

Later, when Mugge was to be married atop the Peabody Hotel, "Al was supposed to conduct the ceremony . . . we were such good friends."* Green had wanted him to do a music video for a new gospel album, and Al "was supposed to wire money to my account for me to hire a crew, but the money never came." Mugge decided against having a Memphis service

---

* Mugge even managed to rope Green into recording a message for his answering machine: "Hi, this is Al Green. Bob Mugge can't come to the phone right now, but if you leave a message for him at the tone, I'll make sure he calls you back." A brief snippet of "Call Me" ensues before the beep.

officiated by the Reverend as it would leave his wedding party "depending on a guy who may not be there."

In discussing Green, Mugge compared him to Sun Ra, an equally maverick subject of one of his other documentaries. "Al is one of those people that maintains a childhood innocence that allows them to go places in their creative work, but it can also make them temperamental, undependable . . . they haven't been socialized like other people." That childlike quality "is a double-edged sword for those around them."

❖

"A Polish kid from Chicago," Paul Zaleski was the newest edition to Al Green's menagerie. Zaleski had recorded a lot of black music, some of it for the infamous Gene Lucchesi Sr. at the Sounds of Memphis studio. "When disco was hitting, we were doing R&B—Ollie Nightingale, the Masqueraders, Sam the Sham. We were the last ones, we never gave up."

A soulful person with a deep understanding of Memphis music and its history, Zaleski's life was coming apart in April 1983. An investor in his music projects had died unexpectedly, and Paul had become paralyzed on one side of his face. So when Green's office manager Renee Kirk called offering him a job, Zaleski didn't want to go—"I looked like a freak, I had a patch over my eye, I talked funny"—but he went. Next thing Paul knew he was "workin' on a fuckin' Christmas album in July." When Green walked in, Zaleski greeted him with "Hi, Rev." Green instructed Paul to call him Al. "We hit it off from there," said Paul.

Zaleski had been hired to replace engineer William Brown, an ex–Mad Lads singer who had one too many quarrels with Al. Zaleski's first production credit was *Trust in God,* which came out in January 1985. A mélange of still more pop covers as spirituals, some weak originals, and a title cut (with, don't ask me why, seagulls-and-waves sound effects) which was reprised for no apparent reason a la *Lord Will Make a Way,* somehow the album didn't win a Grammy, although it was nominated.

There's always at least one hidden gem lurking on any Al Green album, and in this case it is a lovely, understated cover of Joe South's "Don't It Make You Want to Go Home" that makes one wish Green would enlist a producer with taste and restraint who could pull an entire country album out of him. "A lot of people don't know that Al loves country music," said Zaleski, who tried to get him to cut more of it. "We were in the studio together on many occasions when he would bring out the guitar and sing country songs."

Trust in God was more evidence of a disorganized mind than any sort of cohesive album, and the reason for this was Green "had one more album to do for Myrrh, but he didn't want to spend any money," said Zaleski. "He had tracks that were cut in the vault, but the drummer on the original tracks couldn't keep time." Al wanted to keep some of his vocals, "so we had to redo the tracks," said Paul, who called the experience a "nightmare, but I did it." Zaleski also recorded Green's sermons every Sunday and edited them for a syndicated radio program and helped out on the sound for the documentary. "My life was just total Al Green."

According to Paul, Al "liked havin' a white producer." The two men bonded. Zaleski would ride around with Green in a Rolls-Royce they'd loaded up with hay to feed his bull, Ralph. They'd go to Sears and buy cologne. Or hop into Al's white Comet and eat at the Catfish Cabin.

"He'd wear a stocking cap and glasses," said Paul. "Nobody knew him." Zaleski is a golf fanatic, and on breaks in the studio, he'd take his club and hit a few balls in the backyard, which butted up to the runway of the Memphis airport. "Al thought it was stupid. He would sit and read his Bible. I'd chip, and he'd read his Bible."

❖

It hadn't gotten any easier being a member of Al Green's band. Reuben Fairfax Jr. had left a few times but was now drifting away for good, with Johnny Brown assuming the role of bandleader. "I was never fired; I quit," said Fairfax. "It was my fault . . . I was probably a bit too arrogant and got a little too big for my britches. The other problem was people in the band getting into drugs. Everything changed."

In Philadelphia, Reuben "couldn't get the guys out of the hotel to go to the show." By the time Fairfax got the band to the gig, Al was onstage with a local choir. Figuring he'd lost control of the musicians, he left for good, never saying good-bye to Al or explaining why. Later he'd learn what the problem was: drugs. "People smoking crack get hung up, won't come out of the hotel . . . I wasn't part of it, I didn't understand 'til many, many years later. At the time I thought I had done somethin' wrong."*

---

* Although I could find no one to verify the story and Reuben has no memory of it, Johnny Brown insisted that Green had a falling out with Fairfax over a woman. "This one night we had a show, it was real late at night, Al didn't want to pay for a hotel room, and he takes the van over to this girl's house. We're all sittin' in the van, and Al went in. Reuben was all quiet, and we realized this was Reuben's ex-girlfriend's house. And while Al was in the house, the girl's mama told Al every bad thing that Reuben had said about him." A livid Green charged back onto the bus and chewed Fairfax out. "The whole band thought that was funny. Reuben didn't."

For a brief period in 1984 Green hired two white musicians that had been in the Amazing Rhythm Aces, best known for their 1975 hit "Third Rate Romance" (former Green keyboard alumni James Hooker had also been a member). First to arrive was Reuben's replacement, bass player Jeff "Stick" Davis. Then Al got into some kind of beef with Johnny Brown, so he hired keyboard player Billy Earheart. The band gave both men a warm welcome. Ex–Enterprise Orchestra guitarist James Bass was back in the fold (according to Earheart, he had a choice piece of advice: don't mess around with Al's backup singers).

Like most musicians who've had the chance to play with Al, Davis and Earheart spoke of Green's talents with great admiration. "When he says break it down, he ain't kidding," said Earheart. Al would wave the band down to playing "so low you can't hear it . . . the whole house is just silent." Then he'd "lay the mic down on the stage and start singing." Al would wander off five feet from the mic, still singing. "It was intense, man," said Billy with admiration. The rule of thumb was: watch the singer. "You gotta pay close attention to him, because it was not exactly the same every night. He'd be quoting scripture; it would turn into a church service almost. You just had to watch him."*

Outside of the music and the camaraderie with band members, the gig was less than a joy. After his bus burned down, Green didn't get another. "He would fly and we would go in a rented van, about ten of us having to sit up all the way. No one could even lay down." There was little advance warning for gigs. Band members would get notice a few days before for a lone gig that might be off in New York.

And Green himself seemed suspicious and standoffish. One band member felt some of Green's paranoia "had to do with leisure-time activities. We were doing two shows at the Beverly Theatre. Al wouldn't come outta his dressing room. Curtis Mayfield was backstage, famous actors, but he was just in his dressing room. His brother Lonel kept coming in and out." When it was time to do the second set Green "finally came out and he was pretty blazed, eyes glazed over."**

---

* For a look at just how great Green could be in this period, see the tremendous *Live in Tokyo* DVD, recorded at the Black Heritage Festival in 1987. A drenched-in-sweat Al sings off-mic as he lies on the floor as well as dances around holding one of his shoes to his face, throwing in a bit of James Brown–style funk along the way. Even usually poker-faced backup singer Linda Jones cracks up over Al's antics.

**According to a *Los Angeles Times* review of this January 26, 1985, performance, Al was an hour late getting onstage. "The Beverly announced his plane had been late, but then Green mentioned that he'd been in Oxnard the night before," wrote reviewer Richard Cromelin. "The Lord isn't the only one who moves in mysterious ways."

Band members allege Green had gotten deep into cocaine at the time, although few wanted to talk about it. At one point the band had to stop off in Los Angeles because Al had to catch a flight. It was one of the rare times he rode in the van. According to one musician, he was on the pipe the whole ride down. "He'd let somebody else have a little," said the source, who didn't want to judge Green as cocaine was so prevalent at the time. They were halfway across Arizona when "all of a sudden Al goes, 'DAMN! I was supposed to get out in LA!'" Green appeared to be totally in the grips of the drug. He was "sitting there smoking blow for two days straight. All the way back . . . it was kind of sad, actually." One depressing result was that Al "couldn't sing as good when he got all gacked up on that shit."

Who knows when this period began; who knows when it ended. "It was only when I found Al Green in a Rolls-Royce sobbing his eyes out that I knew I had to leave these things behind," Green told interviewer Jon Wilde in 2005. "Al Green turned to Al Green and asked: What is that cocaine in your pocket? Why don't you roll down that window and throw that packet away?' Well, I didn't want to throw that away. That was five hundred dollars worth of coke. My hand was in the pit of hell."

During a 2000 *Rolling Stone* interview, Scott Spencer would describe an Al Green "bent over his desk, a maniacal look over his face" as he mimed chopping up lines and snorting them before throwing the imaginary blow out the window. "I got clean," Green claimed. "No rehab got you into it, Al, and no rehab's gonna get you out . . . "

One Los Angeles show was more than a little hair-raising. Green showed up very late and nearly got into an argument with Johnny Brown. "When Al came in he said, 'Johnny, take me to the dressing room, I gotta change clothes.' I said, 'Al, you can't change . . . you have to go straight onstage, you have no choice—they have been waiting almost an hour.'" Although Brown got the haggard-looking singer out in front of the crowd, "whatever Al had did, Al could barely sing. He was standin' next to the organ, just leanin' on the organ . . . the first two songs they were booin' him."

Suddenly, said Johnny, it seemed like "a switch popped in his head." Green proceeded to put on a fantastic show. "I never seen Al sing and dance like that *ever*. Al did the splits, he did the moonwalk . . . the whole place was hollerin' and screamin'." Apparently Green put the blame for the shape he'd been in on a particular girlfriend. "You didn't see her for years after that incident," said Johnny.

❖

Earheart and Davis soon left the band for the reason most musicians left Green. "A couple of times he got funny with my money," admitted Earheart. "It was tough to get paid, and I didn't understand that, 'cause everyone gave one hundred and ten percent." There was a New Year's Eve show in Dallas at "a really nice theater. The place was packed to the gills and we didn't play. The guy didn't have all the money. Well, Al said, 'I ain't playing.'" The band squeezed back into the van and went home. Unpaid.

Earheart and Davis marched into Hattie Angel's office and demanded that Green reimburse them for their time. "Sure enough, he paid us . . . a bad check," said Earheart. "He eventually made it good. But he didn't give the other guys nothing. And they all played with him at his church services . . . if they said anything or upset him a little, he wouldn't let them do the church service either."

Word soon got out among the rest of the band that "the white guys got money," said Earheart. "No one else did. They'd have an attitude but never said anything." It happened a time or two more. Eventually Green paid everybody but "I'd had enough of it," said Earheart.* Al just treated musicians "shitty," said Paul Zaleski. "He didn't treat 'em good at all! Number one, you're lucky to get paid. You had no job security . . . you have to understand: these guys didn't have another gig."

❖

On December 7, 1983, in Miami, Green married again, this time to Clover (aka Vivice Beverly) Dixon, a Jamaican woman a few months older than Al. Little is known about her beyond the fact that they had a son in 1984, and that on March 30, 1985, Clover "took the parties' minor child, Adam Green, and abandoned plaintiff without cause . . . the defendant has not returned to the marital home since that day," stated Al's divorce request, which was granted on "grounds of desertion" October 21, 1986. His attorneys had searched for her in New York City, Miami, and Memphis. After less than two years of marriage, Clover took their child and simply disappeared.**

---

* Johnny Brown claimed that Davis and Earheart threatened to tell the press some of Green's more unflattering secrets. "Al paid 'em their money and you never saw 'em again."

** Attempts to contact Dixon as well as members of her family were unsuccessful. In 1998, unaware of the divorce that had been granted Green, Clover filed for divorce in New York. She claimed Al had engaged in "extrinsic fraud" as she was not made aware of the 1987 divorce, although Green had run a small notice in the Memphis paper *Daily News* four weeks in a row to notify her as required. The court ruled in Al's favor in 1998, dismissing her case and denying her request for alimony and child support.

"Al had a hard time keepin' wives," notes Johnny Brown. One day—Johnny thinks it might've been during the marriage to Clover, but given the way Al kept his band separate from his wives, he's not sure—Green and Brown were flying back from a tour and once they got off the plane, "my wife was standin' there and his wasn't." Green began to seethe. "Every time we pull up, your wife is sittin' there waitin' for you," said Al. "Here I got everything in the world, my wife's gonna show up when *she* gets ready." Finally Mrs. Green appeared at the airport. "They went to their car, I went to mine," said Johnny. "I drove home and turned on the TV. It was on the news—Al had gotten into a big fight with his wife at the airport."

Drugs. Another divorce. Fleeing band members. Even though he'd left his pop career, bought a church, become a reverend, and done all that he said the Lord had asked of him, it seemed that peace of mind still eluded Al Green.

"My problem is and always was overcoming Al," Green confessed to Scott Spencer. "I can get over the world. I can get over my backsliding, my forwardness of mind.

"But there's always Al, I gotta deal with Al."

GET BEHIND ME, SATAN

I'm a cat that does things by impulse. Half insane,
but sometimes a genius.
—AL GREEN

Arthur Kohtz was pissed off at Al Green. Over money.

A pal of Paul Zaleski's, Kohtz had been a jingle writer at Pepper Tanner in Memphis, and was helping Paul work on various projects at Green's studio. Arthur "was a nut," said Zaleski's daughter, Jennifer Carstensen. "He was so awesome. The dirtiest car ever. Shit everywhere, four hundred bags of chips, pop cans. I think at some point he was living out of his car." But when it came to music, "Kohtz had the same passion my dad had, he just kind of went all in—at the expense of money."

In order to supplement whatever income he managed to squeeze out of Green, Zaleski had a side business at his studio where he'd cut quickie albums for inexperienced and unknown gospel groups. "We'd record an album in a day," said Kohtz, laughing. Some of the bands were so lacking in chops they'd tell the members to go relax at their hotel. Meanwhile they'd record the instrumentation themselves. "They'd come in and listen to the music and go, 'Wow, man—did we play that? We never sounded so good!'"

Not that renting Al's studio to outside clients always went well—take the death metal band from Kansas, for example. Green was very fastidious when it came to his studio, and these satanic rockers brought more than just their instruments with them. "Honest to God, they took boxes of live roaches into the studio," said Zaleski. "Al came in, saw the roaches, heard the music, and fucking flipped. We had to fumigate the place. Al said a bunch of prayers."

Zaleski and Kohtz also operated a jingle company out of Al's studio. "I was getting the clients and writing the music, and I was giving him a cut." Kohtz wasn't getting his, however. "A check came in and Al cashed it. It was for Arthur and me," said Zaleski, who claimed it was a misunderstanding, that Green didn't know it was theirs. It didn't matter to Kohtz. "Arthur goes into the office and goes, 'Look, you motherfucker—you took my three thousand dollars,'" said Zaleski. "Al says, 'I didn't take your three thousand.'"

Things went downhill from there. "Money was coming in and I wasn't seeing any of it," said Arthur. "Anytime I'd ask him, he'd have an excuse—'Oh baby, don't you worry 'bout it, I'm gonna pay you.' I went through so much bullshit with him. Finally I said, 'Listen, motherfucker, you gotta pay me!'"

Around this time Kohtz, who'd been to church maybe five times in his life, managed to write a gospel number for Al called "Let It Shine."* "Baddest motherfucking song you ever heard," insisted Zaleski. "It was a hit." Paul dragged Green over to the better-equipped Ardent studio where he'd bought time, and cut two vocal tracks—a cover of "He Ain't Heavy, He's My Brother" and the Kohtz song. They were the first tracks with Zaleski in the role of producer. When Green started in on the vocals, Paul felt he was walking through the performance. "I said, 'Look, you're not mouthing this shit. *I'm* producing this time. You're gonna go out there and sing it.' Because Al, he will do that to you. You do not know what he is capable of until you push him." So right there at Ardent, Zaleski told Green "to go out there and sing the song like it's supposed to be sung—so no one else will ever sing the song again."

Green did just that, and everybody was wowed by the results. "Let It Shine" in particular got an A&M Records executive salivating. "When David Anderle heard it, he said it was the best thing Al's ever done in his fuckin' life and it would cross over into pop," said Zaleski.

Then came the beef with Kohtz. Later they'd be working on Al's *Soul Survivor* album and Green would drop the song. "Al said, 'Let's knock out

---

* Not to be confused with the Teenie Hodges–Al Green song also titled "Let It Shine" on the 1976 album *Full of Fire*.

'Let It Shine.'" I told him, 'You can't do that, it's a hit!' He said, 'I ain't dealin' with Arthur.'" Thus the world has never heard what some consider to be one of Green's finest performances. "My song got bounced," said Arthur. "It was like a silent payback—'I'm gonna show you, white boy.'"

But that was in the future. The first two songs Zaleski had produced for Green got him a major-label deal. So what did Al do? He went off and made a gospel album with Willie Mitchell. "I became super-depressed," said Paul, who had expected to produce his next album. "Al said he needed a hit. And he thought Willie could give him one."

❖

A&M was definitely not Myrrh. "They wanted me to do pop music," said Green in 1985. Green steadfastly refused, feeling that doing a pop album now would render him a phony. "It'd say that I was lying, it'd say that I retract all I've preached for the last eight years. That I was just kidding; that everybody's got a price. Believe me, I could use the money, but I don't think so."

Instead, he managed to talk Mitchell into producing a gospel album, a first for Willie. *He Is the Light* came out in April 1985. It's one of Green's most solid (if low-key) gospel offerings. A melancholy mood permeates; mortality comes up often. "You know, sometimes it seems like everything is going wrong . . . and sometimes we don't know how we'll make ends meet," Al intones in his deepest, most earnest voice on the spoken intro to the slow ballad "Power." Outside of a synth-heavy cover of the annoyingly exuberant 1981 Clark Sisters hit "You Brought the Sunshine," Mitchell brought his usual taste and economy. There was a different crew of musicians, namely Steve Potts on drums and Perry Michael Allen (whom Willie had once asked to leave the studio for discussing his own religious conversion) handled keyboards, percussion, arranging, and additional (uncredited) production work. Neither Howard Grimes nor Charles Hodges contributed, although Teenie and Leroy did.

Green pays tribute to Sam Cooke on a couple of Soul Stirrers covers, particularly an impassioned "Nearer My God to Thee." The spooky "Going Away" is one of Al's most striking original gospel songs and benefits from a classic Mitchell arrangement. The song won Green another Grammy, and the album received major-label promotion, A&M pushing the record not on gospel stations and public television but with Green performing on *Saturday Night Live*.

❖

According to Paul Zaleski, *He Is the Light* "was one of the lowest-selling re-cords of all time. Al came up to me and says, 'You wanna be my producer?'"

Soul Survivor was cut at Al's studio (with some additional recording elsewhere), but this was not another quickie gospel album. "That was well over a year in the making," said Zaleski. All the songs we cut did not make the album—we probably cut twenty. We worked so hard on 'em." Just like during his very first session with Green, Zaleski pushed Al. Paul would not accept lazy, first-take vocals from him. "We'd listen to it, I'd say, 'I think you could do better.' Al would say, 'Fuck you! Where?'" Paul would point out a line that needed improvement, and Green would do it again. "I'd turn his voice up in his headphones loud to make him sing soft so he wouldn't sing out his voice. You get more emotion when you have Al singin' soft."

Contrary to the album credits, Zaleski maintains that, outside of back-ground singers, most of the album was recorded by just four people*—"Al, me, Errol Thomas, and Michael Toles." Toles, a member of the Bar-Kays, was a guitarist, and Thomas, a bass player who'd worked a lot with Zaleski (and with Al on *Truth n' Time*), was particularly important to the album. Thomas was "very good at arranging," said Arthur Kohtz, who did un-credited work on the album. "Errol was our guy on the floor," explained Zaleski, who joked that Thomas could "interpret my Polishness" to black musicians. Outside of some tracks with esteemed Memphis percussionist Willie Hall on the skins, "there was no drummer," said Zaleski, who used drum machines. "We didn't program, we played 'em with our fingers so we would get the feel. Al and I would do it."

They were a close-knit group. "Al, myself, and Errol used to sit out by the B3 and we would just talk music until four o'clock in the morning. Al would bring in his guitar." Zaleski saw the value of Green's guitar play-ing. "He's great. Because Al doesn't know what he's doin'. He's got a very unique way. Al picks up a guitar, feels it, plays it, one take, done." Which is how stunning versions of the traditional "Yield Not to Temptation" and Laura Lee's "Jesus Will Fix It" came about. "'Jesus Will Fix It' took four months. That's Al Green, a drum machine, and Errol playin' bass, a little

---

* As far as the actual list of credits, "We put a bunch of people's names on it that had nothin' to do with the fuckin' album," said Zaleski, who felt that if there were only four names listed it might "slant" critics against it. "Was there any logic to it? I doubt it. I'm not a very logical person."

of Michael Toles overdubbing. That's *it*. That song was very hard to mix. You had five Al Green vocals and five Al Greens on guitar."

Zaleski wrote the music for "You Know and I Know," an affecting love song to Christ. "You think that I don't listen to a word you say," Al tells God. Paul had written the track one night as his daughter was going to sleep. "When I got done writing, I called Al up, played it for him over the telephone. He said, 'Let's go to the studio.'" Paul got out the drum machine, Al wrote the words, and the next day Michael Toles overdubbed a guitar part. The song title became something of a touchstone for Al; whenever he saw Paul, he'd start laughing and say it. "We'd be on a plane, I'd walk by, and he'd say, 'You know and I know.'"

It was all great stuff, but with "Let It Shine" gone, they "still didn't have a hit," said Zaleski. One day on the band bus headed for Washington, DC, he heard a few instrumental tracks done by friends of the piano player. The homemade music appealed to Paul. "It was made with a real little machine, a Yamaha thing that plays keyboard and a beat at the same time." They'd been recorded by Jimi Randolph and Eban Kelly, a pair from nowhere who wound up with production credits on the album cuts. "I think we paid seven grand for all the tracks," said Zaleski. "I played 'em for Al, I said, 'Here are the hits.'"

One of the tracks turned into a song on the spot in the studio when Errol had gone to grab some food. He was late returning, and Paul was getting antsy. "Al said, 'Don't worry, everything's gonna be all right, he's comin' back just like he said he would.'" Zaleski thought if they just capitalized those pronouns, they'd have a hit gospel song. "I said, 'Son of a bitch, that's the title, write it down!'" It took a minute for it to click with Green. "That's the title—sing it," Paul told him. Al did so, halfheartedly. "I said, 'Jesus Christ already . . . c'mon, *sing* the *song*! SING IT! You're wastin' money.' He kept singin', we kept on punchin'." "Everything's Gonna Be Alright" became the first single off the album, earned Green another Grammy, and became a staple of his live shows.

The album closed with "23rd Psalm," Psalm 23 set to music. Zaleski loved the track until Al mangled it. "We had violins, it was beautiful," said Paul, still pained. "That was a classic—*without* the kick drum." While Zaleski was away, Green overdubbed a drum machine. "I accidentally left my Yamaha drum machine there, and he stuck that son of a bitch on, mixed that thing, and edited it himself. Al loved to hear a kick drum. It's not in time either." When Zaleski heard it, he blew a gasket, but Al had made up his mind. According to Paul, Green told him, "Baby, we have to have that. We're doing black music, you have to have the kick." Zaleski came back at him: "'Al, this is crossover shit. I'm trying to get you to *white people*. White people don't need that shit. This is cool shit, leave it alone.' About five years later he said, 'Y'know, you were right.'"

If you can manage to ignore the cursed eighties drum machines as well as a couple of particularly excruciating pop-as-gospel covers, "He Ain't Heavy, He's My Brother" and "You've Got a Friend" (not produced by Zaleski), *Soul Survivor* is one of Green's most original and cohesive gospel albums. Unfortunately one of the best songs, the very Hi-sounding "So Real to Me," plays for less than a minute. (The full recording is available only as a single B-side. When I asked Zaleski why it was so truncated on the album, his response was "For suspense.") When the album was done, Zaleski listened to it with Green and David Anderle. Al's verdict, according to Paul? "That's a bad motherfucker . . . a *bad* motherfucker." The album was number one on the gospel charts for three months, and "Everything's Gonna Be Alright" made it to number twenty-two on the R&B charts. It was Green's first Top 40 R&B hit in over a decade, and he'd done it with a gospel song. "*That's* when he said thanks," said Zaleski. "That was cool."

❖

In a May 1988 interview, Green announced an album due out the next month, *Family Plan*. He boasted it had been recorded in Memphis, Atlanta, and Boston—the latter city because, as he ladled on the bullshit to interviewer Simon Witter, "You only get the very sophisticated 1990ish music out of Boston . . . very hip, digital, Mitsubishi-type tracks." Zaleski said a number of great tracks were cut for this album, among them "I Remember When," "You Got the Love," and "Was It Something I Said?" *Family Plan* has never seen the light of day. "I don't know why it never came out," said Paul. "They were hits."

Around this time Green recorded a gospel album on an aspiring young singer from his Grand Rapids stomping grounds, Denise Flippin. "She just appeared one day and we cut an album on her," said Johnny Brown. "Her father came with her—a preacher friend of Al's, I think he was contributing to the church," noted Zaleski. Flippin was "beautiful, Whitney Houston beautiful. She looked wholesome as apple pie. I don't think she was more than twenty or twenty-one. [If public records are accurate, Flippin was closer to eighteen or nineteen.] She would come to the studio a lot. A lot. They had somethin' goin' on, I just don't know what . . . it was a strange, strange relationship. He put her down as writer on a couple of songs, but she didn't have anything to do with them." And then one day Flippin was just "gone," said Brown, who suggested that it "might have something to do with some relatives . . . they accused him of bein' with her." Flippin would share cowriting credit with Green on four songs on his next album, *I Get Joy*, then vanish. Said Zaleski, "She faded into the sunset, just like she came in on the sunrise."*

❖

In October 1988 Green recorded a duet with Annie Lennox, "Put a Little Love in Your Heart." Produced by then-ubiquitous pop-rock leprechaun Dave Stewart, it's a piece of manufactured fluff to fill the soundtrack of the Bill Murray vehicle *Scrooged*. The singers were on different continents when they recorded it, nor do they ever share the same shot in the video, and the results are inoffensive and instantly forgettable. However, the track provided a major boost to Green's career—it was a number-nine pop hit, the first time he'd been in the Top 10 since "Sha-La-La" in 1974. Not everybody was happy, though; Green had crossed a line. "People said you can't sing with Annie Lennox. That's wrong for you to do that,'" he admitted. Who thought it was wrong? "Some people in the church."

Nevertheless, now that Green had managed another bona fide hit, Zaleski noticed that there were "people trying to talk Al into going more modern. I didn't feel comfortable with 'em." Green now had a William Morris agent, Marshall Resnick, and he was pushing for more commercial opportunities. "When Marshall got involved they wanted him to start doing pop . . . there was a lot of pressure."

❖

Around twelve at the time, Jennifer, Paul Zaleski's daughter, was allowed to visit Al Green's studio on occasion. Despite her age, she was an astute observer. "Al had a charisma and an infectiousness that drew people to him. He didn't really listen to other people very much, he was in his own little world—'You're either on my boat or not on my boat. And if you're not on my boat, I don't know you.'" Sometimes Jennifer would sneak over

---

* In 2002 Denise Flippin released a gospel album, *Simply Denise*. There is nary a mention of Al Green in the extensive thank yous. All attempts to reach Denise were unsuccessful.

to Green's hair salon. "Those ladies carried on like Al Green was not next door. Everyone treated him like a normal person. Lots of chatter, ladies in all the chairs, curlers everywhere. I would sneak in the back and put a quarter in the Nehi machine."

But life under Al could be a trial for the Zaleski family. Green would summon Paul, and he'd be gone for days on end. They never knew when or if he'd get paid. "It was a hard life!" said Jennifer, who grew to hate it when Green called the house. "First of all, he never spoke . . . he only sang. He'd call the house and would start singing to me—'Jenny, Jenny.' I hated it—I'm a Jennifer." I kept telling him, 'Nobody calls me Jenny, don't call me Jenny.' He kept doing it, he did not care. He would just laugh. I would hang up on him sometimes and he would just keep calling back. And my Dad would say, 'You can't be that rude to him, he's a really important person.' I'd say, 'I don't care, *he won't quit calling me Jenny!*'"

As Al and Paul started working on another album, Zaleski's team was disintegrating. First Arthur Kohtz went, then Errol Thomas. Paul said that he and Thomas were promised "three percent of the gross forever" for *Soul Survivor*. "I think I got three grand, Errol got a grand. Errol got into a fight with Al Green about money and he left. Errol sued." Zaleski didn't. "Errol leaving changed a lot of dynamics. That was bad."

Still, Zaleski hung in there. Paul's dedication to Al was "over the top," said Arthur Kohtz, who was dismayed by the way Green treated him. "There would be times I'd look at Paul and I'd say, 'Has he ever given you any money, Paul? An advance, something?'" Zaleski told him no.

Although Zaleski maintained that drugs were banned from the studio, Arthur and Jennifer felt cocaine abuse was rampant. "I know there were a lot of drugs during those sessions . . . a lot of blow," said Kohtz. "I think I did it one time just to keep myself awake . . . that was the downside of the whole thing." Said Jennifer: "I remember going into the studio and seeing coke lines and razor blades. In fact, I took one of the razor blades." Her father out of the room, Jennifer had looked at the tapes on the mixing board and, having seen her dad splice edits in the analog tape, thought she'd help out. "I took the razor blade that had white powder on it and I sliced the tape. I'm just helping . . . I literally cut through the work they had just spent three days doing."

Released in May 1989, *I Get Joy* was another disorganized, lesser work. Green had written most of the forgettable material. By this point it was inevitable that he would bruise up against the gaudy, gold-plated interstellar universe known as hip-hop. The Mitchell/Green recordings would be sampled by a plethora of artists, particularly throughout the nineties: Ghostface Killah, Nas, Notorious B.I.G., Jay Z, Diddy, Kanye West. Not that the Reverend was a fan. "It seems violent and full of violent gestures. We don't believe in that." Al found some of it "just too sex oriented. Sex, sex, sex, sex, sex. You can tell someone you love them without speaking under their belongings."

Former quarterback-turned-singer/rapper/producer/actor Al B. Sure! was brought in on the track "As Long as We're Together" to "remix that song when we'd already spent five Gs to mix," said a disgusted Zaleski. "I didn't have a say-so. They got a ton of money to do that. Al B. Sure! took off half the instruments. Who the hell is he now? When that thing came back, I looked at Al, I said, 'This *sucks*.'" "As Long as We're Together" won Green yet another Grammy.

There was one exception to the rampant mediocrity. "To me that album was nothing but 'Mighty Clouds of Joy,'" said Zaleski proudly. The song had been a Top 40 hit for B. J. Thomas in 1971, but Al would make it his own. Zaleski had cut the track minus Al with guitar ace Wayne Perkins demoing the vocal. "I called Al up, I didn't push it on him—I said, 'Listen to this,'" Zaleski recalled. Al liked the song, and they cut it. But it wasn't there yet. "Let me sleep on it a couple of days," said Green. A few days later Al called him at one o'clock in the morning: "I'm ready." They hit the studio and recorded a take. It was better, but not great. "You don't have it yet," Paul told him, who felt the end of the song needed to build like dark clouds overhead. So Al did it again.

"The hair on the back of my head stood up the next time, especially during the vamp. Al was twirling on his foot while he did the vocal. You can hear his voice go around the speakers. He had that song nailed and Al *knew* he had it nailed—he said, 'I got it *now!*' My whole heart and soul went into that song. And his did. That's the best Al's ever sung. He'll always be remembered for 'Let's Stay Together,' but he's never sung better than 'Mighty Clouds of Joy.'

"When he was done singin' it, we just looked at each other and walked outside the studio. I handed him my keys. I hadn't been home in a long time. I said, 'I'm goin' to Chicago. I'm done. I cannot do any better.'" Zaleski was in the middle of a rough personal period that included drugs and divorce, and Green finished the album without him. Paul's name is misspelled in the credits.

"Everybody loved Paul," said Arthur Kohtz, who wasn't fond of the way Green had treated Zaleski. "As far as I was concerned, he destroyed him, because Paul went into a downhill slide after that. He took advantage of Paul. When it was all said and done, Paul's wife divorced him, he ended up addicted. Paul made the ultimate sacrifice for that guy. And Al didn't give a shit. All Al Green cared about was Al Green. And I'll take that to my grave. I have no respect for the man. None. I think he's a phony."

Jennifer Carstensen also feels that Green turned his back on her father. "Al cut him out. Wouldn't return his calls. That was the part I think that was just really terrible. Al never knew what my dad truly gave up to work with him. Not only did Al break his heart, he broke his spirit. You can't repair a spirit."

Before Zaleski left, he'd told Al, 'Y'know what, Al? I could sue you to the hilt. I'll write a book. I know enough shit. One day I'm gonna come to you and say, 'Look, I need a little bit of money.' There was an occasion I got into trouble—I got into drugs pretty bad. I needed three grand, and it was there within two hours. Within two hours!" As far as Paul's concerned, "Al did me a favor by holding on to my money."

When it comes to the dark side of Al Green, Paul Zaleski prefers not to look. "He's always come through for me. This guy helped me out so much, not only professionally but personally with his Bible teachings. He's always been a brother to me, even to this day. Do I get mad at him? Fuck, yeah. Do I show respect to him? Yeah. Would I ever do somethin' to hurt him? No."

They'd meet again in a few years, and Paul Zaleski would get burned once more.

❖

On April 28, 1989, Green was granted another divorce. He had married Martha Gibson* on December 14, 1987, in Indianapolis, Indiana. They separated three days before the divorce was issued. There were no children. Another mystery woman in Green's life, Martha received "a lump sum cash payment of $1,000" and was gone.

❖

Ponytailed, bearded Arthur Baker looked like a heavy out of a Steven Seagal movie. He'd be the one to get Green back to recording pop music

---

* Attempts to reach Martha went unanswered.

again, but oddly enough, Al would have to guest star on two of Arthur's records before that happened. Nine years younger than Green, Boston-born Baker made a name for himself as a deejay, moving to New York, where he produced seminal hip-hop record "Planet Rock" for Afrika Bambaataa and the Soul Sonic Force. He remixed dance versions for Cyndi Lauper, Bruce Springsteen, and the Pet Shop Boys, produced many hits for New Order, and oversaw Bob Dylan's much-maligned *Empire Burlesque* as well.

Baker had been an Al Green fan since he nabbed a promo copy of *Let's Stay Together* while working at a record store as an adolescent. Signed to A&M in 1989 to make an album himself, Baker had cut a song he'd written called "The Message Is Love." A singer by the name of Will Downing had sung the vocal, but he was on another label and a deal couldn't be worked out. Jerry Moss suggested another artist on A&M—Al Green. Baker was excited by the idea and sent Al a cassette of the song.

They met in the studio. "He went in, did a take, it was pretty lively," Baker recalled. "But he just made up his own melody. He didn't really sing the song." Asking Al to listen to the melody, Arthur played him Downing's version again. Green, who preferred the take he'd just recorded, immediately went into Third-Person Al. "He ain't gonna do it any better than that," said Al of himself.

Baker rose to the occasion. "Could the second guy who knows the melody tell the first guy to sing the melody, and you two guys get it together?" That got a laugh from Green, who recorded it again. "It was a great take," said Baker.

An inoffensive piece of catchy, post–"We Are the World" fluff, "The Message Is Love" was an international hit (if not in America). The video starts in black-and-white with Arthur releasing a dove in slow motion, then comes Al singing and dancing around a lit-up globe, intercut with shots of extremely undernourished third-world denizens. The song was credited to Arthur Baker and the Backbeat Disciples featuring Al Green. Green accompanied Baker on a promotional tour of Europe. Second fiddle was an odd position for Al to be in, but Arthur deduced A&M was "paying him for these trips. Why else would he do it?" The song was a massive hit in Germany, where the Berlin Wall had just come down. "It became kind of the anthem there."

Promoting the song in the States in May 1989, Baker learned how quickly Green could turn. He'd assembled an all-star band for Green to perform the song on *The Arsenio Hall Show*. When they met at the airport to fly to Los Angeles, it became apparent that whoever booked the tickets had screwed up. Baker had a first-class ticket; Green did not. "And he got pissed off at me—'Al Green—twenty-million records and they put him in the back of the bus!' The A&R guy talked to someone and they were gonna upgrade him to first class, but he wouldn't do it. He was getting really pissed off; the A&R guy had to literally get in between us.

"We land, and he won't talk to me. I'm thinking, 'Oh, what a nightmare this is.' He wouldn't get in the limo." Green caught a cab and pulled a disappearing act. He resurfaced but would only appear on the show on one condition. "The next morning we're supposed to do rehearsal," Baker recalled. "The A&R guy calls and says, 'Sorry, man, but Al doesn't want you at the rehearsal. Because of the ticket.'" Thus Arthur did not appear on his own song on *The Arsenio Hall Show*. He sat in his room at the Mondrian Hotel and stewed. "I don't remember if I even watched it, I was so fuckin' pissed off. Then I get a phone call that night after he's back—'Artie, where were you, how come you weren't there?' I'm like, 'Dude, *really*? Seriously?!'"

In 1991 came "Leave the Guns at Home," a message song written by Baker and keyboard whiz Greg Phillinganes that is as painfully literal as the title implies (there's also a twelve-inch with "Dissolving Rap" and "Churchapella Mix" versions). The song begins with that omnipresent syncopated nineties drumbeat, signaling an overblown production with gospel superstars the Winans overdubbing backing parts. It sounds like—well, countless other dull recordings of the time. Green's vocals were recorded at Royal, and a mystified Baker watched Willie Mitchell in action with his funky equipment: as usual, "the tape machine was not working one hundred percent, and Willie was using his finger to make sure the machine would keep rolling."

Green and Baker made a trip to First Ebenezer Baptist Church, where they received an award for the song from shooting victim and gun-control advocate James Brady. "Being in Harlem with Al Green is an experience you can't imagine," said Baker. "Women were coming up to him, taking out baby pictures saying, 'That's because of *you*.'" Both of the message songs that Green had recorded with Baker were a good fit for a singing reverend, easy sells to his congregation back in Memphis. The next material they'd record together would be Jesus-free. He'd make another gospel album first.

❖

Green re-signed with Word Records (which was now distributed by Sony) in 1991. Late that year Word's vice president, Tom Ramsey, met with Al and asked him what he wanted to do next. "I really want to reach everybody . . . I don't want to single out anybody," said Green. Ramsey took that to mean as mainstream an album as possible, and put Green together with Tim Miner, a Caucasian Oklahoma preacher's kid eighteen years younger than Al. Miner had cut a solo record for Motown and produced various artists for Word. *Contemporary Christian Music* dubbed him "gospel's long-haired *wunderkind* of funky music."

When Green entered Miner's Knightlight Studios in Dallas, he was immediately enamored by the lit candles everywhere. "I walk in and he wants to have a prayer. Prayer!" said Al. "That knocks me out." Green and Miner wrote ten songs in the studio, enlisting the help of various other white Texas gospel musicians. "We were like kids sitting together on the floor writing songs," said Green. "We were fasting while we recorded this one. It makes for a better album."

Al would declare *Love Is Reality* "the most exciting thing I've done in ten years." The reality is that this album gets my vote for the worst Al Green album of all time. "We wanted to make it 1992, give it the Infiniti-Lexus style," boasted Al. "You got to change with the times." Yet the sound is strictly eighties: pointlessly busy arrangements, sheeny synth, and that fat, flabby reverb snare drum. The sound is so physically fatiguing it's hard to get through the whole thing in one sitting. Obviously Green put his heart into this, as did a legion of other people, and I drove around in my car blasting this thing trying to like it. Impossible. Aside from a few guests of color—namely El DeBarge and Kirk Whalum—it sounds like a whole lot of white Christians flapping away attempting to get funky. Goody-good music. In the middle of "You Don't Know Me," Green even performs an awkward and ill-advised rap, telling of people "living a lie and dealing in contrary ways. Don't let it stop your stuff!" To hear a singer of Al's stature trapped in such a rinky-dink nightmare is hard to stomach.

One song cuts through the computerized cacophony, however. "A Long Time" may be the most melancholy song Al has ever written or recorded (producer Miner gets a cowriting credit). He reflects on the "marks" on his back left by Mary Woodson and, pleading for help, tosses in a verse of "Amazing Grace." It appears that being saved did not end Green's torment. Like elsewhere on the album, Al boasts that nobody knows him yet refuses to reveal himself. "There are surprises that I keep / Some things I'll never tell,"* he sings, a riddle to the end. It is an intriguing, deeply felt song, naked in its despair. Al sounds like the loneliest man on earth.

❖

Despite a big push from the label, *Love Is Reality* "never really took off," said Tom Willett, who worked in Sony marketing at the time. "They even spent twenty-five grand for Dr. Dre to do a twelve-inch remix of the title track, although nobody could tell what he'd actually done to it. We played it, and damned if any of us could hear anything different from this mix than from what we turned in. We even played it backwards. The promo guy said, 'What you're buying is Dre's *name* for twenty-five K. It doesn't matter if he mixed it or not.'"

Willett recalled taking Green to lunch so he and another executive could suggest that Al "write some songs that would integrate his faith with topical issues of the day . . . he was pretty quiet." In a limo on the way to an appearance on *The Tonight Show,* Willett unwisely broached the subject once more. Green, who obviously saw this as another attempt to coax him into secular music, "threw up his hands, made the sign of the cross with his fingers, and said, 'GET BEHIND ME, SATAN!'" When they got to Burbank, Carson's second banana, Ed McMahon, trotted out to welcome them, but Al wouldn't "introduce me. And refused to talk to me the rest of the day. I'd been blessed by Little Richard, but I was now cursed by Al Green."

Nothing was easy with Green, including getting him anywhere. "I learned you can't say, 'Al, your ticket is at the airport' . . . You had to physically FedEx his ticket—and not just one. Usually about five different flights had to be arranged. There had to be a stack of tickets in his possession so that finally, eventually, he would show up."

Willett was ecstatic when *Rolling Stone* committed to doing a story on Green. A writer was sent down to Al's church, expecting to talk to him after the service. After hours of church, "one of the deacons came up and said, 'Al has been called away to Fort Lauderdale. I'll be preaching today.' He'd just blown off these writers 'cause he wanted to go to Florida."

Green had a show at the Beacon Theatre in New York City. Willett had wined and dined a bunch of Sony executives that night before the show to get them pumped to work Green's album. "I went backstage to see him

---

* That's the lyric as performed. In the CD booklet it's written (and sung by the background vocalists) as "There are surprises that I keep / I could never tell."

before he went on and I told him, 'Hey, it would be really great if you would give a shout-out to the Sony people . . . tell them thank you.' So he goes out and does his show, and I can tell—he forgot." Willett rushed backstage to remind Al, but he was blindsided by what happened next. "Al said, 'It's been a great night. I just wanted to thank my label . . . RCA Records.' He was actually announcing he was going into business with *another* major!"

Needless to say, the Sony people were a little stunned. "We found out the next day he actually did sign with RCA," a mortified Willett recalled. Al had a contract with Word/Sony, but the fine print specified it was only for gospel music. Out of nowhere, Green had signed an overseas deal with RCA to record R&B once more. Said Willett, "He had told me he was not going to do anything but gospel records!"

Such are the whimsical ways of Al Green. "We shot a video for a sales conference the next day," said a woeful Willett. "I literally got a pie in the face."

AL GREEN DON'T DO CATS

*People say, 'Well, you can sing this and you can't sing that.' I think
you can sing what God tells you to sing.*
—AL GREEN, BEACON THEATRE, 1989

In 1992 Al Green changed his mind. He began performing his old hits
live, then returned to recording pop music. There were a few numbers
from his Hi days that he'd deemed suitable for his gospel shows, such as
"L-O-V-E" and "How Can You Mend a Broken Heart?," which he'd end
with a reference to Jesus as he pointed upward. During a raucous April
9, 1989, show at the Beacon Theatre in New York City, Green teased the
audience with snippets of secular Al, and a year later he was singing "Tired
of Being Alone" during a gospel set at the Apollo.

Why the sudden change? "Somebody talked him into it," theorized
Paul Zaleski, who'd be back to engineer Al's live sound. "He made a lot of
money—a *ton* of money." Green told Zaleski he'd demanded a thousand
dollars per minute to sing the old hits, figuring for that amount "they
won't make me sing." He was wrong. Al's set ran fifty minutes, no encores,
and for that, according to Zaleski, he'd receive "fifty K a show, not count-
ing the band."

The decision had not come easily. To one reporter Al admitted, "I became overburdened by what I could not do. The 'Thou-Shalt-Nots' got
to be too many." One day in the studio he sat down with horn player
Anthony Royal and admitted, "I don't know how I feel about playin' my

R&B stuff." Royal pointed out the content of his music didn't go against anything found in the Bible. "These are all love songs," he told Green. "We're talkin' about love between a man and woman, nothing wrong with that." That logic appealed to Al.

Green told the press that in order to return to secular music he'd sought his congregation's permission, and that he "actually went and sought counseling to see what type of music I was singing in comparison to my faith and beliefs . . . after that, I went to get away by myself way up in the mountains for a week or two, just to get away, pray, get away and listen to the waterfalls. Just get away and see if I could sing my music." Al turned heavenward for the ultimate advice, and God had the same point of view as Anthony Royal. "I had to go talk to the master about it. He said, 'Al, I gave you the songs 'cause they're beautiful songs . . . if people got a problem with what you sing, such as 'Love and Happiness' and 'For the Good Times,' then how did they get here?'" Thus God instructed him: "You got to do *all* of Al Green."

Green returned to the studio to record his first non-gospel album in many years. Arthur Baker got him an overseas deal with RCA, and they started recording, although things got off to a halting start at Baker's New York studio. Green "walked in and there was a cat there," said Baker. "He goes, 'Naw . . . I don't do cats.' There could not be cats in the studio when Al was there. Al was not cat-friendly."

Besides matters feline, Green was still reluctant about the material. "The thing was convincing Al to sing any songs that weren't religious," said Baker. There was a line in one of the new songs that used "baby" as a term of endearment. "Al said, 'He can't sing that,' speaking about himself. 'He can't sing *baby*—he'll sing *maybe*.' So it still was spiritual love, not sexual love. I thought, 'Okay, whatever works. He's Al fucking Green, he can do what he wants."

A brief, uncomfortable impasse occurred over the song "Keep On Pushing Love," which had been written by Baker, Tommy Faragher, and Lotti Golden. The day they were to record, the writers were sitting around the piano with Green discussing the number. "He goes, 'This really sounds like Al,'" said Faragher. So much so that Green wanted in on the writing and publishing. He felt the song was "a pastiche of his stuff," said Baker. "He wanted twenty-five percent before he recorded."

"It was a really odd moment," recalled Faragher, who said they offered Green a cut. "He really went into third person—'I don't know if my publisher could agree, because it sounds so much like *Al*.' We couldn't quite figure out what he was saying . . . when he agreed to take the writing credit, we all breathed a sigh of relief." The very first line of the song is Green talking, saying, "Ooooh, I love this—somebody, somebody say blessing." It was an ad-lib that came out of his mouth directly after the matter of credit was settled. "He was laughing and I pressed record," said Baker. "We were fine with him getting his piece."

Al came to the sessions with no entourage, no handlers. He'd show up, record, and then "he would just disappear," said Faragher. "We did background vocals in Jersey, and he would or wouldn't show up. You never knew. When he was there, you dropped everything to get as much done as possible." At times he seemed lost in Dimension Al. "He was always cool, but he would drift and you weren't quite sure he knew who you were."

Recording Green's vocals was "an unbelievable experience," said Faragher, who said you couldn't get Al to stand in front of a mic "like a normal singer. He would not do it. It's not like, 'I'm a professional, I'm gonna stay on mic, stand three inches away.' He doesn't give a shit about any of that. He literally walks around a six- to eight-foot area. He'll start to sing something off mic, then he'll move in, do these little things, clap his hands—he has these antics he does while he's singing, it's all part of the package, it's part of the Al Green sound. It fades in slowly, it builds. When it's fading out, he's literally walking off mic. I got it after working with him—'Oh my God, that's part of his brilliance.' It's a performance."

The songs Baker cut this time were reasonable nineties facsimiles of Al's old Hi hits, particularly "Love Is a Beautiful Thing."* Most interesting of all, however, were the seven cuts produced by David Steele and Andy Cox of the Fine Young Cannibals ("I must admit their group's name sounded mighty odd to me at first," confessed the Reverend). On "Best Love," "What Does It Take," "Waiting on You," and "One Love," these two Brits managed to do what so many of their American counterparts had failed at, and that was to pay homage to the Hi past while updating Green's sound in a way that was neither grating nor obnoxious but intriguing.

---

* Tchad Blake mixed two of Baker's songs for the album. Al "didn't say much," Blake recalled. Listening to one of the mixes, he moved around the room "with a smile on his face. When it finished playing back, he looked at me, then turned to Arthur and said, 'Wow, you know what this is? It's a cheeseburger, not a hamburger. That's a cheeeeeseburger.' And he left the studio."

"The Cannibals do have the Memphis soul sound down pat," conceded Al. "But I want you to know they have it on a computer!"

"Mix hip-hop with Hi was the aim," said Steele, and thus the beats were all programmed. "When I listen back, that's my only regret—I wish we had used live drums." The sessions were done at Sorcerer, a low-key New York studio in Soho, then finished in London with some overdubs by the Memphis Horns. Most of the striking background vocal samples were done by Wincy, an unheralded singer who'd sung on Monie Love's 1990 hit "It's a Shame (My Sister)."

David found working with Al whirlwind-fast and free of drama. "A lot of singers today, you have to get them a yoga room before they start. Al was just like, 'Give me some coffee and I'll sing." They started out working on just one song for the album but wound up recording the majority of Green's next album. "He was just so fast," said Steele. "He'd finish the vocal, it would be great, and we'd have another two days booked in the studio. He'd say, 'What else have you got lying around?'" David would play him a demo and if Green took to it, Steele prepared a track as Al went back to his hotel to write words. Whatever Green delivered the next day was the lyric. "It wasn't like a normal writing process—'Hey, that line's no good,'" admitted Steele, who received cowriting credit on the songs.

One thing Steele remembered most vividly was the way the RCA executives walked on eggshells around Al, as they worried Green might back out of recording anything that wasn't gospel. "Everybody was scared of him, terrified he was gonna quit at any second," said Steele. "The whole idea was to try and make him comfortable." *Don't Look Back* came out in England in 1993, and in November 1995 MCA rereleased it in the States as *Your Heart's in Good Hands,* using eight tracks (four of them remixed) from the original album, plus two lackluster new ones produced by Narada Michael Walden and DeVante Swing.

Green's return was hitless and underwhelming to many. As beautifully as he sings on some of this material, it feels like he's holding back, that he isn't giving his all. Al certainly knew the difference. "This isn't *Trust in God.* What we really tried to get was family values—it's about the husband, the wife, the kids, the dog, the good car, going on vacation." Once more he saw his pop music career as a stealth mission to get a Christian message across, creating an album "that will speak to the hearts of a lot of people that you may not find in the sanctuary on a Sunday morning." The bland title video shows Green crooning in the park intercut with Hallmark-card scenes of a couple falling in love. Flat, one-dimensional notions of "perfect love" seem important to Green.

In 1994 Green was part of the *Rhythm, Country and Blues* album. The overhyped gimmick here was pairing an African American artist with a white one for duets on country and R&B chestnuts. Thus Green re-recorded "Funny How Time Slips Away" with clown-haired alt-country precursor Lyle Lovett (if you're going to bother with such an idea, at least pair Green with a singer worthy of his talents—such as George Jones, who was sentenced to crooning "Patches" alongside B.B. King). Overseen by sunglassed producer du jour Don Was, who even went to the trouble of sticking Teenie Hodges and the Memphis Horns on the track, this was another unnecessary remake that added nothing to the Willie Mitchell–produced version. It provided Green with yet another Grammy.

❖

On September 2, 1995, Green appeared at Cleveland Stadium for his in-duction into the Rock and Roll Hall of Fame. This was the very first ceremony, with a star-studded lineup that included fellow nominees Jerry Lee Lewis and Chuck Berry as well as a slew of superstar guests such as Bruce Springsteen, Bob Dylan, Lou Reed, and Iggy Pop, the whole affair broadcast live on HBO. As part of his duties, Green performed several times during the show. There was an embarrassing "duet" with Aretha Franklin on "Freeway of Love." According to Al, "We rehearsed 'Love and Happiness,' because that's what she said she wanted to sing, and her band had it down pat." At the last moment, Franklin sprang "Freeway of Love" on Al. "I'm like, 'I don't know "Freeway.'" She said, 'Just follow me.'" Off a cliff. Holding court over a small city of musicians sprawled across the stage, Franklin charged through the number, with Green, who clearly didn't know the song, bouncing onstage toward the end to join in. Al and Aretha just run up and down the stage outshouting each other. As it's just one more televised awards show, one has to gauge expectations accordingly, but since it is the only onstage union for the two performers thus far, one might have hoped for something a little more dignified.

Somewhat better was Green's solo performance of Sam Cooke's "A Change Is Gonna Come," backed by Booker T. and the MG's plus various and sundry other pros (as always with these affairs, too many musicians end up adding nothing). Apparently the choice of song was the Hall of Fame's idea, an unexpected detour into something actually exciting. "I never sang that before I rehearsed it that evening," Green admitted. It was an interesting opportunity—Stax meets Hi—and many felt Al stole the show, a knee-jerk opinion from those not well versed in his incendiary live performances. Since Cooke is one of Green's idols, you wanted him to crush it—the TV world was watching. Truth be told, Al—bejeweled and resplendent in shades and wearing something that resembled an intergalactic Chairman Mao suit—engaged with the lyric only intermittently, nervously prowling the stage, pointing at and waving to the sea of people. Green thrives on the intimacy he creates with an audience, and often seems lost performing on cavernous stages where the crowd is far out of reach. For a deeper, more melancholic reading of the Sam Cooke song, watch Al's October 21, 2001, performance during the post-9/11 United We Stand concert in Washington, DC. Wearing a spiffy gold suit, Al fully concentrates on the song, building the kind of emotional arc Willie Mitchell could appreciate, although his voice cracks on the last note (only mentioned because it's such a rare occurrence).

Green's acceptance speech at the Hall of Fame was brief. "I just decided to write some songs about my little life . . . I don't know about all this *greatness* . . . I'd just like to keep on keepin' on." Other than the Hall of Fame itself, he thanked no one. Clearly some part of him relished his outsider status. "It's controversial, isn't it?" he said later. "The *Reverend*. Somebody said to me, 'How many preachers do you know that are in the Hall of Fame?' And I cracked up."

❖

The Hall of Fame show reunited Green with Paul Zaleski, who had remarried and gotten his life back together. Out of the blue Al had "called the office where I was working and said, 'Let's go to the Hall of Fame induction.'" Green paid for everything, and in the limo to the airport afterward they discussed working together again. Al wanted Paul in the studio and on tour as his soundman. "I told him I'd only go on the road for fifteen hundred dollars a gig." Surprisingly, Green acquiesced, and for a while Zaleski said it was "a blast." But then came a disastrous European tour. Paul's new wife had taken time off from work to join him on the road.

In Belfort, France, Green fired his assistant. "She was a true pro," said Zaleski. "He was treating her like shit for about a week before." Green "just went nuts. He was clean and sober, I know that, so it wasn't drugs that set him off in France." Green made one of the male background singers his new assistant. "He was a pretty boy," noted Paul, who said once this happened "everything changed." Zaleski claimed Al slashed the band's pay from $250 a show to $250 a week. And Paul's pay went from $1,500 to $300. "You can't fight because you don't have another gig set up," said Zaleski. "When you're overseas with an itinerary, with plane tickets that he's got, what are you gonna do?"

Once they'd returned home, Zaleski bailed. "We were supposed to go from Chicago to Canada and I said—right to his face—'Fuck you! I've been fucked by you before, you ain't fuckin' me again.' That was the end of that." Paul hasn't spoken to Al since, yet he just can't get the bug out of his system. All these years later, Zaleski is still dreaming up potential collaborations with Al Green.

❖

Green's personal life grew even murkier. David Gest in his book writes that Al's "Shelby farm burned down in the 1990s and I remember his girl-friend went back to Chicago immediately after." Green lived behind his church while his home was being repaired.

In 1997 came *Anthology,* the first Al Green box set of (mostly) Hi re-cordings, an idiosyncratic four-CD set attractively encased in faux white leather and featuring a booklet with notes by Robert Gordon that finally shone a light on the members of Hi Rhythm (two more boxed sets would follow in England in 2001 and 2003, with notes by Colin Escott).

Green had a recurring television role on the *Ally McBeal* show in 1999—as an apparition Al Green that appeared whenever Ally got weepy. In one episode, she awakens from a bad dream to see a bathed-in-blue, tux-and-bow-tied Al (complete with background singers), standing in her bedroom crooning "How Can You Mend a Broken Heart?" to her, after which Al and Ally slow dance.

Green would also have the misfortune to appear alongside NSYNC relics Lance Bass and Joey Fatone in a mediocre 2001 film entitled *On the Line,* playing himself once again. Over the end credits, Al—outfitted in oversized, floppy cuffs and acting like a daffy pied piper—leads the cast in "Let's Stay Together," complete with a cringe-inducing a guest rap.

In 2000 Green's autobiography was released. A highlight from the press tour was an appearance on an ABC morning show where Green, accompanied only by a piano player, sang snippets of his hits. Hearing his voice unencumbered by indifferent clutter revealed how little his vocal power had diminished over the years. During the interview he once more referenced "You Ought to Be with Me" to illustrate how his consciousness had changed: "I used to sing 'you'"—Al pointed above—"'ought to be with *me*,'" pointing at himself. He said it again, reversing it to indicate that these days, Green knew who was boss.

❖

In 2002 Green went to Philadelphia to record with gospel singer Ann Nesby. "Put It on Paper" was a brooding, five-minute-plus duet that celebrated "the opportunity to be married and be pleasing in God's sight," as Nesby explained to *Jet*. She even included a brief track called "Al Green Interlude" on the *Put It on Paper* album, which was an impromptu blast of Green preaching after being egged on in the studio. "A *good* wife is from the Lord," declares Al. One has to wonder about Green's requirements for a "good" wife. Apparently no one's passed the test thus far. Critic Michael Awkward felt Green had a "stagnant" view of women: "Even after his religious rebirth, he never seems to move far beyond an adolescent view of them either as objectified itch-scratchers or unproblematic sites of maternal comfort."

A low-down, tough piece of music far better than any of his recent gospel or message songs, "Put It on Paper" was a mild R&B hit in spite of Green's indifference. As far as Nesby goes, Al "treated her like a dog," said Willie Bean. "She told me herself, 'Willie Bean, I don't understand—he helped me with the record, just came in and did it, no money, no nuthin'.'" But when Nesby wanted Green to make appearances with her, "he wouldn't even call her up. She sat there waiting." When Al did take her out on the road to do the song, it was less of a duet and more like two solo performances. "Most artists, they're singin' it to each other, like Marvin Gaye and Tammi Terrell," said Johnny Brown. Green "wouldn't sing like that. They would do the song, but he'd be on the middle of the stage, she'd be on one side. If she came over to his side of the stage, he'd go to the other." At one show in Chicago, Ann "had her whole family there. And when he called on her song and she wasn't in the spot that she was supposed to be, he went on to the next song. She made it out thirty seconds later and figured he'd call on the song next." Green never did.

Footage of a live performance has surfaced on YouTube, and it's strange. Green summons Nesby onstage like he's calling cattle: "Where's Ann at? Ann, ya here? Come on." His pallor a bit deathly, Al seems disoriented at times, forgetting the lyrics of the song. "My doctor told me to take it easy . . . stop tryin' to push so hard," he says after the song is done. "Al was high as gas," claimed one YouTube viewer.

Rumors of drugs continued to swirl around Green. Margaret Foxworth finally left around 2004. "The paranoia had started before that. You saw a progression of it—2003 was really bad." According to Foxworth, "drugs and him being paranoid made him a different person. He was *so* paranoid. He had a bodyguard outside the door. Eventually he accused me of stuff, like breaking the windows in his car. I was like, 'Your car is in a storage bin, locked up. I don't have the keys to it.' He would imagine all this stuff. He accused me of having an orgy with all these men—'I was at *your* house. When did this happen? Who are you talking about?' You couldn't talk to him . . . if you're in it, you don't see it. He believed everything he was thinking. I never thought he and I would be at odds. He was someone I talked to every day."

Johnny Brown left as well. Being in Green's band hadn't gotten any less rocky. At one point the band, who, according to Brown, "hadn't had a raise in years, went on strike." Johnny claimed he didn't want to do it but the band "talked me into it." The result was Al fired the band and hired the Bar-Kays. "Al was gonna prove something to you—'Okay, I'll hire somebody else. And pay them twice as much.' We couldn't understand that. He could've given us fifty more dollars a week, but he refused to budge."

Matters between Brown and Green deteriorated further when a band member hijacked the band bus, selling everybody's instruments for crack. "Even though Al acted at first like, 'Well, Johnny, I know you didn't do it,' it created a real strained relationship." Brown had divorced, and he was living in Florida with a new paramour. "Al decided he was no longer gonna pay for my plane tickets or my gas to get to the rehearsals, and he wasn't gonna pay for me to have a hotel room—because Al wanted me to go back to my first wife. By takin' the hotel room from me, he figured that was gonna make me go back home. I made up my mind—'this is it, I can't take this any longer.'" They were about to go out on the road, and as usual Johnny was to be paid part up front and the rest when it was over. Brown picked up the advance check and "got in my car and went home. That was it. Never went back."

❖

Awards started to roll in for Green—a Lifetime Achievement Grammy in 2002, induction into the Songwriters Hall of Fame and the Gospel Music Association's Hall of Fame two years later. Usually delivering dialed-in versions of his old hits, Green was a frequent guest on the late-night talk shows—*Late Night with David Letterman* and *The Tonight Show with Jay Leno*. And he remained as cantankerous as ever. Frank "Poncho" Sampedro, guitar player for Crazy Horse, was band leader Kevin Eubanks's second-in-command on the show, and he says three guests got the audience to their feet like no others—Robin Williams, Little Richard, and Al Green. But dealing with Green proved difficult. One day he called the office to speak about an upcoming appearance. First he corrected Sampedro for not addressing him properly—"it's Reverend Green"—then demanded to speak to Eubanks, who was onstage at the time. By the time Poncho returned with Kevin, Green had hung up.

Despite the continual chaos, Al Green had achieved the status of legend. Now in his fifties, Green had entered that peculiar station in show business where one is offered quizzical opportunities just because. TV shows, movies, duets. But the inevitable hadn't happened yet—a secular music reunion with Willie Mitchell.

PUT YOUR HAT ON THE FLOOR

I would love to get married again. Because I am the
Love & Happiness man.
—AL GREEN

For Willie Mitchell, the battles had all been fought, the races won. Willie was parked at Royal, "sittin' down there with nothin' to do," said his old Hi cohort Ace Cannon. "He'd drink a couple of fifths a day. He was drinkin' himself to death."

Mitchell had kept Royal Studios running. Occasionally he'd record albums for his on-again, off-again Waylo label, or record visiting artists like Buddy Guy, John Mayer, or Keith Richards, all of whom no doubt hoped some of that old Hi magic would rub off. But as Reuben Fairfax Jr. points out, Royal was not for "somebody who was tryin' to make a career. Pops just maintained the space. It was his hangout."

After leaving Al Green, Reuben had done a stint in Albert King's band, and had now branched out into producing (and driving a cab on the side). He'd go to Royal and, using the four-track machine in the back, build rhythm tracks by himself. Pops "had never seen that," said Fairfax. Soon he was hanging out with Mitchell every day. It was a different relationship from the one with Green. "Al, I don't know what we'd talk about unless we were doin' music," said Reuben, who felt so at home at Royal "I might fall asleep in the chair, or any damn thing." No longer was he just the upstart who'd been part of the *Belle* showdown. Playing with Green and King had instilled in him with a musical knowledge Mitchell appreciated. "Pops used to say, 'You're the only person here who knows how to turn the song around, get from one part of the song to the other.' That's why me and Pops were so close: I knew how to play major over minor."

Willie—who no longer drove, due to his alcohol intake—would be dropped off at Royal by a family member around ten or eleven "and stay 'til the wee hours of the morning," said producer/guitarist Mark Bingham. In the front lobby his cronies would gather. "The peanut gallery," Bingham recalled. "Bunch of ol' guys sittin' around telling jokes and lies. If you could tell a good joke, you definitely had a seat in the middle of that. Sometimes Pops would tell the same joke over and over, but everybody would laugh away." By late afternoon the Grey Goose vodka had taken effect. "You could tell when Pops had really got in the juice," said Mark. "He'd come down the hall and it looked like he was walkin' a tightrope."

Willie's grandsons—Lawrence "Boo" Mitchell and Archie Mitchell, sons of Willie's daughters Lorrain "Lo" Mitchell and Yvonne "Von" Mitchell—were becoming active at Royal. Boo, despite his ponytail, is the spitting image of Willie, but it's his bald-headed cousin, two years Boo's senior, who reminds people most of Pops. "You can bullshit with Archie," said Royal regular Gene Mason. "I feel at home with him like I did with Willie." Willie legally adopted both Archie and Boo at an early age. As Archie told Andria Lisle, "Apparently I wanted to be adopted, too, because when Pops asked me to do something one day, I got smart and said, 'Why don't you get your son to do it?'" Next thing five-year-old Archie knew, they were before a judge, and Pops had made it official.

Archie and Boo had a rap outfit called M-Team, and in 1991 Mitchell released their only album, *For Deposit Only,* on his Waylo Records label. The cover showed the pair handcuffed together next to a vault, bags of cash and bills in their hands, being led away by an armed chick in a red leotard. M-Team's video of "Rolling Samurai" got them on *Yo! MTV Raps*; this led not to stardom but to a plethora of local rappers filing into Royal to be produced by Archie. Pops, who was credited as executive producer on *For Deposit Only,* did not care for rap, to put it mildly. "It's too fast," declared Willie, who liked to refer to the rappers scuttling about Royal as "Rooty-Poots," or simply the "Poots." At the end of the night he'd look at Archie and the rappers going at it and call it a day, telling Fairfax, "'I'm gonna leave it to the Poots.' They could be in there all night, he didn't care."

In 1993 Willie Mitchell's Rhythm and Blues Club opened at 326 Beale. Mitchell had little to do with the enterprise and was rarely there. "Willie would be getting drunk, they'd always want to be hurryin' him home," said Gene Mason, a longtime Memphis club owner. Friends considered the nightclub an outlet Willie'd given to his relatives so they'd have something to do and, in Mason's opinion, they "fucked it up." It ran for five years—Green even played there—before closing "following a controversial decision to stage a lingerie show that was in violation of Beale Street's ban on sexually-oriented entertainment." It reopened under new management, then vanished.

In 2001 Pops lost Anna, his wife of fifty-two years. His brother James had died three months before that. James had contributed so much to the Hi arrangements, and he'd taken a lot of shit from his brother in the process. "When James died, I went to the funeral," said Gene Mason. "Willie was cryin' because he had treated James so mean. He cried like a baby. Boo was holdin' him as he walked down the aisle. I told him, 'I love you . . . I loved James.' He said, 'Thank you so much, Gene. I miss my brother.'"

Now in his midseventies, Mitchell's own health was failing. "He wants to have diabetes and also drink vodka," judged Al Green in 2004. "I told him, 'The doctor said that you can't drink the vodka if you're going to take the medicine.' Willie said, 'Forget you *and* the doctor.' He's kind of crazy like that, but you've got to pay for your crazy, too. That's why he's in the hospital."

Friends claim it was after one of these long hospital stays that some family members moved Willie out of circulation for a bit. "They took him to one of the relatives' houses and kept him there against his will," said Mad Lads singer John Gary Williams, who'd gotten close to Mitchell in the later years. It was suggested that this was to protect Pops from himself, not to mention the bottle, but friends claim nobody could actually speak to him to see if he was all right.

Eventually Willie reached out to Williams. "He finally got ahold of a phone and called me—'Man, come get me and take me home.'" Another relative wanting to help called to let John know Willie was there alone, and the coast was clear. "I went, got him, put as much of his clothes and awards in the trunk of my car as I could, and I got my boy outta there, took him home."

People had run up a lot of charges on his credit card while he'd been indisposed. According to Williams, authorities told Mitchell in order to get the funds back "they would have to prosecute everybody." Pops talked it over with John. "I told him, 'Man, you ain't never had no bad name with your family, no bad karma. If you do this, it's gonna be publicized and ridiculed and everything else.' He decided not to do it." The situation caused Willie a lot of pain. "It was deep, man. It was really deep . . . I think it affected him up until the day he died."

According to Reuben Fairfax Jr., there were times Pops "went to the bank and couldn't get any of his money out. He did some things legally to straighten out what was goin' on. It was just a crazy time. See, every time he got sick, they'd have a family meeting and make preparations. They thought he was gonna die. He *didn't* die." Reuben laughed. "Pops was like a cat. He had nine lives."

❖

One person kept calling Willie while he was in the hospital. Al Green. "When I got out, he came into the studio, sat in that chair there, and said he wanted to make a record," said Mitchell, who laid down the law. "I told him, 'Al, if you want to make another gospel album, you can get the fuck out of here right now.'"

In January 2003 they began work on an album—without a label, funding it themselves to the tune of sixty grand. Mitchell insisted they write songs together at the piano like the old days. That spring they recorded. Mitchell dusted off old mic number nine. From the old crew, he brought back Teenie and Leroy Hodges*; Jack Hale and Andrew Love on horns; Rhodes, Chalmers, Rhodes on backing vocals; and then added other select Memphis players: Skip Pitts, Steve Potts, and Lester Snell on piano and arrangements. "There was a lot of history there, but there was some apprehension," said musician Scott Bomar, an assistant engineer on the project. "Al hadn't been in there for years. People were a little worried. After a couple of days, stuff was sounding so good. After one of the playbacks, Al

---

* The reason Charles did not participate was money. "Mitchell called me, I told him I'd do it," said Hodges, who backed out when he was told his pay would be $2,500. "I said, 'You know I love you, Willie, but I can't do it for no twenty-five. Give me fifty thousand dollars, I'll probably do it.'" Mitchell declined. When they were preparing Green's second Blue Note album, Al personally called and asked Charles to play. Charles told him the same figure: fifty grand. When Green balked, Charles told him, "'I won't do it for any less.' End of the conversation." Why Howard Grimes didn't play on the Blue Note albums, I do not know. Supposedly Teenie wrote a great song for *I Can't Stop*, but it was left off in favor of all Green-Mitchell originals.

was just running around the control room, jumping up and down, yelling, going crazy 'cause he was so excited about the track. Willie said, 'Al Green, shut the fuck up and sit down!' Al didn't say another word."

By this time Al and Willie were like an old married couple. "Pops and Al would argue all the time, like a man and his woman would argue," said John Gary Williams. "Pops knew how to push Al's buttons—'Man, that sounds like shit, Al. Come back tomorrow 'cause you just don't got it today.' Typical Pops. He knew if he aggravated Al, he'd do his best." Said Willie at the time, "Ain't no reverend when he's in my studio. I drive him like a golf ball." But Al had his own way of showing Willie that the dynamic had changed. "Al was always really late," said Bomar. "The musicians were getting paid by the hour, on the clock. That was frustrating to Willie . . . he had to pay musicians for being there two or three hours."

After hearing the results, Blue Note signed Green for the first of three albums he'd do for the label, *I Can't Stop*. Everybody loves a reunion story, and Green and Mitchell did a lot of press. Reporters flocked to Memphis to hear the album. Richard L. Eldredge caught the Royal ambience best: "Walls of heavy, dingy, sound-absorbing orange felt hang from the high ceiling. Fifty-year-old cigarette burns dot the faded carpeting . . . four boxed reels containing the master tapes of the tracks on *I Can't Stop* sit on the floor next to rows of empty Grey Goose vodka bottles."

Who wasn't excited to see these two back together? Reunions like these rarely amount to anything other than enforced nostalgia, however, and despite rave reviews, *I Can't Stop,* released November 18, 2003, is no exception. The songs are mediocre, Al seems only intermittently engaged, and the arrangements are cluttered and generic, with some uncharacteristically busy playing throughout. Only "Rainin' in My Heart" comes close to the bull's-eye, and even that arrangement sounds a bit stiff—search out the acoustic performance Green did of the song for VH1 instead (accompanied only by a second guitarist, Al did a stunning "Simply Beautiful" as well).

Everything's OK, the second Green-Mitchell Blue Note album, arrived March 14, 2005, and is a marked improvement, with some occasionally impassioned singing from Al. One song Green wrote with the band, "I Can Make Music," could even pass for an outtake from *Al Green Is Love.* But outside of passing moments, it fails to maintain any sort of intensity. The songs aren't there; neither are magic and emotion. According to Reuben Fairfax Jr., Green would later admit to Willie that he hadn't given his all.

"They weren't hungry anymore, they were just on autopilot," said Fairfax. It didn't really matter. Al Green and Willie Mitchell had already climbed all the mountains. There was no way to top that past. "Pops used to say if you get one hit record in a lifetime, that's pretty good," said Fairfax. "To have two or three, even better. But all of the records they had? That's unbelievable."

❖

Willie Mitchell was set to produce the third Blue Note album, but things went in an entirely different direction due to a bunch of interlopers known as the Roots. One of the most damning reviews of *I Can't Stop* had come from their drummer, Ahmir "Questlove" Thompson, who'd been anxious to hear it after reading a rave in *Rolling Stone*. Questlove, a great admirer of Willie's work, had a scathing (but accurate) reaction to the comeback album once he'd heard it: "This sounds like the House of Blues house band."

Questlove, who had watched producer Rick Rubin pump oxygen into Johnny Cash's career and Jack White do the same with Loretta Lynn, thought, "Why can't that happen on the black side of music?" Then Blue Note's A&R vice president, Eli Wolf, called to ask if the Roots would be interested in working with Green. They leapt at it, even though attempts at working with Stevie Wonder and Earth, Wind and Fire had left them a bit leery of resuscitating superstars by the time it came to Al Green. "Some artists of his stature have done things on the comeback trail trying to be too contemporary," Questlove told *Jet*. "I don't want to hear him on the record rapping." Fearing the record company would "oversaturate" the album with guest-star bloat, he told them to "cap it at three.'" John Legend, Anthony Hamilton, and Corinne Bailey Rae filled these slots, and for the most part they'd be used in a subdued fashion in support of Al and the song.

Over twenty-five years Green's junior, Questlove is six foot four with a wild Afro and beard straight off the *Let's Stay Together* cover, a self-described "black nerd" and "music snob" who possesses a lethal knowledge of music in general and a deep understanding of Al Green's work in particular. "Most black singers go zero to 100, rushing to the big payoff. But Al Green is like a soufflé that takes 45 minutes to rise," Thompson told *Rolling Stone*. Questlove was cognizant of the fact that when it came to the Hi sound, "less is more." He'd also issue this audacious throwdown: "I wanted to make the true follow-up to *Belle*, which is considered the last quote-unquote *real* Al Green record."

Things got off to a rough start. Roots keyboard player and producer James Poysner and executive producer Rich Nichols went to meet with Green at his hotel after a gig in Philadelphia. Due to "a mix-up in communication," Al was hot. As Nichols told Matt Rogers, "We got to really see first-hand the true Al Green . . . in five minutes! And we saw that Al Green is in charge and is really, really demanding." *Lay It Down* would take three years to complete—by far the longest time ever taken on any Al Green creation.

In fall of 2005 work began with three loose jam sessions at Electric Lady Studios in New York City. Outside of the wacky *Love Is Reality* sessions, Green had done nearly all his recording the way Mitchell had produced sessions: writing the songs, the band recording the tracks, then Green overdubbing his vocal. Since *Voodoo,* the D'Angelo album they'd cut in 2000, the Roots had created from scratch, live in the studio, and they insisted on doing things the same way with Al (and save one number written solely by Green, all the song credits would be split, not unlike on *Belle*, with the band).

It turned out that Al took to the Roots' recording style immediately— as in the moment he walked in the door. Questlove didn't even meet Al until after they'd recorded the first—and best—song on the album, "Lay It Down." The band had gotten to the studio two hours early to set up and Al caught them off guard with his early arrival. "We're just playing, and next thing I know, I hear: 'Don't mind me, I'm going to sing with y'all,'" said Questlove. "He started singing, and he damn near free-styled about 70 percent of the title cut." They were onto something "really spontaneous" with Al that "wasn't overthought," said James Poysner. "Whatever came out, came out." Green, who claimed he wrote eight songs that first night, thrived in this atmosphere. "He wanted to do every song like that," said Questlove. "He was a little addicted to the real-time thing." Green even claimed that "I'm Wild About You," an ode to the feral side of procreation inspired by a nature program, had been censored by his young band, who "didn't let me say all the things I wanted to say! They wanted to keep it civilized."

Before Green ventured into the deep, dark kingdom of the Roots, Willie Mitchell had cautioned him: "Al, be sure you sing you. They gonna try and play it hip-hop . . . just be you." But once they'd unleashed Green in the studio, Questlove detected a bit of natural hip-hop in Al's approach. "Truth be told, Al Green could give most freestyle rappers a run for their money," he confessed to Matt Rogers. By the second day Questlove was "thinking, 'Man, Al Green and Ghostface could do a duet together.'" Wu-Tang Clan was a constant reference in Questlove's head because he thought RZA's use of Hi samples had made him "the one figure that has made the most sense out of Willie Mitchell's catalog more than anybody else." He fought hard to retain the instrumental intro to "What More Do You Want from Me?" on *Lay It Down* because "I heard Raekwon and Ghostface all over it." Yet Questlove tread carefully. "I didn't want to reveal to Al what my agenda was . . . a name like Ghostface Killah could possibly scare Al to death."

The Roots joined the club of those dazed and confused by Third-Person Al. Green would mumble to himself on the mic as he wrote lyrics, and at first it was hard to ascertain if he was talking to them or not. As Questlove recalled, "He'll sit there and argue with himself about pronouns—'*Now, if I say "she" here that will limit the appeal of the song.* But if I say "you," then men and women can relate. *But then again, Al, you're a man. So I don't know if a man would take it that way.* So let's make it "she." *Yeah, yeah, make it "she."'* I'm talking about 20 minutes of this . . . His whole thought process is just . . . wow."

None of it was easy. There was one song Questlove felt "Al was over-singing: we wanted him to go subtle, and he was going rough and intense." They sent Rich in to deliver the news. "It didn't go well," wrote Questlove in *Mo' Meta Blues.* "I'm not going to do it any other way, no matter how many times you ask," pouted Green. The Roots responded by packing up their instruments and heading for the door. "Al didn't like that," writes Questlove. "He wanted us to beg him to stay."

Green's fury only increased. "If you motherfuckers put your computers away, and concentrate on your job, and stop worrying about my job, then you might see how things fit," he snarled. "The more we tried to placate him, the madder he got. He was mad at us, mad at the computers, mad at technology and the passage of time and the nerve of young producers who dared ask him to do something that he, Al Green, didn't feel in his bones." But once the smoke cleared, Green did exactly what they wanted. "Replay that ad infinitum, and that will give you some sense of how *Lay It Down* got done," Questlove reported.

In the press, Green waved off the hip-hop factor—he'd been confident all along that "once you start wrapping any song around Al, it's gonna sound just like 1974." That had not been occurring in recent years, of course, and in this case I think it has more to do with the care and respect the Roots paid to creating the appropriate accompaniment for Green. They played live in the same room with Al, insuring plenty of leakage on the tracks, which only adds the kind of authentic grit lacking from the pristine, squeaky-clean recordings of the digital age. They enlisted Philadelphia legend Larry Gold, who'd not only played cello for MSFB but had done strings for Lana Del Rey, to do string arrangements; the Dap-Kings supplied horns. The latter had been a big part of Mark Ronson's retro-yet-modern production for Amy Winehouse's *Back to Black,* an album that was a major signpost for Questlove.

The Roots remained fanatically faithful to a Hi-era sound without turning it into a boring museum piece or sacrificing anything current. *EQ* magazine wrote an entire article on the machinations of the production. Questlove's overcompressed drum sound fit in with any current hip-hop sample, yet in his playing he reached back for "an understated, Charlie Watts-ish, nonchalant feel." Some of the Roots had been raised playing in church and thus knew the vibe they were after, but when it came to their highly schooled bass player, Mark Kelley,* Questlove felt moved to give this instruction: "You're a twenty-nine-year-old cat from Memphis named Purvis . . . you only have three strings on your bass . . . you can't play that good, but you can hold a melody." Keep it simple, stupid. And that's what's best of all about *Lay It Down*'s instrumentation, they keep the playing simple and stay the hell out of Green's way.

The end result is exactly what Questlove promised: Al Green's best since *Belle.* It's a quiet album that is (unlike so many of Green's post-Hi releases) tastefully done, as warm as a woodstove. I can remember the exact moment I popped in the CD and heard the opening of "Lay It Down." An actual chill ran down my spine. This was the Al Green I'd thought would never return. The feeling, the mystery, the soul—it's all right there. That line "put your hat on the floor" elicits a laugh every time (as Green laughs himself a little later at another great line in the song). It's a throwaway, yet conjures up so much in that eccentric Al way. When he performed the song on *Late Night with David Letterman,* he forgot the line, yet added

---

* Kelley is not credited on the album. Adam Blackstone, Gabriel Roth, and Owen Biddle are listed as the bass players.

a new stage move—pulling the hankie out of his suit pocket and, with a dramatic flourish, throwing it to the floor.

While nothing else on the album meets that high standard, none of the other songs are so sketchy or generic as to be embarrassing, and some of them, like "Just for Me" and "You've Got the Love I Need," push Al's voice in interesting new directions. The Roots also adhere to another Hi technique—to keep things rhythmically intricate when Green falls back into his bag of lyric "love" clichés, which is fairly often. Released May 27, 2008, the album went to number nine on the *Billboard* album charts, Green's first Top 10 album since 1973. At the same time Al Green had left his mark on Questlove. "I'm under the impression that all musical geniuses are crazy. And Al is no exception to the rule. He's channeling something that's not normal. . . . He's from another planet."

But the Roots had delivered another win. "I promised I would get him his first R&B Grammy," said Questlove. "I lied. He got two." *Lay It Down* was a triumph, and if Green never records again, he goes out as a champ. As Al himself put it, "We cut some baaaaad shit. Pardon the Reverend!"

❖

On February 8, 2009, Green not only received his two Grammys for *Lay It Down,* he appeared on the awards show performing "Let's Stay Together" with Justin Timberlake as a last-minute substitution for no-show couple Rihanna and Chris Brown, who had suddenly cancelled (Brown would subsequently be arrested for assaulting her). Timberlake, who had grown up down the street from Green's estate, gushed to *Rolling Stone* that "hearing Al as a kid made me want to become a singer and showed me that it was OK to have a softer, more falsetto voice." When the Grammy staff reached out to Green just hours before the broadcast, he was in the shower. "I just threw my suit in a bag and went over." At the rehearsal Timberlake saw "this mink coat coming down from the rafters, almost like the angels." Green said, "I'm sorry I'm late . . . I was in the tub." That night, joined by Boyz II Men and Keith Urban, they got a standing ovation. It was your typically overblown TV nonevent, although it must be noted that Al seemed far more comfortable onstage with superstar Timberlake than he had been with any of his female duet partners.

Although Al Green will surely go down in history as one of the greatest live performers ever to have graced a stage, his recent appearances are not the ones to seek out. Backed by an assortment of Memphis veterans plus a flashy white guitarist, Green is frequently joined by three daughters from his first marriage—Rubi, Alva, and Kora—who sing backup (all are active online and appear to be pursuing careers in gospel).* Inexplicably, Green also brings along a pair of male dancers to strut their stuff during the show. Al has gained considerable weight in recent years, and to be fair, he's a much older individual. Along with the ever-present shades, he's sometimes taken to wearing white gloves onstage (sometimes only one, perhaps in tribute to Michael). Al seems content to race through the hits and let the audience do much of the singing. Angry concert attendees have posted a torrential amount of negative reviews online, and they are excoriating:

"A Concert Without Songs: Al Green tried to avoid singing as much as he could. Talking, band solos, making the audience sing—he used every trick. 'Sing it, sing it' screamed a lady in a seat behind me. Well, he didn't . . . it was more of a campfire singalong."

"Why am I giving Al one star? He didn't sing! He avoided singing like the plague."

"Al sucked. His voice is still fantastic, but he wouldn't sing. He'd do a line or two from each song, then make the audience sing the rest. If I wanted to sing along, I would have stayed in my shower and saved some money. We all felt totally ripped off."

"Al Green did have us sing-a-long . . . something was definitely wrong with him, he looked incoherent and shaken."

"If I were to estimate the total time Al sang, it would probably be about fifteen minutes. Maybe twenty."

Green's old bandleader Johnny Brown has seen some of the shows in recent years and feels that Al's musicians "play too fast. They zip through. Everything was, 'Hurry up and get to the next song.'" As Brown hung around backstage, he detected a different environment from the old days. He feels Al's current band doesn't "have the same interest in playin' for Al as we did. We taped as many shows as possible. When the bus was on

---

*The addition of his daughters would provoke from Green a rare, if off-handed, compliment for ex-wife Shirley. "I sing this way," their mother "sings that way, and the kids sing both ways. That's a wonderful thing." In 2014 Green would tell Chris Roberts of the *Washington Post* his relationship with Shirley was no longer "distant and hateful," and that she'd even visited his church and sang a number. Shirley returned again to perform at the fortieth anniversary of Full Gospel Tabernacle in December 2016.

"We love each other very much," Al said just days before, going on to praise Shirley for trying to calm him down back in his wilder days. "She's an evangelist . . . she was a big help to me, too, in reference to, 'Sit down . . . and pray about it. Sit down and think about it. Decide what you wanna do before you jump the track and start runnin' all over the place.'"

the way to the hotel we'd be listenin'—'We shoulda done this, we shoulda done that.' We took pride in wantin' to be the best band out there. It seemed like it was just a job to them. They weren't really into Al Green music."

Reuben Fairfax Jr. feels that young players of today's Memphis don't have the background the old cats had. Instead of relying on computers, samples, and effects, "they actually had to play *music*." Reuben said the times were already changing when he joined the Enterprise Orchestra. He relied on big Marshall amps; the old Memphis musicians "could play without all that. They had a foundation in all kinds of music, all styles— blues, cha-cha, ballads." The situation has only deteriorated further in the digital age. "I get some young guys together today, they just gonna play loud. It's not gonna have that sweetness. Music used to be finesse. Now music is power."

❖

Those who had made the long journey with Al Green were starting to die. On November 22, 2006, his mother, Cora Lee Green, passed away. She was eighty-seven. At the memorial at Full Gospel Tabernacle, Al's daughter Rubi stood up and said "Belle" was Cora's favorite song. "I was just through after that," said Reuben, who felt that Green's relatives had treated him like family when he'd joined the band. "Mama Green[e] was my mama too." Green, who'd recently been ordained as a bishop,* "preached his mama's funeral," said Fairfax. "Al sang a song in complete falsetto. He was completely mourning his mother's death. He made it all the way to the cemetery—when it got to 'dust to dust, ashes to ashes,' he just couldn't go any further. Bishop Reed took it from there."

Before the service, Green and Fairfax shared a rare moment of reflection. "We just sat and talked . . . I remember Al looked at the wall the whole time we were sittin' beside each other. He didn't look at me." According to Reuben, Green had "hurt his back, and they'd given him steroids—that's why he gained all that weight." Fairfax tried to talk to him about the evils of junk food and the virtues of green tea, but Al was suspicious, which Fairfax chalked up to the Green family's "slight belief in voodoo." Al told him green tea "didn't fit with his lifestyle."

---

* Fairfax recalled this happening around the time of the 2006 *Belle* expanded edition. When Reuben was playing the finished version for Al in his car, Green "was just actin' so silly, I didn't know what was wrong with him." Afterward Fairfax found out he'd been made a bishop.

When it came time for the sermon, however, Green "preached on everything I talked to him about—'McDonald's, Kentucky Fried Chicken, Taco Bell come in our neighborhood and what do we get out of the deal? We get high blood pressure, diabetes, strokes!' Our whole conversation, he preached it at his mama's funeral. I said, 'Well, I'll be damned.' Afterwards he thanked me for comin'."

Green's old bandleader and guitar player Larry Lee died October 30, 2007. Lee had been in the hospital, and Al "never took time to see him. Not one day," said his wife, Jackie. "The rest of the musicians came. My kids were hysterical about it." Green did attend the funeral, and she claims that a week after that, he assured her that he'd make sure she got the royalties on the two songs of Larry's that he'd recorded. She received just one payment shortly thereafter. "I haven't seen anything since then. I write, call his church . . . I'm in the process of suing him."

Green officiated over another Full Gospel Tabernacle memorial service following his brother Walter's death on May 20, 2008. And Al's beloved sister Maxine Eve Green went missing in Grand Rapids, Michigan, in September 2013. Maxine, a diagnosed schizophrenic who battled drug and alcohol addiction, was sixty-one when she disappeared from her assisted living home. Green refused to comment on the matter to the press. "I can't answer why Al Green has not ever reached out," said Maxine's daughter Lasha. "Let the public know that your sister is missing." She also claimed Green had "promised" to send money to contribute to a reward fund. "He never sent anything," said Lasha. Johnny Brown felt the criticism Al got in the press was undeserved when it came to Maxine. "Al did help her a whole lot . . . it just got to a point you couldn't do nothin' for Maxine. I heard she had called and asked for help for about the millionth time and this time Al didn't help her and she disappeared." (In October 2015 Al's lookalike younger brother, Lonel, also went missing in Memphis. He was later found safe at a local shelter, and apparently had just become disoriented, perhaps due to a spider bite.)

❖

Willie Mitchell's health continued to deteriorate. In 2007 he released *Anytime Anyplace Anywhere,* an album on his Waylo label, by Mashaa, aka Erma Shaw, his girlfriend at the time and a very unpopular figure with the Mitchell clan. "Some people weren't too happy about the relationship," said John Gary Williams. "But it made Willie happy." When they were cutting a session on Gene "Poo Poo Man" Anderson at Royal, Erma came in and, according to Gene Mason, you could hear a pin drop. "She said, 'How come all you motherfuckers get quiet when I come in here?'" Shaw was known as a feisty, salty character, and according to Thomas Bingham, "that kind of intrigued Willie, because he couldn't control" Shaw. "She'd jump through there and raise hell and he'd just look at her—'Okay, baby, okay, baby.'" Mitchell produced the album and gave her the full superstar treatment, using many of the top-flight players from the recent Green sessions and cowriting five songs with her, some of which were appealingly low-down. He even played the keyboard and xylophone. Mashaa has a pleasant if limited voice, a bit like Deniece Williams with dentures. The cover shows her in a blazing red outfit that channels Native America by way of Cher. On the whole, the album sounds like 1979 on a bad day. It went nowhere.

In 2008 Mitchell received a Grammy Trustees Award (the year before, the stretch of South Lauderdale that Royal resides on had been rechristened Willie Mitchell Boulevard). He also broke his ankle, and a fire forced him out of his home. "A string of bad luck" is how Willie put it to Hi aficionado Red Kelly. In June of 2009 Reuben Fairfax Jr. paid a visit to Royal. "Pops was lying on the couch." Mitchell had fallen and "thought he just bruised himself." In the wake of the house fire, "he was stayin' at the studio, wouldn't go to a hotel." At the time, the Fat Possum label was reissuing the Hi catalog and wanted another Green/Mitchell album. John Cleaves, a longtime associate of both Green and Mitchell, brought Al by for a visit. Willie would tell Reuben afterward it was the first time he'd seen Al in two years.

The guys shot the shit for a while. "I remember Al was probably about two hundred sixty pounds and Pops asked him, "Al, how much you weigh?' Al said, 'Ohhhh, two eighteen . . . two ten . . . one ninety-five . . . one eighty-five.' And I'm lookin at Al, his arms are bigger than my legs. Al was talkin' about how he was runnin' ten miles. I got ready to say somethin', but Pops gave me the evil eye and put his finger up to his lips."

Willie wanted to play something for Al. "Pops had a little CD player in the back office," said Reuben. He put on "Something," that mournful 1976 ballad Green had cowritten with Teenie, who'd accompanied on sitar. For a few minutes the air was full of magic and emotion, the greatness of their past. "He had put that song on to go back and reflect," said Fairfax. "We sat there and listened to that with Pops layin' on the couch. Al's like, 'Wow.'"

Al and Willie agreed to undertake a new album that fall. "That's what Willie was really holdin' on for," said Reuben. "He was gonna get some rest and we were gonna do one more Al Green album." It was not to be.

Soon Willie was back in the hospital. The fall he had taken was worse than anyone thought. "He had osteoporosis," said Reuben. "He didn't know his pelvis was broken." His condition only grew worse over the next few months. "It seemed like after they amputated one of his legs, he gave up hope," said John Gary Williams. Thomas Bingham visited him in the hospital. "They weren't letting everybody see him, just a very few people. You had to have a special password." Bluesman Preston Shannon had just left, and when Thomas walked into the room, Willie was asleep. "He just kinda looked bad, kinda weak," said Bingham haltingly. "Pops always kept that hair. He had not only been dyin' his hair, but maybe his eyebrows. It was all gray."

Mitchell woke up. Thomas asked him how he was. "I'm here, boy . . . I'm here. I'm getting tired." Then Willie looked at him "dead in the eye and said, 'Have you seen Bingham?' I smiled. 'Ah, you mean Roubaix.'" That was Reuben Fairfax's nickname. "Yeah, yeah, yeah," muttered a slightly confused Mitchell.

A few days later, Fairfax, driving his cab, got a call from a distraught Erma Shaw. Willie Mitchell had died at 7:25 a.m. at Methodist University Hospital. "When he died I was more shocked than anybody. I just never thought he was gonna die. He told me, 'Roubaix, I'm gonna bury all y'all.' I just held him to it." Fairfax was working at B.B. King's Blues Club on Beale Street that night. "Halfway through the set I called the engineer. I said, 'Man, my dad died. This is it for me. I'm not doing this anymore.' Pops told me when you make a decision, you just make it right there. When he died, I changed everything—'I'm gonna keep my cab, I'm gonna keep workin' in the studio, and that's it.' Any type of authority, I'm through with that. Pops just treated me so well. I never been treated that well in life."

On January 13 there was a three-hour memorial celebration at Hope Presbyterian Church. Hi Rhythm, Don Bryant, J. Blackfoot, Preston Shannon, Willie Clayton, Solomon Burke, and Otis Clay performed (Al Green was en route to an Australian tour when Willie passed). Politicians offered tributes; letters were read from John Mayer and Robert Cray. A tearful Al Bell spoke of the desperate days following the collapse of Stax.

"Willie Mitchell came looking for me." Willie had "put food on the table for my family and a roof over our heads."

John Gary Williams, who had been one of the pallbearers at Mitchell's funeral, did not attend the tribute—out of deference to Willie. "I knew Pops didn't like fanfare, and I knew how he felt about all the fake people that would be there. I probably would've gotten pissed, so I decided I wouldn't go." Those who loved Mitchell grappled to find the words to discuss his passing, but invariably a silence took over. He had been such an elemental force for so many years, not only in Memphis music but in their personal lives. "It wasn't 'was he happy or a good guy'; Pops was always positive," said Fairfax. "He never spoke in the negative."

As far as Hi Records went, Willie Mitchell was Hi. His death ended an era of Memphis music and left a massive void. "I would compare it to the same hole that was left when Stax closed," said Williams. "He was a genius. And a genuine, beautiful person. The best friend you could ever have."

❖

On June 22, 2014, Memphis music was dealt another blow. Mabon "Teenie" Hodges died in a Dallas hospital due to complications of emphysema after an improbable performance backing Snoop Dogg. Teenie was a musician 'til the end, and didn't let the emphysema he'd struggled with for years slow him down. When I interviewed him in 2013, Teenie was skinny as a rail and carting an oxygen tank nearly as big as he was, but full of plans for the future. Gene Mason remembered a recent night at B.B. King's club when Teenie was on fire to "kill some motherfucker." Gene asked, "Who's gonna carry your oxygen as you run down the street?" The comment elicited a grin from Teenie.

In recent years he'd played on an acclaimed 2006 Cat Power album, *The Greatest,* and lived to see a homemade, heartfelt short documentary by Susanna Vapnek in 2012, *Mabon "Teenie" Hodges: A Portrait of a Memphis Soul Original.* In one telling and highly amusing scene, Teenie ventures over to see Al Green at Full Gospel Tabernacle for the benefit of the camera. Green, just coming off the pulpit after a service, hugs Hodges and tells him he'll be right back after he changes. But even though he's just walked through the door, Teenie's already had enough of Al. As soon as Green is out of earshot he tells the camera, "We can go now." End of visit.

As with Willie, everybody was crazy about Mabon Hodges. "The thing I loved about Teenie was he was so encouraging to other musicians, whether they were great or not. The quality of his attention made them feel like they *were* great," said Memphis music and film veteran Joe Mulherin. "He made a big difference in a lot of people's lives."

Teenie had given heart and soul to the Hi sound, and to Al's music in particular. Now he was gone too.

❖

Royal Studios has kept going since Willie's death, but it is not easy to maintain a vision when the auteur is gone. In 2004 Willie Mitchell had established a trust, and in 2005 he formed Willie Mitchell, LLC. Upon his death he wanted all proceeds to be split equally between Boo, Archie, and a granddaughter, Oona. For reasons unknown Mitchell's two daughters, Yvonne and Lorrain, were specifically excluded in his will. He put Boo in charge of all financial decisions.

The cousins continued to work together at Royal after Willie's death. "Archie does all the rap, Boo does the R&B," said Gene Mason. Boz Scaggs, Paul Rodgers, and Canadian singer-songwriter Frazey Ford have all cut there in recent years. Boo proved to be quite the hustler, arranging for a historical marker to be put in front of Royal, helping produce the Memphis music documentary *Take Me to the River*, and undertaking an as-yet-unfinished one on his father. And in 2014 Royal was part of an international hit—Mark Ronson's single with Bruno Mars, "Uptown Funk." The song was recorded in six cities around the world, one of the locations being Memphis and Royal Studios. Boo Mitchell was one of eleven engineers credited, and all won a Grammy.

Without Willie steering the ship, though, problems developed at Royal. "It's a little bit tense over there," Mason told me in 2013. "They don't get along too good, Boo and Archie. How it started, Archie was goin' with this titty dancer. Apparently this did not sit well with the rest of the Mitchells, who felt that was a bad image for the company." Boo also complained that Archie drank and smoked with reckless abandon in the studio, endangering, according to court documents, "delicate vintage equipment, including the irreplaceable microphone on which Al Green sang his hits." Oona sided with Boo. Apparently Willie had foreseen Archie's troubles. Said Gene Mason, "I was there when Willie told Archie, 'When I die, it's gonna be tough on you.'"

The matter was soon tangled up in probate court. In June 2013 Archie was served with legal papers "to cease and desist holding himself as an agent [of Royal] and damaging Royal property." Archie then petitioned the court to have Boo removed from his role as financial executor. He told the court that "he had been locked out of the studio, unable to work" and "that Lawrence [aka Boo] has ruined his reputation in the industry." Archie "claimed that Lawrence did not like his clients and that was the real problem." Boo claimed that when Willie was alive, he had banished Archie from the studio due to his bad habits and that Archie had squandered his adopted father's money.

The court issued an order that Archie be allowed back into Royal as long as no drink or drugs were involved.* In January, Boo and studio employee Chris Jackson filed affidavits that they'd seen Archie imbibe in the studio the very next month. "I personally witnessed Archie Mitchell drinking alcohol in the studio," declared Boo's statement. The family was clearly at each other's throats. Royalties, property, the studio—everything Willie had left his children was in dispute, down to a Hummer Archie claims he put five grand on out of proceeds from Green's *I Can't Stop* album, but that he said had been put in Willie's name due to "obtaining financing on the vehicle and to obtain a tax deduction for a car owned for business purposes." (Archie pointed out Willie had not only bought Boo a Ford Expedition and Oona a Mercedes, he'd bought them both homes in nearby Cordova.)

In a January 2015 ruling, the court found that Boo "breached his fiduciary duties to the beneficiaries of the trust," citing ten examples, which included "failed to file timely tax returns," "commingled the LLC funds with his own personal funds," "paid members of the family, including Archie, when they did not work," and "made payments of some of his personal expenses and some of Archie's and Oona's from the LLC or accounts in the name of the trust." The court was equally critical of Archie, finding that "some of his statements are not truthful" when it came to alcohol and drug issues, noting that even his mother, Yvonne, had testified against him in this regard. But no one was left off the hook, even the daughters excluded from the will. "This court is concerned that the management of the real

---

* Of course, had this rule had been in effect for Willie Mitchell, he would've been locked out of Royal in 1962. At least one musician felt that Archie Mitchell was being treated unfairly in this situation. "Archie was the one that actually did the work in the studio," said Reuben Fairfax Jr.

estate has been delegated to Lorraine [*sic*] and Yvonne Mitchell . . . real estate taxes were not paid for several years." Overall, the court felt "that neither Lawrence nor any of the trustees were concerned about making sure the Trust terms were honored."

As of late 2016 the matter appears to be moving toward an out-of-court settlement (although rumor has it one party has yet to sign the agreement). Hopefully Royal can continue on as it has for the past sixty years. As even the probate court pointed out, it is "clear throughout all the documents that Willie Mitchell did not want his children to fight." In July 2016 Boo and Oona Mitchell announced they were starting Royal Records, an independent label with an emphasis in hip-hop. Given how Pops felt about the genre, Rooty-Poot Records might've been a better moniker.

❖

Al Green has laid low in recent years. He's threatened to put out a jazz album and another gospel album, but nothing's materialized. Al seems content to preach every Sunday at Full Gospel Tabernacle. There was said to be a longtime girlfriend from Cleveland who, according to Margaret Foxworth, "left her husband" for Al, but lately he's told his congregation he lives alone. When asked about relationships during a recent interview, his voice grew sharp. "I'm not tryin' to figure out anything about *a woman*. A woman? That's pretty hard to figure out . . . make sure you're in line with the man upstairs, then you'll be happy. See, I'm not tryin' to go to the moon. I've already been—twice." His relationship with God is more important than any of that, or any more touring. "I did this for thirty-five years. You burned me out, baby." As far as ambitions go, looking back is good enough these days. "I done did alotta stuff . . . I'm not hankering for anything. Not really."

His only recent appearance in the news was in a November 2014 news article entitled "Violent Bull Escapes Al Green's Property, Infuriating Residents." It was the second time his cattle were loose, and an unidentified neighbor declared it "terrifying . . . I have small children." There was no comment from Al.

These days Green seems benign, if slightly daffy—the crazy-old-coot uncle who can be counted on to say or do something bizarre at family get-togethers. One recent Memphis article states the best place for a Green sighting is the local Krispy Kreme. Gene Mason was at a Burger King when he spotted Al ahead of him in line. "He didn't know I was behind him. He said, 'I'll take a Double Whopper.'" When asked if he wanted pickles and mustard on it, Green "started singin', 'I'm so *tired* of pickles . . . ' That's when they recognized who he was. It was funny as hell."

❖

On January 20, 2012, Al Green got a boost from an unexpected fan—Barack Obama, who was attending a fundraiser at the Apollo Theater when he broke into an impromptu bit of "Let's Stay Together." The crowd went wild, and according to press reports, Green's digital sales jumped 490 percent. Obama would also make public a Spotify playlist that included Al's rendition of "How Can You Mend a Broken Heart?"

Although Al made an occasional appearance for Jesse Jackson or Al Gore, Johnny Brown maintains he "didn't want to do nothing political, didn't want to be involved in it at all. He'd say black people need to vote in church." Paul Zaleski considers Green a conservative, although the one president Al's been enthusiastic about in the press has been Bill Clinton, whom he felt was "an excellent president . . . Mr. Clinton has the kind of charisma that makes the stock market go up."

Green claimed to be unable to attend Obama's January 2013 inaugural ball due to "scheduling conflicts," so Jennifer Hudson warbled "Let's Stay Together" instead. But the president finally nabbed him in December 2014, when Green received the Kennedy Center Honors award alongside fellow nominees Tom Hanks, Lily Tomlin, Sting, and ballerina Patricia McBride. The televised ceremony held no surprises. Whoopi Goldberg introduced Green's segment with some ersatz down-home patter, although she managed one truth, which was about to be proven once more: "No one can cover Al Green."

Then came Usher, Jennifer Hudson, Sam Moore, and Earth, Wind and Fire, trotted out to perform Al's songs. Hudson's overwrought massacre of "Simply Beautiful" and Moore stumbling over the lyrics of "Take Me to the River" (the latter complete with choir) were the most felonious, and one had to endure the unsightly spectacle of gold-plated celebrities and politicians twitching in their seats and mouthing along. It was an emphatic—if not terribly believable—display, and it added up to a thimbleful of soul.

Gazing down from on high in the balcony was Albert Leorns Green, stuffed into a tux and sporting his garish medal. There was a modest smile fixed on that now-round face, a face whose mouth can exhibit a pouchy disapproval not dissimilar to latter-day Jerry Lewis. And a dim twinkle in his eye. Al appeared to be enjoying the pomp and circumstance on his behalf, but in the back of his mind he had to be saying to himself, "Once there was a time I ruled any stage. And guess what? I can *still* cut your asses. I don't need no fancy dancers and bright lights. Or even a band. Just my God-given voice."

What was going on in Al Green's head? His life had been so endlessly chaotic and strange. He'd answered to no one—except the Lord—and we only know one side of that conversation. Is he proud of his work, his life? Has there been a moment of peace within? Al remains inscrutable. Defiantly so.

Creep through the few blurry, artless snapshots of Green hidden away on the Facebook pages of his children and former lovers and a feeling emerges. Here's Al backstage in a tux. Here's Al in his tracksuit riding the bus. He looks so solitary in these pictures, so without a friend.

"I'm still a loner," he boasted to the *Washington Post* in 2014.

And is the Love and Happiness Man ever lonely? they asked.

"Yeah. Every day."

HOLY ROLLER

I'm different. I'm not made to be everyone else. I didn't come here to do what I'm told to do—except by God.
—AL GREEN

On just about any Sunday in Memphis, you can go see one of the world's greatest singers for a voluntary donation—or nothing, if you're cheap. Al Green pastors at Full Gospel Tabernacle every week, usually showing up around noon or so. The crowd is divided between a small, faithful group of Memphis regulars and the fans and tourists who come from all over the world. He addresses the latter with Vegas-like patter. "Where y'all from—Amsterdam? England? Give 'em a hand. Where you from, honey? Chicago! Thank you, Jesus! Wales? Give Wales a hand. Amen."

During the sermons I have witnessed or heard, Green does a plethora of songs he's never recorded, gospel songs associated with James Cleveland and the Mighty Clouds of Joy, as well as more contemporary artists like VaShawn Mitchell, such as "I've Got One Thing You Can't Take Away," "That's Enough," "Call Him Up," "I'm Going Home to Live with Jesus," "One Day at a Time," "Just Another Day the Lord Has Kept Me," "Jesus Is All over Me," "Nobody Greater," and "Near the Cross."

Sometimes he'll just throw out a line or verse and move on; other times the band and choir will kick it, and they'll go for twenty minutes. There are no obligations or expectations—Green can just sing whatever the hell he wants. ("Anybody here like country music, raise your hand," I saw him ask the congregation before letting loose with a "yee-haw" and a bit of "I Saw the Light.") Want to record a great album on Al Green right now? It's simple, here's how. Tape his sermons for nine or ten Sundays. Spread the dates out so you get a few different Als. Keep the musicians he's already comfortable with as well as his choir, then record it using a great engineer. And change nothing.

But don't just come for the music, or Al will get mad. "There's a whole lot of people who try to sing their way to heaven. You can't get to heaven on a song." And he'll get testy if you start snapping photos. "Let me take *your* picture—put you on the other end, see how it feels."

The first service I attended, there was a baby crying loudly. "*Shut up, kid,*" snapped the Bishop. People gasped; a few busted out laughing. Green used the same exact line a few Sundays later. There are a few bits of business Al likes to return to over and over again: how he prefers his old wooden pulpit to the fancy new glass ones ("I haven't changed buildings five or six times like most ministers," he says proudly). Or how he demands his flock relax: "This is the Sabbath day. I don't want nobody doin' nuthin'. Go home, kick your shoes off, pop the TV on, put in a pizza, open a cold beer."

Occasionally he'll cuss, as on the day he decreed gangbangers the product of "parents not raisin' their kids worth a damn." More gasps and giggles from his congregation, who are obviously accustomed to Al's quirks. "What did I say? Whatever I said, I meant it." Green enjoys his role as outlaw preacher. "I'm *glad* to be a holy roller. My daddy, when I was a little boy, he said, 'Don't have nothing to do with the holy rollers.' He'd be shocked to see me now."

Most of all Green likes to return to a line from his father, who had this advice when Al told him he was going to preach. "You cannot raise grown people. You can tell 'em what's in the Bible, but *you cannot raise grown people.*" Al will quote an unfinished line of scripture, letting his congregation fill in the missing word or phrase, then do the same for the next passage. It's hypnotic. "I'm just here to tell you what thus sayeth the Lord. I'm not here to run your life . . . I can't even run my *own* life, how am I gonna run yours? Somebody say amen." At Full Gospel Tabernacle they whoop and holler and talk in tongues. One member of his flock remains instantly recognizable due to the short, dramatic "Yessssssss!" he shouts out after nearly every utterance by Al.

As mercurial as Green is, the message he imparts is fairly straightforward—follow the Bible. "I've been readin' this book thirty-seven years and I still don't know nothin' about it. You got to *live* the book, not learn the book . . . every time I read it I think He's talking directly to me." Al lays out blunt, practical advice. "I try to be realistic about religion," he's said. "I don't want people to think that I believe that leading a religious life is easy. . . . It's work—boy, is it work. But it's also so rewarding."

Bishop Green is antiviolence. "Sometimes you just want to wring a neighbor's neck, a pastor's neck, a choirman's neck. That's not in the Commandments, so put your hands in your pockets and walk on by." He is against drugs and alcohol. "You can get spirits at the liquor store but you can't get the Holy Spirit." At the same time he'll tell his flock, "I like wine. Sorry 'bout that." Looking up, he paraphrases Timothy 5:23. "You said drink a little for thy stomach's sake and often infirmities. Well, I have 'often infirmities.'" Self-righteous "goody-goods" he has no patience for. "Gets me to my bones, these do-right Christians."

Green peppers his sermons with comments on current events. Al seemed dubious of Obamacare. "When you start tryin' to insure everybody in the United States, that's a lotta money. . . . It doesn't matter who's throwin' the politics at you, you still have to pay the bill." (Later Green referred to bin Laden as "Obama bin Laden." Whoops.)

Al remarked on recent altercations at Donald Trump rallies, expressing his thankfulness that things were peaceful at his church. "We don't raise a lot of Cain. Fussin', fightin', with black eyes. I had my days for that. Whoooo. I gave up on it." Al knows Judgment Day is approaching. "The world is goin' the way God said it's going to go . . . God is the only someone you can count on in these last and evil days . . . you notice that all the folks that don't go to church, they think you're crazy? In the end, we'll see who's crazy."

Green sings, rambles, and generally seems to say whatever pops into his head. "Some people preach for *style*. I don't have too much style. Because when the Holy Ghost gets ahold of you, your style will go right out the window." I've sent many people over to Full Gospel to experience Green's sermons, and reviews are mixed. Some enjoy his irreverent delivery; others feel he's scatterbrained. "He never seems to have any real point to his sermons," said Molly Whitehorn, a research assistant who attended some services for me. She felt Al opened the Bible only to "pick passages at random, and stop at every other word to go on a tangent."

For a biographer, though, his sermons are fascinating. Green frequently references himself. At times it feels like a therapy session, with Al working out whatever's roiling inside before the brethren. One Sunday he lectured on the evils of gossip. "Talkin' about folks you don't *know*. *Jesus will put a little* trouble *in your way.* You want to talk about other folks, you want to talk about me; you don't even *know* me. You know AL GREEN, but you don't know me . . . you only know what you *heard* about me." The Bishop paused for dramatic effect. "I'm gonna tell you right now—what you heard is probably true." Laughter from the parish. Another Sunday, Al felt compelled to reveal that "I live by myself. If I don't fix the bacon right, too bad. Ain't nobody gonna fix it . . . I ain't got nobody and I ain't *lookin'* for nobody."

On Sunday, October 6, 2013, Al gave his congregation a tongue-lashing for not attending his weekly Bible class. That previous Wednesday it had just been Al and his right-hand man Taylor sitting there, although two out-of-towners eventually showed up. Apparently this was a chronic problem, and this Sunday Al was steaming. "If this is going to be a Bible-based church, you're gonna need to study the Bible. Maybe you need somebody else to be your teacher—I'll let *you* do it. You know everything—your last name is *Einstein*? You don't want to study the word of God? I'm ashamed of you."

When I finally heard one of Green's Bible classes—from February 19, 2014—I understood why even the faithful might not want to attend.* Here in this intimate setting, before a small group of church members, Al seemed much harsher and more unhinged. After sharing a few lines of scripture from Ephesians 2:20 and telling the class "hate will destroy you," he lurched into a long, toxic rant on the burdens of being Green. He complained about people calling him at home late at night for advice, favors, salvation. "I got people in *New York* with problems, I got people in *Virginia* with problems, now I got people in *Georgia* with problems." All his callers were women. He occasionally impersonated them in a high, ridiculous voice.

Green had particularly harsh words for an ailing ex-paramour (I'm assuming) with whom he'd traveled to Jamaica long ago. "Now she wants

---

* Whitehorn, my previously mentioned assistant—a young, attractive woman—attended the class, and before he started, Al stared straight at her and said, "You will like me before all this is over."

somebody to come *pray* for her," he said dismissively. "You done smoked yourself into a coma. You make your own bed."

Jumping from topic to topic in an almost stream-of-consciousness fashion, for some unknown reason Al proceeded to recount asking his cleaning ladies if they were illegal aliens, mocking their Spanish accents. "I don't even know what they talkin' 'bout." He claimed one of his cleaners broke into song—what else but an Al Green number, "Let's Stay Together." "I said, 'Honey, you are *off-key*! Clean the table, I'm *gone.*'" He belittled an African American doing construction work at his home for being uneducated. "The white guys are laughin'—he done laid the foundation *over* the septic tank." Clearly Green sided with them. He felt Hispanics on the crew were more industrious and intelligent and had "taken the place of the black workers."

Al turned to a recent trip he'd made to a fast-food restaurant and the starstruck female behind the counter. "The woman was so busy lookin' at me she put *three buns* on my hamburger," insisted Green, who was now yelling. "So I got *two* tops, *one* bottom. . . . She put pickles on and *everything,* she don't even *look.*" The indignity of it left Al weary, but he understood her amazement at the superstar across the counter. "I laughed and went on my way. She didn't mean it."

This morphed into a critique of the potentially nonbelieving fans that stream into his church. "Maybe people come to church just *to look.*" The notion disturbed him. "They don't get the prayer right, they don't know *nuthin'*—'*I just want to* see *Al.*' I want to do more than *see.*" Green had his sights set heavenward. "I want to get up *there.*"

In February 2016, at the tail end of a long sermon, Al slipped into one of my favorite and most poignant bits of business. "Sometimes I stay by myself, and I walk around in the kitchen going, 'Whoooo.'" Walking back and forth behind the pulpit, eyes closed, face dripping with sweat and what seemed to be tears, Green hung onto that last word for a while, singing it in falsetto. He seemed oblivious to the congregation, that high, ghostly voice floating eerily in the air. "Whooooooooo." For a minute he looked up, and I thought I caught a brief glimpse of little Albert Leorns Greene hiding in there. He looked as haunted as ever.

Eventually Green will ask those present to donate a little something to the church. "Go and get your wallet and get a love offering. . . . Help the poor Reverend. I'm not really poor, but I can act like it. . . . We ain't got nothin' to sell ya. All the religious folk always got a book, a video, drink somebody's water, anointin' cloth. We got salvation, and it's free." He might tease the congregation by singing a brief bit of "Tired of Being Alone." The ladies in big hats will swoon a little.

This church is Al's home, his mission in life. It wouldn't surprise me if one day he just keels over midsermon during one of those high, lonesome "whoooooo"s. My guess is he'd be pleased by such an exit.

"I really don't care how I'll be remembered," Green told a reporter back in 1996. "Because our flame is eternal, and we came down and ascended back up, and we plan to come again. So, therefore, the love and faith in us is eternal, and there is no beginning and there is no end."

ACKNOWLEDGMENTS

This was a very challenging project and there are many people to thank.

Sarah Heldman was an unrelenting detective, unearthing many legal documents around the country. She is an excellent researcher and this book would've suffered greatly without her involvement. There will be no pie but plenty of roosters, Sarah. Stephanie Kreutter sifted through mountains of digital recordings to do transcriptions in record time. It's a relief to be able to rely on Stephanie for a job I'd only entrusted to myself in the past.

As with my last few books, author David K. Frasier tracked down all sorts of books and articles. Charlie Beesley read the manuscript and made many pertinent suggestions. My brother John McDonough also tracked some useful court documents and provided some astute advice.

In Memphis: Bob Mehr helped me in innumerable ways, contacting people, sharing research, making calls. Robert Gordon, who even gave me panicked directions over the phone so I wouldn't be late to an interview, did the same, sharing much of his research and making many a suggestion. I owe both of these guys. They never said no to a request and opened their research to me, as did Andria Lisle, who shared her excellent interviews concerning Al Green/Hi Records. Thanks to the McWherter Library at the University of Memphis and to Chris Ratliff in particular.

I thank the many writers who've covered various aspects of this beat long before me. Colin Escott, Martin Hawkins, Hank Davis, David Nathan, Bill Dahl, Rob Bowman, Matt Rogers, Denise Hall, Sue C. Clark, Peter Guralnick, Stanley Booth, Pete Nickols, Don McLeese, Lynn Norment,

Richard L. Eldredge, Aliya S. King, Colin Dilnot, Robert Palmer, Ben Fong-Torres, Scott Spencer, and T. Bruce Wittet. Bob Mugge shared much information regarding the making of *Gospel According to Al Green* as well as access to his lengthy interview with Green. I'd like to thank the Smithsonian for making its tremendous Rock 'n' Soul Audiovisual History Project archive available. Special thanks to the excellent interviewers: David Less, Pete Daniel, Charles McGovern, and John Meehan. Thanks to John Ridley and his amazing website, Sir Shambling's Deep Soul Heaven (www.sirshambling.com).

Harvey Kubernik shared an incredible interview with Willie Mitchell. Patrick Berkery did likewise with a great interview of Howard Grimes. Roben Jones helped with information/sources, as did David Whiteis. David Cole provided me with interviews from his late, lamented *In the Basement*. David Less helped fill in some blanks and provided help with photos by Rick Ivy, as did Rick's sister Carole Givens. Preston Lauterbach was an early sounding board and an immense help. Jaan Uhelszki provided her interview with Green, as did Karen Schoemer, who went to great trouble to dig out her interview tape. Rob Hatch-Miller, director of *Syl Johnson: Any Way the Wind Blows,* provided my favorite Johnson publicity shot. Pat Rasberry of the Tupelo Convention and Visitors Bureau helped with locating Ray Harris pictures, as did Ray's daughter, Ryta Harris. Special thanks to Kenneth Christian for the great shot of Ray. For other photos, thanks to Paul Zaleski, Bernard and Angie Staton, Nikki Walker, Harris Lentz, and the mighty Bob Mehr. I thank the many interviewees. They are listed in the source notes.

For help with documenting Green's sermons, thanks go to Molly Whitehorn, Chris Ratliff, Carole Nicksin, Frank Bruno, and David Leonard. I'd also like to thank Andrew Ballard, Pier Dominguez, Bill Carpenter, Sherman Wilmott, the great Rudolph Grey, Joel Selvin, Kim Rush, Kevin Kiley, Zach Myers, James McLennan of the Irving Police Department, Dominique "Imperial" Anglares, Alain Mallaret, William "Marty" Willis III, Frank "Poncho" Sampedro and Ipo Carvalho, Shane Malsom, Buster, Pebble, Molly Scott, Tad Bennicoff, Leo Trombetta, Allen "Charmin'" Larmin, Gene and Diana Nitchman, Nate Fridena, Mary Jo Berner, Megan McDonough, Amy Hanson, Chris Stovall Brown, Jamie Laughlin, Craig Leibner, Brian O'Hara, Tess Alexander, Brittany "the Tool" Karas, Margaret Dollrod, Nicki Walters, and Liz Main. Thanks to David Peck for keeping me supplied with rare Al Green video all those many years ago, and to Dale Lawrence for playing me so much fantastic music back in that swampy Hoboken apartment with the picturesque wallpaper.

Sometimes you run into a person who kicks your ass in the best possible way. Stephanie Worth of Acupuncture Northwest has helped change my life much for the better. An amazing individual, and a great inspiration. (Thanks as well to A.N.'s Wade Kimble and Louise Reynoldson.)

Ben Schafer was the perfect editor for this book. He let it play without lifting the needle, all the way to the run-out groove. Thank you, Ben. My gratitude to the rest of the Da Capo crew: Julie Ford, Michael Clark, Susan VanHecke, Michael Giarratamo, Justin Lovell, Jeff Williams, and Alex Camlin. As far as the editorial/production process goes, this has been the best experience I've ever had in the book world. Thank you all.

My fabulous agent, David McCormick, took care of all the details. Thanks to everyone at the agency: Bridget McCarthy, Susan Hobson, Leslie Falk.

My wife, Natalia Wisdom, understands music a great deal more than I ever will. She spent countless hours driving around with me, listening to and discussing Al Green and other Hi records. For that and so much else I thank her.

APPENDIX: LEGAL DOCUMENTS

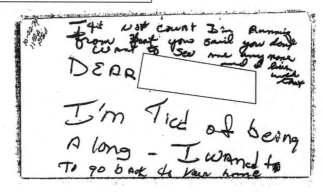

Mary Woodson's suicide note and envelope.

CHANCERY NO. D-3405-2
GREEN vs. GREEN   EXHIBIT "A"

PRE-MARITAL AGREEMENT

THIS AGREEMENT made and entered into this _____ day of
_____, 197_, by and between the REV. AL GREEN and
_____; WITNESSETH:

WHEREAS, at the present the Rev. Al Green and
_____ are not engaged to be **married**;
but

WHEREAS, in consideration for _____
entering into this agreement in which she will release all of
her marital rights in and to the property of the Rev. **Al Green**
by virtue of their marriage, the Rev. Al Green agrees to and
shall enter into marriage with _____; and

WHEREAS, the Rev. Al Green has disclosed to _____
_____ the nature and extent of his various property
interests and the sources of his income;

IT IS, THEREFORE, AGREED:

1. Release of Dower. The Rev. Al Green shall hold all
real property which he now owns or may hereafter acquire free from
any claim of dower, inchoate or otherwise, on the part of _____
_____, and this agreement shall evidence the right
of the Rev. Al Green to convey any of his real estate free from any
such claim of dower. At the request of the Rev. Al Green, _____
_____ shall execute, acknowledge, and deliver such
other instruments as may be reasonably required to accomplish the
transfer by the Rev. Al Green of any of his real property free from
any such claim of dower or to divest any claim of dower in such
property.

2. Release of Marital Rights. _____
shall accept the Rev. Al Green's promise to marry her and his marriage
to her in release and in full satisfaction of all rights which, by
reason of the marriage, she may acquire in the property or estate of
the Rev. Al Green, and in consideration thereof she does hereby waive
and relinquish all rights which, as widow of the Rev. Al Green, she

Al Green's "pre-marital agreement."

-2-

would otherwise acquire in his property or estate, under the law now or hereafter in effect in any jurisdiction, whether by way of dower, distributive share, right of election to take against will, widow's allowance or otherwise.

3. During the continuance of said marriage relations each of the parties is to have the full right to own, control, and dispose of his or her separate property the same as if the marriage relations did not arise and each of the parties is to have the full right to dispose of and sell any and all real or personal property now or hereafter owned by each of them without the other party joining and said transfer by either of the parties to this contract shall convey the same title that said transfer would convey had the marriage relations not existed. This contract limits the right of either party to participate in the estate of the other.

4. _____ acknowledges that she has been advised that the net worth of the Rev. Al Geeen is substantial and that his yearly income is also substantial and that she has given consideration to these facts and that she is entering into this agreement freely and with the full understanding of its provisions.

5. Effective Date. This agreement shall come into effect only if the contemplated marriage between the Rev. Al Green and _____ is solemnized, and upon coming into effect shall bind, and inure to the benefit of, the parties and their respective heirs, executors and administrators.

IN WITNESS WHEREOF the parties have signed and acknowledged, this agreement on the day and date first above written.

WITNESS: _Hattie Angel_

WITNESS: _Maxine_

Rev. Al Green

X _Shirley June Green_

DISCOGRAPHY

The Al Green/Hi Records discography below is a rather rudimentary one. I suggest searching out the vinyl albums/singles if you want to hear the Hi Records sound in all its glory. The Hi material has been reissued countless times both in this country and overseas. Audio aficionados have been extremely critical of most Al Green/Hi releases on CD, although the Capitol twofers from the mideighties and the first batch of Right Stuff releases (those remastered by Larry Walsh in the nineties rather than those by Bob Norberg from the mid-aughts) rate better than some. The one reissue exception is the Steve Hoffman remaster of Al Green's *Greatest Hits*, which is out of print and fetches very high prices.

For the most part this discography does not include straight reissues of albums/CDs, nor soundtracks/compilations that include previously released songs. Some of the releases below come with extensive liner notes, and if they add something, the authors are noted. In the case of artists other than Al Green, if the album includes a song mentioned in the text, I try to list it. For earlier release dates I have relied largely on Pete Doggett's excellent discography "Al Green on CD" in the December 2001 issue of *Record Collector*.

Albums

Back Up Train (as Al Greene) (1967) Hot Line Music Journal, HLS 1500S/1500. Back Up Train/Hot Wire/Stop and Check Myself/Let Me Help You/I'm Reachin' Out/Don't Hurt Me No More//Don't Leave Me/What's It All About?/I'll Be Good to You/Guilty/That's All It Takes (Lady)/Get Yourself Together

Green Is Blues (April 1969) Hi, SHL-32055. One Woman/Talk to Me/My Girl/ The Letter/I Stand Accused//Gotta Find a New World/What Am I Gonna Do with Myself?/Tomorrow's Dream/Get Back Baby/Get Back/Summertime (There are two covers for this album; the first version has a picture of a moody young Al Green in a tie and suit; the second shows Green at the mic.)

Gets Next to You (January 1971) Hi, SHL 32062. I Can't Get Next to You/Are You Lonely for Me Baby?/God Is Standing By/Tired of Being Alone/I'm a Ram//Driving Wheel/Light My Fire/You Say It/Right Now Right Now/All Because

Let's Stay Together (January 1972) Hi, SHL 32070. Let's Stay Together/La-La for You/So You're Leaving/What Is This Feeling/Old Time Lovin'//I've Never Found a Girl/How Can You Mend a Broken Heart?/Judy/It Ain't No Fun to Me

I'm Still in Love with You (December 1972) Hi, XSHL 32074. I'm Still in Love with You/I'm Glad You're Mine/Love and Happiness/What a Wonderful Thing Love Is/Simply Beautiful//Oh, Pretty Woman/For the Good Times/Look What You Done for Me/One of These Good Old Days

Call Me (July 1973) Hi, XSHL 32077. Call Me (Come Back Home)/Have You Been Making Out O.K.?/Stand Up/I'm So Lonesome I Could Cry/Your Love Is Like the Morning Sun//Here I Am (Come and Take Me)/Funny How Time Slips Away/You Ought to Be with Me/Jesus Is Waiting

Livin' for You (November 1973) Hi, ASHL 32082. Livin' for You/Home Again/Free at Last/Let's Get Married/So Good to Be Here//Sweet Sixteen/Unchained Melody/My God Is Real/Beware

Explores Your Mind (October 1974) Hi, SHL 32087. Sha-La-La/Take Me to the River/God Blessed Our Love/The City/One Nite Stand//I'm Hooked on You/Stay with Me Forever/Hangin' On/School Days

Greatest Hits (February 1975) Hi, SHL 32089. Tired of Being Alone/Call Me (Come Back Home)/I'm Still in Love with You/Here I Am (Come and Take Me)/How Can You Mend a Broken Heart?//Let's Stay Together/I Can't Get Next to You/You Ought to Be with Me/Look What You Done for Me/Let's Get Married

   The much-coveted Steve Hoffman remaster of *Greatest Hits* came out in 1998 on DCC Compact Classics, GZS-1125.

Al Green Is Love (September 1975) Hi, SHL 32092. L-O-V-E (Love)/Rhymes/The Love Sermon/There Is Love/Could I Be the One?//Love Ritual/I Didn't Know/Oh Me, Oh My (Dreams in My Arms)/I Gotta Be More (Take Me Higher)/I Wish You Were Here

Full of Fire (April 1976) Hi, SHL 32097. Glory, Glory/That's the Way It Is/Always/There's No Way/I'd Fly Away//Full of Fire/Together Again/Soon as I Get Home/Let It Shine

Have a Good Time (December 1976) Hi, SHL 32103. Keep Me Cryin'/Smile a Little Bit More/I Tried to Tell Myself/Something/The Truth Marches On//Have a Good Time/Nothing Takes the Place of You/Happy/Hold On Forever

Al Green's Greatest Hits, Volume II (June 1977) Hi, SHL 32105. Love and Happiness/Sha-La-La (Make Me Happy)/Take Me to the River/L-O-V-E (Love)/Rhymes//For the Good Times/Keep Me Cryin'/Livin' for You/Full of Fire

The Belle Album (December 1977) Hi, HLP 6004. Belle/Loving You/Feels Like Summer/Georgia Boy//I Feel Good/All N All/Chariots of Fire/Dream

Truth n' Time (December 1978) Hi HLP 6009. Blow Me Down/Lo and Behold/Wait Here/To Sir with Love//Truth n' Time/King of All/Say a Little Prayer/Happy Days

The Lord Will Make a Way (1980) Myrrh, MSB-6661. The Lord Will Make a Way/Pass Me Not/Too Close/Highway to Heaven//Saved/None but the Righteous/In the Holy Name of Jesus/I Have a Friend Above All Others/Highway to Heaven

Tokyo . . . Live! (1981) Hi, HCD 5001. L-O-V-E (Love)/Tired of Being Alone/Let's Stay Together/How Can You Mend a Broken Heart?/All N All//Belle/Sha-La-La/Let's Get Married//God Blessed Our Love/You Ought to Be with Me/For the Good Times//Dream/I Feel Good/Love and Happiness. Recorded live at Nakano Sun Plaza Hall, Tokyo, Japan, on June 23 and 24, 1978.

Higher Plane (February 1981) Myrrh, MSB-6674. Higher Plane/People Get Ready/By My Side/The Spirit Might Come—On and On//Where Love Rules/Amazing Grace/His Name Is Jesus/Battle Hymn of the Republic

Precious Lord (October 1982) Myrrh, MSB-6702. Precious Lord/What a Friend We Have in Jesus/The Old Rugged Cross/Morningstar/How Great Thou Art//Glory to His Name/Rock of Ages/In the Garden/Hallelujah (I Just Want to Praise the Lord)

I'll Rise Again (1983) Myrrh, MSB-6747. It Don't Take Much/Jesus Is Coming (Back Again)/Leaning on the Everlasting Arms/I Close My Eyes and Smile/Ocean Blue (I'll Rise Again)//Look at the Things That God Made/I Just Can't Make It By Myself/I Know It Was the Blood/Straighten Out Your Life

White Christmas (1983) Myrrh, WR-8117 (vinyl), Epic, EK 48597 (CD). White Christmas/The Christmas Song/Winter Wonderland/I'll Be Home for Christmas/Jingle Bells//What Christmas Means to Me/O Holy Night/Silent Night/It Feels Like Christmas

Trust in God (January 1985) Myrrh, SPCN 7-01-678306-5 or WR-8118. Don't It Make You Wanta Go Home?/Up the Ladder to the Roof/Ain't No Mountain High Enough/Trust in God/No Not One//Lean on Me/Never Met Nobody Like You/Holy Spirit/Trust in God (Reprise)/All We Need Is a Little More Love

Going Away (late 1985, possibly January 1986) A&M, 395 102-1 (rereleased as *He Is the Light*, A&M, SP-5102). Going Away/True Love/He Is the Light/I Feel Like Going On/Be with Me Jesus/You Brought the Sunshine/Power/Building Up/Nearer My God to Thee

Soul Survivor (April 1987) A&M, SP-5150. Everything's Gonna Be Alright/Jesus Will Fix It/You Know and I Know/Yield Not to Temptation/So Real to Me/Introduction—Soul Survivor//Soul Survivor/You've Got a Friend/He Ain't Heavy/23rd Psalm

I Get Joy (May 1989) A&M, SP-5228. You're Everything to Me/All My Praise/The End Is Near/Mighty Cloud of Joy/I Get Joy//As Long as We're Together/Praise Him/ Blessed/Tryin' to Do the Best I Can/Tryin' to Get Over You

Love Is Reality (March 10, 1992) Word/Epic, EK 48860. I Can Feel It/Love Is Reality/Just Can't Let You Go/You Don't Know Me/Again/Positive Attitude/Sure Feels Good/Long Time/Why/I Like It

Don't Look Back (UK, 1993) BMG, 74321 16310 2. Best Love/Love Is a Beautiful Thing/Waiting on You/What Does It Take/Keep On Pushing Love/You Are My Everything/One Love/People in the World (Keep On Lovin' You)/Give It Everything/Your Love (Is More Than I Ever Hoped For)/Fountain of Love/Don't Look Back/Love in Motion

Your Heart's in Good Hands (1995) MCA, MCAD-11350. Your Heart's in Good Hands/Keep On Pushing Love/Could This Be the Love/Love Is a Beautiful Thing/ One Love/Don't Look Back/Best Love/ Your Love (Is More Than I Ever Hoped For)/ What Does It Take?/People in the World (Keep On Lovin' You)

Testify: The Best of the A&M Years (2001) A&M. All the best (and some of the worst) of Green's gospel recordings for A&M. Includes "Mighty Clouds of Joy."

I Can't Stop (November 17, 2003) Blue Note, 7243 5 93556 2 7. I Can't Stop/Play to Win/Rainin' in My Heart/I've Been Waitin' on You/You/Not Tonight/Million to One/My Problem Is You/I'd Still Choose You/I've Been Thinkin' 'Bout You/I'd Write a Letter/Too Many

Everything's OK (March 14, 2005) Blue Note, 7087 6 18870 2 0V. Everything's OK/ You Are So Beautiful/Build Me Up/Perfect to Me/Nobody but You/Real Love/I Can Make Music/Be My Baby/Magic Road/I Wanna Hold You/Another Day/All the Time

Lay It Down (May 27, 2008) Blue Note, 0946 3 48449 2 5. Lay It Down/Just for Me/You've Got the Love I Need/No One Like You/What More Do You Want from Me?/Take Your Time/Too Much/Stay with Me (By the Sea)/All I Need/I'm Wild About You/Standing in the Rain

Singles Discography (US Only)

Back Up Train/Don't Leave Me (as Al Greene and the Soul Mates) (October 1967) Hot Line Music Journal 15,000/8345/8346

Don't Hurt Me No More/Get Yourself Together (as Al Greene) (1968) Hot Line Music Journal 15,001/8604/8605

A Lover's Hideaway/I'll Be Good to You (as Al Greene) (1968) Hot Line Music Journal 15,002/8726/8727

Want to Hold Your Hand/What Am I Gonna Do with Myself? (April 1969) Hi 2159

One Woman/Tomorrow's Dream (June 1969) Hi 2164

You Say It/Gotta Find a New World (December 1969) Hi 2172

Right Now, Right Now/All Because (I'm a Foolish One) (May 1970) Hi 2177

I Can't Get Next to You/Ride Sally Ride (September 1970) Hi 2182

Drivin' Wheel/True Love (February 1971) Hi, 2188

Tired of Being Alone/Get Back Baby (May 1971) Hi 2194

Let's Stay Together/Tomorrow's Dream (November 1971) Hi 2202

Look What You've Done for Me/ La-La for You (February 1972) Hi 2211

Guilty/Let Me Help You (September 1972) Bell 45,258

Hot Wire/Don't Leave Me (December 1972) Bell 45,305

I'm Still in Love with You/Old Time Lovin' (June 1972) Hi 2216

You Ought to Be with Me/What Is This Feeling? (October 1972) Hi 2227

Call Me (Come Back Home)/What a Wonderful Thing Love Is (February 1973) Hi 2235

Here I Am (Come and Take Me)/I'm Glad You're Mine (June 1973) Hi 2247

Livin' for You/It Ain't No Fun to Me (November 1973) Hi 2257

Let's Get Married/So Good to Be Here (March 1974) Hi 2262

Sha-La-La (Make Me Happy)/School Days (September 1974) Hi 2274

L-O-V-E (Love)/I Wish You Were Here (February 1975) Hi 2282

Oh Me, Oh My (Dreams in My Arms)/Strong as Death (Sweet as Love) (June 1975) Hi 2288

Full of Fire/Could I Be the One? (October 1975) Hi 2300

Full of Fire (special disco version) (1975) Hi 5N-2300 (10-inch single-sided 45 rpm promo issue only)

Let It Shine/There's No Way (April 1976) Hi 2306

Keep Me Cryin'/There Is Love (October 1976) Hi 2319

I Tried to Tell Myself/Something (January 1977) Hi 2322

Love and Happiness/Glory, Glory (July 1977) Hi 2324

Belle/Chariots of Fire (October 1977) Hi 77505

I Feel Good/Feels Like Summer (March 1978) Hi 78511

I Feel Good/I Feel Good (1978) Hi 78510 (12-inch)

To Sir with Love/Wait Here (December 1978) Hi 78522

To Sir with Love/Wait Here (1978) Hi 78523 (12-inch)

Going Away/Building Up (November 1985) A&M 2786

True Love/He Is the Light (February 1986) A&M 2807

Everything's Gonna Be Alright/So Real to Me (March 1987) A&M 2919

You Know and I Know/True Love (June 1987) A&M 2952

Soul Survivor/Jesus Will Fix It (September 1987) A&M 2962

White Christmas/Winter Wonderland (2001) Hi 72438-77680 (clear vinyl)

Duets and Guest Appearances

Shirley Caesar and Al Green. Sailin' on the Sea of Love/Lord Let Your Spirit Fall on Me (1984) Myrrh 9016253262 (single). Green does not appear on the B-side.

Deniece Williams with Al Green, Patti Austin, Roberta Flack, Melba Moore. Lift Ev'ry Voice and Sing (1985), Lite/Miller Brewing 503081X (single).

Annie Lennox and Al Green. Put a Little Love in Your Heart/A Great Big Piece of Love (by the Spheres of Celestial Influence; Green is not on the B-side) (1988), A&M 1255 (single). Also on the *Scrooged* soundtrack (1988) A&M CD 392.

Arthur Baker and the Backbeat Disciples featuring Al Green. The Message Is Love (12-inch Cupid mix)/The Message Is Love (7-inch edit)//The Message Is Love (12-inch Message Is Club)/The Message Is Love (12-inch Message Is Dub)/The Message Is Love (12-inch Message Is Instrumental) (1989) A&M SP-12323.

Arthur Baker and the Backbeat Disciples featuring Al Green. Leave the Guns at Home (edit)//Leave the Guns at Home (extended version)/ Leave the Guns at Home (album version) (1991), RCA 62120-1 (12-inch single).

Various artists, *Our Christmas* (1991) Word, 7019193609. Green sings "The First Noel."

Ann Nesby featuring Al Green. Put It on Paper (radio edit)/Put It on Paper (album version without intro)/Put It on Paper (album version with intro) (2002) Universal 20739-2. Also on Nesby's album *Put It on Paper* (March 19, 2002) Universal, 440 017 391-2, which also includes Al preaching solo on "Al Green Interlude."

Queen Latifah, *The Dana Owens Album* (2004) A&M, B0003435-02. Green duets with Latifah on "Simply Beautiful." He's in the video as well. Album cut only.

Various artists, *The Best of* Soul Train *Live* (2011) Time-Life, 26508. Includes Green performing "Love and Happiness" on the March 3, 1973, show. Somebody needs to release all the Green *Soul Train* performances on DVD. That would be an incredible collection.

Various artists, *Oh Happy Day: All-Star Music Celebration* (2012) EMI/CMG, 5099962436250. Green and Heather Headley perform "People Get Ready."

Outtakes/Unreleased

Listen: The Rarities (UK, 2000) Hi, 251. The best collection of outtakes/rarities from Green's Hi years. Not much here, I'm afraid—I'm told Mitchell recorded over outtakes to save tape. Includes "I'll Be Standing By," "So Good to Be Here," "Love Is Real." Liner notes by Colin Escott.

DVDs

Gospel According to Al Green. Acorn Media, 2009. DVD of the essential 1984 Robert Mugge documentary.

Al Green: Everything's Gonna Be Alright. Xenon, 2004. Pedestrian gospel performance from the Celebrity Theatre in Anaheim, California.

Live in Tokyo. Hudson Street, 2008. Tremendous 1987 performance with one of Green's great gospel bands.

Live in '72. Revolver, 2005. Both of the *Soul!* TV appearances. Utterly fantastic, essential for any serious Green fan. Withdrawn due to rights issues.

Box Sets

Anthology (1997) The Right Stuff/Hi, 72438-53033-2-6. Four-CD set covering Green's career from "Back Up Train" through *Truth n' Time.* Incudes live cuts from the TV shows *Soul!* and *Soundstage, Gospel According to Al Green,* and a few interview snippets. Excellent liner notes by Robert Gordon, producer of the box.

Love and Happiness (UK, 2001) Cream/Hi, FBOOK 26. Three-CD collection of hits, album cuts, oddities. Liner notes by Colin Escott.

The Immortal Soul of Al Green (2003) The Right Stuff/Hi, 72435 90551-2-1. Four-CD collection covering Green's career from "Back Up Train" through *Truth n' Time* in a more straightforward (and less interesting) manner than *Anthology.* Liner notes by Colin Escott, producer of the set.

Hi Times: The Hi Records R&B Years (1995) The Right Stuff, T2 30584. Three-CD set with both hits and obscurities. Liner notes by Robert Gordon, Bill Dahl, Colin Escott, David Nathan, and Cary Baker.

Royal Memphis Soul (UK, 1996) Cream/Hi, HiBOOK 11. Four-CD overview of Hi, including many of its greatest artists as well as unsung wonders like Quiet Elegance, Jean Plum, and Erma Coffee. Includes the Joint Venture (Rhodes, Chalmers, Rhodes) cut "When the Battle Is Over." Excellent liner notes by Peter Nichols. Out of print and expensive, but well worth finding.

Hi Records: Other Artists

Hi Records: The Early Years, Vols. 1 and 2 (UK,1999) Cream/Hi, HEXD44. Compilation of nearly all the early Hi recordings discussed in this book, including those by Carl McVoy, Jay B. Loyd, Gene Simmons, Bill Black Combo, Jerry Jaye, and others. Liner notes by Colin Escott, Martin Hawkins, and Hank Davis.

The Ray Harris Sun sides are on *Let's Bop: Sun Rockabilly Volume 1* (1995) Avi, AVI CD 5003. This album also includes cuts by the equally unhinged rockabilly genius Jimmy Wages. Apparently Harris attempted to cut some tracks with Wages during Hi's early days but failed to come up with anything releasable. A tragedy of Herculean proportions.

Ace Cannon, *The Best of Ace Cannon: The Hi Records Years* (2001) The Right Stuff/Hi, 27837. Liner notes by Colin Escott. Includes "Tuff."

Willie Mitchell, *The Memphis Rhythm 'n' Blues Sound of Willie Mitchell* (UK, 2010) Stomper Time, STCD 26. Collection of Mitchell's pre-Hi recordings. With Don Bryant. Includes the original version of "The Crawl." Liner notes by Tony Wilkinson.

Willie Mitchell, *Poppa Willie: The Hi Years/1962–74* (UK, 2001) Cream/Hi, HEXCD 48. Liner notes by Colin Escott. Just what it says; includes "20-75" and "Soul Serenade."

Don Bryant, *The Complete Don Bryant on Hi Records* (UK, 2000) Cream/Hi, HEXCD 50. Liner notes by David Cole.

O. V. Wright, *Giant of Southern Soul 1965–1975* (UK, 2001) Connoisseur, VSOP CD353. The Backbeat hits on a single disc.

O. V. Wright, *O. V. Box* (Japan, 2007) P-Vine, PCD-7303/7. Hard to find now, but all the Backbeat material on five CDs. It'll put your hair in curlers.

O. V. Wright, *Memphis Unlimited* (2009) Universal Music Special Markets, B0012329-02. Wright's Hi Records masterpiece, with "I've Been Searching," "Nothing Comes to a Sleeper," "You Must Believe in Yourself," "I'd Rather Be (Blind, Cripple and Crazy)," and the unbelievable "He's My Son (Just the Same)," apparently a true story.

O. V. Wright, *The Complete O. V. Wright on Hi Records, Volume 1: In the Studio* (UK, 1999) Cream/Hi, HEXCD 47. Includes "I Don't Know Why."

O. V. Wright, *The Complete O. V. Wright on Hi Records, Volume 2: On Stage (Live in Japan)* (UK, 1999) Cream/Hi, HIRS 169.

The pair of two-CD sets above collects Wright's entire Hi output. Not as strong as the Backbeat material, but it's still O. V.

Ann Peebles, *The Best of Ann Peebles: The Hi Records Years* (1996) The Right Stuff/Hi, 52659. Good single-CD collection of Peebles's Hi material. If you want everything Peebles cut for Hi, get the next pair of two-CD collections.

Ann Peebles, *The Complete Ann Peebles on Hi Records, Volume 1: 1969–1973* (UK, 2003) Cream/Hi, HEXCD 55. Includes "I Still Love You," my favorite Peebles ballad.

Ann Peebles, *The Complete Ann Peebles on Hi Records, Volume 2: 1974–1981* (UK, 2003) Cream/Hi, HEXCD 56.

Denise LaSalle, *On the Loose/Trapped by a Thing Called Love* (UK, 1996) Westbound, CDSEWD 018. LaSalle's work recorded at Royal but not released by Hi. Includes "Man Sized Job."

Syl Johnson, *The Complete Syl Johnson on Hi Records* (UK, 2015) Cream/Hi, HEXCD 51. Incudes "Any Way the Wind Blows," "Take Me to the River," "Let Yourself Go." Liner notes by John Ridley.

Syl Johnson, *Complete Mythology* (2010) Numero, NUM032. Four CDs/six LPs. Johnson's pre-Hi recordings (some produced by Willie Mitchell, including the outtake "Your Love Is Good for Me," which Johnson feels influenced the Hi Al Green sound) in an extensive, beautifully produced box set. Liner notes by Bill Dahl. A staggering work.

Otis Clay, *The Best of Otis Clay: The Hi Records Years* (1996) The Right Stuff/Hi 7243-8-36027-2-8. Includes "Trying to Live My Life Without You" and "The Woman Don't Live Here No More."

Hi Rhythm, *On the Loose* (1976) Hi, SHL 32099. Hi Rhythm's idiosyncratic album. You'll either love it or hate it. I fall into the former category. Includes "Superstar."

Hi Rhythm, Black Rock/Save All My Lovin' (1975) Hi 5N-2275. Their earlier single, equally nutty.

Hodges Brothers and Hi Rhythm, *Perfect Gentlemen* (1992) Velvet Recordings of America, VR-CD 001. Hi Rhythm's totally obscure last effort (try finding a copy). Worth it for one cut: "Best in Town," with Percy Wiggins on vocals. Hot stuff!

Detroit Emeralds, *Greatest Hits* (UK, 1998) Westbound, CDSEWD 119. Includes some of the recordings done partially at Royal (and not released on Hi) with Willie Mitchell, including the divine "Feel the Need in Me."

Laura Lee, *That's How It Is* (1991) MCA/Chess, CHD-93005. Liner notes by David Nathan. Lee's Chess material, pre-Al. Incudes "Dirty Man." Not produced by Willie Mitchell, but you should hear it anyway.

Laura Lee, *Women's Love Rights/I Can't Make It Alone/Two Sides of Laura Lee* (UK, 2010) Edsel, EDSD 2050. Lee's feistier Invictus albums recorded during and after Al. Liner notes by Tony Rounce.

The year 2017 brought two unexpected surprises: Reggie Young, the guitar player central to Hi's early days and so influential on the players that came after, put out his first instrumental album at age eighty, *Forever Young* (Whaling City Sound, WCS094-P). Young is still plucking sounds out of a guitar no one's heard before, and these days I doubt he's using a pencil to do it (check out the exquisite ballad "Jennifer"). And seventy-four-year-old Don Bryant, a singer many feel never got his due at Hi (his one 1969 solo album, *Precious Soul*, was an inexplicable collection that ignored his early singles for generic soul covers), released an album of mostly original material, *Don't Give Up on Love* (Fat Possum, B01MV01JKT). Dedicated to Ann Peebles, Don's wife, the album features Hi Rhythm alumni Charles Hodges, Archie "Hubbie" Turner, and Howard Grimes.

Warning: there is much more Hi out there to explore . . .

SOURCE NOTES

EPIGRAPH

ix   **"Beware of men":** AG to Stanley Booth, *Rhythm Oil: A Journey Through the Music of the American South.*

TALKING IN TONGUES

Author interviews: Davin Seay, Dale Lawrence, Don McLeese, Lynn Norment, Paul Zaleski, Reuben Fairfax Jr.

1   **"I'm a mystery . . . half the time":** AG to Jaan Uhelszki, *Harp,* March 2005.

3   **"read my own . . . the real life":** AG to Adam Higginbotham, "Soul Survivor," *Telegraph,* June 13, 2005.

4   **"is that of an anxious . . . not to be hurt":** Michael Awkward, *Soul Covers: Rhythm and Blues Remakes and the Struggle for Artistic Identity (Aretha Franklin, Al Green, Phoebe Snow).*

5   **"might like a photo . . . the shower":** David Nathan, "Al Green: Soul Minister Al Aims to Get Next to You," *Blues & Soul,* July 1976.

5   **"The man has . . . distracts him":** AG to Kristine McKenna, "Al Green—The Prince of Love," *Los Angeles Times,* July 30, 1989.

5   **"I've never been unhappy":** Ibid.

6   **"I'm not happy":** AG to Lynn Norment, "How Tragedy Affected the Life of Al Green," *Ebony,* October 1976.

6 **"an exercise in forbearance . . . of this world":** Peter Guralnick, *Sweet Soul Music: Rhythm and Blues and the Southern Dream of Freedom.*

6 **"People don't need . . . about now?'":** AG to Mary Ann Lee, *Memphis Press-Scimitar,* December 29, 1972.

6 **"I live in town . . . bunch of folks":** AG to Pete Wells, "Q&A with Al Green," *Details,* July 2007.

7 **"I'm just a guy . . . that's all":** AG to Walter Dawson, "Al Green: I Don't Care About Being in the Top Ten," *Commercial Appeal,* January 11, 1981.

7 **"We don't deal . . . not our thrust":** AG to Kristine McKenna, "Al Green— The Prince of Love," *Los Angeles Times,* July 30, 1989.

7 **"I put the truth . . . write about":** AG to Mark Mobley, "Al Green and the Clouds: Sacred and Secular," *Virginian-Pilot,* June 23, 1991.

7 **"Knowledge of his eventual . . . spiritual salvation":** Awkward, *Soul Covers.*

7 **"is cited as evidence . . . entire popular oeuvre":** Awkward, *Soul Covers.*

7 **"Daddy, if you . . . what's important?":** AG sermon, July 28, 2013.

8 **"The greatest thing . . . I found peace":** AG to Larry Getlen, "What I've Learned: Al Green," *Esquire,* September 2001.

8 **"It can only be one . . . they already know":** AG video interview, "Green Room Tales," *House of Blues,* www.youtube.com/watch?v=KCJoahItGbI.

8 **"I could be considered eccentric . . . figure out":** AG to Stephen Wilding, "The New Al Green," *Black Stars,* May 1978.

8 **"I'm a weirdo . . . knows me":** AG to Jacqueline Trescott, "Singer Al Green: Those Complexities Behind the Silk and Romance," *Washington Post,* August 15, 1975.

8 **"I guess I really don't . . . know myself":** AG to William Earl Berry, "Singer Al Green: Inventing Master of Rhythm & Blues," *Jet,* November 23, 1972.

9 **"He demands to . . . in the water":** Robert Christgau, "Al Green," *The Rolling Stone Illustrated History of Rock & Roll,* 1976. Quote specifics vary between "He demands to have his feet in the ground and walk in the water" and "He demands to have his feet on the ground and walk on the water" across multiple sources.

LITTLE AL, COUNTRY BOY

Author interviews: Reuben Fairfax Jr, Jackie Lee, Johnny Brown, Lee Virgins, George Lowe, Larry Redd, Dale Lawrence, David Steele, Curtis Rodgers, Phil Roberts.

10 **"I had that boy on the floor":** Cora Greene to Scott Spencer, "Al Green's Gotta Serve Somebody," *Rolling Stone,* September 28, 2000.

10 **"I dropped . . . be a color":** AG to Sue C. Clark, "Getting Next to Al Green," *Creem,* March 1972.

11 **"Animals make . . . the time":** AG to Alan Light, "In the Studio: Al Green," *Rolling Stone,* April 21, 2008.

11 **"I was taught to raise cattle . . . the same thing":** AG to uncredited, "Talking to Al Green," unknown publication.

11 **"Really, I'm just . . . bales of hay":** AG to Tom Bailey Jr., "Friendly Rancher Al Green Calls Shelby Forest Home," *The Commercial Appeal,* September 12, 1996.

11 **"I learned . . . a bike":** AG to unknown interviewer, *Now You Can Interview Al Green* promo album, produced by Fred Robbins, Hi Records SHL-1, 1972.

11 **I've also seen his name:** Lynda Green vs. Lonel Green, December 18, 1984 divorce filing, D12463-3, Shelby County Chancery Court.

11 **"When I was . . . to be poor":** AG to William Ruffin, "100,000 for a Week's Work," *Soul,* April 1, 1974.

11 **"My father . . . of none":** AG to Jacqueline Trescott, "Singer Al Green: Those Complexities Behind the Silk and Romance," *Washington Post,* August 15, 1975.

11 **"was [just] like me . . . a loner":** AG to Juan Williams, "Singer, Songwriter, and Preacher Al Green Discusses His Musician Career and When He Became a Christian," *Talk of the Nation,* September 18, 2000.

11 **"My daddy...and sorrows":** Al Green to Davin Seay, *Take Me to the River,* hereafter AG/DS, *TMTTR.*

11 **"It was like . . . to flick it":** Ibid.

12 **"My mother and . . . in church":** AG to Geoffrey Himes, "Al Green: Stepping Back in the Future," *American Songwriter,* July/August 2016.

12 **"the eyes of the overseer":** Ibid.

12 **"In those days . . . the church":** Knight to Jerma A. Jackson, 1992 interview quoted in *Singing in My Soul* (see bibliography)

12 **"We used . . . a wooden floor":** AG sermon, November 24, 2013.

12 **"He wasn't . . . family":** AG to Don McLeese, "Al Green Is Still in Love with Him," *Chicago Sun-Times,* June 25, 1985.

12 **"Diligence . . . steadfastness":** AG to Ben Fong-Torres, "Make This Life Work for You," *Parade,* June 19, 2005.

12 **"I measure . . . mama":** AG to Larry Getlen, "What I've Learned."

13 **"I was raised . . . in my cornbread":** AG to Geoffrey Himes, " "Al Green: Stepping Back in the Future."

13 **"We'd just get . . . *for real*":** AG to Charles Waring, "Love & Happiness," *Blues & Soul,* June 8–21, 2007.

13 **"My momma could . . . a jaybird!":** AG to Matt Rogers, "Labor of Love: Reverend Al Green Strives for Perfection," *Waxpoetics* 28 (2008).

13 **"My father played . . . music at home":** AG to Gene Santoro, "Once a Soul Man, Always a Soul Man," *Pulse,* July 1989.

13 **Strangely enough . . . figure that":** AG to Don McLeese, "Al Green Is Still in Love with Him."

13 **"He looked at . . . to show them":** AG to Alan Carson, "Al Green Turns Soul to Gold," *Black Stars,* June 1975.

13 **"I said, 'When . . . that song'":** AG to Sue C. Clark, "Gettin' Next to Al Green."

14 **"Nobody ever . . . little kid":** AG to Franklynn Peterson, "Al Green: Pop's Most Versatile Singer," unknown publication, March 1973.

14 **"beat me . . . nine times":** AG to Matt Rogers, "Labor of Love: Reverend Al Green Strives for Perfection."

14 **"He'd say . . . the desire":** Ibid.

14 **"All I knew . . . without anyone":** AG to G. Fitz Bartley, "Al Green Sets the Stage for Superstardom," *Black Stars,* June 1973.

14 **"After a while he'd . . . say anything":** AG to Larry Getlen, "What I've Learned."

14 **"spitting curses and throwing punches, aiming to break Mama's jaw":** AG/DS, *TMTTR.*

14 **"that one of them . . . calling the police":** Ibid.

14 **"the kid . . . by himself":** AG to Phil Symes, "Shades of Green," *Disc and Music Echo,* January 1, 1972.

15 **"always the weird . . . in trouble":** AG to unknown, "Al Green: A Superstar's Life Isn't All Glamor," *Phonograph,* January 1975.

15 **"We were having . . . ever tasted before'":** AG to Jon Wilde, "The Jon Wilde Interview: Al Green," *Uncut,* June 2005.

15 **"cracking up with laughter . . . was eating":** Ibid.

15 **"I've never . . . since":** Ibid.

15 **"worried in . . . bad influence":** AG to Robert Hilburn, "Al Green: Walk On, Superstar," *Los Angeles Times,* March 31, 1974.

15 **"They didn't . . . after me":** AG to Robert Hilburn, "The Gospel According to Ex-Soul Star Al Green," *Los Angeles Times,* March 1, 1981.

15 **"My brothers . . . just different":** AG to unknown, "Al Green: A Superstar's Life Isn't All Glamor."

15 **"My brothers . . . how to show it":** AG to Matt Rogers, "Labor of Love: Reverend Al Green Strives for Perfection."

15 **"My momma . . . the children'":** Ibid.15

16   **"something out of the *Beverly Hillbillies*"**: AG/DS, *TMTTR*.

16   **"When we got . . . need anybody"**: AG church sermon, October 6, 2013.

16   **"God made . . . a job"**: Ibid.

16   **"still make me shudder"**: AG/DS, *TMTTR*.

16   **"repeated warnings of unnecessary roughness"**: AG/DS, *TMTTR*.

18   **"'Deacon Jones, I'm . . . gets back"**: Deacon Jones to Charley Honey, "Al Green's Grand Rapids' Upbringing Made Him Part Preacher, Part Soul Singer, and All Joy," *Grand Rapids Press,* June 12, 2012.

18   **"I first got really . . . the house"**: AG to Robert Hilburn, "The Gospel According to Ex-Soul Star Al Green."

18   **"sneak away . . . go home"**: AG to Alan Carson, "Al Green Turns Soul to Gold."

18   **"He had such . . . move mountains"**: AG to P. Bailey, "Al Green: Apostle of Love and Happiness," *Ebony,* November 1973.

19   **"hit the high . . . them tingle"**: AG to G. Fitz Bartley, "Al Green Sets the Stage for Superstardom."

19   **"I dug James . . . strong stand"**: *Now You Can Interview Al Green.*

19   **"I thought that . . . be great"**: AG to Franklynn Peterson, "Al Green: Pop's Most Versatile Singer."

19   **"I was an Elvis . . . every movie"**: AG to unknown, "Talking with Al Green."

19   **"Nine brothers . . . tripped out'"**: AG to Roger Catlin, "Soul + Salvation: Al Green Brings It Home," *Hartford Courant,* August 6, 1996.

19   **"didn't make . . . their music"**: AG to Ken Tucker, "Al Green: His Life and Music Have Come Full Circle," *Miami Herald,* August 24, 1984.

19   **"at a club . . . your music'"**: AG to Bob Mehr, unedited interview for "Al Green: 40 Years at Full Gospel Tabernacle," *The Commercial Appeal,* December 16, 2016, www.commercialappeal.com/story/entertainment/music/2016/12/16/soul-call-al-green-marks-40-years-church-pastor/95146078/.

19   **"I'd like to . . . right time"**: AG to Jon Wilde, "The Jon Wilde Interview: Al Green."

19   **Solomon Burke first record**: AG to Andria Lisle, "Al Green: The Reverend," *Mojo,* date unknown.

19   **"When he'd . . . back on"**: AG to Russ Mitchell, "Al Green Changes His Tune," *CBS News*, June 31, 2005.

19   **"My mother . . . Play 'em!'"**: AG to unknown, *Soundstage,* 1978.

20   **"asked me . . . hear me?'"**: AG to Bob Mehr, unedited interview for "Al Green: 40 Years at Full Gospel Tabernacle."

20   **"He caught . . . it again"**: AG to Don McLeese, "Al Green Is Still in Love with Him."

21 **"I was the terrible . . . old-fashioned family group":** AG to David Dalton and Lenny Kaye, *Rock 100,* 1977, online at www.rocksbackpages.com.

21 **"I left home . . . ever since":** AG to Phil Symes, "Shades of Green."

21 **"I wanted to . . . my father":** AG to Ben Fong-Torres, "Al Green Is Still in Love with You," *TONEAudio,* June 2008.

21 **"You're not . . . gonna be":** AG to unknown, *VH1 Classic Interviews,* www .vh1.com/video/interview/69497/al-green-part-1.jhtml#id=1518000.

21 **"Brought in a guy . . . Golden Harmonaires":** AG to Roger St. Pierre, "Al Green: The Soul Story," *Beat Instrumentals,* December 1971.

24 **"little kid" . . . "sang jazz . . . Chicago":** AG to unknown, "Al Green: The Reverend," unknown publication.

24 **"I had no money . . . a nobody":** AG to Joe Smith and Mitchell Fink, *Off the Record* (see bibliography).

24 **"It was like . . . of heaven!":** AG to Roger Catlin, "Soul + Salvation: Al Green Brings It Home."

24 **"I spent the last . . . my heart":** AG to Stanley Booth, *Rhythm Oil.*

24 **"was one of . . . in Al Green":** AG to unknown, "Soul Man: Al Green Ready to Entertain at Blues Fest," *Wisconsin State Journal,* August 17, 2003.

25 **"pimp and whore":** AG/DS, *TMTTR.*

25 **"sex was sort of a distraction":** Ibid.

25 **"flamboyant costumes":** Ibid.

25 **"I learned more . . . pass along":** Ibid.

25 **"a scar upon my soul":** Ibid.

30 **"scared me to death":** AG, *Soundstage,* 1978.

30–31 **"four of those . . . next act":** AG to Chris Charlesworth, "Green Light," *Melody Maker,* April 19, 1975.

31 **"I tried to do . . . 'Back Up Train'":** Ibid.

31 **"a dressing . . . the tenth":** Ibid.

32 **"The walls of . . . with it":** AG, *Now You Can Interview Al Green.*

32 **"I was a . . . one record act":** AG to Andy McKaie, "Al Green: The New King of Sweet Soul Music," *Rock,* April 23, 1973.

32 **"I didn't have . . . no plan":** AG to Jacqueline Trescott, "Singer Al Green: Those Complexities Behind the Silk and Romance."

32 **"only weighed . . . take my money":** AG to Robert Hilburn, "Al Green: Walk-On Superstar."

32 **"This guy would . . . car and leave":** AG to unknown, *VH1 Classic Interviews.*

33 **"My girlfriend . . . out about it":** AG to Juan Williams, "Al Green Discusses His Musician Career and When He Became a Christian."

33   "So the guy . . . going nowhere'": Ibid.

33–34 "Al weighs . . . construction worker": Ibid.

34   "The guy . . . go home'": Ibid.

34   "I left that night . . . came to Memphis": Ibid.

HIT INSTRUMENTALS

Author interviews: Quinton Claunch, Hayward Bishop, Gene Mason, Jerry Arnold, Reggie Young, Ace Cannon, Martin Willis.

35   "Stax had everything . . . across town": AG to Joe Smith, *Off the Record.*

35   "Memphis despised . . . made us unique": Robert Gordon, *Respect Yourself: Stax Records and the Soul Explosion* (see bibliography).

35   "Oppression is . . . encapsulated here": Gordon, *It Came from Memphis* (see bibliography).

36   "Memphis has . . . independent, renegade": Ibid.

37   "where nothing . . . always does": Gordon, *Respect Yourself.*

37   "Tall and imposing . . . demands subtitles": Colin Escott, *Tattooed on Their Tongues: A Journey Through the Backrooms of American Music.*

37   "some boy named Presley": Ray Harris to Colin Escott, 1986, www.rocka billy.nl/?artists/rharris.ht.

37   "I thought . . . I can't do'": Ibid.

37   "couldn't sing . . . didn't care": Bill Cantrell to Colin Escott, *Tattooed on Their Tongues.*

38   "wearing nothing . . . and sweating": Ibid.

38   "looked like . . . he played . . . intense": Sam Phillips to Colin Escott and Martin Hawkins, *Good Rockin' Tonight: Sun Records and the Birth of Rock 'n' Roll.*

38   "the more we drank, the better it sounded": Ray Harris, uncredited, www.rockabillyhall.com/RayHarris1.html.

38   "finally decided that I was on the wrong side of the mic," Ray Harris to Adriaan Sturm, 1971 interview, http://archive.is/vFozi#selection-195.1-240.115.

38   "We took a . . . behind the barn": Quinton Claunch to David Whiteis, "Quinton Claunch: Life of a Record Man," *Living Blues,* October 2015.

39   "Women and booze": Quinton Claunch to David Whiteis, "Hi Records," unedited manuscript of *Goldmine* article, May 12, 1995.

39   "That little mistake . . . our own record company": Bill Cantrell to Colin Escott, Martin Hawkins, and Hank Davis, notes to *The Sun Country Years: Country Music in Memphis 1950–1959,* Bear Family BFX 15211, 1986.

40   **"We took in exactly $5.63 . . . the demand was,":** Joe Cuoghi to Elton Whisenhut, "Hi's Cuoghi: Dynamo of Industry," *Billboard,* November 27, 1967.

40   **"just had a . . . the beginning,":** John Novarese to David Less and Charles McGovern, Memphis, August 10, 1992, Box 2 of 8, RnS000M0066, Rock 'n' Soul Video History Project Collection, Smithsonian Institution Archives, Accession 06-013, Smithsonian Productions, Washington, DC, hereafter RNSVHPC.

40   **"to ninety-five percent . . . the Mid-South":** Elton Whisenhut, "Memphis Operators Report R&R Making Strong Comeback on Jukes," *Billboard,* September 4, 1961.

40   **"get yourself a . . . Phillips sent you":** Uncredited, "Three Historical Markers Were Dedicated in August," West Tennessee Historical Society, https://wths-tn .org/2015/07/16/three-historical-markers-will-be-dedicated-in-august. Peter Guralnick quotes it slightly differently in his Sam Phillips biography.

41   **"legendary, a household name":** Milton Pond to Robert Gordon, *It Came from Memphis.*

41   **"You can't go on . . . same stage":** John Novarese to David Less and Charles McGovern, RNSVHPC.

41   **"Chief, look . . . his feelings":** Ibid.

41   **"You sure he's not black?":** Ibid.

41   **"the sales . . . doubled":** Ibid.

42   **"lone architectural purpose . . . no sound":** Preston Lauterbach, *The Chitlin' Circuit and the Road to Rock 'n' Roll.*

43   **"As you go down that slope the music gets bigger, it separates":** WM to Robert Palmer, "Memphis Magic: The Al Green Sound," *Rolling Stone,* October 15, 1975.

43   **"Finally somebody kicked it and got it going":** Fred Burch to Ken Burke and Dan Griffin, *The Blue Moon Boys: The Story of Elvis Presley's Band.*

43   **"didn't even have an echo chamber":** Scotty Moore to Randy McNutt, http:// homeofthehits.blogspot.com/2012/12/vintage-recording-studios-pt-1.html.

43   **"I'd come . . . got off":** Harris to David Whiteis, "Hi Records," unedited manuscript of *Goldmine* article, May 12, 1995.

44   **"We couldn't . . . another take":** Ray Harris to Hank Davis and Martin Hawkins, "Disc One: Notes on the Recordings," liner notes, *Royal Memphis Soul,* Hi/Demon, HiBOOK 11, 1996.

44   **"Hear that . . . walking out":** Ray Harris to Hank Davis, "The Hi Records Sound," liner notes, *Royal Memphis Soul.*

44   **More on Claunch exit from Hi:** Colin Escott has written in *Tattooed on Their Tongues* that Claunch "was forced out of the Hi partnership soon after cutting

Bill Black sound-alikes for another label." (He also writes about it in the liner notes to *Hi: The Early Years Vol 1–2*, adding that Bill Cantrell surmised that Claunch was piqued because Ray Harris "was assuming a greater amount of the production work after the success of 'Smokie.'") When David Whiteis asked him about it at my request, he responded "that was Bill Robin and the Blue Jays. I never even put that out. I got about ten sides on 'em. . . . He sounded exactly like Bill Black, that instrumental did. That didn't have anything to do with Hi . . . it was just one of the songs that we did down at Muscle Shoals, we put that Bill Black sound to it, you know. They just got the wrong impression what was going on . . . we got that resolved. It was resolved, and everybody, everything was okay after I explained it."

A 45 by Bill Robin and the Blue Jays was released on MGM in 1961, but Claunch's name isn't on it. Claunch wasn't happy to have the matter brought up, and told Whiteis he felt that Ray Harris and Willie Mitchell "had blown the whole thing out of proportion" in interviews. I've never found interviews with either where they discuss the matter. Perhaps the source of the information is Bill Cantrell, who is long deceased.

45   **"gave":** Willie Mitchell to David Whiteis, "Hi Records."

45–46 **"just kept on . . . developed a sound":** Ray Harris to Adriaan Sturm, 1971 interview, http://archive.is/vFozi.

46   **"We would do take . . . thirty or forty":** Mike Leech to Roben Jones, *Memphis Boys: The Story of American Studios.*

46   **"so many times . . . I couldn't play":** Martin Willis to Ken Burke and Dan Griffin, *The Blue Moon Boys.*

46   **"crazy about . . . distortion":** Ray Harris to David Whiteis, "Hi Records."

46   **"Y'all sing . . . your belt":** Dwight Twilley to the Popmatters staff, "20 Questions with Dwight Twilley," December 2, 2010, www.popmatters.com /feature/132559-20-questions-dwight-twilley/.

47   **"needed twenty . . . light bill":** Ray Harris to Colin Escott, liner notes to *Hi Records: The Early Years, Vols. 1 and 2.*

47   **"About 90 percent . . . those records?":** Gene Simmons to Burke and Griffin, *The Blue Moon Boys.*

47   **"Harris sent . . . Klan outfit."** Bob Mehr, "For the Good Times," *Mojo,* January 2013. To add further to the Ray Harris intrigue, according to Rob Bowman's *Soulsville, USA,* when David Porter cut a Hi single under the name Kenny Cain at Royal in 1962, Harris informed him—in a reverse of the infamous declaration by Sam Phillips—"that he wanted to develop a black artist that sounded white."

47–48 **"I put in an order . . . Combo, all right":** Ibid.

49   **"they set fire underneath my truck":** Ibid.

THE REDUCER

Author interviews: Scott Bomar, John Gary Williams, Wayne Jackson, Jack Hale Jr., Jack Hale Sr., Thomas Bingham, Gene Mason, Reuben Fairfax Jr., Terry Manning, Charles Hodges, Leroy Hodges, Teenie Hodges, Sandy Rhodes, Lawrence "Boo" Mitchell, Pete Mitchell, Reggie Young, Jerry Arnold, Earl Banks, Denise LaSalle, Donna Rhodes, Charles Chalmers.

51   **"I know Al . . . I created him":** WM to Richard L. Eldredge, "Reuniting with Legendary Producer, Al Green Steps Reverently Up to Soul-Music Mike Again for the Good Times," *Atlanta Journal-Constitution,* December 7, 2003. Fantastic article.

53   **"Willie Mitchell . . . any difference":** Teenie Hodges to David Less and John Meehan, Memphis, April 2, 2000, Box 1, RNSVHPC.

59   **Ma Rainey gig:** unnamed Bearsville recording artist produced by WM, by way of Bill Bentley.

59   **"At 14 I organized . . . big band":** WM to Pete Daniels and Charles McGovern, RNSVHPC.

59   **"He was . . . piano player!":** WM to Andria Lisle, "Solid Soul Poppa: Willie Mitchell," *WaxPoetics,* Summer 2004.

59   **"He was so . . . scare you":** WM to Pete Daniels and Charles McGovern, RNSVHPC.

59   **"He had his . . . great he was":** Ibid.

59   **"He was a motivator . . . of a band":** Ibid.

59   **"If a guy come . . . somethin' to it":** Ibid.

59   **"I always found . . . the chords":** Ibid.

60   **"I came up playing . . . underneath it":** WM to Larry Nager, *Memphis Beat: The Lives and Times of America's Musical Crossroads.*

60   **"I don't . . . blee-blop stuff":** Howlin' Wolf by way of WM to Peter Guralnick, *Sweet Soul Music.*

60   **"tried to steer . . . fancy him":** Chris Davis, "The Swinging Sixties," *Memphis Flyer,* April 14, 2004, www.memphisflyer.com/memphis/the-swinging-sixties/Content?oid=1113954.

61   **"We'd play pop . . . play anything":** WM to Pete Daniels and Charles McGovern, RNSVHPC.

61   **the most . . . ever saw":** WM to Colin Escott, liner notes to *Poppa Willie: The Hi Years/1962–74,* Hi/Demon HEXD 48, 2001.

62   **"a hole . . . in the morning":** Ernie Barrasso to Chris Davis, "The Swinging Sixties."

62   **"A swing . . . family":** Robert Gordon, *Respect Yourself: Stax Records and the Soul Explosion.*

62 **"was really . . . went there":** Wayne Jackson to David Less and Pete Daniel, Memphis, November 9, 1999, Box 2 of 8, RNSVHPC.

62 **"A lot of people . . . people dance":** Wayne Jackson to Bob Mehr, "Plantation Inn: Where Stars Rose in the West," *Commercial Appeal,* October 19, 2007, http://archive.commercialappeal.com/entertainment/plantation-inn-where-stars-rose-in-the-west-ep-398547400–323989421.html.

62 **"We wanted . . . Mitchell's band":** Don Nix to Robert Gordon, *Respect Yourself.*

63 **"Cherry wore his . . . of Reuben Cherry'":** Pete Daniel, *Lost Revolutions: The South in the 1950s.*

63 **Elvis stealing a rubber snake:** Robert Gordon, *It Came from Memphis.*

63 **"havin' problems":** Willie Mitchell to Pete Daniels and Charles McGovern, RNSVHPC

63 **"I became Bill Black's arranger . . . began to record":** Ibid.

63 **"He used to say":** WM to Harvey Kubernik, "Willie Mitchell: Soul Music Pioneer," unedited manuscript for *Mojo* article, 2004.

63 **"He respected . . . a hit record":** Ibid.

63 **"I changed the rhythm":** Ibid.

63 **"Dig in hard":** Ray Harris to Colin Escott, *Poppa Willie: The Hi Years/1962–74.*

64 **"He would find . . . the left or right of it":** Reggie Young to Roben Jones, *Memphis Boys.*

64 **"I guess you . . . way it was":** Joe Arnold to David Mac, "Joe Arnold—Out of the Shadows," undated, http://bluesjunctionproductions.com/joe_arnold_-_out_of_the_shadows.

66 **"knew how good . . . shit smell good":** Sam Moore to Andy Doerschuk, Robert L. Doerschuk, and Wally Schnalle, "Al Jackson Jr.: The Sound of '60s Soul," April 12, 2011, http://drummagazine.com/al-jackson-jr-the-sound-of-60s-soul/.

66 **"I think he's . . . ever lived":** Willie Mitchell to Pete Daniels and Charles McGovern, RNSVHPC.

66 **"Al is remembered . . . guitar and bass":** T. Bruce Wittet, "Al Jackson: Memphis Backbeat," *Modern Drummer*, October 1987. An incredible article.

66 **"fast hands . . . he was simple on records":** WM to Harvey Kubernik, "Willie Mitchell: Soul Music Pioneer."

66 **"Hell, I played . . . Al Jackson":** Steve Cropper to T. Bruce Wittet, "Al Jackson: Memphis Backbeat."

66–67 **"Al was the . . . used to copy":** Steve Cropper to Andy Doerschuk, Robert L. Doerschuk, and Wally Schnalle, "Al Jackson Jr.: The Sound of '60s Soul."

67 **"Al had a way . . . cymbal straight":** Ibid.

67 **"We all lived . . . asses off":** Wayne Jackson, ibid.

67   **"You didn't play . . . the dynamics":** Steve Cropper to T. Bruce Wittet, "Al Jackson: Memphis Backbeat."

67   **"If I would rush . . . was off":** Booker T. Jones to Robert Gordon, *Respect Yourself.*

67   **"He can't . . . couldn't play":** Willie Mitchell to Pete Daniels and Charles McGovern, RNSVHPC.

67   **"By the time . . . really learned":** Ibid.

67   **"It was almost . . . all bassy":** Steve Cropper to T. Bruce Wittet, "Al Jackson: Memphis Backbeat."

68   **"played a different . . . more creative":** Ibid.

68   **Part of the secret, Willie . . . drum kit:** Ibid.

68   **"They have . . . hard sound":** Ibid.

68   **"was hitting the drums different":** Ibid.

69   **Spelling of Archie "Hubbie" Turner's name:** "Archie 'Hubbie' Turner: MBS Feature Story," Mark E. Caldwell, Memphis Blues Society, http://www.memphisbluessociety.com/content.aspx?page_id=22&club_id=539640&module_id=190187.

72   **"I don't like . . . the music":** WM to Teenie Hodges, author interview.

72   **"Like the great . . . was done":** Colin Escott, *Poppa Willie: The Hi Years/ 1962–74.*

73   **"Dear, dear Teenie . . . pure sunshine":** Rita Coolidge with Michael Walker, *Delta Lady: A Memoir.*

74   **"there was . . . *that* cool":** Jim Dickinson to Robert Gordon, "Teenie Hodges," *Spin,* March 1988. Emphasis mine.

77   **"There were times . . . play it *raggedy*":** WM to Andy Doerschuk, Robert L. Doerschuk, and Wally Schnalle, "Al Jackson Jr.: The Sound of '60s Soul."

77   **"He said, 'Howard . . . soaking in":** Howard Grimes to Andria Lisle, "Solid Soul Poppa."

77   **"He said, 'You're . . . like that!":** Ibid.

77   **"When you see Popeye . . . a crazy motherfucker'":** Howard Grimes to Robert Gordon, unedited interview transcript, May 1, 1995.

79   **"When I cut . . . to hear":** WM to Colin Escott, *Hi Records: The Early Years, Vols. 1 and 2.*

79   **"I would always . . . than this":** WM to Harvey Kubernik, "Willie Mitchell: Soul Pioneer," unedited interview, 2004.

79   **"I told Joe . . . somewhere else'":** WM to Colin Escott, *Hi Records: The Early Years, Vols. 1 and 2.*

79   **"When he left . . . then on":** WM to Pete Daniels and Charles McGovern, RNSVHPC.

79   **"The biggest . . . I had":** WM to Robert Palmer, "Memphis Magic: The Al Green Sound," *Rolling Stone,* October 25, 1975.

79   **"I would turn . . . check it":** WM to Robert Gordon, liner notes to *Hi Times: The Hi Records R&B Years,* The Right Stuff T2 30584, 1995.

79   **"The Memphis sound . . . and so forth":** Duck Dunn to T. Bruce Wittet, "Al Jackson: Memphis Backbeat."

80   **"I wanted to . . . and white":** WM to Peter Guralnick, *Sweet Soul Music.*

I'VE BEEN SEARCHIN'

Author interviews: Charles Hodges, Reuben Fairfax Jr., Don Bryant, Quinton Claunch, George Journigan, Gene Mason, John Gary Williams, Syl Johnson, Denise LaSalle, Leroy Hodges.

81   **More on the song "You Must Believe in Yourself":** Texas bluesman Johnny Copeland cut an earlier version of this number for a single B-side in 1971. I tried to find out more about the song itself—the only songwriting credit I could find was for another Texan, Charles Jerue—but got nowhere. I'd love to know who Jerue was and what inspired him to write it.

83   **"You just close . . . the old blues":** O. V. Wright to James Cortese, "On the Record: 'It's Only Old Blues' Says O. V. Wright," *Commercial Appeal,* September 10, 1967.

83   **"He's so emotional":** WM to Pete Daniels and Charles McGovern, RNSVHPC.

83   **"that hurtin' . . . voice":** Ibid.

83   **"could take . . . a stylist":** Ibid.

83   **"We worked . . . 13 years":** Ibid.

84   **"He just wanted . . . fine cars":** Edward Wright to Peter Guralnick, *Sweet Soul Music.*

84   **"severely beat . . . and body":** Divorce Filing, Norma Louise Wright vs. OV Wright, Shelby County Circuit Court, 27663, September 27, 1971.

84   **"struck her in . . . medical attention":** Ibid.

84   **"frequently beat . . . or medication":** Divorce Filing, Norma Louise Wright vs. OV Wright, Shelby County Circuit Court, 17550, July 1, 1969.

85   **"O. V. once casually . . . the joint":** JM interview, confidential source.

85   **Wright was arrested for theft, forgery, stealing a woman's purse:** Jeff Colburn, "Lost in the Shuffle: The O. V. Wright Story," *Goldmine,* October 16, 1992. Excellent article.

85   **"distributing a controlled substance":** Ibid.

85   **More on the death of Arthur Brown:** Suspected by police of trafficking in drugs and prostitution" (according to the *Memphis Press-Scimitar*), Arthur Brown was a colorful character worthy of further research. "Mr. Brown was sharp," said singer John Gary Williams, who went over to visit Brown one day and found him standing out in the street with a pistol in his hand, facing down some punk. "I pulled up and said, 'Hey, Arthur, maybe I caught you at a bad time.'" Brown told him to get out of the car and help him. Somebody had come to Brown's door and tried to get him outside on the ruse his car was on fire. Brown had said he'd be out after he put on his pants. In the meantime, he looked out the window and saw his car wasn't on fire.

"This cat Arthur's got [the punk] by the collar with a pistol in his face and he says, 'Now show me where it's burning!'" Williams recalled. There was another guy up the street, and Brown fired a shot in his direction. Dragging the first guy by the collar, Brown confronted the new arrival. And he said, "'John, search him! Look up under his coat.' I said, 'Mr. Brown, I can't do that.' I said to the guy, 'Mister, I don't know you, but I know this man right here—if you don't show him what you got under your coat, he's definitely goin' to shoot you!' So the guy goes, 'Oh, help me, Lord Jesus, help! Somebody please call the po-lice!'"

At which point a third assailant, lurking across the street behind the hedges of a church, ran in and started firing. "And the guy he was askin' me to search had a sawed-off shotgun on a string up under his coat, and *he* started firing! I broke and run and Mr. Brown ran up underneath a viaduct," said Williams. "It was just a mess." Before escaping, one of the three had managed to shoot Arthur Brown in the leg. "He thanked me and said if I hadn't have came by when I did he probably would've got killed."

Around a year later Mr. Brown was finally rubbed out. Robert Lee Wright was convicted of the murder, even though two other men were reportedly at the scene. Why was Brown killed? "I heard it was about a gambling debt," said Williams. "Those were interesting times, man."

85   **Willie Mitchell and Al Green, pallbearers:** Garth Cartwright, *More Miles Than Money: Journeys Through American Music*.

85   **"...was incredible":** AG to Fred Shuster, "Al Green Takes Soul Full Circle," *Pittsburg Post-Gazette*, December 17, 1995.

86   **"We always ... a ghost":** Howard Grimes to Bill Dahl, "Notes on the Recordings," liner notes to *Syl Johnson: Complete Mythology*, Numero Group 032, 2010. A tremendous achievement on every level. Do these guys love Syl!

86   **"You sing ... the highway'":** Willie Walker to Martin Goggin, "Reaching for the Real Willie Walker," *Juke Blues*, date unknown.

87   **"stay in focus ... two records":** Howard Grimes to Bill Dahl, "Notes on the Recordings."

89 **"Willie was . . . something":** Howard Grimes to Patrick Berkery, unedited interview for *Modern Drummer,* "What Do You Know About? . . . Howard Grimes," September 2014.

90 **"the girl with . . . of these people!":** WM to Pete Lewis, *Blues & Soul,* October 1987.

90 **"I looked out . . . love you":** Ann Peebles to Pete Daniel and David Less, November 9, 1999, and Memphis Horns/Ann Peebles interview, October 15, 1997, original master DAT, Box 2 of 8, RNSVHPC.

90 **"I saw him . . . head":** Ibid.

92 **"Everything was concentrated on Al Green":** Otis Clay to David Cole, "Otis Clay: There's Always Something in the Can!" September 11, 2003, interview, *In the Basement* 32, November 2003–January 2004.

92 **"Joe was . . . he loved me":** WM to Pete Daniels and Charles McGovern, RNSVHPC.

92 **"I called all . . . 'Joe's gone'":** WM to Pete Daniels and Charles McGovern, RNSVHPC.

92–93 **"I'll put you . . . days a week":** Ibid.

93 **"called in . . . cut records'":** Ibid.

93 **"that sissy voice":** Ray Harris to Colin Escott (by way of Bill Cantrell), *Tattooed on Their Tongues* (also mentioned in liner notes to *Hi Records: The Early Years, Vols. 1 and 2*).

SILKY ON TOP, ROUGH ON THE BOTTOM

Author interviews: Charlie Hodges, Leroy Hodges, Teenie Hodges, Willie Bean, Terry Manning, Roland Jones, Sandra Rhodes, Donna Rhodes, Charles Chalmers, James Brown, Bettye Berger.

94 **"I'd rather be . . . with a past":** AG to William Earl Berry, "Singer Al Green: Inventive Master of Rhythm & Blues," *Jet,* November 23, 1972.

94 **"Al need his hair fixed":** Howard Grimes to Robert Gordon, unedited interview transcript, May 1, 1995.

94–95 **"I was a lone . . . player, nuthin'":** AG *Soundstage* interview, 1978.

95 **"I didn't know . . . band to me":** AG to Vince Aletti, "His Name in Lights," *Rolling Stone,* March 2, 1972.

95 **"Before he finished . . . found my man,":** AG to Robert Hilburn, "Al Green: Walk-On Superstar."

95 **"had mid-range . . . very unique":** WM to John Abbey, "Willie Mitchell," *Blues and Soul,* January 1970.

95 **"I said, 'Come over . . . that long'":** WM to Harvey Kubernik, "Willie Mitchell: Soul Pioneer."

95 **"was real cocky, but I liked his attitude":** Ibid.

95 **"I wouldn't . . . wouldn't like it":** AG *Soundstage* interview, 1978.

95 **"I didn't know Willie Mitchell . . . singing along":** Al Green profile from unknown book, mid-1970s vintage.

96 **"Really, it . . . with ya!":** WM to John Abbey, "Willie Mitchell."

96 **"We are about ten . . . need some money'":** WM to Harvey Kubernik, "Willie Mitchell: Soul Pioneer."

96 **"Al Green might get lost":** AG to Robert Palmer, "Memphis Magic: The Al Green Sound."

96 **"no artists":** Ibid.

96 **"Joe Cuoghi owned half the durn town":** Ibid.

96 **"You're the motherfucker who got my money":** WM to David Whiteis, "Hi Records."

96 **"We started working . . . the morning":** WM to Robert Gordon, "Spirit Filled Al Green," liner notes to *Anthology,* The Right Stuff 72438-53033-2-6, 1997.

97 **December 3, 1968; January 3, 1969:** Colin Escott, liner notes to *The Immortal Soul of Al Green,* The Right Stuff 72435-90551-2-1, 2003.

97 **"A great song—for the Beatles":** AG to Terry Gross, *Fresh Air,* June 21, 1991.

97 **"come over to . . . the album":** AG to unknown, from unknown book, mid-1970s vintage.

97 **"didn't like all . . . interfered too":** Howard Grimes to Patrick Berkery, unedited interview.

98 **"fixated on . . . my drums":** Ibid.

98 **"He'd call . . . the sound":** Ibid.

98 **"He liked the snare . . . so big":** Ibid.

98 **"We was still lost at that time":** WM to Robert Gordon, "Spirit Filled Al Green."

98 **"The biggest thing . . . need to scream'":** Ibid.

98–99 **"If you want . . . own thing":** WM to Pete Daniels and Charles McGovern, RNSVHPC.

99 **"He was getting real frantic":** Ibid.

99 **"I knew he was gonna get there":** Ibid.

100 **"They don't work . . . too often.":** WM to John Abbey, "Willie Mitchell."

100 **"Ike was at . . . Bring him back!'":** AG to Andria Lisle, unknown Ike Turner profile supplied by author.

100 **"I have had . . . with God,"** AG to Lynn Norment, "How Tragedy Affected the Life of Al Green."

100 **"down and out":** Ibid.

100 **"We got together . . . ever wanted":** AG to Paul Niemark, "Did Al Green Make a Deal with the Devil?" *Sepia,* April 1974.

100 **"God told me . . . all that money":** AG to Scott Spencer, "Al Green's Gotta Serve Somebody."

100 **"I'd get everything . . . pay for it":** AG to Paul Niemark, "Did Al Green Make a Deal with the Devil?"

101 **"is convinced some . . . soul to Mephistopheles":** Ibid.

101 **"I wasn't satisfied . . . own thing'":** WM to Harvey Kubernik, "Willie Mitchell: Soul Pioneer."

102 **"I did what . . . did my job":** Howard Grimes to Patrick Berkery, unedited *Modern Drummer* interview.

102 **"shifted on me . . . do the firing'":** Ibid.

102 **"I was kind of . . . like women":** Ibid.

102 **"There's two people . . . Howard Grimes":** WM to John Abbey, "Willie Mitchell."

103 **"He was still . . . such command":** WM to Harvey Kubernik, "Willie Mitchell: Soul Pioneer."

103 **"With a gospel . . . three-way encounter":** Anthony Heilbut, *The Gospel Sound: Good News and Bad Times.*

103 **"I wrote my first million seller because of her":** AG to Joe Smith and Mitchell Fink, *Off the Record: An Oral History of Popular Music.*

103 **"It took a long . . . was it":** WM to Harvey Kubernik, "Willie Mitchell: Soul Pioneer."

104 **"skinny beanpole with lots of hair":** Laura Lee to Colin Dilnot, "Laura Lee: Winning Hearts," *In the Basement* 31, April–May 2003.

104 **"the first gospel group to sing in nightclubs":** Laura Lee to David Nathan, liner notes to *Laura Lee: That's How It Is.*

104 **"the little girl with the big voice":** Lois Wilson, liner notes to *Laura Lee: The Chess Collection,* Chess 983 229-4, 2006.

104 **"weary of being dominated":** Laura Lee to Colin Dilnot, "Laura Lee: Winning Hearts."

104 **"A little shack . . . hillbilly musicians":** Laura Lee to David Nathan, liner notes to *Laura Lee: That's How It Is,* Chess CHCD-93500, 1990.

104 **"Al Green . . . of mine":** Laura Lee, online interview, "This Is Laura Lee," defunct Laura Lee website. I suspect the interviewer is Dilnot.

104 **"My reply . . . up here":** Ibid.

104 **"I was sitting . . . said, 'No'":** Ibid.

104 **"I kept telling . . . at him":** Ibid.

104 **"We lived together":** Ibid.

104 **"we would just create together":** Ibid.

104 **"soul mate":** AG/DS, *TMTTR*

104–105 **"Miss Lee, decked . . . for the altar":** Anonymous, *Jet*, October 18, 1973.

105 **"They tried to . . . advocating women's love!":** Laura Lee to Colin Dilnot, 2003 interview.

105 **"This shy guy . . . to my mother . . . ":** Intro to "Since I Fell for You."

105 **"I was singing about Mr. Green":** Laura Lee to Colin Dilnot, "Laura Lee: Winning Hearts."

105 **"This lady used . . . that song":** AG to Joe Smith, *Off the Record.*

105 **"I say, 'Man . . . pay the rent'":** AG to Juan Williams, "Al Green Discusses His Musician Career and When He Became a Christian."

105 **"I kicked . . . hurt about it":** Laura Lee, online interview, "This Is Laura Lee," defunct Laura Lee website.

106 **"Larry would say . . . as possible'":** Thriller website, now defunct, 2008.

106 **"love, emotional . . . phony about it":** AG to William Earl Berry, "Singer Al Green: Inventing Master of Rhythm & Blues," *Jet*, November 23, 1972.

106 **"After we got . . . my own":** AG to Terry Gross, *Fresh Air*, June 21, 1991.

107 **"So Willie told . . . with the band":** Ibid.

107 **"When I heard the song":** WM to Harvey Kubernik, "Willie Mitchell: Soul Pioneer."

107 **"Willie says . . . Sing mellow":** AG to Terry Gross, June 21, 1991.

107 **"Willie sat me down . . . raw vocal strength":** AG to unknown author, unknown article.

110–111 **"People dance . . . it thunder!'":** WM to Pete Daniels and Charles Mc-Govern, RNSVHPC.

111 **"We sold about . . . be a hit'":** WM to Harvey Kubernik, "Willie Mitchell: Soul Pioneer."

111 **"Everybody was after . . . she refused":** WM to Richard L. Eldredge, "Al Green Steps Reverently Up to Soul-Music Mike Again."

111 **"buying her . . . started ringing":** Ibid.

111 **"We did 30,000 . . . 1.5 million":** WM to Harvey Kubernik, "Willie Mit-chell: Soul Pioneer."

112 **"Al will try and impress me":** WM to Tom Moon, "Hello Ladies! Al Green Says the Lord Has Ordained His Return as a Love Man," *Rolling Stone*, November 13, 2003.

112 **"going over some mellow changes"**: AG to Sue C. Clark, "Getting Next to Al Green," *Creem*, March 1972.

112 **"was beating . . . beat out of"**: Ibid.

112 **"They were just playing"**: *Now YOU can interview AL GREEN on your own program promo album* . . . Hi Records Demo SHL-1, produced by Fred Robbins, 1972.

112 **"I thought he . . . but hours?"**: AG to Robert Palmer, "Memphis Magic: The Al Green Sound."

113 **"where all . . . open up!"**: AG to Sue C. Clark, "Getting Next to Al Green."

113 **"I sat down . . . build it again'"**: AG to Juan Williams, "Al Green Discusses His Musician Career and When He Became a Christian."

113 **"just started writing about my baby"**: Ibid.

113 **"It makes it . . . get his lesson"**: WM to Tony Jones, "Willie Mitchell: A Few Words with the Genius Behind Hi Records," *Memphis Flyer*, April 4, 2003, www.memphisflyer.com/CityBeat/archives/2003/04/04/willie-mitchell.

113 **"some sharp suits"**: AG to Peter Guralnick, *Sweet Soul Music.*

113 **"you got to . . . it soft"**: Ibid.

113 **"He said, 'Man . . . damnedest fights"**: Ibid.

113 **"just wouldn't . . . who Al Green is'"**: WM to Richard L. Eldredge, "Al Green Steps Reverently Up to Soul-Music Mike Again."

113 **"I got so upset . . . the top down"**: AG to unknown, VH1 Classic Q&A, http://www.vh1.com/video/interview/69497/al-green-part-1.jhtml#id=1518000.

113 **"I'm not even . . . it at all"**: AG to Russ Mitchell, CBS News, July 31, 2005.

113 **"sang the shit . . . what I wanted,'"**: WM to Richard L. Eldredge, "Al Green Steps Reverently Up to Soul-Music Mike Again" Deleted expletive added back by me.

113 **"a hundred hours . . . at a time"**: Robert Palmer, "Memphis Magic: The Al Green Sound."

114 **"I wanted 500,000 . . . it was gold"**: WM to Harvey Kubernik, "Willie Mitchell: Soul Pioneer."

114 **"When people used . . . the music happen"**: WM to Robert Gordon, "Spirit Filled Al Green."

114 **"was after . . . playing the kit"**: Howard Grimes to Patrick Berkery, unedited *Modern Drummer* interview.

114 **"pound on the . . . was *there*, man"**: Ibid.

114 **"If Willie . . . more volume"**: Wayne Jackson, *In My Wildest Dreams (Takes 1, 2, and 3).*

115 **"Willie was trying . . . started recording"**: Teenie Hodges to Robert Gordon, unedited interview for liner notes to *Anthology*, May 1995.

117   **"laughed in my . . . do with it":** WM to Barney Hoskyns, *Say It One Time for the Broken Hearted: Country Side of Southern Soul.*

117   **"all this music . . . kind of delayed":** WM to Robert Palmer, "Memphis Magic: The Al Green Sound."

118   **"We've now gotten . . . got into music":** WM to John Abbey, "Willie Mitchell."

118   **"There's a bunch . . . it's the winos":** WM to Robert Mugge, *Gospel According to Al Green* unedited interview, hereafter AG to Robert Mugge, *GATAG* unedited interview.

119   **"Once he got . . . song was dead":** WM to Harvey Kubernik, "Willie Mitchell: Soul Pioneer."

119   **"We had six . . . with Al":** Ibid.

119   **"This man . . . to the sound":** AG to unknown, *VH1 Classic Q&A*, www.vh1.com/video/interview/69497/al-green-part-1.jhtml#id=1518000.

119   **"It has a . . . warm sound":** WM to Seth Mnookin, "No. 9," *New Yorker,* December 8, 2003.

119   **"I was drinking vodka":** Ibid.

119   **"As long as . . . eight-track":** WM to Robert Palmer, "Memphis Magic: The Al Green Sound."

120   **"dressed in an . . . foot shaking":** Roger St. Pierre, "Front Row: Al Green," *New Musical Express,* December 18, 1971.

120   **"Then it started . . . love you'":** AG to Rose Rouse, "Saved by the Belle: Green Wants to Take You Higher," *The Face,* date unknown.

120   **1973 petition:** Helen Cameron, "208 Girls Petition Al Green, 'Please, Don't Get Married,'" *Commercial Appeal,* June 9, 1973.

120–121   **"Your music makes . . . my brain":** P. Bailey, "Al Green: Apostle of Love and Happiness," *Ebony,* November 1973.

121   **"Hordes of . . . Says Al":** Henry Edwards, "Al Green: Heaven's on His Side," *After Dark,* November 1974,

121   **"The police had . . . top of me":** AG to Sue C. Clark, "Getting Next to Al Green."

MASCULINE AL, FEMININE AL

Author interviews: Paul Zaleski, Jeff Davis, Teenie Hodges, Buddy Jarrett, Roland Jones, Johnny Brown, "Bongo" Eddie Folk, Michael Baker, Margaret Foxworth, Charles Hodges, Reuben Fairfax Jr., Davin Seay, Bettye Berger, Syl Johnson.

122 **"I may not . . . this planet":** AG to Simon Witter, "I May Be from Another Planet . . . Al Green," *NME,* July 16, 1988.

123 More on **Sounds of Friction:** before joining Al Green, the Sounds of Friction cut one single in Louisville as the Detroit Sounds of Friction with Buddy Jarrett on vocals: www.youtube.com/watch?v=vOJf4eQdPdM.

131 **"Some of the . . . almost impossible":** WM to uncredited, "Al Green Believes in the Man," *Zoo World,* August 15, 1974.

131 **"nothing but jazz changes":** Ibid.

131 **"used a C-minor . . . the B-natural":** WM to Robert Palmer, "Memphis Magic: The Al Green Sound."

131 **"It's very, very . . . really low":** AG to Alan Light, "Love and Happiness," *Vibe,* June/July 1995.

131 **"Part of what . . . in that aspect":** Stan Lathan to Elyse Eisenberg, "Interview: Director Stan Lathan," WNET, January 2009. www.thirteen.org/soul/interview-soul-director-stan-lathan/.

132 **"We got him . . . gonna go somewhere":** Ibid.

132 **"I'd be so . . . I'd be okay":** AG to David Less, "Al Green: Soul Reborn but Sales Waste Away," *Downbeat,* April 5, 1979.

136 **"a friend of mine":** AG to Kristine McKenna, "Al Green, the Prince of Love," *Los Angeles Times,* July 30, 1989.

138 **"I like to be . . . I want to":** AG to Vince Aletti, "His Name in Lights," *Rolling Stone,* March 2, 1972.

138 **"We seldom rehearse . . . how I feel":** AG to Chris Charlesworth, "Green Light," *Melody Maker,* April 19, 1975.

138 **"Green's sexiness . . . jolt that transcends identification":** Robert Christgau, "Al Green," *The Rolling Stone Illustrated History of Rock & Roll.*

138 **"lean body . . . sexual confidence":** Ibid.

139 **"I live way out in the woods":** AG to Stephen Wilding, "The New Al Green," *Black Stars,* May 1978.

139 **"I didn't want . . . this house'":** AG to uncredited, *Now You Can Interview Al Green.*

140 **"I met Miss . . . to her house":** AG to Bob Mehr, unedited interview for "Al Green: 40 Years at Full Gospel Tabernacle."

140 **"used to have . . . leave country out'":** Ibid.

141 **"played so . . . Good Times'":** AG to Paul Kingsbury, April 1994 interview, liner notes to *From Where I Stand: The Black Experience in Country Music,* Warner Bros. Records 9 46428-2, 1998.

141 **"of instances . . . to blows":** WM to John Abbey, "Willie Mitchell."

141 **"not for":** Teenie Hodges to Robert Gordon, unedited interview for liner notes to *Anthology*, May 1995.

141 **"because of this girlfriend of mine":** Ibid.

141 **"I wanted to screw . . . the grocery store":** Ibid.

141 **"We need to go . . . we come back":** Ibid.

141 **"Jerry Lawler was . . . whole chorus . . . ":** Ibid.

141 **"the hook, for sure":** Ibid.

141 **"we needed one . . . I got a song'":** Teenie Hodges to David Less and John Meehan, April 2, 2000, Box 1, Memphis, RNSVHPC.

142 **"He said no . . . turn it around":** Teenie Hodges to Robert Gordon, unedited interview for liner notes to *Anthology*, May 1995. The rest of the quote: "I said, 'It'll make you do right' first." He turned it around—"make you do wrong" came from my interview with Hodges.

142 **"We drove . . . 'Love and Happiness'":** AG to Travis Atria, "Al Green—Everything's OK," *Glide*, September 19, 2007.

143 **"Teenie and Al . . . messing around":** Teenie Hodges to Robert Gordon, unedited interview for liner notes to *Anthology*, May 1995.

143 **"Willie said, 'Wait . . . right *here*'":** Ibid.

143 **"We'd been working . . . it was":** Ibid.

143 **"marks the place . . . the blues":** Craig Werner and Rhonda Mawhood Lee, *Love and Happiness: Eros According to Dante, Shakespeare, Jane Austen, and the Rev. Al Green.*

144 **"boils the *Divine* . . . followed in":** Ibid.

144 **"responsible for . . . 40 people":** Peter Bailey, "Al Green: Apostle of Love and Happiness," *Ebony*, November 1973.

144–145 **Al Green the singer . . . and stays late":** Ibid.

145 **"I try to help . . . help someone else":** AG to Lynn Norment, "How Tragedy Has Affected the Life of Al Green," *Ebony*, October 1976.

145 **"all that killing, dope, and girls":** AG to unknown, profile chapter in unknown book.

145 **"take my family to":** AG to Lynn Norment, "How Tragedy Has Affected the Life of Al Green."

AL AND THE WOMEN

Author interviews: Roland Jones, Johnny Brown, Margaret Foxworth, Willie Bean, Miss Mercy Fontenot.

146 **"I don't beat . . . good songs":** AG to anonymous, "Al Green: Right On, Al Green," *Zoo World*, March 29, 1973.

146 **"I had a woman . . . the same thing'":** AG to Travis Atria, "Al Green—Everything's OK."

147 **"Well, I am composed . . . That's it":** AG to Karen Schoemer, unedited interview for "Praise Be to Al Green," *Newsweek,* November 13, 1995.

147 **"She's a wonderful . . . blew it":** AG to Adam Higginbotham, "Soul Survivor."

147 **A few unnamed wife mentions:**
    "Saturday Night and Sunday Morning," *Commercial Appeal,* November 10, 1995 (which also mentions his three-year-old son, Al Jr.).
    "Al Green: The Preacher Superstar—18 Years After Going Gospel, the Reverend Is Singing 'Baby' Again," *Entertainment Weekly,* December 1, 1995.
    "Al Green's Gotta Serve Somebody," Scott Spencer, *Rolling Stone,* September 28, 2000.

147 **"10,000 girlfriends":** AG to anonymous, "Words of the Week," *Jet,* August 17, 1987.

147 **Anonymous posts online; Jackie Ware-Green:** www.answers.com/Q /How_long_has_Al_Green_and_Jackie_Ware_Green_been_married.

147 **"his oldest daughter . . . result in marriage":** AG to Don McLeese, "Al Green Is Still in Love with Him."

147 **"Is This Al Green's Son?":** www.youtube.com/watch?v=qTnJ6P0YNXA.

148 **"I just want . . . my father":** Shaun Bobo, ibid.

148 **"the wonderful . . . crazy about her!":** AG to Kristine McKenna, "Al Green, the Prince of Love."

148 **"I personally . . . mild and obedient":** AG/DS, *TMTTR.*

148 **"There was something . . . over the years":** Ibid.

148 **"There are thousands . . . do anything!":** AG to Henry Edwards, "Al Green: Heaven's on His Side," *After Dark,* January 1974.

150 **"mentor":** David Gest, *Simply the Gest.*

150 **"Al did not always go for the most beautiful women":** Ibid.

150 **"David Gest's All-Star Holiday Extravaganza":** www.realitytvworld.com /news/soul-singer-al-green-sues-former-producer-david-gest-1000336.php.

151 **"Because my dick don't know no better":** Ibid.

151 **"clearly trying . . . his harem":** Ibid.

151 **"was the only . . . him mayhem":** Ibid.

151 **"We used to . . . hard to trust!":** AG to Henry Edwards, "Al Green: Heaven's on His Side."

151 **"It was a magical . . . freaking fantastic":** Linda Wills, *The Great Record Promoter: Behind the Scene in the Record Industry.*

151 **"stable of women":** Ibid.

152 **"devious people":** Ibid.

152   **"wanted to end my life":** Ibid.

152   **"Nothing or nobody":** Ibid.

152   **"in the boondocks":** Ibid.

152   **"Sometimes Al . . . do the norm":** Ibid.

152   **"There were times . . . a good look":** Ibid.

152   **"beat her repeatedly":** "Al Green, Ex-Secretary Settle $100,000 Suit," *Jet*, August 7, 1975.

152   **"Wills was allegedly . . . by Green's sister":** "Singer Al Green Charged in $25,000 Civil Suit," *Jet*, August 15, 1974.

152   **"treated for contusions, bruises and bleeding":** Ibid.

152   **"struck her with a bottle and kicked her":** "Charges Dismissed Against Singer," *Commercial Appeal*, August 28, 1974.

153   **"pray over the garment":** "Al Green, Ex-Secretary Settle $100,000 Suit."

153   **"vehemently denied":** Ibid.

BLACK ELVIS

Author interviews: Jim Cummings, Teenie Hodges, Bill Bentley, David Less, Buddy Jarrett, Roland Jones.

155   **"Women crave . . . with my body":** AG to Paul Niemark, "Did Al Green Make a Deal with the Devil?"

155   **"playing with God . . . be with *me*":** AG to Juan Williams, "Al Green Discusses His Musician Career and When He Became a Christian."

156   **"tears runnin' down both sides of my face":** AG to Karen Schoemer, unedited interview for "Praise Be to Al Green."

156   **"Everybody on the . . . the audience":** AG to Jim Carroll, "Archive: Al Green," *Irish Times*, 2005, interview reprinted online 1/11/10.

157   **"cliché ridden . . . rapid-fire succession":** Michael Awkward, *Soul Covers*.

157   **"more as parody than as heartfelt engagement":** Ibid.

157   **"As far as racial . . . more pop":** AG to Andy McKaie, "Al Green: The New King of Sweet Soul Music," Andy McKaie, *Rock*, April 23, 1973.

158   **"I like to record . . . the real you":** AG to Phil Symes, "Shades of Green," *Disc and Music Echo*, January 1, 1972.

158   **"fervor that . . . spiritual ignorance":** AG/DS, *TMTTR*.

159   **"doing 525 . . . little jay":** AG to Paul Byrne, "Get the Green Light," *Irish Herald*, October 16, 2008.

159   **"I got scared . . . this world!'":** Ibid.

159 **"I was singing . . . my personality!":** AG to Rose Rouse, "Saved by the Belle: Green Wants to Take You Higher."

159 **"like a charge of electricity":** AG to Robert Mugge, *GATAG* unedited interview.

159 **"I'm saying. . . .that before":** Ibid.

159 **"Then I got embarrassed . . . you, Jesus!'":** AG to Sandra Pointer-Jones, "Al Green: The Holy Ghost Speaks Through His Soul," *King Biscuit Times,* September 2003.

159 **"I heard . . . ashamed of me?'":** AG to Robert Mugge, *GATAG* unedited interview.

159 **"I come out there . . . *will* be ashamed!":** Ibid.

159 **"My Daddy asked . . . was amazing":** AG to Bob Mehr, unedited interview for "Al Green: 40 years at Full Gospel Tabernacle."

159 **"still second-billed . . . auditorium concerts":** Ben Fong-Torres "Al Green: I've Got to Be Free and Then I Can Sing," *Rolling Stone,* March 15, 1973, as reprinted in *Becoming Almost Famous.*

159 **"casually stole . . . Smokey Robinson":** Ibid.

159 **the only year Al Green played Disneyland . . . :** As reported by Chris Strodder, *Disneyland Book of Lists.*

159 **"I got a book I want you to read . . . it's a Bible":** AG to Robert Mugge, *GATAG* unedited interview.

159 **"happy, a little high—joints. Kind of loose":** Ibid.

159 **"I sat down . . . readin' it":** Ibid.

160 **"I went to . . . born-again":** AG to Sandra Pointer-Jones, "Al Green: The Holy Ghost Speaks Through His Soul."

160 **"I was feelin' . . . as I could":** AG to Robert Mugge, *GATAG* unedited interview.

160 **"He said to me, 'I kept my side'":** AG to Scott Spencer, "Al Green's Gotta Serve Somebody."

160 **"We sat down . . . be born-again!'":** AG to Robert Mugge, *GATAG* unedited interview.

160 **"I've never been . . . that night":** AG to Juan Williams, "Al Green Discusses His Musician Career and When He Became a Christian."

161 **"I wasn't ready . . . on the wall":** AG to Denise Hall, "Troubled Genius of Soul," *Black Music,* February 1975. Fantastic article. I tried to find you, Denise.

161 **"I was going . . . my word":** Ibid.

161 **"I ran for . . . couldn't get away":** AG to Juan Williams, "Al Green Discusses his Musician Career and When He Became a Christian."

161 **"play my music perfectly"**: AG to John Abbey, "Al Green: Superstar," *Blues and Soul,* June 1972.

162 **"Keys to city . . . motorcade to begin"**: Robert Heaton, "Green Draws 10,000 to Benefit," *Commercial Appeal,* September 1, 1973.

163 **"We didn't really . . . tune alone"**: WM to David Nathan, "Willie Mitchell: Changing Sounds in Memphis," *Blues and Soul,* June 1976.

164 **"commands a power . . . frightening"**: Robert Palmer, "The Pop Life: Al Green and Shirley Caesar Together in Person," *New York Times,* July 25, 1984.

165 **"Both Green . . . do the robot"**: Flo Jenkins, "Come to Al Green's Party . . . and Get Down!" *Right On!,* January 1975.

165 **"I just said . . . lot to say"**: AG to Bob Mehr, unedited interview for "Al Green: 40 years at Full Gospel Tabernacle."

166 **"with the simplicity and feeling . . . Memphis tradition"**: Robert Palmer, "Al & Aretha: Soul Survivors," *Rolling Stone,* January 30, 1975.

166 **"thinking about being baptized"**: Teenie Hodges to Jason Gross, Perfect Sound Forever, December 2013, www.furious.com/perfect/teeniehodges.html.

166 **"He was a teacher . . . That's Teenie"**: AG to Bob Mehr, unedited interview for "Al Green: 40 years at Full Gospel Tabernacle."

167 **"a poor man's Al Green"**: Syl Johnson to David Cole, "Different Strokes: Syl Johnson," September 7, 2010 interview, *In the Basement,* Fall 2010.

167 **"total smash"**: Ibid.

167 **"Fuck Al Green . . . this was a conspiracy by *him*"**: Syl Johnson to unknown, 2008 Australian online interview, since disappeared.

168 **"Junior listened to it, and he thanked us"**: Teenie Hodges to Bill Dahl, "I Gotta Be More: Al Green—The Hi Records Years," *Goldmine,* October 23, 1998.

168 **"It's almost a gospel song"**: WM to Tim de Lisle, "Lives of the Great Songs: Soul with Plenty of Body—Take Me to the River," *Independent,* February 5, 1994, www.independent.co.uk/arts-entertainment/lives-of-the-great-songs -soul-with-plenty-of-body-take-me-to-the-river-some-songs-are-born-great -and-1392391.html.

169 **"his biggest payday"**: Andria Lisle, "Love and Happiness," *Memphis Flyer,* July 17, 2004.

170 **"Sometimes onstage . . . winds me up"**: AG to Phil Symes, "Shades of Green."

170 **"Cultivating something . . . flower blooming"**: AG, *Midnight Special* television interview, 1974.

171 **"millions upon millions"**: David Gest to Ben Fong-Torres, "Deputy Al Green's Recovery," *Rolling Stone,* January 16, 1975.

171   **"peddle tapes concerning the performer's sex life":** *Jet,* November 21, 1974.

171   **"It's a very beautiful . . . family to see":** Flo Jenkins, "Come to Al Green's Party . . . and Get Down!"

171   **"I thought my ass . . . out of gold":** AG to Wes Orshoski, "Parting Shots: Al Green: I Thought My Ass Was Gold," *Relix,* June 2008.

STRONG AS DEATH

Author interviews: Bill Bentley, Ben Whitney III, Charles Hodges, Margaret Foxworth, Buddy Jarrett, James Cole, Cheryl Crump, Kimberly Williams, Johnny Brown, Paul Zaleski, Teenie Hodges, Bettye Berger.

172   **"You don't know . . . love someone":** Woodson suicide note, FBI file FOIA request 1330831-0, file 95-HQ-196351, Section 1.

172   **"A .38 . . . ":** Described by James Cole, "Spurned Woman Throws Hot Grits on Singer, Kills Self, Officials Say," *Commercial Appeal,* October 19, 1974.

172   **Cream of Wheat:** AG to Don McLeese, "Al Green Is Still in Love with Him."

172   **Malt-O-Meal:** AG to Sandra Pointer-Jones, "Al Green: The Holy Ghost Speaks Through His Soul."

172   **"to fix grits":** AG to Bart Bull, "Amazing Grace," *Spin,* June 1987.

172   **"loved Mary then . . . always love Mary":** AG to Pete Wells, "Wiseguy: Al Green," *Details,* April 2005.

173   **"aggravated assault with gun, threat to take own life":** FBI to Roy C. Nixon, December 11, 1974. FBI file FOIA request 1330831-0, file 95-HQ-196351, Section 1.

173   **"If I ever . . . no mistakes":** Mary Woodson via sister, Aliya S. King, "Love and Unhappiness," *Vibe,* December 2004.

174   **"You have to be . . . Yeah":** AG to Sophie Harris, "Al Green on His Ministerial Duties, Victoria's Secret Undies, and His New Record," *Time Out,* October 11, 2009, www.timeout.com/newyork/music/al-green-on-his-ministerial-duties.

174   **"fond of wearing . . . like burnt orange":** AG/DS, *TMTTR.*

174   **"The way she . . . to the mystery":** Ibid.

174   **"unexpectedly" and Tom Jones:** "Autopsy Awaited on Woman Found Dead at Singer's Home," *Memphis Press-Scimitar,* October 19, 1974.

174   **"She was the . . . and members":** AG to Malcolm R. West, "Al Green Buys Church, Preaches His First Sermon," *Jet,* January 20, 1977.

174   **"She told me . . . first usher":** Ibid.

174   **"I kept telling her . . . no preacher'":** AG to Sandra Pointer-Jones, "Al Green: The Holy Ghost Speaks Through His Soul."

175   **"I said, 'Well . . . you, too!'":** AG to Robert Mugge, *GATAG* unedited interview.

175   **"I never knew . . . incident happened":** Ibid.

175   **This is contradicted . . . :** See Ben Fong-Torres, "Deputy Al Green's Recovery," *Rolling Stone,* January 16, 1975.

175   **Green grew tired of Woodson:** See Denise Hall, "Troubled Genius of Soul."

175   **$15-a-night room at the Admiral Benbow Inn; room 25:** Hotel receipts, FBI file FOIA request 1330831-0, file 95-HQ-196351, Section 1.

175   **"Because I am . . . home, I don't":** AG to Denise Hall, "Troubled Genius of Soul."

175   **Colin Escott dates the recording . . . :** See liner notes to *Al Green: Love and Happiness* box, Hi Records/Demon/Westside FBOOK 26, 2001.

175   **Woodson/Franks arrest:** "Young Woman Found Shot to Death in Singer Al Green's Country Home," *Memphis Press-Scimitar*, October 18, 1974.

175   **Green says he was in the studio:** AG/DS, *TMTTR.*

175   **$250 bail, Al Green Enterprises:** FBI file.

175   **Mary came back to Royal:** AG/DS, *TMTTR.*

175–176   **"Green had flown . . . to sign autographs":** Elizabeth M. Oliver, "Jilted Lover Burns Al Green, Kills Self," *Baltimore Afro-American,* October 22, 1974.

176   **Mary had a room at the Memphis Airport Sheraton Inn:** James Cole, "Spurned Woman Throws Hot Grits on Singer, Kills Self, Officials Say," *Commercial Appeal*, October 19, 1974.

177   **"any of that stupid mess":** AG to Denise Hall, "Troubled Genius of Soul."

177   **"This put the first party in the back seat":** Ibid.

177   **"just getting out of the tub":** "Girlfriend Scalds Singer, Kills Self," *Wisconsin State Journal*, October 19, 1974.

177   **taking a shower:** AG to Larry Getlen, "What I've Learned."

177   **"All of a sudden here comes":** AG to Ben Fong-Torres, "Deputy Al Green's Recovery, *Rolling Stone,* January 16, 1975.

177   **"I'm in total . . . on my skin":** AG to Robert Mugge, *GATAG* unedited interview.

177   **"I'm screaming . . . hit the floor":** AG to Larry Getlen, "What I've Learned."

177   **"three times"; William Maley:** "Young Woman Found Shot to Death in Singer Al Green's Country Home," *Memphis Press-Scimitar,* October 18, 1974.

177   **"a wall and couch":** Ibid.

177–178   **"Green and Mrs. Williams . . . hearing the shots":** Elizabeth M. Oliver, "Jilted Lover Burns Al Green, Kills Self."

178   **"nerve pills":** Carlotta Williams quoted by James Cole, "Spurned Woman Throws Hot Grits on Singer, Kills Self, Officials Say."

178   **"retraced Green's steps":** Ibid.

178   **found Woodson's body, "playing possum":** Ibid.

178   **"I'm sayin' . . . in the room":** AG to Sandra Pointer-Jones, "Al Green: The Holy Ghost Speaks Through His Soul."

178   **"pounding down the hall":** AG/DS, *TMTTR.*

178   **Green calling Bill Green:** AG to Robert Mugge, *GATAG* unedited interview.

178   **"Green's relatives"; 2:20 a.m.:** James Cole, "Spurned Woman Throws Hot Grits on Singer, Kills Self, Officials Say."

178   **2:20 a.m. call:** Ibid.

178   **3:57 a.m. call:** Ibid.

178   **"Sergeant J.R. Roberts . . . plush home":** "Green: Woman Threw Grits at Him, Then Killed Self," *Abilene Reporter-News,* October 19, 1974.

179   **emergency-room police interview; 9 a.m. neuron test:** James Cole, "Spurned Woman Throws Hot Grits on Singer, Kills Self, Officials Say."

179   **Gun test results:** "Gun Not Fired By Al Green, Tests Indicate," *Commercial Appeal,* October 24, 1974.

179   **"His voice was . . . believe me'":** David Gest, *Simply the Gest.*

179   **"grabbed my . . . kill her'":** Willie Mitchell to Aliya S. King, "Love and Unhappiness."

179   **"They tell me . . . don't believe it'":** AG to Denise Hall, "Troubled Genius of Soul."

179   **"gruesome":** David Gest, *Simply the Gest.*

179   **"had all these . . . the bone":** Ibid.

179   **"I'm all burned . . . what hot is":** AG to Bob Mehr, unedited interview for "Al Green: 40 Years at Full Gospel Tabernacle."

179–180   **"torment to me . . . do no more":** Ibid.

180   **"said to be Green's":** uncredited, "Young Woman Shot to Death in Singer Al Green's Country Home," *Memphis Press-Scimitar,* October 18, 1974.

180   **"was running about the yards . . . back and ears":** Ibid.

180   **City Hall; awards ceremony:** Ibid.

181   **"solely in charge of the investigation":** Sergeant Earl Strauser quoted in "Woman Shot Dead in Al Green's Home; He Tells Conflicting Stories; Faces FBI Probe," uncredited, *New York Amsterdam News,* October 26, 1974. What's interesting about this article is the fact that in the first police report Green told them that he "ran to a neighbor's house after hearing gun shots." There were no nearby houses around Green's property. "The information must've gotten twisted around somehow," said Captain William Maley.

181   **"Evidence collected from . . . removed from a wall":** "Scalded Woman Threw Grits, Then Shot Herself," *Arizona Republic,* October 19, 1974.

181 **"After we complete . . . a grand jury":** Maley quoted in "Singer's Lover in Suicide," *Lebanon Daily News,* October 19, 1974.

181 **"We've got enough . . . a suicide":** Dan Jones quoted by James Cole, "Spurned Woman Throws Hot Grits on Singer, Kills Self, Officials Say."

181 **Different bullets; cleaning gun:** "Hit Singer Green Recovering from Burns," *Sumter Daily Item,* October 21, 1974.

181 **"courage shot":** James Cole, "Spurned Woman Throws Hot Grits on Singer, Kills Self."

181 **"Frequently suicide . . . for themselves":** Ibid.

181 **Autopsy details:** Shelby County Chief Medical Examiner Report, case A79-589.

182 **"taped statement played on some radio stations":** "Green #2 Suicide Note," *Baltimore Afro-American,* October 29, 1974.

182 **"I am deeply . . . love you all":** "Shooting Death Ruled a Suicide," *Commercial Appeal,* October 20, 1974.

182 **Suicide note to Sue Franks details:** "Singer's Secretary Gets Suicide Note," *Memphis Press-Scimitar,* November 22, 1974, and FBI file.

182 **"Apparently . . . delayed in the mail":** "Ibid.

182 **Sheriff Roy C. Nixon sent the notes off:** October 31, 1974, letter, FBI file.

182 **"It was something . . . message to you":** AG to Ben Fong-Torres, "Keeping 'Deputy Al Green' Safe," *Lakeland Ledger,* undated clip, presumably January 1975.

184 **"a brilliant writer":** Jesse Jackson to Bob Goldsbrough, "Earl Calloway, 1926–2014, Chicago Defender's Longtime Arts Columnist," *Chicago Tribune,* August 24, 2014, www.chicagotribune.com/news/obituaries/ct-earl-calloway -obituary-met-20140824-story.html.

184 **"was treated like . . . didn't improve":** Earl Calloway, "Recordings and Stuff," *Pittsburgh Courier,* November 2, 1974.

185 **"The informer also . . . were extremely high":** Ibid.

186 **"a dress she wouldn't be caught dead in":** Jo James to Aliya S. King, "Love and Unhappiness."

186 **"wasn't to let this affect his career":** AG to Denise Hall, "Troubled Genius of Soul."

186 **"It could not . . . Woodson wrote":** December 17, 1974 FBI letter, FBI file.

186 **"more than the usual variations":** Ibid.

186 **"numerous specimens should be obtained":** Ibid.

186 **"They are not . . . didn't, either":** William Maley to uncredited, "Companion of Green Shot Self, Police Say," *Memphis Press-Scimitar,* January 24, 1975.

187 **"You got to consider . . . her handwriting":** William Maley quoted in "Suicide Ruling Closes Probe," *Commercial Appeal,* January 24, 1975.

187 **"due to mutilation . . . it was fired":** December 14, 1974, FBI letter, FBI file.

187 **"We're satisfied . . . was a suicide":** William Maley to uncredited, "Suicide Ruling Closes Probe."

187 **"For a while . . . committed suicide":** David Gest, *Simply the Gest.*

187 **"the impact on . . . sales dipped":** Ibid.

187 **"Benefit Show By Al Green Plays to Small Audience":** *Commercial Appeal,* November 14, 1974.

188 **"if that actually . . . it happened":** AG to Robert Mugge, *GATAG* unedited interview.

188 **"had fourteen, fifteen . . . Mary is gone'":** AG to Bob Mehr, unedited interview for "Al Green: 40 Years at Full Gospel Tabernacle."

189 **"That wasn't a . . . with no woman":** AG to Paul Byrne, "Get the Green Light."

ON THE RUN

Author interviews: Teenie Hodges, Jim Trombetta, Roland Jones, Arthur Baker, Johnny Brown, Reuben Fairfax Jr., Lee Hildebrand, Cynthia Lane, Leroy Hodges, Charles Hodges, Lee Housekeeper, Howard Bloom.

190 **"There were knocks . . . it meant":** AG to Denise Hall, "Troubled Genius of Soul."

190 **"a woman . . . for two hours":** "Gun-Toting Second Cousin Threatens Al Green," *Indianapolis Recorder,* November 23, 1974.

190 **"and drove for . . . or four pills":** AG to Denise Hall, "Troubled Genius of Soul."

190 **"Please lift . . . is killing me":** Ibid.

190 **"She took me . . . rented a chalet":** AG to Lee Hildebrand, "Al Green Sings, Preaches to Own Soulful Beat," *SFGate,* August 30, 2009, www.sfgate .com/entertainment/article/Al-Green-sings-preaches-to-own-soulful-beat -3287828.php.

190–191 **"was gonna stay . . . a green Cadillac!":** AG to Bob Mehr, unedited interview for "Al Green: 40 Years at Full Gospel Tabernacle."

191 **"sat on the . . . stream every day":** Ibid.

191 **"No phone, no TV, no Coca Cola":** AG To Scott Spencer, "Al Green's Gotta Serve Somebody."

191 **"didn't eat for forty days":** Ibid.

191 **"Lord, what are you trying to do to me?":** Ibid.

191   **"Al Green performs . . . victim of threats?":** Lynn Van Matre, "Green's on Guard in Niles," *Chicago Tribune,* December 20, 1974.

191   **"I haven't reacted . . . should stay away":** AG to Bob Fisher, "Eaten Something Funny, Al?" *NME,* April 26, 1975.

191   **"I work on . . . sheriff's department":** AG to Jim Trombetta, "The Love Ranger: A Visit to the Memphis Manse of Al Green, the Sheriff of Soul," *Crawdaddy,* November 1975.

191   **"would dilute my projects":** Ibid.

191   **"We do *own* . . . is the police!":** Ibid.

191   **"To live is . . . a lot, okay?":** Ibid.

191   **"This in turn . . . places to go":** Ibid.

193   **"I really didn't . . . all instrumental":** John Abbey, "Willie Mitchell: Gettin' High Again," *Blues and Soul,* March 1978.

194   **"Al Green is an . . . in the fall . . . ":** AG to Jim Trombetta, "The Love Ranger: A Visit to the Memphis Manse of Al Green, the Sheriff of Soul."

194   **"my act . . . suit and tie":** AG to Robert A. DeLeon, "Al Green Sings Again," *Jet,* December 12, 1974.

195   **"I was writing without a piano or anything":** James Mitchell to Robert Gordon, unedited interview for liner notes to *Anthology*, May 1995.

195   **"Andrew and Jack said . . . play it'":** Ibid.

195   **"Willie said, 'Motherfucker . . . kinds of ways":** Ibid.

195   **"He complimented . . . me before!":** Ibid.

195   **"Willie wouldn't let me venture out":** Ibid.

195   **"sounded a little like Tex Ritter's band":** Ibid.

196   **"absolutely . . . I'm busy prayin'":** AG to Bob Mehr, unedited interview for "Al Green: 40 Years at Full Gospel Tabernacle."

197   **"Being a millionaire . . . ":** AG to Lynn Norment, "How Tragedy Has Affected the Life of Al Green."

197   **"Psychologically I was . . . what to do":** AG to Andria Lisle, "Soul Searching," *Mojo,* April 2004.

197   **"I was in a trauma . . . such turmoil":** AG to Chet Flippo, "Soul Raptured," *Tennessee Illustrated,* Summer 1990.

197   **"Every Sunday morning . . . and everything . . . I had to go":** AG to Robert Mugge, *GATAG.*

197   **"any Pentecostal . . . I could find":** AG to Sandra Pointer-Jones, "Al Green: The Holy Ghost Speaks Through His Soul."

197   **"dress up in these disguises":** Ibid.

197   **"so overcome . . . incognito'd be gone":** Ibid.

197   **"Fame can be . . . they'll forget I'm there":** AG to Paul Lester, "Al Green on Fame, God and Michael Jackson," *Guardian*, July 23, 2009.

197   **"My man Curtis . . . it was wonderful":** AG to Chet Flippo, *Tennessee Illustrated*, Summer 1990.

197   **"The spirit came . . . I'm rejoicing":** AG to Robert Mugge, *GATAG* unedited interview.

198   **"then, when I'd . . . shall be saved'":** Ibid.

198   **"this weird little . . . were gone":** AG to Andria Lisle, "Soul Searching."

198   **"No, no, no . . . your personal savior":** Author interview with Lee Hildebrand, also mentioned in contemporaneous *Rolling Stone* article.

198   **"And so the concerts . . . into this thing":** AG to Robert Mugge, *GATAG* unedited interview.

198   **"I had producers, promoters . . . come back *later*'":** AG to Andria Lisle, "Soul Searching."

198   **"I had to walk . . . he was making":** Bob Schwaid to Harry Weinger, "Twenty Years of Career Guidance: Schwaid Manages to Succeed," *Billboard*, November 24, 1984.

199   **"At every concert . . . in my life":** AG to Geoffrey Himes, " "Al Green: Stepping Back in the Future."

199   **"came to my house . . . anything about it'":** WM to Karen Schoemer, unedited interview for "Praise Be to Al Green."

199   **"to avoid . . . be a preacher":** AG to unknown, "Al Green Blends Religion, Entertainment in Every Area of Life," *Memphis Press-Scimitar,* December 10, 1977.

199   **"I was instructed . . . rock star":** AG to Walter Dawson, "I Don't Care About Being in the Top Ten," *Commercial Appeal,* January 11, 1981.

199   **"got to me . . . to take it'":** AG to Robert Mugge, *GATAG* unedited interview.

200   **"will be the . . . divine power":** AG quoted in "Singer Buys Hale Road Church," *Commercial Appeal,* October 20, 1976.

200   **"I shall be one . . . around the world!":** AG to Robert Mugge, *GATAG* unedited interview.

200   **"I'm a religious . . . with preachers":** WM to Karen Schoemer, unedited interview for "Praise Be to Al Green."

200   **Atlantic offer:** Colin Escott, liner notes for *The Immortal Soul of Al Green.*

200   **"I was under . . . questioning myself":** WM to John Abbey, "Willie Mitchell: Gettin' High Again."

200   **More on Hi Rhythm:** Before *On the Loose* there was a fantastic 1975 single, "Black Rock," www.youtube.com/watch?v=D8934atYTdU.

201 **"conservative projection":** Al Bennett to Gerry Wood, "Memphis on Rise, Bennett Convinced," *Billboard,* June 25, 1977.

202 **"We've basically . . . a change":** WM to David Nathan, "Willie Mitchell Changing Sounds in Memphis," *Blues and Soul,* June 1976.

203 **"moved to a squalid little cubbyhole":** Harvey Kubernik, "Willie Mitchell: Soul Pioneer."

203 **"the people that . . . went bankrupt":** Ann Peebles to David Cole, "Ann Peebles: Tellin' It," *In the Basement,* August 2000.

204 **"I hadn't had no . . . can come up with":** Howard Grimes to David Less, Memphis, November 12, 1999, Box 1 of 8, RNSVHPC.

HAND LOTION AND DEAD DOGS

Author interviews: Johnny Brown, Paul Zaleski, Reuben Fairfax Jr., "Bongo" Eddie Folk, Buddy Jarrett, D. E. "Hutch" Hutchison.

205 **"I was a fornicator . . . the terrestrial":** AG to Scott Spencer, "Al Green's Gotta Serve Somebody."

205 **"He took *the rock* . . . name is *Jesus*":** AG to Viv Broughton, "Music for the Soul: Al Green," Royal Albert Hall tour book, July 13, 1984, emphasis mine.

205 **"somewhat dilapidated . . . far from Graceland":** Gene Santoro, "Once a Soul Man, Always a Soul Man," *Pulse,* July 1989.

205 **"parallelogram-obsessed architecture":** Jack W. Hill, "Service with Soul," *Arkansas Democratic-Gazette,* February 2, 1996.

206 **"to promote the . . . and charitable work":** Charter of the Al Green Full Gospel Tabernacle Church, court filing LG 5058, October 20, 1976.

206 **"the corporation shall . . . independent status":** Ibid.

206 **"in league with the devil":** Patrick Donovan, "Got a Soul Lot of Love," *Melbourne Age,* November 5, 2009.

206 **Full Tabernacle rejection of gays, footnote:** "if you're gay, you go to hell, and Al Green wasn't shy in letting you know that you disgust him": Kevin E. of Palo Alto, CA, February 1, 2015, Full Gospel Tabernacle Church Yelp page, www.yelp.com/biz/full-gospel-tabernacle-church-memphis.

206 **"We have some . . . for a sinner":** AG to anonymous, "Al Green Blends Religion, Entertaining in Every Area of Life."

206 **"I think it's the commitment . . . a goody two-shoes":** AG to Larry Nager, "With His Whole Soul Now," *Commercial Appeal,* November 4, 1995.

206 **"I felt . . . embarrassed by it":** AG to Simon Witter, "I May Be from Another Planet . . . Al Green" interview tape, www.rocksbackpages.com.

206 **"It's not always . . . now and then":** Lynn Norment, "Al Green's Mission: 'Have a Good Time,'" publication unknown, December 18, 1976.

206 **"If I'm totally . . . my music"**: AG to Bob Billbourn, "The Number One Spot? ' . . . It Can Be Pretty Lonely,' Says Al Green," *Blues and Soul,* December 11–24, 1979.

206–207 **"I feel at home . . . enlightened"**: AG to Bob Darden, "Al Green's Transcendent Reality," *Contemporary Christian Music,* May 1992.

207 **"There's a tremendous . . . from the word"**: AG to Clint Roswell, "Al Green," unknown publication.

207 **"In church . . . don't want to"**: AG to Stephen Wilding, "The New Al Green," *Black Stars,* May 1978.

207 **"fell right . . . help me'"**: David Gest, *Simply the Gest.*

207 **"Boy, you haven't . . . the church"**: AG to Stanley Booth, *Rhythm Oil.*

207 **"There seem to . . . church world"**: AG to David Nathan, "Minister of Soul," *Blues and Soul,* July 11–24, 1989.

207 **"a prophet without honor . . . eyes"**: AG to Lynn Norment, "Born Again Al Green," *Ebony,* March 1978.

207 **"Al Green . . . there's . . . That's wrong"**: Willie Morganfield to Alan Young, *Woke Me Up This Morning.*

207 **"years before . . . show them"**: AG to David Nathan, "Minister of Soul."

208 **"I had always . . . beauty shine"**: AG to unknown, www.songfacts.com /detail.php?id=30833. I have no idea where the quote originally came from.

208 **"women who come . . . in mind"**: AG to Lynn Van Matre, "A Star Is Reborn from Pop Singer to Pastor Al Green," *Chicago Tribune,* June 14, 1987.

209 **"A lot of my people . . . the musicians"**: AG to Joe Smith, *Off the Record.*

215 **Texas arrest, May 30, 1977:** Irving, Texas, police arrest record 25176 /A46357.

215 **"Robinson stated that . . . with his fists"**: Ibid.

215 **"eye was puffed up and swollen shut"**: Ibid.

215 **"the actor Al Green"**: Ibid.

216 **"It was basically . . . particular occasion!"**: Patti LaBelle to David Nathan, "Patti LaBelle: Going Straight," *Blues and Soul,* August 1978, www.rocksback pages.com/Library/Artist/patti-labelle.

217 **"church bird"**: AG to Lynn Norment, "'I Can't Stop' Making Soul Music and Praising God," *Ebony,* April 2004.

217 **"I saw her . . . shake her hand"**: AG to Michael Copley, "For a Song: The Subject Was Rosebuds; Now, Green's the Reverend Al, Ringing Church and Wedding Bells," *People,* December 19, 1977.

218 **"complete God's work"**: Shirley Green memory by way of John W. Fountain, "Silent No Longer," *Chicago Tribune,* January 3, 1995.

218 **"I asked, 'What . . . How 'bout it?'":** AG to Michael Copley, "For a Song: The Subject Was Rosebuds; Now, Green's the Reverend Al, Ringing Church and Wedding Bells."

218 **Kyles/Green marriage ceremony details:** Otis L. Sanford, "Green Reported Wed to Singer," *Commercial Appeal,* June 24, 1977.

218 **"determined to get . . . much in love":** Ibid.

219 **"and kill the story":** Ibid.

219 **"it wasn't true":** Ibid.

219 **introduced Shirley as his sister:** John W. Fountain, "Silent No Longer."

219 **"We sing great together":** AG to Michael Copley, "For a Song: The Subject Was Rosebuds; Now, Green's the Reverend Al, Ringing Church and Wedding Bells."

220 **"My dogs are . . . listened to me":** Jacqueline Trescott, "Singer Al Green: Those Complexities Behind the Silk and Romance," *Washington Post,* August 15, 1975.

220 **"He was terrified":** AG to Jim Trombetta, "The Lone Ranger: A Visit to the Memphis Manse of Al Green, the Sheriff of Soul."

220 **"just went out . . . on my guitar":** AG to Paul Niemark, "Did Al Green Make a Deal with the Devil?"

HIM THAT I NEED

Author interviews: Paul Zaleski, Reuben Fairfax Jr., Jim Shackleford, Johnny Brown, Margaret Foxworth, Bernard Staton, Carol Staton, Buddy Jarrett.

221 **"If the wages . . . afford it":** AG to David Nathan, "Soul Minister Al Aims to Get Next to You," *Blues and Soul,* April 1978.

221 **"With the *Belle* . . . with *my* band":** AG to Nick Kent, "Al Green—the Record Mogul in the Sky," *NME,* 1979.

221 **"'Belle' was Mary":** AG to Bart Bull, "Amazing Grace"; also **"I was singing about Mary":** AG to Andria Lisle, "Soul Searching."

222 **"an old straw . . . picking cotton":** AG to Robert Palmer, "Al Green, Country Boy, Comes Home," *Rolling Stone,* March 9, 1978.

222 **"Willie has everything . . . confining for me":** AG to Judy Spegelman, "Al Green: The Preacher Who Sings," *Soul,* November 27, 1978.

223 **"The sound is homemade and eccentric":** Robert Palmer, "Al Green, Country Boy, Comes Home."

223 **"The *Belle* album . . . seriousness about it":** AG to Don McLeese, "Al Green Is Still in Love with Him."

224   **"There's no ad . . . back cover":** Greil Marcus, "Al Green: The Belle Album," *Rolling Stone,* February 23, 1978, www.rollingstone.com/music/albumreviews/the-belle-album-19780223.

224   **"I think *Belle* . . . them so well":** AG to Viv Broughton, "Music for the Soul: Al Green."

224   **"I thought that . . . girl that's irrelevant":** AG to Stanley Booth, *Rhythm Oil.*

224   **"under circumstances . . . established,"** other DeWitt Jordan information: http://faculty.southwest.tn.edu/ejones/content/dewitt_jordan/biography.html.

225   **"I can understand . . . glory to God":** AG to Ken Tucker, "His Music Has Come Full Circle," *Philadelphia Inquirer,* July 5, 1994.

225   **"We may someday . . . Al Green's best":** Greil Marcus, "Al Green: The Belle Album."

225   **Lou Reed, "Belle" and "Georgia Boy":** www.helsinkiklub.ch/jukebox/lou-reeds-favorite-100-singles/; www.vh1.com/news/51820/lou-reed-ballot-100-greatest-songs/.

225   *The Belle Album/Truth n' Time* **unreleased recordings:** Somewhere during this period, Muhammad Ali attended a Green show in Chicago. Al was invited to record a song for Ali's 1979 TV movie, *Freedom Road,* the story of ex-slave Gideon Jackson, who gets elected to the Senate. Reuben Fairfax Jr. recalls cutting a title track for the movie with Fred Jordan. "We had a big boat chain and beat on it to get the sound of the slaves." "Freedom Trail," a song from these sessions, has escaped, but it's definitely not Al singing (it might even be Shirley Green). I hear no evidence of Al's music in the movie itself. Fairfax remembers Ali coming by the studio but not having much interaction with Al. "I just remember how big his head was. He never looked right at you, but from the corner of his eye."

225   *Jet* **photo of Mason gathering:** "Reverend T. J. Jemison Honored by Black Freemasonry Group," *Jet,* December 5, 1983.

225   AL GREEN'S WIFE SEEKS DIVORCE, **ran the headline:** "Al Green's Wife Seeks Divorce," *Commercial Appeal,* May 9, 1978.

225   **May 4, 1978, divorce filing:** Shirley Anne Watts Kyles Green vs. Albert Leorns Green, D3405-3, Chancery Court, Shelby County, TN.

225   **"because of fear":** Ibid.

226   **"cruel and inhuman treatment":** Ibid.

226   **"on numerous occasions . . . the Defendant":** Ibid.

226   **"I detest . . . personal story":** Shirley Green e-mail to author, February 25, 2013.

226   **Protection order:** Shirley Anne Watts Kyles Green vs. Albert Leorns Green.

226   **abuse started the day after they got married:** John W. Fountain, "Silent No Longer."

226   **"set him off":** Ibid.

226   **alleged Green slapped her repeatedly:** Ibid.

226   **"my eyes were black":** Ibid.

226   **"afraid":** Ibid.

226   **"Defendant did indeed . . . or 3 days":** Shirley Anne Watts Kyles Green vs. Albert Leorns Green.

226   **"Pre-Marital Agreement":** Shirley Anne Watts Kyles Green vs. Albert Leorns Green.

227   **"release all her marital rights in and to the property of the Defendant":** Ibid.

227   **As Shirley's lawyer pointed out . . . :** Ibid.

227   **"Defendant has been guilty . . . of said child":** Ibid.

227   **"approximately the end . . . adulterous relationship":** Ibid.

227   **"a misunderstanding . . . from Shirley":** AG to unknown, "Al Green, Wife Together Again After Splitting over 'Misunderstanding,'" *Jet,* May 10, 1979.

229   **"I'd start singing it and Willie would say, 'Everyone break'":** AG to Terry Gross, date unknown, as quoted by Colin Escott, liner notes to *The Immortal Soul of Al Green.*

229   **"When Job was . . . right by you":** AG to David Less, "Soul Reborn but Sales Waste Away."

230   *Truth n' Time*–period **unreleased recordings:** During the press for *Truth n' Time,* Green mentioned he'd cut some tracks with the great soul singer Spencer Wiggins that he'd put "some guitar on." Hopefully they'll be released one day. He also mentioned he'd written a song for Rod Stewart called "Dance to the Disco."

230   **"was still in . . . wasn't together":** AG to Walter Dawson, "Al Green: I Don't Care About Being in the Top Ten."

230   **"there are things . . . cannot do . . . ":** AG to David Less, "Soul Reborn but Sales Waste Away."

230   **"give him a chance . . . Cadillac cars. *No.*":** Ibid.

232   **Bernard Staton deal:** Regarding the "quarter of a million" deal Green offered Bernard Staton, he might've been better off not signing the agreement. Along with Lois Reeves and Mildred Vraney, Yvonne "Frankie" Gearing was one of the singers in Quiet Elegance, a trio that recorded a number of tracks (a couple of Al Green covers among them) that are beloved to Hi fanatics. Quiet Elegance toured with Green in 1975 (his first female backup group on the road, I believe), and he signed the vastly underappreciated Gearing to a contract. "From [illegible word] to Four, Their Star Is Rising," a 1978 article in

Florida's *Evening Independent* newspaper, quotes a friend of Gearing's stating that Frankie had been reduced to bussing tables at a motel restaurant as she "was still under a contract to Al Green she couldn't get out of."

231 **More on Quiet Elegance:** A Green TV appearance on the terminally bland Dinah Shore–hosted *Dinah!*, where he performs "Sha-La-La" and "Full of Fire," is the only recorded evidence I know of where he performs with Quiet Elegance singing backup. There is also the special discomfort of watching Al endure sitting on the couch attempting show-biz small talk with the beyond-whitebread trio of Dinah, Dr. Joyce Brothers, and Ruth Buzzi. Blind country singer Ronnie Milsap is present as well.

   Hi staff producer Dan Greer had tried to rope Green into singing a duet with Gearing one day at Royal, on the song "You Brought the Sunshine Back into My Life." As Greer told David Cole, "Al came in and I said, 'Al, I want you to sing this song with us.' He didn't say no, and I gave him the lyrics . . . and he went downstairs. About ten minutes later I said, 'Where's Al gone?'" Green had vanished without recording a note. Greer ended up singing the song with Gearing himself, and it remained unreleased until 1990. Dan Greer to David Cole, "Frankie Gearing: Making Out O.K.," *In the Basement,* October 3, 2011.

232 **The music of Bernard Staton:** www.cdbaby.com/Artist/BernardAngelaStaton.

233 **"inner self":** AG to Don McLeese, "Al Green Is Still in Love with Him."

233 **"not to go . . . do a revival":** Ibid.

233 **"went anyway . . . on faith":** Ibid.

234 **"That was the final . . . in that fall":** AG to Robert Hilburn, "The Gospel According to Ex-Soul Star Al Green."

234 **"I was being . . . hurry up":** Ibid.

TOO CLOSE

Author interviews: Reuben Fairfax Jr., James Bullard, Paul Zaleski, Johnny Brown.

235 **"We're all pulled . . . and evil":** AG to David Waters, "Al Green to Bless City that Blessed Him," *The Commercial Appeal,* October 3, 2014, http://archive .commercialappeal.com/columnists/david-waters/david-waters-al-green-to -bless-city-that-blessed-him-ep-648277122–324321681.html.

235 **"I don't care . . . of the Lord":** AG to Walter Dawson, "Al Green: I Don't Care About Being in the Top Ten."

238 **"After seven years . . . *million records*":** AG to Chris Roberts, "Al Things Bright and Beautiful," *Melody Maker,* July 23, 1988.

240 **"He said, 'I'm . . . to do that'":** AG to Robert Mugge, *GATAG* unedited interview.

242   **"You take all . . . spiritual fire":** Ibid.

243   **March 26, 1981, arrest:** Memphis Police Department, report 81084532.

243   **July 26, 1979, warrant:** Ibid.

243   **"The defendant did . . . about the body":** Ibid.

243   **"she received surgery on her right hand (finger)":** Ibid.

244   **"treated for severe bruises to the body":** Ibid.

244   **"After being released . . . his wife":** "Gospel Singer Al Green Arrested on Assault Charge," *Commercial Appeal,* March 26, 1981.

244   **April 1, 1981, divorce filing:** Shirley Green vs. Albert Leorns Green, #80424 Shelby County Circuit Court.

244   **a hundred dollars:** Ibid.

244   **"throughout the marriage . . . including hospitalization":** Ibid.

244   **March 1981, "when the plaintiff . . . months pregnant":** Ibid.

244   **Another order of protection was granted:** Countercomplaint on June 8, 1981, 80424-2, Shelby County Circuit Court.

244   **"admits that he . . . of the plaintiff":** Ibid.

244   **AG testimony; "I was raised . . . being belittled":** John W. Fountain, "Silent No Longer."

244   **"justifiable under any circumstances":** Ibid.

244   **"The beating of the wife . . . on the surface":** Ibid.

245   **"there was literally . . . her for that":** AG to unknown, "Rev. Al Green Denies Beating," unknown publication, May 2, 1981.

245   **"The devil will try":** Ibid.

245   **"a wonderful, wonderful person":** Ibid.

245   **"You're talking about . . . and abusive relationships":** AG to Karen Schoemer, "Praise Be to Al Green."

245   **Al isolated her from her family, hid her Bibles, and chastised her for singing out during service:** John W. Fountain, "Silent No Longer."

245   **she shot at her husband:** Ibid.

245   **she'd still get back together:** Ibid.

245   **settlement details:** #80424-II R.D., January 29, 1982, Shelby County Circuit Court.

245   **Shirley was back in court in May 1983:** #80424-2 RD, May 16, 1983, Shelby County Circuit Court

245–246   **Details on Green finances:** June 3, 1981 affidavit, Shirley Green vs. Albert Leorns Green, Complaint 80424, Shelby County Circuit Court

246   **"I anticipate . . . $8,000 net":** AG in January 26, 1981 affidavit: Ibid.

246 **Tour bus fire:** Edward M. Poag and Jennie M. Poag vs. Al Green and Easley Equipment Company, Complaint 00546-8 TD, Shelby County Circuit Court.

BOXING WITH GOD

Author interviews: Richie Becker, Quinton Claunch, Johnny Brown, Paul Zaleski, Reuben Fairfax Jr., Robert Mugge, David Appleby, Erich Roland, James Hooker, Jeff "Stick" Davis, Billy Earheart.

249 **"I'm here to . . . or Palestine":** AG to Cecilia Payne-Wright, "Al Green Moves Ministry Right Along to Broadway," *Memphis Press-Scimitar,* October 28, 1982.

249 **"I had broken . . . for the jugular":** Patti LaBelle with Laura B. Randolph, *Don't Block the Blessings: Revelations of a Lifetime.*

249 **"Everyone understood . . . all I cared":** Ibid.

250 **"He demanded . . . carrying the burden":** Ibid.

250 **"I couldn't believe . . . a single matinee":** Ibid.

250 **"If you don't . . . go to Hollywood":** Ibid.

252 **"The producers finally . . . Bob Hope?":** AG to uncredited, "Words of the Week," *Jet,* August 17, 1987.

252 **"Mr. Green transforms . . . a revival meeting":** Robert Palmer, "Stage: 'Your Arms Too Short,'" *New York Times,* September 10, 1982.

252 **"And he proves . . . of our time":** Ibid.

252 **"Too often she falls back . . . sheer overkill":** Ibid.

252 **"glitzy showboating":** Ibid.

257 GUN CONFISCATED: "Gun Confiscated from Entertainer," *Memphis Press-Scimitar*, April 7, 1983.

257 **Bob Dylan and Al Green:** Rumors of a Dylan/Green recording session have kicked around for years due to a July 24, 1984, studio date at Intergalactic Studios in New York City, where Dylan cut Harold Dorman's song "Mountain of Love." Green's bass player at the time, Jeff "Stick" Davis, says it happened after his first gig with Al at the Beacon Theatre July 28, 1984. Ron Wood attended the show and asked some of the guys in the band to join him at Electric Lady Studios (not Intergalactic, and not on the twenty-fourth) after the show. "We went out on the floor and were literally jamming. After a while, Bob Dylan comes in . . . and I've just played with Al Green my first time and I'm here with a Rolling Stone—and now Bob Dylan!" Davis felt like Dylan's impromptu appearance didn't add up to much recording-wise, although he felt one of the tracks they cut might've ended up on a Ron Wood solo album. Green was not present, nor did producer Arthur Baker know about the session

when I asked him, even though it's been credited as a session for Dylan's *Empire Burlesque.*

257 **"I had to chase . . . he said yes":** Bob Mugge to Terry Gross, *Fresh Air,* November 11, 1985.

259 **"over and over . . . 'Let's Stay Together'":** Ibid.

260 **"I think of a . . . childish things":** AG to Robert Mugge, *GATAG* unedited interview.

264 **"It was only . . . pit of hell":** AG to Jon Wilde, "The Jon Wilde Interview: Al Green," *Uncut,* June 2005.

264 **"bent over his desk, a maniacal look over his face":** AG to Scott Spencer, "Al Green's Gotta Serve Somebody."

264 **"I got clean . . . get you out . . . :** Ibid.

265 **Divorce from Clover Dixon:** A. L. Green vs. Beverly Dixon Green, Shelby County Circuit Court, case 107858rd2.

265 **"took the parties' . . . since that day":** Ibid.

265 **"grounds of desertion":** Ibid.

265 **Clover Green divorce filing ruling:** Vivice Green aka Clover Green vs. Albert Lee [*sic*] Green, Nassau, NY, Supreme Court, 1/26/98, http://caselaw.findlaw .com/ny-supreme-court/1147333.html#sthash.4Ys6taId.dpuf.

265 **"extrinsic fraud":** Ibid.

265 **Green had run a small notice:** A. L. Green vs. Beverly Dixon Green, Shelby County Circuit Court, case 107858rd2.

GET BEHIND ME, SATAN

Author interviews: Arthur Kohtz, Paul Zaleski, Jennifer Zaleski, Arthur Baker, Frank "Poncho" Sampedro, Tom Willett, Tchad Blake, David Steele, Willie Bean, Margaret Foxworth, Johnny Brown.

267 **"I'm a cat . . . a genius":** AG to Mary Ann Lee, "Al Green Rates as Today's Hottest Singer," *Memphis Press-Scimitar,* January 19, 1972.

269 **"They wanted me . . . don't think so":** AG to Don McLeese, "Al Green Is Still in Love with Him."

272 **"You only get . . . Mitsubishi-type tracks":** AG to Simon Witter, "I May Be from Another Planet . . . Al Green."

273 **"People said you . . . in the church":** AG to Michael [last name illegible], "Al Green Uses His Music to Spread Word of Divine Love," *Birmingham Post-Herald,* May 18, 1992.

275 **"It seems violent . . . believe in that":** AG to Deborah Wilker, "Take It on Faith: The Reverend Al Green Delivers a Scorching Sermon on Rhythm and Blues, Pop . . . and Love for His Fellow Human Being," *Sun Sentinel,* July 24, 1992.

275 **"just too sex . . . their belongings":** Simon Witter, "I May Be from Another Planet . . . Al Green."

276 **Divorce from Martha:** Al Green vs. Martha Green, Shelby County Circuit Court, #123800td, April 28, 1989.

276 **"a lump sum cash payment of $1,000":** Ibid.

279 **"I really want . . . out anybody":** AG to Bob Darden, "Al Green's Transcendent Reality."

279 **"gospel's long-haired . . . funky music":** Ibid.

279 **"The most . . . in ten years":** Ibid.

279 **"We wanted to . . . the times":** AG to Larry Nager, "Al Green Festivalgoers Will Witness a 'Total' Singer," *Commercial Appeal,* May 1, 1992.

AL GREEN DON'T DO CATS

Author interviews: Paul Zaleski, Arthur Baker, Tommy Faragher, Tchad Blake, David Steele, Willie Bean, Margaret Foxworth, Johnny Brown.

282 **"People say . . . to sing":** AG to audience, Beacon Theatre concert, New York, NY, author tape, April 9, 1989.

282 **"I became overburdened . . . be too many":** AG to Dan DeLuca, "Down to Earth: After Singing Nothing but Gospel for 16 Years, the Rev. Al Green Has Lent His Sublimely Sexy Voice to a Collection of Soul," *Philadelphia Inquirer,* January 3, 1996.

283 **"actually went and . . . sing my music":** AG to Larry Nager, "With His Whole Soul Now," *Commercial Appeal,* November 4, 1995.

283 **"I had to go . . . they get here?'":** AG to uncredited, "The Righteous Rev. Al Green Still Spreads Love & Happiness," *Sacramento Observer,* July 6, 2012, http://sacobserver.com/2012/09/the-righteous-rev-al-green-still-spreads-love-happiness/.

283 **"You got to do *all* of Al Green":** AG to Dan DeLuca, "Down to Earth: After Singing Nothing but Gospel for 16 Years, the Rev. Al Green Has Lent His Sublimely Sexy Voice to a Collection of Soul."

285 **"The Cannibals do . . . on a computer!":** AG to Roger St. Pierre, "Green At Peace," *Blues and Soul,* December 29, 1982–January 12, 1983.

285 **Al Green/David Steele production:** Steele felt he'd fully realized the kind of production he wanted for Al Green on *Fried,* a UK album he did in 2004 with New Orleans singer Jonte Short (there is an American edition called *Things Change;* I prefer *Fried*).

285 **"This isn't . . . going on vacation":** AG to Robert Wilonsky, "Can He Get an 'Amen'? Al Green Returns with His First All-Secular Album Since 1977," *Dallas Observer,* January 14, 1995.

285   **"that will speak . . . Sunday morning":** Ibid.

286   **"I'm like, 'I don't . . . follow me'":** AG to George Varga, "Al Green's Soulful Rock of Ages," *San Diego Union-Tribune,* June 20, 1996.

286–287   **"I never sang that before I rehearsed it that evening":** Ibid.

287   **"I just decided . . . on keepin' on":** AG Rock and Roll Hall of Fame speech, September 2, 1995.

287   **"It's controversial . . . I cracked up":** AG to Chris Willman, "Al Green: The Preacher Superstar—18 Years After Going Gospel, the Reverend Is Singing 'Baby' Again," *Entertainment Weekly,* December 1, 1995.

288   **"Shelby farm burned . . . Chicago immediately after":** Gest, *Simply the Gest.*

289   **"I used to sing 'you'"—Al pointed above—"'ought to be with *me*'":** AG to unknown interviewer, unknown ABC TV morning show, YouTube clip no longer accessible.

289   **"the opportunity . . . in God's sight":** Ann Nesby to uncredited, "In the Spotlight: Ann Nesby Tells Fans to 'Put It on Paper,'" *Jet,* June 3, 2002.

289   **"stagnant":** Michael Awkward, *Soul Covers.*

289   **"Even after his . . . maternal comfort":** Ibid.

289   **"Where's Ann . . . Come on":** www.youtube.com/watch?v=X7ROcwVTVZk.

290   **"My doctor told . . . song is done":** Ibid.

290   **"Al was high as gas":** Shameka Good, viewer comments on above video.

PUT YOUR HAT ON THE FLOOR

Author interviews: Ace Cannon, Reuben Fairfax Jr., Lawrence "Boo" Mitchell, John Gary Williams, Charles Hodges, Scott Bomar, Johnny Brown, Gene Mason.

292   **Hi Rhythm end period:** In 1992 Hi Rhythm released one more album, *Perfect Gentlemen.* There's one killer cut on this hard-to-find CD, "Best in Town," with Percy Wiggins on vocals.

292   **"I would love . . . Happiness man":** AG to Clarence Watkins, "Al Green: Singer Lays It Down on Music, Why He Wants to Marry Again," *Jet,* July 21, 2008.

293   **"Apparently I . . . do it?'":** Archie Mitchell to Andria Lisle, "'Everything's Coming Full Circle' as Willie Mitchell's Sons Carry On His Memphis Music Legacy," *Commercial Appeal,* February 5, 2008, http://archive.commercial appeal.com/entertainment/everythings-coming-full-circle-as-willie-mitchells-sons-carry-on-his-memphis-music-legacy-ep-3976013-323978561.html.

294   **"He wants to have . . . in the hospital":** AG to Peter S. Scholtes, "What's That in Your Shirt Pocket? The Rev. Al Green Talks About His Spirit and

What Happened When God Found His Stash," Minneapolis-St. Paul *City Pages,* March 24, 2004.

294 **"following a controversial . . . sexually-oriented entertainment":** uncredited, "Famed Blues Club Reopens on Beale Street," Bizjournals.com, April 27, 1998, www.bizjournals.com/memphis/stories/1998/04/27/daily3.html.

295 **"When I got out . . . here right now'":** WM to Richard L. Eldredge, "Al Green Steps Reverently Up to Soul-Music Mike Again." I filled in the expletive.

296 **"Ain't no . . . a golf ball":** Ibid.

296 **"Walls of heavy . . . Goose vodka bottles":** Ibid.

297 **"This sounds . . . house band":** Questlove Thompson to Michael Roberts, "Q&A with Ahmir ?uestlove Thompson of the Roots," *Westword,* May 28, 2008, www.westword.com/music/qanda-with-ahmir-uestlove-thompson-of-the-roots-5688923.

297 **"Why can't that . . . side of music?":** Questlove Thompson to Alan Light, "In the Studio: Al Green," *Rolling Stone,* April 21, 2008.

297 **"Some artists of . . . record rapping":** Questlove to Clarence Waldron, "Al Green: Singer Lays It Down on Music, Tells Why He Wants to Marry Again," *Jet,* June 2, 2008.

297 **"oversaturate":** Questlove to Matt Rogers, "Laying It Down," *WaxPoetics* 28, 2008. Excellent article.

297 **"cap it at three":** Ibid.

297 **"black nerd":** Questlove Thompson to Jon Caramanica, "'O.K., Let's Make Something Great': Chris Rock and Questlove Discuss 'Top Five,'" *New York Times,* November 26, 2014.

297 **"music snob":** Questlove Thompson to Michael Roberts, "Q&A with Ahmir ?uestlove Thompson of the Roots."

297 **"Most black singers . . . minutes to rise":** Thompson, "14. Al Green" in "100 Greatest Singers of All Time," *Rolling Stone,* December 2, 2010, www.rollingstone.com/music/lists/100-greatest-singers-of-all-time-19691231/al-green-20101202.

297 **"less is more":** Questlove Thompson to Michael Roberts, "Q&A with Ahmir ?uestlove Thompson of the Roots."

297–298 **"I wanted to . . . Green record":** Questlove Thompson to Alan Light, "In the Studio: Al Green."

298 **"a mix-up in communication":** Rich Nichols to Matt Rogers, "Laying It Down."

298 **"We got to really . . . really demanding":** Ibid.

298 **"We're just playing . . . the title cut":** Questlove Thompson to Bob Mehr, "Tuning In Al Green's Channel: Singer Knows How to 'Lay It Down,'" *Commercial Appeal,* July 5, 2008.

298   **"really spontaneous":** James Poysner to Matt Rogers, "Laying It Down."

298   **"wasn't overthought . . . came out":** Ibid.

298   **"He wanted to . . . real-time thing":** Questlove to John Jurgensen, "Al Green Goes for the Gold," *Wall Street Journal,* May 24–25, 2006.

298   **"I'm Wild About Your Love"; "didn't let me . . . keep it civilized":** AG to Alan Light, "In the Studio: Al Green."

298   **"Al, be . . . just be you":** AG to Bob Mehr, "Tuning In Al Green's Channel: Singer Knows How to 'Lay It Down.'"

299   **"Truth be told . . . for their money":** Questlove to Matt Rogers, "Laying It Down."

299   **"thinking, 'Man . . . a duet together":** Ibid.

299   **"the one figure . . . than anybody else":** Ibid.

299   **"I heard Raekwon . . . all over it":** Ibid.

299   **"I didn't want . . . Al to death":** Questlove to Michael Ross, "Here I Am Again: ?uestlove and Crew Bring Retro Styles and Modern Beats to a Soul-Renewed Al Green," *EQ,* August 2008.

299   **"He'll sit there . . . is just . . . wow":** Questlove Thompson to Bob Mehr, "Tuning In Al Green's Channel: Singer Knows How to 'Lay It Down.'"

299   **"Al was oversinging . . . rough and intense":** Ahmir "Questlove" Thompson and Ben Greenman, *Mo' Meta Blues: The World According to Questlove.*

299   **"It didn't go . . . times you ask":** Ibid.

299   **"Al didn't like . . . things fit'":** ibid

299   **"The more we . . . feel in his bones":** Ibid.

299   **"Replay that . . . got done":** Ibid.

300   **"an understated . . . nonchalant feel":** Questlove to Michael Ross, "?uestlove and Crew Bring Retro Styles and Modern Beats to a Soul-Renewed Al Green," *Electronic Musician,* July 24, 2008.

300   **"You're a twenty . . . hold a melody":** Questlove to Matt Rogers, "Laying It Down."

301   **"I promised . . . He got two":** Ahmir "Questlove" Thompson and Ben Greenman, *Mo' Meta Blues.*

301   **"We cut some . . . the Reverend!":** AG to Wes Orshoski, "Parting Shots: Al Green: I Thought My Ass Was Gold," *Relix,* June 2008.

301   **"I'm under the . . . from another planet":** Questlove Thompson to Bob Mehr, "Tuning In Al Green's Channel: Singer Knows How to 'Lay It Down.'"

301   **"Hearing Al . . . falsetto voice":** Justin Timberlake, "66. Al Green" in "100 Greatest Artists of All Time," *Rolling Stone,* April 20, 2011, www.rolling stone.com/music/lists/100-greatest-artists-of-all-time-19691231/al-green -20110420.

301 **"I just threw . . . went over":** AG to Korin Miller, "Al Green Rushes from Shower to Last-Minute 'Let's Stay Together' Grammy Duet with Justin Timberlake," *Daily News,* February 9, 2009, www.nydailynews.com/entertainment /gossip/al-green-rushes-shower-last-minute-stay-grammy-duet-justin-timber lake-article-1.389506.

301 **"this mink coat . . . the angels":** Justin Timberlake to Billy Johnson Jr., "Justin Timberlake Jokes About Stalking the Reverend Al Green," April 9, 2013, www.yahoo.com/music/bp/justin-timberlake-admits-stalking-al-green -234123787.html

301 **Green said, "I'm sorry I'm late . . . I was in the tub":** Ibid.

302 **"I sing *this* . . . wonderful thing":** AG to Chris Richards, "Al Green, the Soul Legend and Kennedy Center Honoree, Is Still Tired of Being Alone," *Washington Post,* December 5, 2014, https://www.washingtonpost.com/entertainment/music/al-green-the-soul-legend-and-kennedy-center-honoree-is-still-tired -of-being-alone/2014/12/05/457f2c3e-75b6-11e4-a755-e32227229e7b_story .html.

302 **"distant and hateful":** Ibid.

302 **Negative Al Green concert reviews:** www.watermelonpunch.com/algreensucks/ and www.ticketmaster.com/Al-Green-tickets/artist/735206#BVRRWidgetID.

304 **"I can't answer . . . ever reached out":** Lasha Green to Annmarie Laflamme, "Soul Singer Al Green's Sister Missing 18 Months, Family: 'Let the Public Know Your Sister Is Missing,'" WXMI Fox17, February 21, 2015, http://fox 17online.com/2015/02/21/soul-singer-al-greens-sister-missing-18-months -family-let-the-public-know-your-sister-is-missing/.

304 **"Let the public . . . sister is missing":** Ibid.

304 **"promised":** Ibid.

304 **"He never sent anything":** Ibid.

305 **"A string of bad luck,"** WM to Red Kelly, "Willie Mitchell—Bum Daddy (Hi 2147)," The B Side, August 18, 2009, http://redkelly.blogspot.com/2009/08 /willie-mitchell-bum-daddy-hi-2147.html. Kelly is extremely knowledgeable on the subject of Hi and other labels. Visit his blogs.

307 **"Willie Mitchell came . . . over our heads":** Al Bell, *Willie Mitchell Memorial Celebration,* January 22, 2010, www.youtube.com/watch?v=oajDcNWDJUQ.

308 **daughters excluded from will:** Willie Mitchell Last Will and Testament, admitted to probate October 28, 2013, Cause # D-16957, Probate Court case PR000387, Shelby County, Tennessee.

309 **"to cease and . . . damaging Royal property":** "Archie" L. Mitchell, Sr. vs Willie Mitchell, LLC; Lawrence A. Mitchell; Oona Bean, January 13, 2015, Docket #PR-387-1, "Rule 52 Findings of Fact, Conclusions of Law, and Order," Probate Court case PR000387, Shelby County, Tennessee.

309 **"he had been . . . unable to work":** Ibid.

309 **"Archie testified that . . . in the industry":** Ibid.

309 **"He claimed that . . . the real problem":** Ibid.

309 **Archie be allowed back into Royal . . . :** Consent Order D-16957, October 17, 2013, Probate Court case PR000387, Shelby County, Tennessee.

309 **Boo and Chris Jackson affidavits . . . :** Affidavits, No D-16957/PR 387, January 3, 2014, Probate Court case PR000387, Shelby County, Tennessee.

309 **"I personally witnessed . . . in the studio":** Ibid.

309 **Hummer; "obtaining financing on . . . for business purposes":** "Response of Archie L. Mitchell Sr, to Motion for Order Compelling Sale of Probate Assets," Docket #D16957, June 30, 2014, Probate Court case PR000387, Shelby County, Tennessee.

309 **Boo, Ford Expedition; Oona, Mercedes;** homes: Ibid.

309 **"breached his fiduciary . . . of the trust":** Archie L. Mitchell, Sr. vs. Willie Mitchell, LLC; Lawrence A. Mitchell; Oona Bean.

309 **„failed to file timely tax returns":** Ibid.

309 **"commingled the LLC . . . own personal funds":** Ibid.

309 **"paid members of . . . did not work":** Ibid.

309 **"made payments of . . . of the trust":** Ibid.

309 **"that some of his statements are not truthful":** Ibid.

309–310 **"This court is concerned . . . for several years":** Ibid.

310 **"that neither Lawrence . . . terms were honored":** Ibid.

310 **"clear throughout all . . . children to fight":** Ibid.

310 **Royal Records:** Bob Mehr, "Memphis Music Beat: Mitchell Siblings Set to Launch Royal Records Label," *The Commercial Appeal,* July 27, 2016, http://archive.commercialappeal.com/entertainment/music/memphis-music-beat/memphis-music-beat-mitchell-siblings-set-to-launch-royal-records-label-388ea9c6-967e-18f1-e053-01000-388460881.html.

310 **"I'm not tryin' . . . Not really":** AG to Bob Mehr, unedited interview for "Al Green: 40 Years at Full Gospel Tabernacle."

310 **"Violent Bull . . . small children":** uncredited, I Love Black People, November, 2014, http://iloveblackpeople.net/2014/11/violent-bull-escapes-al-greens-property-infuriates-residents/.

311 **"an excellent . . . market go up":** AG to uncredited, "The Righteous Rev. Al Green Still Spreads Love & Happiness," *Sacramento Observer,* September 7, 2012, http://sacobserver.com/2012/09/the-righteous-rev-al-green-still-spreads-love-happiness/.

311 **"scheduling conflicts":** Lauren Sexton, "Al Green Declines Request to Sing for Barack Obama at Inaugural Ball," *Digital Spy,* January 23, 2013,

http://www.digitalspy.com/showbiz/news/a453244/al-green-declines-request
-to-sing-for-barack-obama-at-inaugural-ball/.

311 **"No one can cover Al Green":** Whoopi Goldberg, Kennedy Center Awards,
December 8, 2014.

312 I'm still . . . **Every day":** AG to Chris Richards, "Al Green, the Soul Legend
and Kennedy Center Honoree, Is Still Tired of Being Alone."

HOLY ROLLER

For assistance in documenting Green's sermons at Full Gospel, thanks to Chris
Ratliff, Molly Whitehorn, Carole Nicksin, David Leonard, Frank Bruno.

313 **"I'm different . . . except by God":** AG to Chet Flippo, "Soul Rapture,"
Tennessee Illustrated, Summer 1990.

314 **"I haven't changed buildings":** AG to Bob Mehr, unedited interview for "Al
Green: 40 Years at Full Gospel Tabernacle."

315 **"I try to be realistic . . . also so rewarding":** AG to Ken Tucker, "His Music
Has Come Full Circle."

316 **"You will like . . . this is over":** Molly Whitehorn, e-mail to author, February
21, 2014.

318 **"I really don't . . . is no end":** AG to George Varga, "Al Green's Soulful Rock
of Ages: He Sings of Love, Spiritual and Secular."

318 **Other Al Green at Full Gospel Tabernacle quotes:** Full Gospel Tabernacle
services/classes, April 7 and 14, 2013; June 9, 2013; July 28, 2013; September
9, 2013; October 6, 2013; November 3, 2013; November 24, 2013; January
19, 2014; February 29, 2014; April 4, 2015; and March 14, 2016, "Afflicted—
One from the Heart—Al Green Testifies," www.youtube.com/watch?v
=VqsV6alg4Sc

PHOTO INSERT

"Al does what God tells him": AG to Jon Bream, "Music a Fine Medley of
Pop, Gospel," *Minneapolis Star Tribune*, September 22, 1989.

BIBLIOGRAPHY

Awkward, Michael. *Soul Covers: Rhythm and Blues Remakes and the Struggle for Artistic Identity (Aretha Franklin, Al Green, Phoebe Snow)*. Durham: Duke University Press, 2007.

Beard, Steve, Chad Bonham, Jason Boyett, Scott Marshall, and Denise Washington. *Spiritual Journeys: How Faith Has Influenced 12 Music Icons*. Lake Mary, FL: Relevant Books, 2003.

Blassingame, John W. *The Slave Community: Plantation Life in the Antebellum South*. New York: Oxford University Press, 1972.

Booth, Stanley. *Rhythm Oil: A Journey Through the Music of the American South*. New York: Pantheon Books, 1991.

Bowman, Rob. *Soulsville, U.S.A.: The Story of Stax Records*. New York: Schirmer Books, 1997.

Broven, John. *Record Makers and Breakers: Voices of the Independent Rock 'n' Roll Pioneers*. Urbana: University of Illinois Press, 2009.

Burke, Ken, and Dan Griffin. *The Blue Moon Boys: The Story of Elvis Presley's Band*. Chicago: Chicago Review Press, 2006.

Carpenter, Bill. *Uncloudy Days: The Gospel Music Encyclopedia*. San Francisco: Backbeat Books, 2005.

Cartwright, Garth. *More Miles Than Money: Journeys Through American Music*. London: Serpent's Tail Books, 2010.

Coolidge, Rita, with Michael Walker. *Delta Lady: A Memoir*. New York: Harper, 2016.

Daniel, Pete. *Lost Revolutions: The South in the 1950s*. Chapel Hill: University of North Carolina Press, 2000.

Danois, Ericka Blount. *Love, Peace, and Soul: Behind the Scenes of America's Favorite Dance Show Soul Train*. Milwaukee, WI: Backbeat Books, 2013.

Des Barres, Pamela. *Let's Spend the Night Together: Backstage Secrets of Rock Muses and Supergroupies*. Chicago: Chicago Review Press, 2007.

Dickerson, James L. *Mojo Triangle: Birthplace of Country, Blues, Jazz, and Rock 'n' Roll.* New York: Schirmer, 2005.

———. *Goin' Back to Memphis: A Century of Blues, Rock 'n' Roll, and Glorious Soul.* New York: Cooper Square Press, 2000.

Escott, Colin. *Tattooed on Their Tongues: A Journey Through the Backrooms of American Music.* New York: Schirmer Books, 1996.

Escott, Colin, and Martin Hawkins. *Sun Records: The Brief History of the Legendary Recording Label.* New York: Quick Fox, 1980.

———. *Good Rockin' Tonight: Sun Records and the Birth of Rock 'n' Roll.* New York: St. Martin's Press, 1991.

Farley, Charles. *Soul of the Man: Bobby "Blue" Bland.* Jackson, MS: University of Mississippi Press, 2011.

Fong-Torres, Ben. *Becoming Almost Famous: My Back Pages in Music, Writing, and Life.* San Francisco: Backbeat Books, 2006.

Freeland, David. *Ladies of Soul.* Jackson, MS: University Press of Mississippi, 2001.

Freeman, Sarah Wilkerson, and Beverly Greene Bond. *Tennessee Women: Their Lives and Times.* Athens: University of Georgia Press, 2009.

Gest, David. *Simply the Gest.* London: Headline Book Publishing, 2007.

Gordon, Robert. *It Came from Memphis.* Boston: Faber and Faber, 1995.

———. *Respect Yourself: Stax Records and the Soul Explosion.* New York: Bloomsbury, 2013.

Green, Al, with Davin Seay. *Take Me to the River.* New York: Harper Entertainment, 2000.

Green, Laurie Boush. *Battling the Plantation Mentality: Memphis and the Black Freedom Struggle.* Chapel Hill: University of North Carolina Press, 2007.

Guralnick, Peter. *Sweet Soul Music: Rhythm and Blues and the Southern Dream of Freedom.* New York: Harper & Row, 1986.

Hall, Ron, and Sherman Wilmott. *Memphis Rocks: A Concert History, 1955–1985.* Memphis: Shangri-la Projects, 2014.

Heilbut, Anthony. *The Gospel Sound: Good News and Bad Times.* New York: Limelight Editions, 1985.

Heimbichner, Craig, and Adam Parfrey. *Ritual America: Secret Brotherhoods and Their Influence on American Society.* Feral House, 2012.

Hildebrand, Lee. *Stars of Soul and Rhythm & Blues: Top Recording Artists and Show-stopping Performers, from Memphis and Motown to Now.* New York: Watson-Guptill, 1994.

Hoskyns, Barney. *Say It One Time for the Broken Hearted: Country Side of Southern Soul.* London: Bloomsbury, 1998.

Hughes, Charles L. *Country Soul: Making Music and Making Race in the American South.* Chapel Hill: University of North Carolina Press, 2015.

Jackson, Jerma A. *Singing in My Soul: Black Gospel Music in a Secular Age.* Chapel Hill: University of North Carolina Press, 2004.

Jackson, Wayne. *In My Wildest Dreams (Takes 1, 2, and 3).* Published by Wayne and Amy Jackson, 2012–2013.

Jones, Roben. *Memphis Boys: The Story of American Studios.* Jackson: University of Mississippi Press, 2011.

LaBelle, Patti, with Laura B. Randolph. *Don't Block the Blessings: Revelations of a Lifetime.* New York: Riverhead Books, 1996.

Lauterbach, Preston. *The Chitlin' Circuit and the Road to Rock 'n' Roll.* New York: W. W. Norton, 2011.

LaVette, Bettye, with David Ritz. *A Woman Like Me.* New York: Blue Rider Press, 2012.

Lisle, Andria, with Mike Evans. *Waking Up in Memphis.* London: Sanctuary, 2003.

Miller, Jim, ed. *The Rolling Stone Illustrated History of Rock & Roll.* New York: Random House, 1976.

Nager, Larry. *Memphis Beat: The Lives and Times of America's Musical Crossroads.* New York: St. Martin's Press, 1988.

Pruter, Robert. *Chicago Soul.* Urbana: University of Illinois Press, 1991.

Questlove. *Soul Train: The Music, Dance, and Style of a Generation.* New York: Harper Design, 2013.

Redd, Lawrence N. *Rock Is Rhythm and Blues: The Impact of Mass Media.* East Lansing: Michigan State University Press, 1974.

Ridley, Jasper. *A Brief History of the Freemasons.* London: Robinson, 2008.

Smith, Joe, and Mitchell Fink. *Off the Record: An Oral History of Popular Music.* New York: Grand Central, 1989.

Stowe, David W. *No Sympathy for the Devil: Christian Pop Music and the Transformation of American Evangelicalism.* Chapel Hill: University of North Carolina Press, 2011.

Strodder, Chris. *Disneyland Book of Lists.* Solana Beach, CA: Santa Monica Press, 2015.

Thompson, Ahmir "Questlove," and Ben Greenman. *Mo' Meta Blues : The World According to Questlove.* New York: Grand Central, 2013.

Werner, Craig Hansen. *A Change Is Gonna Come: Music, Race, and the Soul of America.* New York: Plume, 1998.

———. *Higher Ground: Stevie Wonder, Aretha Franklin, Curtis Mayfield, and the Rise and Fall of American Soul.* New York: Crown, 2004.

Werner, Craig, and Rhonda Mawhood Lee. *Love and Happiness: Eros According to Dante, Shakespeare, Jane Austen, and the Rev. Al Green.* Ashland, OR: White Cloud Press, 2015.

Whiteis, David. *Southern Soul-Blues.* Urbana: University of Illinois Press, 2013.

Williams, Lycrecia. *Still in Love with You: The Story of Hank and Audrey Williams.* Nashville: Rutledge Hill Press, 1989.

Wills, Linda. *The Great Record Promoter: Behind the Scene in the Record Industry.* Xlibris, 2015.

Young, Alan. *Woke Me Up This Morning: Black Gospel Singers and the Gospel Life.* Jackson: University of Mississippi Press, 1997.

Younger, Richard. *Get a Shot of Rhythm and Blues: The Arthur Alexander Story.* Tuscaloosa: University of Alabama Press, 2000.

INDEX